REGIONAL AND GLOBAL REGULATION OF INTERNATIONAL TRADE

STUDIES IN EUROPEAN LAW AND INTEGRATION

General Editors

Professor Francis Snyder
Professor Miguel Maduro

Advisory Editors

Professor Christian Joerges (EUI, Florence)
Professor Jo Shaw (Leeds)
Professor Joseph Weiler (Harvard)
Professor Stephen Weatherill (Oxford)

Titles in this Series

Rein Wesseling: *The Modernisation of EC Antitrust Law*

Candido Garcia Molyneux: *Domestic Structures ad International Trade: The Unfair Trade Instruments of the United States and the European Union*

Francis Snyder (ed.): *The Europeanisation of Law: The Legal Effects of European Integration*

Regional and Global Regulation of International Trade

Edited by
FRANCIS SNYDER

·HART·
PUBLISHING

OXFORD – PORTLAND OREGON
2002

Hart Publishing
Oxford and Portland, Oregon

Published in North America (US and Canada) by
Hart Publishing c/o
International Specialized Book Services
5804 NE Hassalo Street
Portland, Oregon
97213-3644
USA

Distributed in the Netherlands, Belgium and Luxembourg by
Intersentia, Churchillaan 108
B2900 Schoten
Antwerpen
Belgium

Hart Publishing is a specialist legal publisher based in Oxford, England.
To order further copies of this book or to request a list of other
publications please write to:

Hart Publishing, Salter's Boatyard, Folly Bridge,
Abingdon Road, Oxford OX1 4LB
Telephone: +44 (0)1865 245533 or Fax: +44 (0)1865 794882
e-mail: mail@hartpub.co.uk
WEBSITE: http//www.hartpub.co.uk

British Library Cataloguing in Publication Data
Data Available
ISBN 1–84113–218–7 (hardback)

Typeset by Hope Services (Abingdon) Ltd.
Printed and bound in Great Britain on acid-free paper by
Biddles Ltd, www.biddles.co.uk

Contents

List of Contributors

Frederick M Abbott—Professor of Law, Chicago–Kent College of Law and Visiting Professor, University of California at Berkeley School of Law. Rapporteur, International Trade Law Committee, International Law Association.

Richard Blackhurst—Adjunct Professor at the Graduate Institute of International Studies, Geneva since 1974. Member of the GATT/WTO Secretariat 1974-97 and Director of Economic Research for the last 12 years of that period.

Suthiphand Chirathivat—Associate Professor of Economics and Dean, Faculty of Economics, Chulalongdorn University.

François Gipouloux—Senior Research Fellow of the National Centre for Scientific Research (CNRS) in Paris and, since 1997, Director of Research at the French Centre for Research on Contemporary China (Hong Kong).

Rajendra K Jain—Associate Professor, Centre for American and West European Studies, School of International Studies, Jawahorlal Nehru University, New Delhi.

Zeng Lingliang—Professor of Law and Dean, Wuhan University School of Law; Director of Studies, Wuhan University.

Miguel Poiares Maduro—Professor of European Law, Faculdade de Direito, Universidade Nova de Lisboa.

Candido Garcia Molyneux—Associate at Covington and Burling, Brussels; External Professor of International Trade Law at the College of Europe.

Sung-Hoon Park—Professor of Economics and International Trade, Graduate School of International Studies, Korea University.

Francis Snyder—Professor of Law, College of Europe, Bruges; Centennial Professor of Law, London School of Economics; Profeseur associé Universite d'Aix-Marseille III; Fellow, Wissenschaftskolleg zu Berlin 2000–2001; US Attorney (Bar of Massachussets).

Mary L Volcansek—Professor of Political Science, Florida International University.

Huang Weiping—Professor and Dean, School of Economics, Renmin University of China, Beijing.

Shang Yuejiao—Special Advisor to the General Counsel, Asian Development Bank.

Han Zhen—Research Student of International Law at Wuhan University.

Table of Cases

International Court of Justice

GATT Panel

WTO Panel

NAFTA Dispute Settlement Panel

European Court of Justice

Court of First Instance

EC Commission (Anti-dumping decisions)

Hong Kong Courts

Table of Legislation

INTERNATIONAL

BILATERAL TREATIES

EUROPEAN COMMUNITIES

Treaties

Directives

Regulations

NATIONAL LEGISLATION

China (People's Republic of)

Indonesia

Korea

Netherlands

Thailand

United States

1

Governing Economic Globalisation: Global Legal Pluralism and EU Law

FRANCIS SNYDER

How is globalisation governed? Focussing on economic globalisation, this chapter tries to answer this question. It presents a case study of the international commodity chain in toys, identifies the various segments or boxes in this international commodity chain, and then gives examples to illustrate how each of them is governed. The chapter argues that economic globalisation is governed by the totality of strategically determined, situationally specific, and often episodic conjunctions of a multiplicity of sites throughout the world. These sites, for example, include EU law, US law, Chinese law, multinational corporation and trade association codes of conduct, international customs conventions, and WTO law. Each of these sites has institutional, normative and processual characteristics. Although the sites are not isolated from each other, each has its own history, internal dynamics and distinctive features. Taken together, they represent a new form of global legal pluralism.

I INTRODUCTION

How is Globalisation Governed?

How is globalisation governed?[1] I suggest that it is governed by the totality of strategically determined, situationally specific, and often episodic conjunctions

---

[1] Early versions of parts of this chapter were presented at the Institute of International Studies, Stanford University, 2 April 1999, while I was Visiting Senior Fellow at the Stanford Law School Program in International Legal Studies; the Conference on "Transatlantic Regulatory Cooperation", Inaugural Conference of the European Studies Center of New York, held at Columbia Law School, 16–17 April 1999; the Conference on "The Regional and Global Regulation of International Trade", Institute of European Studies of Macau, 10–11 May 1999; the Guangdong International Research Institute for Technology and Economy, 13 May 1999, Guangzhou, China; the Workshop on "Governance and Globalisation in Theory and Practice", European University Institute and the Danish Research Project on "Globalisation, Statehood and World Order", Florence, 1–2 October 1999; and as the Inaugural Lecture for the 1999–2000 Academic Year,

of a multiplicity of sites throughout the world. These sites have institutional, normative and processual characteristics. The totality of these sites represents a new global form of legal pluralism. This chapter aims to explore and, within limits, to substantiate this claim. It invites us to think systematically about how globalization is governed by global legal pluralism.

The chapter forms part of a broader research project on the governance of globalisation. The project analyses the resolution of trade disputes between the European Union (EU) and China.[2] It focuses on a series of case studies, one of which concerns the international trade in toys between the EU and China. Here I draw on this case study selectively for the purpose of my theoretical argument.

The chapter aims to increase our understanding of how globalization is governed and to improve our capacity to analyse these new forms of governance. It is not intended to promote law reform, or advance a specific political or institutional agenda. Consequently, its perspective is more sociological than normative. It adopts, as a useful starting point, the standpoint of strategic actors. Relations among strategic actors can be envisaged as involving different types of organisations, whether firms, states, or regional or international organisations. Alternatively, we can see them as implicating different structures of governance, whether market-based structures or polity-based structures. From a third perspective, these relationships put into play global economic networks and various sites of global legal pluralism. This chapter is intended to highlight all of these perspectives.

European Academy of Legal Theory, Brussels, 4 October 1999. I wish to thank in particular George Bermann, Coit Blacker, Maria do Ceu Esteves, Jill Cottrell, Chen Yong Quan, Cao Ge Feng, Candido Garcia Molyneux, Tom Heller, David Holloway, Hans Henrik Holm, Emir Lawless, Cosimo Monda, Jens, Ladefoged Mortensen, Francois Ost, Song Ying Georg Sorensen, Anne-Lise Strahtmann, Mark van Hoeck, Yang Zugong, the Hong Kong Trade Development Council, staff of the European Commission in Brussels, and several government and toy industry representatives in the Shenzhen, China, Special Economic Zone, for their contributions to the chapter. Jill Cottrell kindly provided helpful material on Hong Kong law. An earlier, shorter version of the theoretical argument of the chapter will be published as "Global Economic Networks and Global Legal Pluralism", in G. Bermann, M. Hedeger, and P. Lindseth (eds), *Transatlantic Regulatory Cooperation*, (Oxford University Press 2001).

[2] The basic legal framework is discussed in F. Snyder, *International Trade and Customs Law of the European Union* (Butterworths, 1998), *passim*, in particular 594–600 (hereafter *International Trade*). For other publications resulting from the project, see my "Legal Aspects of Trade between the European Union and China: Preliminary Reflections", in N. Emiliou and D. O'Keeffe (eds), *The European Union and World Trade Law after the GATT Uruguay Round* (John Wiley & Sons, 1996), 363–77; "Global Economic Networks and Global Legal Pluralism", in G. Bermann, M. Hedeger, and P. Lindseth (eds), *Transatlantic Regulatory Cooperation*, (Oxford University Press 2001); "Europeanisation and Globalization as Friends and Rivals: European Union Law and Global Economic Networks", in F. Snyder (ed.), *The Europeanisation of Law* (Hart Publishing, 2000) (hereafter "Friends and Rivals"); "Chinese Toys in the European Court of Justice", in D. O'Keeffe and A. Bavasso (eds), *Liber Amicorum for Gordon Slynn: Judicial Review in European Law* (Chancery 1999) (hereafter "Chinese Toys"); "Legal Issues in EU-China Trade Relations", *Wuhan University Law Review*, forthcoming (in Chinese); and (with Song Ying), *Introduction to European Union Law* (Peking University Press, 2nd ed., forthcoming 2000 (in Chinese)).

The Meaning of Globalisation

Thinking about how global economic networks are governed requires a concept of globalisation. By globalisation, I refer to an aggregate of multifaceted, uneven, often contradictory economic, political, social and cultural processes which are characteristic of our time. This chapter concentrates primarily on the economic aspects, but these need to be set within a more general framework.

In economic terms, the most salient features of globalization, driven by multinational firms, are for the present purposes the development of international production networks (IPNs),[3] dispersion of production facilities among different countries, the technical and functional fragmentation of production, the fragmentation of ownership, the flexibility of the production process, worldwide sourcing, an increase in intra-firm trade, the interpenetration of international financial markets, the possibility of virtually instantaneous worldwide flows of information, changes in the nature of employment, and the emergence of new forms of work.

Viewed from a political standpoint, globalisation has witnessed the rise of new political actors such as multinational firms, non-governmental organisations and social movements. It has tended to weaken, fragment and sometimes even restructure the state, but has not by any means destroyed or replaced it. Globalization has also altered radically the relationship to which we have become accustomed in recent history between governance and territory. It has thus blurred and splintered the boundaries between the domestic and external spheres of nation states and of regional integration organisations; fostered the articulation of systems of multi-level governance, interlocking politics and policy networks; and helped to render universal the discourse of and claims for human rights. In many political and legal settings, such as the European Union, it has raised serious questions about the nature and appropriate form of contemporary governance.

Among the manifold social processes involved in globalisation are the spread of certain models of production and patterns of consumption from specific geographic/political/national contexts to others. Contradictory tendencies have developed towards internationalisation and localisation within, as well as among, different regions and countries. We have also witnessed the uneven development of new social movements based on different, if not alternative, forms of community.

Seen as a cultural phenomenon, globalisation has implied the emergence of a new global culture, which is shared to some extent by virtually all elite groups.

---

[3] See, in particular, the work of the Berkeley Roundtable on the International Economy: e.g. M. Borrus and J. Zysman, "Globalisation with Borders: The Rise of Wintelism as the Future of Industrial Competition", in J. Zysman and A. Schwartz (eds), *Enlarging Europe: The Industrial Foundations of a New Political Reality* (University of California at Berkeley, 1998), 27–59.

This has enhanced the globalisation of the imagination and of the imaginable.[4] At the same time it has contributed both to the transformation of many local cultures, sometimes strengthening them, sometimes marginalising them, sometimes having both consequences simultaneously. Consequently, it has sometimes increased the range and depth of international and infranational cultural conflicts, as well as resistance to new forms of cultural imperialism.

An Analytical Strategy

The remainder of the chapter is divided into four main parts. Part II introduces the global commodity chain in toys, an empirical anchor for my theoretical argument. Part III then sketches what I consider to be the basic elements of global legal pluralism. Part IV presents in more detail the shape of global legal pluralism, bringing together examples of institutional, normative and processual sites, and the segments of the global commodity chain in toys which they govern. The conclusion briefly summarises the argument and proposes hypotheses for further research.

II   A GLOBAL ECONOMIC NETWORK: THE GLOBAL COMMODITY CHAIN IN TOYS

Global economic networks take various forms. I focus here on the international toy industry. The toy industry's global reach and domestic impact can be illustrated clearly by the Barbie doll. In European countries, imports of toys from Asia have sometimes provoked reactions bordering on xenophobia. In the United States they have triggered outrage against cheap Chinese labour and trade deficits with China, which in the case of the toy trade between China and the United States was claimed by the latter to amount to US $5.4 billion.[5] This has not, however, been true by and large of the Barbie doll, which is usually viewed instead as a US or even global product.

The Barbie doll's label says "made in China". This suggests, correctly, that in the production of Barbie, China provides the factory space, labour and electricity, as well as cotton cloth for the dress. It conceals, however, the facts that: Japan supplies the nylon hair, Saudia Arabia provides oil, Taiwan refines oil into ethylene for plastic pellets for the body, and Japan, the United States, and Europe supply almost all the machinery and tools, most of the molds (the most

---

[4] For this expression, I am indebted to Prof. Pietro Barcellona, oral intervention at the Conference on "*Quelle culture pour l'Euope? Ordres juridiques et cultures dans le processus de globalization*", Réseau Européen de Droit et Société (REDS) and Istituto di Ricerca sui Problemi dello Stato e delle Istitutionzi (IRSI), Rome, 2–3 November 1998.

[5] Rone, "Tempest, 'Barbie and the World Economy", *Los Angeles Times World Report* (special section produced in co-operation with *The Korea Times*), 13 October 1996, 3. There are major differences between US and Chinese estimates of US-PRC trade figures. In 1995 the US Department of Commerce estimated the deficit at US $33.8 billion in China's favour, while China estimated the deficit at only US $8.6 billion: *cf.* ibid.

expensive item), come from the United States, Japan, or Hong Kong; the United States supplies cardboard packaging, paint pigments and molds; and Hong Kong supplies the banking and insurance and carries out the delivery of the raw materials to factories in Guandong Province in south China, together with the collection of the finished products and shipping. Two Barbie dolls are marketed every second in 140 countries around the world by Mattel Inc. of El Segundo, Callifornia. There is a Barbie doll museum in Palo Alto, California. Barbie celebrated her fortieth birthday on 9 March 1999, and the US Post Office released a commemorative US postage stamp in June in her honour.[6] The Barbie doll is quintessentially American in origin, style and culture, and of course is the result of a global commodity chain powered by a US buyer. But Barbie is a global product, if by "global" we refer to the fragmentation of the production process, the dispersion of production facilities among different countries, and the organisation of production within international production networks.

We can understand this industry most easily by conceiving of it as a global commodity chain. By "commodity chain", I mean "a network of labor and production processes whose end result is a finished commodity".[7] Global commodity chains tend to be strongly connected to specific systems of production and to involve particular patterns of co-ordinated trade.[8]

Each global commodity chain, if we follow Gereffi's widely accepted schema, has three main dimensions. The first refers to the structure of inputs and outputs: products and services are linked together in a sequence in which each activity adds value to its predecessor. The second concerns territoriality: networks of enterprises may be spatially dispersed or concentrated. The third dimension is the structure of governance: relationships of power and authority determine the flow and allocation of resources (financial, material, human) within the chain.[9]

Here we are interested especially in the third dimension, the structure of governance, which is internal to the chain. Gereffi distinguishes two distinct types of governance structures within global commodity chains. On the one hand are producer-driven commodity chains, in which the system of production is controlled by large integrated industrial enterprises. On the other hand are buyer-driven commodity chains, in which production networks are typically decentralised and power rests with large retailers, brand-name merchandisers

---

[6] Rapoport, "Barbie at 40", *Sky* (Delta Air Lines, March 1999), 54–7.

[7] Hopkins/Wallerstein, "Commodity Chains in the World-Economy Prior to 1800", (1986) 10 *Review* 157, 159.

[8] G. Gereffi, "The Organization of Buyer-Driven Global Commodity Chains: How U.S. Retailers Shape Overseas Production Networks", in G. Gereffi and M. Korzeniewicz (eds), *Commodity Chains and Global Capitalism*, (Greenwood, 1994), 95, 96 (hereafter "The Organization"). See also G. Gereffi, "New Realities of Industrial Development in East Asia and Latin America: Global, Regional and National Trends", in Appelbaum and J. Henderson (eds), *States and Development in the Pacific Rim* (Sage, 1992), 85–112; G. Gereffi, "Global Commodity Chains: New Forms of Coordination and Control among Nations and Firms in International Industries" (1996) 4 *Competition & Change* 427; G. Gereffi, "Commodity Chains and Regional Divisions of Labor in East Asia" (1996) 12 *Journal of Asian Business* 75.

[9] Gereffi, "The Organization", above at n. 8, 96–7.

and trading companies.[10] This distinction provides a useful point of departure for analysing the global commodity chain in the EU–China toy trade.

The international toy industry is a prime example of an international commodity chain dominated by the buyers. It is hierarchically organised. At the top of the hierarchy are large buyers as well as large retailers. The buyers include several US manufacturers, two Japanese manufacturers and one European company. The most important buyers are two US companies, Mattel and Hasbro. The key elements in the power of buyers are designs and brands. The large buyers are the node in various networks of inventors and creators of toys. Through contract, they control the access of inventors, intermediaries and factories to the market. The most important retailers include large specialist stores such as Toys " Я " Us, discount houses such as Wal-Mart in the United States, and hypermarkets or catalogue stores in the EU. Taking buyers and retailers together, the power of this group lies in its control of design, brands and marketing.

Buyers and retailers compete, however, with regard to access to retail markets. The powerful buyers are dependent to some degree on large retailers, such as Toys " Я " Us and discount stores such as Wal-Mart. As economic downturns reveal, however, the two groups have conflicting interests with regard to the retail market. To maintain market share, and to enhance their dominant position in the global commodity chain, buyers have tried recently to lessen their dependence on retailers. Their strategies for doing so include increased direct-to-consumer sales, including catalogs and Internet sales, either from their own website or from online retailers.[11]

The US firms have regional headquarters and a significant share of the toy market in Europe. The EU toy market is supplied mainly through importer-wholesalers. As at 1995, the EU toy industry comprised about 2,600 firms, producing a great variety of toys, and employing just under 100,000 workers, with only fifteen firms having more than 500 employees.[12] Each country has its own distinctive retail sector, varying from catalogue stores through hypermarkets to independent retailers.[13] Except for LEGO, established in Denmark in 1932 and now one of the world's ten largest toy manufacturers, there are no large manufacturers or specialist retailers based in Europe similar to those based in the United States. Together with LEGO and the Japanese firm Bandai, the US firms dominated the first main peak trade association, Toy Manufacturers of Europe, formed in the early 1990s, and are now the principal players in the current EU peak association, Toy Industries of Europe (TIE).

---

[10] Gereffi, "The Organization", above at n. 8, 97.

[11] *Cf.* Anders/Bannon, "Etoys to join web-retailer parade with IPO", *The Wall Street Journal*, 6 April 1999, at B1.

[12] Commission of the European Communities, "Report from the Commission to the Council on the surveillance measures and quantitative quotas applicable to certain non-textile products originating in the People's Republic of China", COM(95)614 final (6 December 1995), 41.

[13] See Hong Kong Trade Development Council, *Practical Guide to Exporting Toys for Hong Kong Traders* (Hong Kong Trade Development Council, Research Department, March 1999), 34–58.

Further down the hierarchy come the Hong Kong companies which act as inter-mediaries between these multinationals and the toy factories. In East Asia, Hong Kong has been of signal importance in the development of the toy industry. Its role first started in the 1940s as an export platform, then developed in the 1980s as orig-inal equipment manufacturers (OEMs) for overseas importers or as intermediaries between local manufacturers and overseas buyers until, starting in the 1990s, Hong Kong became a re-exporter of toys made in China. In 1998, licensing and contract manufacturing for overseas manufacturers, usually to production specifications and product designs provided by the buyers, accounted for an estimated 70 per cent of total domestic toy exports.[14] US buyers accounted for 51 per cent of Hong Kong's toy exports in the first ten months of 1995.[15] Today Hong Kong is the location of management, design, research and development (R&D), marketing, quality control, finance and usually shipping.[16]

At the bottom of the hierarchy are the factories, most of which are located in China. By 1995 toy production in China involved about 3,000 factories employ-ing more than 1.3 million people.[17] Such factories usually occupy the structural position of OEM producing to other companies' specifications with machinery provided by the buyer. However, some now operate on the basis of original design manufacturer (ODM), producing to designs supplied by the buyer but sharing the cost of machinery and investment as well as markets according to an agreement with the buyer.[18] Today China and Hong Kong account for nearly 60 per cent of the world's toy trade.[19]

III ELEMENTS OF GLOBAL LEGAL PLURALISM

We usually view the legal arrangements which are relevant to such global eco-nomic networks in one of two ways. Often we see them essentially in terms of contracts between nominally equal parties, such as individuals, companies or states, whose agreement is consecrated either in bilateral or multilateral form. Alternatively, we conceive of them in hierarchical terms, for example as consti-tuting various regional or international forms of multi-level governance. I wish to suggest, however, that both of these conceptions, regardless of their force in normative terms, are descriptively inaccurate and analytically incomplete.

[14] "Hong Kong's Toy Industry", *Hong Kong & China Economics*, on the Internet homepage of the Hong Kong Trade Development Council at http://www.tdc.org.hk/main/industries/t2_2_39.htm, last updated 2 July 1998.

[15] *Journal of Commerce*, 13 January 1995.

[16] See the statement by Dennis Ting, who, as of January 1995, was Chairman of Kader Industrial Co. Ltd., a leading Hong Kong toy firm, as well as of the Hong Kong Trading Agency's Toy Advisory Committee and of the Hong Kong Toy Council: *Journal of Commerce*, 13 January 1995.

[17] J. Newton and L. Tse, " 'Kids' Stuff: The Organisation and Politics of the China-EU Trade in Toys", in R. Strange, J. Slater and L. Wang (eds), *Trade and Investment in China: The European Experience* (Routledge, 1998), 147, 154.

[18] Interviews in Hong Kong, Guangzhou, and the Shenzhen Special Economic Zone, China.

[19] "Chinese Toy Making: Where the Furbies come from", *The Economist*, 19 December 1998, 95.

There is a fundamental and growing disjunction between our traditional, normative and hierarchical conceptions of the law governing international trade and the shape of the economic networks which are an integral part of economic globalization. We should not necessarily expect the law and economic relations to be isomorphic. But in order to understand how global economic networks are governed in practice, we need to revise many of our basic ideas about the shape of the global legal order. Global economic networks are the product of, and a form of, strategic behaviour, and they usually have a particular locus of power and a specific hierarchy. Their dramatic growth has placed in question the credibility of lawyers' claims about the hierarchical nature of global economic governance. At the same time it has provoked demands for the constitutionalisation of global governance and debates about its feasibility and desirability.

I suggest that the most adequate concept for understanding the global legal order is global legal pluralism. In order to explore and develop this concept, it is useful to build upon previous research.[20] I focus here on Teubner's theory of *lex mercatoria* as a paradigm of global law.[21] My purpose is not to analyse this work for its own sake, but rather to use it to address two questions. First, what is the author's conception of the law relevant to the global economy? Secondly, what does this conception contribute to our understanding of global legal pluralism?

Teubner's principal thesis is that global law develops mainly outside the political structures of nation states and international organisations.[22] The basic device is contract,[23] and the paradigm is *lex mercatoria*.[24] From Teubner's perspective, global law has several important characteristics. First, its boundaries are not territorial but consist of "invisible" markets, branches, specialised professional communities or highly technical social networks, all of which transcend territorial boundaries.[25] Secondly, its sources are not a legislature, but rather, according to his theory of autopoiesis,[26] "self-organizing processes of 'structural coupling' of law with ongoing globalized processes of a highly specialized and technical nature".[27] Thirdly, global law depends closely on various

---

[20] Of special significance for the present purposes, in addition to Teubner's work (cited below at n. 21) are Shapiro, "The Globalization of Law" (1993) 1 *Indiana Journal of Global Legal Studies* 37; Trubek/Dezalay/Buchanan/Davis, "Global Restructuring and the Law: Internationalization of Legal Fields and the Creation of Transnational Arenas", (1994) 14 *Case Western Reserve Law Review* 407; B. de Sousa Santos, *Toward a New Common Sense: Law, Science and Politics in the Paradigmatic Transition* (Routledge, New York, 1995), esp. ch. 4, "Globalization, Nation-States and the Legal Field: From Legal Diaspora to Legal Ecumenism?", 250–377; A. J. Arnaud, *Entre modernité et mondialisation: Cinq leçons d'histoire de la philosophie du droit et de l'Etat* (LGDJ 1998).

[21] See G. Teubner (ed.), *Global Law without a State* (Dartmouth, 1997).

[22] See G. Teubner, " 'Global Bukowina': Legal Pluralism in the World Society", in G. Teubner (ed.), *Global Law Without a State* (Dartmouth, 1997), 7.

[23] Ibid., 15.

[24] Ibid., 8, 12.

[25] Ibid., 7, 8.

[26] Cf. G. Teubner (ed.), *Autopietic law: a new approach to law and society* (De Gruyter, 1988).

[27] Ibid., 8.

other social fields, instead of being relatively autonomous from political institutions in particular; hence, it is subject to economic pressures and so is not strongly institutionalised in the sense of due process or the rule of law.[28] Fourthly, it consists mainly of broad principles which, though not legally binding, have the great correlative advantages of flexibility and adaptability.[29] Fifthly, at first it is not politicised, but the gradual juridification of economic relations through contract will lead eventually to the interference of political processes.[30] Finally, it is not unified, whether nationally, regionally or on a world scale;[31] instead, due to its dependence on other social processes and its lack of political and institutional support, global law is decentred and non-hierarchical.[32]

This perspective makes several important contributions to advancing our understanding of global legal pluralism. First, it takes seriously the idea that, apart from nation states, there are other sources of economically and socially significant norms that operate across national borders and to a large extent independently of states. Secondly, it recognises that bundles of these norms may be aggregated in the form of a system, and that there are a plurality of such systems, including norm-generating processes. Indeed, in addition to drawing on the literature on legal pluralism,[33] Teubner expressly uses the term "global legal pluralism", though in a different way from that being advanced here. Thirdly, it tries to analyse the organisation of these norms and the systems in which they are embedded as part of distinct networks rather than in terms of hierarchy.[34] Fourthly, it gives due weight and attention to the significance of soft law, "rules of conduct which, in principle, have no legally binding force but which nevertheless may have practical effects".[35]

For the present purposes, however, this useful formulation has several shortcomings. First, its starting point, *lex mercatoria,* leads inevitably to an almost exclusive emphasis on contract. It may be true that, in *lex mercatoria*, contract is not only the central legal device but also the primary source of law and means of self-legitimation.[36] Viewed however from a different perspective, for example that of strategic actors in a global commodity chain, such as multinational

---

[28] Ibid., 8, 19.

[29] Ibid., 21.

[30] Ibid., 21–2; see also G. Teubner, "Foreword: Legal Regimes of Global Non-state Actors", in G. Teubner (ed.), *Global Law Without a State* (Dartmouth, 1997), xiv.

[31] Ibid., 8.

[32] G. Teubner, "Foreword: Legal Regimes of Global Non-state Actors", in G. Teubner (ed.), *Global Law Without a State* (Dartmouth, 1997), xiv.

[33] *Cf.* G. Teubner, "The Two Faces of Janus: Rethinking Legal Pluralism", (1992) 13 *Cardozo Law Review* 1443.

[34] *Cf.* G. Teubner, "The Many-Headed Hydras: Networks as Higher-Order Collective Actors", in J. McCahery, S. Picciotto, and C. Scott (eds), *Corporate Control and Accountability: Changing Structures and the Dynamics of Regulation* (Clarendon Presss, 1993), 41–51.

[35] For this definition, see Snyder, "The Effectiveness of European Community Law: Institutions, Processes, Tools and Techniques", (1993) 56(1) *Modern Law Review* 19, 32.

[36] See G. Teubner, " 'Global Bukowina': Legal Pluralism in the World Society", in G. Teubner (ed.), *Global Law Without a State* (Dartmouth, 1997), 18.

firms, contract is only one among several legal devices, sources of law and forms of legitimation. Secondly, Teubner focuses exclusively on non-state actors; he intentionally neglects the state. For his purposes this methodological choice is useful, if not essential. It is an integral part of his argument that political theories of law are of little relevance to global law.[37] This methodological choice, however, is based on a traditional conception of constitutions, as being associated always with the nation state.[38] It also has the necessary and, for the present purposes, unfortunate consequence that it reveals only part of the picture of global legal pluralism. In particular with regard to international trade, nation states, regional organisations such as the European Union, and international organisations such as the World Trade Organisation, as well as other organisations and networks, play a fundamental role.

Thirdly, a consequence of focusing on *lex mercatoria* and omitting the state and other political structures is an overemphasis on soft law. In the governance of global economic networks, however, both soft law and legally binding norms, or "hard law", are important. Indeed, the relationship between hard law and soft law has long been controversial, and today it is one of the most interesting—and difficult—questions currently raised by the governance of globalization. Fourthly, Teubner's analysis is based a specific conception of legal pluralism. He asks the question, "where are concrete norms actually produced?".[39] Answering it, he defines legal pluralism in terms of discourse, of communicative processes that interpret the world by means of a binary code of legal/illegal.[40] This definition, however, accords relatively little weight to institutions, and it assumes that alternative conceptions of legal pluralism imply "a set of conflicting social norms"[41] and require "an implied delegation of state power".[42] None of these assumptions, as I hope to show, are necessary or indeed helpful in the context of this chapter.

Global legal pluralism, as I use the term, comprises two different aspects. The first is structural, the second relational.

First, global legal pluralism involves a variety of institutions, norms and dispute-resolution processes located and produced at different structured sites around the world. Legal scholarship has traditionally paid most attention to

---

[37] *Global Law Without a State* (Dartmouth, 1997), 7.

[38] In fact, Teubner (ibid., 6) quotes Niklas Luhmann, *Das Recht der Gesellschaft* (Suhrkamp, 1993), 582, to the effect that "the structural coupling between law and politics via constitutions has no correspondence on the level of world society". Compare the different conception of Jean-Philippe Robé, that the world constitutional structure consists of a global legal order comprised of various territorial and functional legal orders, with different goals and hence problems of co-ordination: see J. P Robé, "Multinational Enterprises: The Constitution of a Pluralistic Legal Order", in G. Teubner (ed.), *Global Law Without a State* (Dartmouth, 1997), 45, 70.

[39] Ibid., 12.

[40] Ibid., 12, 14.

[41] Ibid., 14.

[42] Ibid., 18. As to other problems with this definition, see P. T. Muchlinski, " 'Global Bukowina' Examined: Viewing the Multinational Enterprise as a Transnational Law-making Community", in G. Teubner (ed.), *Global Law Without a State* (Dartmouth, 1997), 79, 85.

understanding state, regional and international legal institutions, legally binding norms and dispute-resolution processes involving law. Much of the most
interesting recent work concerns the "constitutionalisation" of international
trade regulation.[43] In addition, international lawyers and related specialists in
international relations have also studied international negotiations, norms that,
at least in principle, are not legally binding, global regulatory networks[44] and
intergovernmental networks.[45] The analysis of international regimes,[46] multi-
level governance and other types of institutional arrangements, such as credit
rating agencies,[47] has largely been the province of political scientists and specialists in international relations. Examples in the field of EU legal and political
science scholarship concern multi-level governance,[48] committees[49] and different types of settings, whether highly institutionalised with specified norms, rules
and procedures, or non-hierarchical and decentralised.[50] While it is possible to
generalise to some extent from this previous work, no one has tried to unite
these different elements. Some basic questions remain therefore to be answered.
What is a site? States and regional and international organisations are included,
but so are a diversity of other institutional, normative and processual sites, such
as commercial arbitration,[51] trade associations and so on. How are sites created
and how do they grow, survive or die? How are they structured? What does it
mean to say that different structured sites are the anchors of contemporary legal
pluralism?

Secondly, the relations among these sites are of many different types, in terms
of both structure and process. For example, in terms of structural relationships,

[43] *Cf.* especially J. II. Jackson, *The World Trade Organization: Constitution and Jurisprudence*
(The Royal Institute of International Affairs, 1998); E.U. Petersmann, "How to Promote the
International Rule of Law: Contributions by the WTO Appellate Review System", in J. Cameron and
K. Campbell (eds), *Dispute Resolution in the World Trade Organisation* (Cameron May, 1998), 75.

[44] *Cf.* S. Picciotto, "The Regulatory Criss-Cross: Interaction between Jurisdictions and The
Construction of Global Regulatory Networks", in W. Bratton, J. McCahery, S. Picciotto, and
C. Scott (eds), *International Regulatory Competition and Coordination* (Clarendon Press, 1996), 89.

[45] *Cf.* Slaughter, "The Real New World Order", (1997) 76 *Foreign Affairs* 183.

[46] A recent example is M. Zacher (with Brent A. Sutton), *Governing Global Networks:
International Regimes for Transportation and Communications* (Cambridge University Press,
1996).

[47] *Cf.* Sinclair, "Passing Judgment:Credit Rating Processes as Regulatory Mechanisms of
Governance in the Emerging World Order", (1994) 1 *Review of International Political Economy*
133.

[48] F. Scharpf, *Governing in Europe: Effective and Democratic?* (Oxford University Press, 1999).

[49] See C. Joerges and E. Vos (eds), *EU Committees* (Hart Publishing, Oxford, 1999).

[50] *Cf.* Risse-Kappen, "Exploring the Nature of the Beast: International Relations Theory and
Comparative Policy Analysis Meet the European Union" (1996) 34 *Journal of Common Market
Studies* 51.

[51] See Y. Dezalay and B. G. Garth, *Dealing in Virtue: International Commercial Arbitration and
the Construction of a Transnational Legal Order* (University of Chicago Press, 1996); see also
A. Casella, "On Market Integration and the Development of Institutions: The Case of International
Commercial Arbitration" (1996) 40 *European Economic Review* 155. For an example concerning
the toy sector, see the 1987 *Award on Dispute over Contract for the Sale of Electric Toys, in Selected
Works of China International Economic and Trade Arbitration Commission Awards (1963–1988)
Updated to 1993* (authorised English Version; English version translated by China Law and Culture
Publications Limited) (Sweet & Maxwell, 1995), 192.

sites may be autonomous and even independent, part of the same or different regimes, part of a single system of multi-level governance, or otherwise inter-connected. In terms of process, they may be distinct and discrete, competing, overlapping, or feed into each other, for example in the sense of comprising a "structural set", "formed through the mutual convertibility of rules and resources in one domain of action into those pertaining to another".[52] These relations of structure and process constitute the global legal playing field. They determine the basic characteristics of global legal pluralism, such as equality or hierarchy, dominance or submission, creativity or imitation, convergence or divergence, and so on. They influence profoundly the growth, development and survival of the different sites.

Global legal pluralism is not merely an important part of the context in which global economic networks are constructed, in the sense that it is a factor to be taken into account by strategic actors; it is an integral part of these global economic networks themselves. In other words, global economic networks are constructed on a global playing field, which is organised or structured partly by global legal pluralism. Global legal pluralism does more, however, than simply provide the rules of the game; it also constitutes the game itself, including the players.

IV THE SHAPE OF GLOBAL LEGAL PLURALISM

Outline

We are now in a position to consider in more detail the interconnection between global legal pluralism and the global commodity chain in toys. Instead of starting with normative systems, I propose to start with social and economic relations. Let us, following Hopkins and Wallerstein, use the term "boxes" to refer to the separable processes involved in any global commodity chain.[53] The separable processes or boxes may include, for example, invention, production, marketing, distribution and consumption. The boundaries of each box are socially defined and so may be redefined.[54] Technological and social organisational changes play a role in these processes. So too does law, conceived broadly to encompass the sites of global legal pluralism, with each site comprising its specific institutions, norms and processes, law. Law helps to construct and to define the boxes which make up the global commodity chain in toys.

---

[52] A. Giddens, "A Reply to My Critics", in D. Held and J. B. Thompson, *Social Theory of Modern Societies: Anthony Giddens and His Critics* (Cambridge University Press, 1989), 253, 299.

[53] T. K. Hopkins and I. Wallerstein, "Commodity Chains: Construct and Research", in Gary Gereffi and Miguel Korzeniewicz (eds), *Commodity Chains and Global Capitalism* (Greenwood Process, 1994), 17, 18.

[54] Ibid.

We can ask a series of questions about the social organisation of the constituent elements of any single box in the chain. They refer, according to Hopkins and Wallerstein,[55] to:

- the number of component units in each box (monopoly or competition);
- their geographic concentration or dispersal;
- membership in one or more chains;
- property arrangements;
- modes of labour control;
- links within a chain

I add two further issues:

- connection between economic relations and specific sites;
- relations between sites and the chain as a whole.

Thus, here I rephrase, elaborate and add to Hopkins' and Wallerstein's questions. I give special emphasis to the institutional, normative and processual components of the sites of global legal pluralism. In the following paragraphs I offer selected examples of the interconnections between these sites and the international commodity chain. The discussion is meant to be illustrative, not exhaustive. It is designed to outline the shape of global legal pluralism.

Monopoly or Competition

First, the *number of component units* in the box. To what degree is a box monopolised by a small number of production units? What are the main factors determining this structure? What incentives for a particular structure are provided by legal and other institutions, norms and processes? For example, to what extent and how does the law provide or permit barriers to entry? To what extent does it facilitate or require market access, for instance with regard to production and/or distribution? Do different sites of global legal pluralism provide conflicting incentives and, if so, how are these conflicts managed, if not neutralised? If demonopolisation of any highly profitable box is an important process in the contemporary world economy, as Hopkins and Wallerstein suggest,[56] what role do the sites of global legal pluralism play with regard to this process, for example by encouraging it, by countering it by redefining the boundaries of the box or by other means, or by creating incentives for shifting capital investment to other boxes, or even other chains?

Several sites of global legal pluralism play a role in shaping or determining the number of component units in any given box in the international commodity chain in toys. Consider some examples.

First, with regard to the invention, production and marketing, US intellectual property law is of crucial significance in determining the number of buyers and

---

[55] Ibid., 18–19.
[56] Ibid., 18.

maintaining their market power. The highest barriers to entry in buyer-driven commodity chains typically concern product conception, design and marketing. Intellectual property law creates or consolidates barriers to entry.

Secondly, antitrust law has an important impact on production, marketing and distribution. In the United States, Europe or Japan, it helps to define the number of key buyers or manufacturers in the international toy industry. US antitrust law in particular affects the possibility of mergers among buyers. When market leader Mattel Inc. acquired the third largest toy manufacturer, Tyco Toys Inc., in 1996, Mattel was quoted in the US media as expressing confidence that the deal would not be blocked by US antitrust law, even though the companies' combined sales represented 19 per cent of the US toy market.[57]

Thirdly, the lack of binding legal regulation of Internet retailing lowers barriers to entry into the retail market in toys. Consequently, when buyers are squeezed by traditional retailers, they turn without great difficulty to the Internet in order to enter the retail sector themselves, either through specialist Internet retailers or by means of the buyers' own websites.

A fourth example, explored in more detail here, concerns EC international trade and customs law concerning the access of importers to the EU toy market.[58] It illustrates clearly the role played by EU legislation and the European Court of Justice in restructuring the EU toy industry. In 1994 the Council of the European Union adopted two major complementary legislative reforms. The first was Council Regulation No. 519/94 on common rules for imports from certain third countries,[59] the general Regulation governing imports from non-market economy countries, except for textile products.[60] The second was Council Regulation No. 520/94 establishing a Community procedure for administrative quantitative quotas.[61] It established a new way of administering quotas, based on a system of licenses issued by the Member States according to quantitative criteria established at Community level.[62] Both Regulations were part of a package deal, designed to secure acceptance of the Uruguay Round multilateral trade

---

[57] Madore, "Mattel confident Tyco deal will pass antitrust scrutiny", *The Buffalo News*, 19 November 1996.

[58] Such importers include both EU and foreign companies, e.g. in joint ventures in foreign countries, outward processing arrangements, or other increasingly complex forms of co-operation which are characteristic of—and indeed create—economic globalization. See Snyder, "Friends and Rivals", above at n. 2.

[59] OJ 1994 L67/89.

[60] Imports of textiles were governed by one of two other regulations. Council Regulation No. 3030/93 on common rules for imports of certain textile products from third countries (OJ 1993 L275/1) covered imports of textile products from countries with which the EC has concluded bilateral agreements, protocols or other arrangements. Council Regulation No. 517/94 on common rules for imports of textile products from certain third countries not covered by bilateral agreements, protocols or other arrangements, or by other specific Community import rules (OJ 1994 L67/1), covered imports of textile products from non-market economy countries with which the Community had not concluded specific arrangements.

[61] Council Regulation No. 520/94 establishing a Community procedure for administering quantitative quotas (OJ 1994 L66/1).

[62] See F. Snyder, *International Trade*, above at n. 2, 190–202.

negotiations, to reinforce existing trade policy instruments, and to complete the EC's Common Commercial Policy.

Both the new quota regime and provisions for administering it exemplified the Europeanisation of law. They involved the total or partial replacement of the law of the Member States by EC law. EC quotas on seven categories of Chinese products, including toys, replaced approximately 6,417 national quantitative restrictions, including 4,700 on more than thirty Chinese products.[63] Council Regulation 519/94 introduced quotas on seven categories of Chinese products, ranging from gloves, footwear, porcelain tableware, ceramic tableware, glassware, car radios and toys. It imposed separate quotas on product categories SH/NC 9503 41 (stuffed toys, such as teddy bears), SH/NC 9503 49 (non-human toys, such as Ninja Turtles), and SH/NC 9503 90 (other toys, such as die-cast minatures). It did not cover, however, certain other toys, such as Barbie dolls.

The adoption of Council Regulation 519/94 inaugurated four years of continuous lobbying, negotiation, litigation, law reform, further litigation and further law reform.[64] The new EC quota regime for toys from China pleased no one, except perhaps the Commission, which had brokered the compromise. The United Kingdom, which had opposed the measure in the vote in the Council of Ministers, brought an Article 173 action in the European Court of Justice (ECJ) to annul the Chinese toys quota.[65] It argued that the new Regulation introduced quotas on imports of Chinese toys into the UK market which previously was free of quotas. Subsequently the Council amended the challenged Regulation.[66] However, this compromise itself was challenged in the ECJ by Spain,[67] one of the main initial proponents of quotas on imports of toys from China. Then the European subsidiary of Tyco Toys Inc.[68] brought an action in the Court of First Instance to annul the toy quota and to obtain compensation for injury.[69]

---

[63] *Agence Europe*, No. 6272, 13 July 1994, 9.

[64] For further details, see F. Snyder, "Chinese Toys", above at n. 2, on which the following paragraphs draw.

[65] Case C-150/94 *United Kingdom of Great Britain and Northern Ireland v. Council of the European Union* [1998] ECR I-7235.

[66] Council Regulation No. 1921/94 amending Council Regulation No. 519/94 on common rules for imports from certain third countries (OJ 1994 L198/1). See also *Agence Europe*, No. 6277, 20 July 1994, 13.

[67] Case C-284/94, *Kingdom of Spain v. Council of the European Union* [1998] ECR I-7309. The Council was supported by the Commission.

[68] Tyco's trade names include Dr Dreadful, Fashion Magic, Kitchen Littles Cookware, Magna Doodle, Matchbox and View-Master. See its Internet website at http://www.matchboxtoys.com. As of February 1999, Tyco Preschool was a Mattel company. See the Internet website of Toy Manufacturers of America at http://www.toy-tma.com/MEMBER/.

[69] Case T-268/94 *Tyco Toys (UK) Ltd. and others v. Commission and Council* (OJ 1994 C254/14); see also *Agence Europe*, No. 6317, 17 September 1994, 13. As of 20 April 1999, this case was still pending, but a hearing was expected to be held soon, according to the services of the ECJ. I am grateful to Emir Lawless of the EUI Library for this information. By May 1999, however, the case had been abandoned: interviews in the European Commission.

The challenge by the United Kingdom to the Chinese toys quota[70] has been ascribed to pressure brought on the UK Government by the largest umbrella trade association, Toy Manufacturers of Europe (TME). Hong Kong firms accounted for the majority of those affected by the quota, but they could not seek the help of the Hong Kong Government, at least directly, because their factories were located in China.[71] Toy multinationals thus lobbied in Europe through the trade association. The TME was formed as a political lobbying group in the early 1990s. It brought together European toy manufacturers, except those in France and Spain, together with German producers of plastic toys, which were grouped instead in the Asociación Española de Fabricantes de Juguetes (AEFJ), established in 1967.[72] The members of TME accounted for approximately 80 per cent of toy manufacturers and distributors operating in Europe. It was dominated by US toy multinationals, together with the Danish firm LEGO and the Japanese firm Bandai. Its members did not manufacture toys in Europe. Their main interest lay in maintaining open markets throughout the world, including the EU, for their main source of production, namely China.[73] They were also concerned to use the EU market and EU law effectively in their strategies for restructuring the international toy sector and ensuring the integration of the EU market into the global commodity chain. The TME had opposed the imposition of quotas from the outset. Its chair, Peter Waterman, considered that the toy industry was being used as a pawn in the debate concerning the accession of China to the World Trade Organisation.[74]

Lobbying and litigation were two facets of the same political strategy. They paid off in a series of continual legislative reforms, six in total during a brief four-year period. The first occurred when, five weeks after the United Kingdom brought its case, the Commission proposed an increase in the quota, largely because of pressure from the TME.[75] The Member States, however, did not agree.[76] Germany, the United Kingdom, the Netherlands and Ireland sought a global solution to the Chinese quota problem, embracing not only toys but also textiles and other products. France, Spain, Portugal and Greece rejected the Commission proposal, both in itself and as a dangerous precedent; they claimed that it favoured traders as against manufacturers. This split between northern and southern countries, between free trade and protectionism, reflected the different Member States' domestic institutional and economic structures.[77] To

[70] Case C-150/94 *United Kingdom of Great Britain and Northern Ireland* v. *Council of the European Union* [1998] ECR I-7235.

[71] *Cf.* Newton and Tse, above at n. 17, 159.

[72] I am grateful to Mr Salvador Miro Sanjuan, President of the AEFJ, for this information.

[73] Newton and Tse, above at n. 17, 156.

[74] *Agence Europe*, No. 6824, 3 October 1996, 5.

[75] *Agence Europe*, No. 6272, 13 July 1994, 9. Newton and Tse, above at n. 17, 159.

[76] *Agence Europe*, No. 6275, 16 July 1994, 14. For the contrasting viewpoint of traders associations, see *Agence Europe*, No. 6289, 6 August 1994, 8.

[77] *Cf.* C. Garcia Molyneux, *Domestic Structures and International Trade: The Unfair Trade Instruments of the United States and the European Union* (Hart, 2001).

break the logjam, the Council adopted a compromise solution.[78] It embraced only the toy sector, but it raised the quota for certain toys from China by almost 30 per cent for the period from 15 March to 31 December 1994.[79] This compromise itself, however, provoked further litigation by Spain[80] and the European subsidiary of Tyco Toys Inc.[81]

The second legislative reform occurred in March 1995, when the Council agreed to raise the toy quota for the year starting 1 January 1995.[82] This was part of a more general revision of quotas on imports from China, in which quotas for some goods were abolished, others increased, and others maintained at the then existing level. The quotas for toys were increased by 36.8 per cent for stuffed toys (ECU 274 764 243 for HS/CN 9503 41), 58.3 per cent for animals (ECU 132 767 177 for HS/CN 9503 49), and 27.8 per cent for other toys (ECU 649 465 212 for HS/CN 9503 90.[83] This included the amounts required to take account of the accession to the EU of Austria, Finland and Sweden. Note that dolls were still free of quota.

The legislative tinkering continued. In April 1996 the Council adopted a third revision, to take effect as of 1 January 1996.[84] This measure was part of a more general revision of imports on goods from China. Like its predecessor, it benefited importers, distributors and processors of Chinese products, met to some extent the demands of the Chinese Government, and conferred new advantages on firms by removing quotas in certain markets. While it did not increase the total quota amount for toys, it fused the three existing quotas into one. This introduced greater flexibility in the implementation of the quotas.[85] Hence it empowered certain firms, notably importers, and increased the free play of the market, while maintaining the overall quota. Arguably, it helped industry to meet changes in consumer demand. As of October 1996 the Tyco Preschool company factory in China was operating six days a week to meet weekly shipments of Tickle Me Elmo, producing 50,000 Elmos a week to sell one million by Christmas Eve. [86] It planned to ship one million dolls from its five factories in China.[87] In 1997 it imported a supply of 300,000 Sing & Snore Ernie

---

[78] Council Regulation No. 1921/94 amending Council Regulation No. 519/94 on common rules for imports from certain third countries (OJ 1994 L198/1). See also *Agence Europe*, No. 6277, 20 July 1994, 13.

[79] Council Regulation 1921/94, Art. 1. The toys in question were those falling within Code HS/CN 9503 41 (stuffed toys representing animals or non-human creatures), such as Furbies.

[80] Case C-284/94 *Kingdom of Spain* v. *Council of the European Union* [1998] ECR I-7309. The Council was supported by the Commission.

[81] Case T-268/94 *Tyco Toys (UK) Ltd. and Others* v. *Commission and Council* (OJ 1994 C254/14), subsequently withdrawn.

[82] Council Regulation No. 538/95 amending Council Regulation No. 519/94 on common rules for imports from certain third countries (OJ 1995 L55/1), Art. 1, Annex II.

[83] Percentage increases are taken from Newton and Tse, above at n. 17, 161.

[84] Council Regulation No. 752/96 amending Annexes II and III of Regulation 519/94 on common rules for imports from certain third countries (OJ 1996 L103/1), Art. 1.

[85] See ibid., Preamble, Sixth Recital.

[86] *USA Today*, 11 December 1996.

[87] Hoye, "Ticke-Me Elmo Hottest Yule Toy", *The Arizona Republic*, 4 December 1996.

dolls from China by plane instead of container ship to get them into stores more quickly for the Christmas season.[88]

Fusion of the three quotas into one also created a greater space for restructuring of the toy sector. The EU toy industry at the time was concentrated geographically in the Jura (France), Milan (Italy), Attica (Greece) and Alicante (Spain). These regions accounted for 50–60 per cent of toy production in their respective countries and included both manufacturers and auxiliary industries. The industry comprised about 2,600 firms, producing a great variety of toys, and employing just under 100,000 workers, with only fifteen firms having more than 500 employees.[89] Their prices were higher than those of toys from China, quite apart from the possibility of producing counterfeit toys anywhere with computer-assigned design programmes.[90] These small EU firms thus were faced from international competition from other producers, as well as being squeezed by the dominant international buyers who controlled the major brands and had easy access to large retailers. They were gradually regrouping and restructuring. The Commission's original proposal for fusing the three quotas was intended partly to encourage these economic and social processes, even though the Commission recognised that its legislative proposals were based on very incomplete information.[91] As a result, the large trade associations in the sector supported the Commission's proposals.

The Commission took a further step towards an open market in May 1996, when it revised the procedures for allocating quota amounts.[92] It reduced the allocations under import licenses for traditional importers by specified percentages, applied to a base equal to average imports for 1992 and 1994.[93] License applications by non-traditional importers were to be met in full within the overall quota limits.[94] In addition, a licence issued for a certain category of toys could also be used for the other categories.[95] This revision, as with the previous reforms, moved EC law closer to meeting the interests of multinational toy buyers and manufacturers, thus gradually undoing the 1994 compromise. It did so,

---

[88] Matzer, "Advertising and Marketing: Holiday '97' ", *The Los Angeles Times*, 6 December 1997, 4.

[89] Commission of the European Communities, "Report from the Commission to the Council on the surveillance measures and quantitative quotas applicable to certain non-textile products originating in the People's Republic of China", COM(95)614 final (6 December 1995), 41.

[90] Ibid., 44–5.

[91] Ibid., 47. In preparing the report, the Commission sollicited information from a wide variety of producers, importers, and traders, either directly or through their trade associations. The response, however, was "incomplete and rather unsatisfactory": ibid., 3. Nearly all the investigated sectors were composed of numerous small and medium-sized enterprises, "of which a significant proportion are not even known by the relevant national federations": ibid., 3. Of the importers, the TME, Toys Traders of Europe (TTE), the Hong Kong Toys Council, the Japan Toy Association, and John Lewis Partnership (UK) submitted remarks: see ibid., 45–6.

[92] Commission Regulation No. 899/96 establishing the quantities to be allocated to importers from the Community quantitative quotas redistributed by Regulation No. 612/96 (OJ 1996 L121/8).

[93] Ibid., Art. 1 and Annex I.

[94] Ibid., Art. 3 and Annex III.

[95] Ibid., Annex I, note 3, and Annex III, note 2.

however, not by increasing or otherwise modifying the quotas themselves, but rather by changing the way they were administered. In particular, it opened more space for new entrants to the import market, while at the same time it increased the flexibility of the administration of licences. In other words, it lowered barriers to entry and the costs of importation, notably for large firms.

In September 1996, litigation in the ECJ bore its first fruit. The Advocate-General gave his Opinion jointly in the two cases brought separately by the United Kingdom and Spain. He proposed that the ECJ should uphold the policy making and legislative discretion of the Council, and thus reject the claims by the United Kingdom and Spain for the annulment of EC legislation. This Opinion was taken by many in the toy sector as a clear signal that the actions brought by the two governments against the Community legislator would ultimately be rejected. At least some academic commentators shared this view.[96] Such a perception neglected the fact that the Advocate-General's Opinion does not state the law, nor is it legally binding on the Court. It captures nicely, however, the real political and symbolic significance of such opinions, in which, rightly or wrongly, the Advocate-General is often seen to be speaking not merely for the public but also for the Court.

Despite its lack of legal force, the Advocate-General's Opinion would seem to have had a decisive impact on further reform of the quota legislation. It encouraged, if not stimulated, the Member States to adjust further the basic 1994 legislation. The Council, the Community legislator, enacted a subsequent reform in mid-1997.[97] While maintaining the same overall quota amount for toys, it excluded toy parts and accessories from the quota. It placed these parts and accessories, as well as certain other categories of toys,[98] under Community surveillance, first for the period from publication of the measure on 14 May 1997 until 31 December 1997,[99] and then for the period from 1 January 1998.[100] These changes followed the main conclusions of the Commission's 1996 annual report.[101] The latter, in turn, presented a somewhat simplified version of the recommendations of what were then the two main trade associations, the TME acting on behalf of importers and the Fédération Européenne des Industries du Jouet on behalf of producers. Together these trade associations represented, in

---

[96] Newton and Tse, above at n. 17, 161. Doubtless the plaintiff governments and the large trade associations were more aware of the legal status of such an opinion and its relation to the eventual judgment by the ECJ. Small businesses, however, are often much less aware of these crucial legal and institutional distinctions.

[97] Council Regulation No. 847/97 amending Annexes II and III to Regulation No. 519/94 on common rules for imports from certain third countries (OJ 1997 L122/1).

[98] HS/CN 9503 30 (other construction sets and construction toys of wood, plastic or other materials).

[99] Council Regulation 847/97 Art. 1, Annexes I and II.

[100] Ibid., Art. 2, Annexes III and IV.

[101] Commission of the European Communities, "Second Report from the Commission to the Council on the surveillance measures and quantitative quotas applicable to certain non-textile products originating in the People's Republic of China", COM(97)11 final, (29 January 1997), 45.

the Commission's view, "almost the entire European toy industry".[102] The legislative reforms testified to the close co-ordination between firms, both independently and through trade associations, and Member States and EC institutions, on the other hand. This co-ordination, in turn, ensured that the adjustments in the law were in step with the changing interests of the EU toy sector, which was then in the process of restructuring within the EU market and of adapting to the new challenges posed by the international market.

The major trade associations had in fact proposed the liberalisation of imports of only "the components of toys which were meant to be subject to further industrial transformation".[103] Articulated for political and other reasons in terms of stimulating employment by local assembly and similar processes, this proposal embodied a very clear recognition of the internationalisation of the toy industry and the role of the EU producers in these increasingly global networks. EU producers were to occupy a place in these new networks that was very similar to that of producers in China, except that Chinese factories were engaged in original equipment manufacturing, whereas EU producers were involved merely in the final (though industrial) transformation of the toys, albeit with the possibility in some instances of moving into own brand manufacturing. This proposal signaled the eventual transformation of many small and medium-sized EU firms, and to that extent the nation states in which they were situated, into flexible, more precarious world factory sites: dependent, as were Chinese toy factories and their Hong Kong owners, on the multinational firms which occupied the dominant positions and which were the key players in the global toy commodity chain. It also implied potentially a shift in legal position. The law governing imports would no longer be the EC quota regulations, but rather EC customs regulations on inward processing and potentially (if China were to accept the relevant annexes) the 1973 Kyoto International Convention on the Simplification and Harmonisation of Customs Procedures.[104] To return to our model of the international toy commodity chain, the legal reforms thus fostered a transformation of the number of production units, an increase in their geographic dispersal, and potentially changes in the property and other arrangements linking various parts of the chain.

A sixth reform followed soon afterwards. Less than a month after the 1997 reform took effect,[105] the Council once again adopted a further Regulation.[106] It abolished entirely, with effect as of 1 January 1998, the quotas of toys falling

---

[102] COM(97)11 final, (29 January 1997), 38.

[103] Quoted in ibid., 38.

[104] Cmnd 5938 (OJ 1975 L100/2). The most convenient source is the Internet edition: World Customs Organisation, *Handbook: of the International Convention on the Simplification and Harmonization of Customs Procedures* (Kyoto, 18 May 1973), 1st edn October 1975; Amending Supplement No. 13, January 1993. In June 1999 the 1973 Kyoto Convention was revised, but the revised Convention has not yet been ratified by all parties: see http://www.wcoomd.org/frmpublic.htm.

[105] It took effect on the date of publication, 14 May 1997: ibid., Art. 3.

[106] Council Regulation No. 1138/98 amending Annexes II and III of Regulation No. 519/94 on common rules for imports from certain third countries (OJ 1998 L159/1).

within HS/CN 9503 41, 9503 49, and 9503 90.[107] It subjected these products (and continued to subject toys of HS/CN 9503 30) to prior Community surveillance to ensure adequate monitoring of the volume and prices of imports.[108]

This final step in our saga of legislative reform occurred in the context of—and contributed to—the transformation of the EU toy industry. By definition, therefore, it also affected the gradual restructuring of the global toy commodity chain, including factories in China. By 1996 the EU toy industry had already adapted its production structures and improved production quality to such an extent that, at least from the standpoint of the Commission and most, if not all, national governments, import quotas were no longer necessary.[109] The EU's restructured toy enterprises imported items that were no longer produced in Europe. As the Commission noted, "most manufacturers in Europe are also becoming importers of some items which may be necessary for them to keep their market share both in the EU and on export markers".[110] EU producers were able to compete in foreign markets: exports of European toys outside the EU grew by a record 16.8 per cent in 1996, while imports in the same year rose by only 3 per cent.[111] The European Commission ascribed this successful adaptation to law. In its view, the temporary protection assured to EU industry by Community quotas permitted the necessary restructuring.[112] It thus also facilitated the redefinition of the role of these EU firms in the global commodity chain.

Changes in the organisation of political representation in the EU toy sector reflected these changes in the organisation of production and marketing. The first major peak association in the EU toy sector was the European Federation of Toy Industries,[113] founded in 1967. It comprised the national associations of the United Kingdom, France, the Netherlands, Germany, Italy, Greece, and Spain. In the early 1990s the UK association, together with the major multi-national toy companies (Hasbro, Mattel, Lego, Tomy, Bandai, etc.), founded the TME. Greece and Italy also joined the TME, as did the German national association composed of larger companies. German producers of plastic toys, France and Spain remained in a separate association, known as the Fédération Européenne des Industries du Jouet (FEIJ). The French and Spanish assocations, however, began negotiations with the TME to form a single peak association. These negotiations culminated in 1997 with the merger of the TME and the FEIJ[114] to form a new peak association, Toy Industry in Europe (TIE). It had

---

[107] Ibid., Art. 1 and Annex I.

[108] Ibid.

[109] See Commission of the European Communities, "Third Report from the Commission on the quantitative quotas and surveillance measures applicable to certain non-textile products originating in the People's Republic of China", COM(98)128 final, (9 March 1998), esp. 26–9, 35.

[110] Ibid., 28.

[111] Ibid., 26.

[112] Ibid., 27–8.

[113] Known in French as the Fédération Européenne des industries du Jouet (FEIJ) and in Spanish as the Federacion Europea del Juguete.

[114] According to the Commission report, it represented national producers, not international buyers. The precise reasons for the merger of FEIJ and TME remain unclear to me. One possibility

essentially the same structure as the TME, with large firms having a major role, but also with representation of indutrial unions, except for those of Germany which remained divided. Subsequently, the Greek association and the small associations of the Nordic countries also jointed the TIE.[115] As of February 1999, the co-presidency of TIE was held by the United Kingdom and Spain. The economic changes in the EU toy sector viewed as part of the global commodity chain thus were mirrored, more or less directly, in terms of industrial associations and political representation.

Since its formation, TIE supported strongly the immediate and total abolition of quotas on toys. In its view, quotas represented an administrative burden, especially for small businesses,[116] and in any event failed to restrict toy imports from China. Rephrasing this view, one might say that quotas were an obstacle to EU firms which sourced partly finished products from abroad, and thus prevented the successful operation of newly articulated global networks. In summary, both the European Commission and the main European trade association agreed by 1997 that toys from China should no longer be subject to quotas; insteads they should be subjected merely to surveillance, requiring only an import licence.[117]

The abolition of quotas was, according to the Preamble of the 1998 Regulation, neither inconsistent with the objective of taking account of the various interests in play nor liable to disrupt the Community market.[118] In fact, it was the culmination of more than a decade of conflict between Member States and between competing firms. It also represented the temporary conclusion of diverse attempts by EU institutions to manage conflicting interests. These conflicts were inherent in the process of market building and market management in the EU, partly because of the changes in the way in which the EU market was integrated into the international toy commodity chain. They began with the Chinese opening-up in 1979, the subsequent restructuring of the international toy industry, and the creation of new economic networks and the thin globalization[119] of this sector of the Chinese economy. Changes occurred in the domestic and international interests in the sector, and the lines between the domestic and the international were not merely blurred but actually

---

was that, despite quotas, it was too weak to be effective. Another is that Spanish and French producers went international: they linked up successfully with China, Hong Kong or other producer firms. A third possibility is that its members were integrated in the global commodity chain on some other terms. A fourth, not inconsistent possibility is that the merger resulted from increased US FDI in the toy sector in Spain and France.

[115] I am grateful to Mr Salvador Miro Sanjuan, President of the AEFJ, for this information.

[116] As to 1996, the EU had 2,000 companies in the toys and games sectors, employing over 100,000 people, of which 55,000 worked in indirect employment: Commission of the European Communities, above at n. 109, 27.

[117] On surveillance, see Snyder, *International Trade*, above at n. 2, 154, 157.

[118] *Cf.* Preamble, Second and Third Recitals of Council Regulation No. 1138/98 amending Annexcs II and III of Rcgulation No. 519/94 on common rulcs for imports from ccrtain third countries (OJ 1998 L159/1).

[119] I am grateful to David Trubek for the expression "thin globalization".

reconfigured. These changes were in turn expressed to some extent in legislative form. Just as the 1994 compromise legislation expressed the balance of interests at the time, changes in the structure of interests led to demands for changes in the law. The gradual legal reforms not only represented these new, changing configurations of interests; they also helped to crystallise and perhaps even to create new interests, especially with regard to the number and nature of units of production.[120]

Geographic Concentration or Dispersal

Second, *geographic concentration or dispersal*. What is the degree of geographic spread of the units in a specific box? In other words, are the units in a specific box geographically concentrated or are they dispersed? For example, are the provision of finance, marketing and retailing geographically concentrated, while production is dispersed? Is the prevailing geographic pattern influenced by the sites of global legal pluralism and, if so, how? For example, what incentives do different institutions, norms and processes provide for either concentration or dispersal of the different sites? Do these institutions, norms and processes play a role in the extent to which boxes shift from the core to the periphery of the world economy, assuming that, as Hopkins and Wallerstein argue, a box is likely to be relatively geographically concentrated in the core, but dispersed on the periphery?

We have already seen that invention, finance, marketing and retailing in the international toy industry are concentrated: the first in the United States, the second and third in the United States and Hong Kong, and the last, so far as control is concerned, in the United States and, to a lesser extent, Europe and Japan. Production has until recently tended to be concentrated mainly in Asia, although it could potentially be much more dispersed. The geographical separation of production from finance, marketing and retailing is encouraged by international norms concerning the customs operations known in the EU as inward processing and outward processing.[121] It is no exaggeration to describe the existence and increased use of these customs rules as the legal basis for what has been called "the new international division of labour".[122]

The overarching international legal framework is provided by the International Convention on the Simplification and Harmonisation of Customs

---

[120] Such a transformation is not unique to the EU. Chinese producers of traditional wooden and other toys are being ousted by international toy companies, such as LEGO: *cf.* Turner, "The Fading Tradition of Tang the Toymaker", *International Herald Tribune*, 8 January 1999, 8. For an account of the heterogeneity of toy producers in China, see also the short story by Zhang Xin, "Where Angels Dare to Tread" (translated by Josephine A. Mathews), in *Contemporary Chinese Women Writers VI: Four Novellas by Zhang Xin* (Panda Books and Chinese Literature Press, 1998), 97–231.

[121] On EU law, see Snyder, *International Trade*, above at n. 2, 83–103.

[122] For case studies from an economic standpoint, see F. Froebel, J. Heinrichs and O. Kreye, *The New International Division of Labour: Structural Unemployment in Industrialised Countries and Industrialisation in Developing Countries* (translated by Pete Burgress) (Cambridge University Press; Editions de la Maison des Sciences de l'Homme, 1980).

Procedures, a veritable international customs code. It was first signed at Kyoto on 18 May 1973 and entered in force on 25 September 1974.[123] An updated version was adopted on 25 June 1999 but has not yet been ratified by all parties.[124] The Kyoto Convention is the fruit of the Customs Cooperation Council (CCC), founded in 1952.[125] Since 1994, the CCC has been known as the World Customs Organisation (WCO). The WCO now oversees the implementation of the Kyoto Convention.[126] Its supervisory functions began with the establishment of the CCC, whose initial *raison d'être* was partly to supervise the application and interpretation of the customs classification system known as either the Brussels Tariff Nomenclature (BTN) or the Customs Cooperation Council Nomenclature.[127]

The WCO as at 1999 had 150 members. The EC Member States have participated since the beginning. However, membership is limited to states, and as a customs union, the EC formally has only observer status, even though the ECJ has taken the view that the Community has replaced the Member States in commitments arising from the Convention.[128] The United States joined the CCC in 1970.[129] Hong Kong and China are also members.

[123] Cmnd 5938 (OJ 1975 L100/2).

[124] The full text is available on the Internet homepage of the World Customs Organization at http://www.wcoomd.org.

[125] 22 UST 320, TIAS No. 7063, 157 UNTS 129. After World War II various European governments, drawing on work previously accomplished under the auspices of the League of Nations, formed in Brussels a European Customs Union Study Group, including a Customs Committee. This led in turn to the Convention establishing a Customs Co-operation Council; the Convention was signed in Brussels on 15 December 1950 and entered into force on 4 November 1952.

[126] See its Internet homepage at http://www.wcoomnd.org. The following three paragraphs are based on the WCO Internet home page at http://www.wcoomd.org: E. McGovern, *International Trade Regulation: GATT, the United States and the European Community,* (Globefield Press, 2nd ed. 1986), 45–7, 150–51; J. H. Jackson, W. J. Davey and A. O. Sykes, *Legal Problems of International Economic Relations: Cases, Materials and Text on the National and International Regulation of Transnational Economic Relations* (West, 3rd ed. 1995), 394; D. Lasok, *The Trade and Customs Law of the European Union* (Kluwer, 3rd ed. 1998), 237–8, 277–8; and F. Snyder, *International Trade,* above at n. 2, 3–9.

[127] The Nomenclature was adopted by the EC Member States and all other major GATT members except the United States and Canada.

[128] Case 38/75 *Nederlandse Spoorwegen* v. *Inspecteur der Invoerrechten en Accijnzen* [1975] ECR 1439. The Community view is expressed either by the Commission or the Member State holding the Presidency of the Council of Ministers.

[129] Though without adopting the Nomenclature. Together with the EC Member States and other countries, the United States participated in the development by the CCC of a new classification system, the Harmonised Commodity Description and Coding System (the Harmonised System), which entered into force on 1 January 1988: see the International Convention on the Harmonised Commodity Description and Coding System, done at Brussels on 14 June 1983, and the Protocol thereto, done at Brussels on 24 June 1986 (OJ 1987 L198/3), 1035 UNTS 3; KAV 2260. The EC is a party to the International Convention on the Harmonised Commodity Description and Coding System: see Council Decision 87/369 concerning the conclusion of the International Convention on the Harmonised Commodity Description and Coding System and of the Procotol of Amendment thereto (OJ 1987 L198/1). Art. 26 and 133 EC (ex Arts 28 and Art. 113) are the legal bases for the Council's power to conclude the Convention: see Case 165/87 *Commission of the European Communities* v. *Council of the European Communities* [1988] ECR 5545. The EC Combined Nomenclature, which is part of the Common Customs Tariff, follows closely the structure of the Harmonised System. The United States adopted the Harmonised System with effect as of 1 January 1989. General similar remarks apply to the Valuation Convention 1950.

The WCO, which is based in Brussels, is virtually the sole international body concerned with the harmonisation of technical customs rules and practices. As currently constituted, its highest body is a Council, composed of the Directors-General of Customs from all members. The Council is assisted by a Finance Committee of 17 members and a Policy Commission of 24 members. In addition, technical committees work in the areas of nomenclature and classification, valuation, customs technique and origin. Council bodies at all levels are helped by a General Secretariat, headed by a secretary-general, assisted by a deputy secretary-general and three directors.[130]

The tasks of the WCO are four-fold.[131] First, it drafts and promotes new agreements, mainly concerning customs techniques. Secondly, it makes recommendations to ensure uniform interpretation and application of its existing conventions, notably with regard to the Convention establishing a Customs Cooperation Council,[132] the Nomenclature Convention[133] and the Valuation Convention.[134] These legal status of these recommendations is ambiguous, and probably not very important from the practical standpoint, but it has been suggested that their acceptance by contracting parties "carries with it an obligation not to arbitrarily resile from the recommendations".[135] Thirdly, the WCO acts as a conciliator in disputes between contracting parties. Fourthly, it provides information and advice to governments in its fields of activity.

The Kyoto Convention is an unusual international agreement. Here I am concerned with the 1973 Convention, since the 1999 revised Convention has not yet been ratified by all Members.[136] One commentator has described it as "the equivalent of a whole series of agreements".[137] The Convention consists of two Parts. Part I contains the Convention itself, including (a) text and commentary, (b) provisions concerning entry into force, (c) obligations of the contracting parties as regards notification, and (d) provisions concerning extensions. Part II comprises numerous annexes, including, for example, Annex E.6 concerning temporary admission for inward processing, Annex E.8 concerning temporary exportation for outward processing, and Annex F.1 concerning free zones. The number of annexes is not fixed once-and-for-all. Existing annexes may be

---

[130] For further details, including a description of the committees, see the WCO website at http://www.wcoomd.org.

[131] This paragraph is based on the WCO website at http://www.wcoomd.org and McGovern, above at n. 126, 45–8.

[132] Convention establishing a Customs Cooperation Council Cmd 9232 (15 December 1950), in force 4 November 1952, 157 UNTS 129; TIAS 7063.

[133] International Convention on the Harmonized Commodity Description and Coding System, done at Brussels on 14 June 1983, and the Protocol thereto, done at Brussels on 24 June 1986 (OJ 1987 L198/3), .1035 UNTS 3, KAV 2260.

[134] Convention on the Valuation of Goods for Customs Purposes, Cmd 9233 (15 December 1950), in force 28 July 1953, 171 UNTS 305.

[135] McGovern, above at n. 126, 48.

[136] References to the Kyoto Convention in the following paragraphs are therefore made to the 1973 Convention. The 1999 revised Convention is broadly similar in structure but not identical. The 1999 Convention contains slightly different annexes and adds a new Specific Annex H on offences.

[137] McGovern, above at n. 126, 47.

amended, and new annexes may be added; this was the work of the Council's Permanent Technical Committee.[138]

These annexes contain the basic substantive rules. Each annex usually consists of an introductory summary, definitions of terms, standards, recommended practices and notes. According to the terms of the Convention,[139] standards are those provisions the general application of which is recognised as necessary for the achievement of harmonisation and simplification of customs procedures. Recommended practices are those provisions which are recognised as constituting progress toward the harmonisation and the simplication of customs procedures, the widest possible application of which is considered to be desirable. Notes indicate some of the possible courses of action to be followed in applying the standard or recommended practice concerned.

The Convention is open to signature by any state member of the Council and any state member of the United Nations or its specialised agencies.[140] A state may become a contracting party by signing the Convention without instrument of ratification, by depositing an instrument of ratification after signing it subject to ratification, or by acceding to it.[141] A state which does so must specify which annexes it accepts, and is required to accept at least one annex.[142] A contracting party which accepts an annex is deemed to accept all the standards and recommended practices in it unless it enters reservations in respect of particular standards or reommended practices, stating the differences between its national legislative provisions and the provisions of the standards or recommended practices in question.[143] States are not permitted to enter reservations against definitions. The Convention does not preclude the application of prohibitions or restrictions imposed under national legislation.[144] At least once every three years, each contracting party bound by an annex is required to review the standards and recommended practices against which it has entered reservations and notify the Secretary-General of the CCC of the results of the review.[145]

The 1973 Kyoto Convention had approximately 30 contracting parties; the number has increased to 114 for the 1999 revised Convention. For the present purposes, let us focus on the EC, its Member States, the United States, and China in relation to the 1973 Convention, Annex E.6 on inward processing,[146]

---

[138] Kyoto Convention, Art. 6.
[139] Ibid., Art. 4.
[140] Ibid., Art. 11(1).
[141] Ibid., Art. 11(2).
[142] Ibid., Art. 11(4).
[143] Ibid., Art. 5(1).
[144] Ibid., Art. 3. This refers only to provisions of general application enacted either by the legislature or the executive and effective at the national level. However, it includes not only the standard exceptions but also restrictions imposed on economic or any other grounds: see the Commentary on Chapter II, Art. 3.
[145] Ibid., Art. 5(2).
[146] Annex E.6 of the Convention concerns temporary admission for inward processing. It was adopted by the Permanent Technical Committee at its eighty-first/eighty-second sessions in October 1973. Subsequently, at its eighty-third/eighty-fourth sessions in March 1974 the Committee addeded a Note to Recommended Practice 43 (compensating products, or setting-off with equivalent

Annex E.8 on outward processing, [147] and Annex F.1 on free zones.[148] As of 1 January 1993, all fifteen EC Member States had ratified the Convention, but not all have accepted all three annexes.[149] The EC was a contracting party, since a customs union was entitled to be a contracting party if its Member States were also parties. The EC had taken advantage of this provision; but it does not have the right to vote.[150] The EC had accepted Annexes E.6, E.8 and F.1, which entered into force for the EC on 26 September 1974. The United States had ratified the Convention and had accepted Annex E.8 on outward processing and Annex F.1 on free zones but not Annex E.6 on inward processing. China had ratified the Convention but had not accepted any of these three annexes. Chinese specialists considered Chinese legislation concerning the special economic zones as not to be recognised under international law,[151] and the European Commission considered it to be incompatible with GATT.[152] It remains to be seen how the 1999 revised Convention will develop after it has been fully ratified.

These legal provisions have encouraged and facilitated the geographical separation from production from invention, distribution and marketing in the international commodity chain in toys. Since the early 1980s, however, Chinese legislation, both central and local, on SEZs has also had a direct influence on the concentration of production facilities.[153] Chinese laws on foreign direct investment (FDI) and labour are of special importance. Most toy factories in China are located in the Shenzhen SEZ. Shenzhen rules on FDI provide for Chinese–foreign joint ventures, Chinese–foreign contractual joint ventures, wholly foreign-owned enterprises, international leasing, compensation trade, and processing and assembling with materials and parts from foreign suppliers.[154] Recently,

goods). This Annex was incorporated into the Kyoto Convention by decision of the Council at its forty-third/fofty-fourth Sessions held in Brussels on 10 June 1974. It entered into force on 6 December 1977 and, subject to certain reservations, it entered into force for the EEC on the same date.

[147] Annex E.8 deals with temporary exportation for outward processing. It entered into force for the EEC, with certain reservations, on 20 April 1978.

[148] Annex F.1 concerning free zones.

[149] Annex E.6 on inward processing has been accepted by all EC Member States except Greece, Luxembourg, Portugal and Sweden. Annex E.8 on outward processing has been accepted by Denmark, France, Germany Ireland, Italy, the Netherlands, Spain and the United Kingdom, but not by Austria, Belgium, Finland, Greece, Luxembourg, Portugal and Sweden. Annex F.1 on free zones has been accepted by Austria, Denmark, Finland, France, Ireland, Italy, Luxembourg, the Netherlands, Portugal, Spain and the United Kingdom, but not by Belgium, Germany, Greece and Sweden.

[150] See Kyoto Convention, Art. 11(7).

[151] See S. Xiuping, C. Wen and L. Xiansheng, *New Progress in China's Special Economic Zones* (Foreign Languages Press, 1997), 54.

[152] See European Commission, market access database available at http://mkaccdb.eu.int/mkdb/chks.

[153] See J. D. Park, *The Special Economic Zones of China and Their Impact on Its Economic Development* (Praeger, 1997).

[154] For an introduction, see the Shenzhen SEZ Internet homepage at http://china-window.com/Shenzhen-w/shenzhen.html. On Chinese FDI law generally, see S. Lubman, "The Legal and Policy Environment for Foreign Direct Investment in China: Past Accomplishments, Future Uncertainties", in *Publication 662: Private Investments Abroad* (Mathew Bender & Co., 1998), ch. 3, 3-1–3-67; P. H. Corne, *Foreign Investment in China: The Administrative Legal System*, (Hong

however, the fact that labour costs in Shenzhen are higher than in the rest of Guandong Province, due partly to law, has encouraged toy companies to establish outside the SEZ, though still in Guangdong.[155]

In fact, however, this part of south China belongs to a wider economic area which includes Hong Kong.[156] Toy factories enjoy very close links with entrepreneurs in Hong Kong and often are part of Hong Kong companies. Production, distribution, quasi-political activities such as participation in trade associations, and often personal or family relations are closely intertwined.[157] Chinese companies, such as Early Light in the Shenzhen SEZ,[158] produce toys on outsourcing contracts for the world's biggest toy companies, not only Mattel but also Hasbro, Fisher-Price, and Ertl from the United States and Bandai and Tomy from Japan. These contracts are often arranged and managed by Hong Kong-based entrepreneurs, who in addition to their role as middlemen sometimes run their own toy manufacturing company in China and are also prominent in the main Hong Kong sectoral trade association, Hong Kong Toys Council.[159] More than half of China's toy production is re-exported through Hong Kong.[160] To the extent that power in the toy chain lies in Asia, it is based in Hong Kong.[161] For this reason, as well as to preserve maximum flexibility in

Kong University Press, 1997). On European trade and investment in China, see R. Strange, J. Slater, and L. Wang (eds), *Trade and Investment in China: The European Experience* (Routledge, 1998).

155 Interviews, Guangzhou and Shenzhen. It was reported that as of 1996 the Barbie doll factories in China were the Meitei factory in Dongguan and the Zongmei toy factory in Nanhai, both in Guangdong Province but outside the Shenzhen SEZ: *cf.* Tempest, "Barbie and the World Economy", *Los Angeles Times World Report* (special section produced in co-operation with *The Korea Times*), 13 October 1996, 3. In 1998, 800 small toy factories closed in Dongguan: "Chinese Toy Making", *The Economist*, 19 December 1998, 95, 98. This did not include Barbie doll factories.

156 See Willem van Kemenade, *China, Hong Kong, Taiwan, Inc.: The Dynamics of a New Empire* (Alfred A. Knopf Inc., 1997).

157 See, e.g. J. Smart and A. Smart, "Personal Relations and Divergent Economies: A Case Study of Hong Kong Investment in South China", (1991) 15 *International Journal of Urban and Regional Research* 216.

158 For a brief historical sketch, see "The tycoon", *The Economist*, 19 December 1998, 99. As of 1993, most of the 2,500 registered foreign-funded businesses in the Shenzhen SEZ were small processing and assembly operators from Hong Kong: see G.T. Crane, "Reform and Retrenchment in China's Special Economic Zones", in Joint Economic Committee, Congress of the United States (ed.), *China's Dilemma's in the 1990s: The Problems of Reforms, Modernization, and Interdependence* (M.E. Sharpe, 1993), 841, 845.

159 As of October 1996, the Chairman of the Hong Kong Toys Council was Edmund K.S. Young, executive vice-president of Perfekta Enterprises Ltd., a leading Hong Kong toy firm: "Barbie and the World Economy", *Los Angeles Times World Report*, 13 October 1996, 3. In January 1995 Mr Young was described as Chairman of Perfekta and Vice-Chairman of the Hong Kong Toy Council: see *Journal of Commerce*, 13 January 1995. As of December 1998, the Chairman was T.S. Wong, head of Jetta, a large toy maker in China: see "Chinese Toy Making: Where the Furbies come from", *The Economist*, 19 December 1998, 95, 99. See also Hong Kong Toys Council, *Federation of Hong Kong Industries, Members Director 1999* (Hong Kong Toys Council, 1999).

160 BBC Monitoring Service: Asia Pacific, 14 June 1995, cited in Newton and Tse, "Kids' Stuff", above at n. 17, 154. See also Hong Kong Trade Development Council, *Practical Guide to Exporting Toys for Hong Kong Traders* (Hong Kong Trade Development Council, Research Department, March 1999).

161 In particular because of the location of branch offices, ownership of local intermediaries and the provision of services.

a highly innovative and rapidly changing market, the production of toys for the export market usually takes place in wholly owned subsidiaries rather than joint ventures.[162]

Multiple Memberships

Third, *membership of one or more chains*. Is a box located in more than one commodity chain? If so, how many? Do specific sites, including institutions, norms and processes, create a structure of incentives so that a particular box tends to be inserted in more than one commodity chain? To what extent, and how, is this insertion of a particular box in different commodity chains encouraged or facilitated by the law? What role do law and other types of norms play in the management of relations between the different commodity chains in which a particular box is located?

Multiple memberships or the arrival into a box of a new entrant from another commodity chain may often lead to conflicts. For example, Mantua, the celebrated maker of collectors' model electric trains, stemmed from a small manufacturer of electric motors for model boats founded in 1926 by John Tyler, the namesake of Tyco Toys Inc. Mantua later merged with the Tyler Manufacturing Company, which was established by John Tyler to sell a new line of electric trains under the name of Tyco Toys. Subsequently it underwent two dramatic changes. First, in 1977 it split off from Tyco when new executives brought in by the company's largest shareholder, the Sara Lee Corporation, imported less expensive, less detailed model trains from Asia. This followed the election of a new president and director of Consolidated Foods, the parent company of Sara Lee, who, starting in the mid-1970s, oversaw the globalisation of the company and its early diversification.[163] Secondly, Mantua contined to produce very detailed historical model trains, but by 1997 much of its own manufacturing was also done in China. The number of its employees had shrunk from 400 during World War II to 25 in 1997.[164] The internationalisation of Mantua's own production and changes in its labour force reflected changes in toy production in Hong Kong and China.

A striking contemporary example of multiple memberships is the expansion of major toy companies into other related but potentially or actually distinct sectors, such as television, cinema and the Internet. Mattel, for instance, started in 1945 as a small California toy manufacturer. Its great success, the Barbie doll, was launched in 1959. By 1998 the Barbie doll accounted for 33 per cent of its sales, or a projected $1.5 billion; pre-school and infant toys, such as Fisher Price

---

[162] See Newton and Tse, "Kids' Stuff", above at n. 17, 149–56; E. Tsui, "Marketing Strategies of the Toy Industry in Hong Kong" (unpublished MBA dissertation, University of Hong Kong, Hong Kong, 1988). As of 1995, OEM, including products made in mainland China, accounted for 75%–80% of Hong Kong toy sales: see *Journal of Commerce*, 13 January 1995.

[163] See the history of the Sara Lee Corporation at http://www.saralee.com/history.

[164] *Cf.* Kent, "Maintaining the Model Train Tradition in a Digital World", *The New York Times*, 7 December 1997, 6.

and Sesame Street, accounted for 33 per cent; and "Wheels", including Hot Wheels, Matchbox and Disney Entertainment, accounted for another 33 per cent. Recently, Mattel has expanded to more high tech toys and e-commerce.[165] Another example is Tickle Me Elmo, heavily marketed during the 1996 Christmas season by Tyco Toys (since acquired by Mattel). This toy was invented by Ron Dubren of New York and Greg Hyman of Florida. Tyco, according to the inventors, recognised the key ingredient, packaging and marketing their product. For their work, the inventors obtained royalties of somewhat less than 5 per cent of the manufacturer's revenue. The largest share of the royalties went to Children's Television Workshop, which owned the licence.[166] Indeed the major toy companies spread like a web and onto the web. To lesson its dependence on a few powerful traditional retailers, Mattel linked up with the Internet retailer eToys Inc.,[167] from Santa Monica, California. It announced a goal of direct-to-consumer sales of $1 billion per year, including catalogues and Internet sales, some from Mattel's own website and some from online retailers such as eToys. In 1998 total toy retail sales were $23 billion, with eToys accounting for only $23.9 million. Now Toys " Я " Us is also developing Internet sales.[168] Sony recently unveiled robotic dogs, which can be trained either through remote control or through a computer programme.[169]

Property

Fourth, *property arrangements*. What property-like arrangements (such as use, ownership, management, control) are associated with the units of a specific box? Which sites of global legal pluralism are the most relevant to these arrangements? Which specific institutions, norms and processes are determinative with regard to the arrangements in a particular site? Why? If different property-like arrangements prevail among the various units in a box, what institutions, norms and processes encourage or tolerate diversity? How is such diversity managed?

Intellectual property is crucial to the international toy industry. The importance of brand marketing in the global commodity chain in toys is illustrated by two recent acquisitions by the leading buyer, Mattel. The first occurred in 1997, when Mattel bought Tyco Toys in the United States for $755 million. According to Mattel, its sales mainly to girls could be complemented by Tyco's "boy-oriented" products. Previously Mattel led the toy industry in overall sales, and

---

[165] See the outline history of Mattel, in Leibovich and Stoughton, "When keeping us isn't child's play; Mattel to acquire Learning Co. as industry pursues digitally savvy children", *The Washington Post*, December 1998, D01.

[166] Balog, "The untold toy success story: Elmo's evolution is a surprise to those involved", *USA Today*, 11 December 1996, 1B.

[167] The web page of eToys Inc. is avaialable at http://www.etoys.com.

[168] *Cf.* Anders and Bannon, "Etoys to join web-retailer parade with IPO", *The Wall Street Journal*, 6 April 1999, B1.

[169] See Agence France-Presse, "No end of a dog's life for robot pets", *South China Morning Post*, 12 May 1999, 10.

its acquistion of Tyco, then in third place, gave it a comfortable margin.[170] Mattel considered that its strength lay in brand-building, and that Tyco was under-marketed around the world. Only a quarter of Tyco's sales were then generated outside the United States.[171] As Mattel's then chairman, John W. Amerman, stated, "The main attraction is Tyco has brands that we can take around the world". Tyco's Matchbox toys were weaker in the United States than elsewhere, and its Sesame Street toys were beginning to be strong in China. Mattel's aim, according to its then president-to-be Jill Bared, was to turn these products into global power brands.[172] Mattel's second important recent acquisition occurred in 1998, when it announced its plan to buy Pleasant Co., the second largest doll maker in the United States, for US $700 million. Mattel's then and current president and chief executive, Jill Bared, announced that "We have acquired probably one of the blue-chip girls' toy brands of all time".[173] Both purchases, as well as its earlier acquisition of Fisher-Price, were consistent with Mattel's strategy of buying companies that were strong in the US domestic market but weak elsewhere. As securities analyst Margaret Whitfield of Tucker Anthony Inc. in New York said, "Mattel has always been looking for strong domestic brands that it can leverage through its global distribution network". Mattel's aim, in her view, was to increase international sales to more than half of all company sales in an effort to cash in on foreign markets that contain 97 per cent of the world's children[174]—in other words China.

It is not surprising, therefore, that a number of intellectual property cases have been brought by international buyers in Hong Kong courts. For example, Mattel, the manufacturer of Barbie dolls, sued Tonka Corporation in the Hong Kong High Court in 1991 for infringement of copyright. It alleged that the defendant's Miss America dolls copied the Barbie dolls' head sculpture and that its packaging infringed registered trade marks by stating that the Miss America doll's clothes also fit the Barbie doll.[175] LEGO brought an action in 1995 against a small Hong Kong company that used the word "Lego" in its business of publishing entertainment and football magazines. The defendant deleted the word "Lego" from its name during the course of the the the court hearing.[176] On the whole, the Hong Kong courts have been favourable to such claims.[177]

---

[170] See the Mattel internet home page at http://www.snc.edu/bsad/ba485/apr1998/group8/history.htm.

[171] Madore, "Mattel confident Tyco deal with pass antitrust scrutiny", *The Buffalo News*, 19 November 1996, 3D.

[172] *The Buffalo News*, 19 November 1996. In 1998 Mattel sold Tyco's science and craft lines to Uncle Milton Industries Inc. See "Former Tyco Toys lines sold to Calif. firm", *Philadelphia Inquirer*, 4 February 1998, C.1.

[173] Gregory, "Mattel plans to buy Pleasant for $700 million: El Segundo firm would acquire the nation's no. 2 doll marker as part of a strategy to cash in on foreign markets", *Los Angeles Times*, 16 June 1998, D.1.

[174] Ibid.

[175] *Mattel Inc.* v. *Tonka Corp* [1991] 2 HKC 411.

[176] *Interlego AG* v. *Lego New Enterprises Ltd.* [1995] 3 HKC 186.

[177] See also *Attorney-General* v. *Hondar Plastic Industries Ltd.* [1976] HKLR 7630 (holding that drawings on which plaintiff's production of toys was based do not need to have an element of

Labour

Fifth, *modes of labour control.* What modes of labour control are found in each box? Which sites of global legal pluralism are most relevant, and why? Which specific institutions, norms and processes are significant, and why? To what extent are different modes of labour control encouraged or faciliated by legal or other institutions, norms and processes? Are there conflicts among different sites with regard to modes of labour control? If so, how are these conflicts resolved in institutional, normative and processual terms?

So far as production is concerned, the labour law of nation states is not the only relevant law, or, in the case of China, even the most important. For example, when Mattel acquired Tyco, analysts said that most of the layoffs would come from outside the United States, where Tyco had most of its operations.[178] The externalities of the acquisition by one US company of another thus occurred mainly in China, where the applicable labour laws for such factories differed radically from those in the United States. In fact, one empirical study of factory regimes in Shenzhen and Hong Kong, albeit in the electronics rather than the toy sector, concluded that the state was much less significant than the social organisation of the labour market as a factor of control of labour and constraint on management.[179]

The codes of conduct elaborated under the aegis of multinational companies and sector-specific trade associations may be much more important in practice than formal national or local legislation. The large toy companies, retailers and trade associations have all adopted sector-specific codes of conduct which are imposed upon or recommended to their factories. Such codes of conduct have been described as "typically book-sized documents that specify working conditions down to the dimensions of the medical boxes on the wall", and as "changing China's toy industry more than anything else".[180]

artistry to qualify for copyright protection); *Video Technology Ltd.* v. *AtariIncorporated* [1982] HKC 504 (allowing an appeal against interlocutory injunction to restrain defendants from dealing in any way with certain electronic games similar to Pac-man); *Core Resources (Far East) Ltd.* v. *Sky Finders* [1992] 1 HKLR 193 (dismissing appeals against summary judgment for the plaintiff for a sum due in respect of a cheque dishonoured by the defendant after the plaintiff refused to respond to a request regarding its trade mark); *Ocean Plastic Manufactory Ltd.* v. *TCA (Hong Kong) Ltd* [1993] 1 HKC 23 (refusing an application to introduce fresh evidence against a order restraining defendants from infringing plaintiff's copyright in a "baby doll" toy); *Navystar (Nagai Shing) Industrial Co. Ltd.* v. *Fairing Industrial Ltd.* [1994] 3 HKC 670 (dismissing an application to strike out plaintiff's statement of claim that it owned copyright in drawings of a toy compact disc player and that defendant had infringed the copyright); *Lanard Toys Ltd.* v. *Winner Toys Manufactory Ltd.* (unreported) HCA No. A11340 of 1994, 18 November 1994, Cheung J. (granting an interlocutory injunction requested by the plaintiff, who, after acquiring the US trade mark from the original owner about 1982, marketed toy airplanes and helicopters worldwide under the name "Prop Shots", to prevent the defendant from marketing identical toys bearing the brand name "Hot Shots").

[178] Madore, "Mattel confident Tyco deal will pass antitrust scrutiny", *The Buffalo News*, 19 November 1996.

[179] C. K. Lee, "Factory Regimes of Chinese Capitalism: Different Cultural Logics in Labor Control", in A. Ong and D. M. Nonini (eds), *Ungrounded Empires: The Cultural Politics of Modern Chinese Transnationalism* (Routledge, 1997), 115–42.

[180] *The Economist*, 19 December 1998, 95, 99.

One example is the Code of Business Practices of the International Council of Toy Industries (ICTI). ICTI was established in 1974 and incorporated under the law of New York. It is an association of toy associations, embracing manufacturerers and marketers. Its members, as of February 1999, comprised the toy associations of Hong Kong, China, the United States, Japan, Denmark, France, Italy, Spain, Sweden and the United Kingdom, as well as Argentina, Australia, Brazil, Canada, Hungary, Korea, Mexico, Philippines, Taiwan and Thailand. The general management functions of ICTI are performed by a president and a secretary, both currently held by Toy Manufacturers of America. English is ICTI's official language.

The ICTI Code of Business Practices, which was revised and approved on 1 June 1998, is a voluntary code of conduct containing specific operating conditions which members are expected to meet, for which members are expected to obtain contractor adherence in advance, and to which supply agreements with firms manufacturing on behalf of ICTI members are expected to provide for adherence. The operating conditions refer to labour practices and the workplace. As with other codes, it borrows from core labour rights set out in International Labour Organisation (ILO) Conventions, though it omits certain other rights from other ILO Conventions, such as the right to organise and collective bargaining and freedom of association.[181] The purpose of the code is to establish a standard of performance, to educate and to encourage commitment, not to punish. The ICTI code of conduct makes elaborate provision for enforcement by the companies through contract. ICTI member companies are expected to evaluate their own facilities, as well as those of their contractors, and request that the latter follow the same with subcontractors. An annual statement of compliance with the code must be signed by an officer of each manufacturing company or contractor. According to the code, contracts for toy manufacture should provide that a material failure to comply with the code, or to implement a corrective action plan on a timely basis, is a breach of contract for which the contract may be cancelled. Annexes to the code provide guidelines for determining compliance; their applicability is to be determined by a rule of reason.[182] These codes have been adopted mainly as a result of pressure from non-governmental organisations (NGOs). For example, the Coalition for the Safe Production of Toys (Toy Coalition) has been instrumental in getting codes of conduct on labour practices adopted by associations of toy manufacturers and companies. The Toy Coalition was started by several Thai and Hong Kong

[181] For a comparison of provisions in four major codes of labour practice with the provisions of ILO Conventions, see "A Comparison of Provisions in Base Codes of Labour Practice", available on the website of the Maquiladora Solidarity Network at http://www.www.web.net/~msn/3codeslg.htm. The four codes in question are the Code of Labour Practices for the Apparel Industry Including Sportswear (the Netherlands), the Ethical Trading Initiative (United Kingdom), SA8000 (United States and United Kingdom), and the Fair Labor Association Workplace Code of Conduct (United States).

[182] This description is based on the ICTI Internet home page at http://www.toy-icti.org. The ICTI Code of Business Practices can be found at http://www.toy-icti.org./mission/bizpractice.htm.

groups in 1994.[183] It was established in response to fires at a Kader toy factory in Thailand and at a doll factory in Zhili, China, and three other factory accidents in Shenzhen and the nearby area in 1993: 188 people died in the Kader fire, 87 people died and 51 were injured in the Zhili fire, and a total of 71 people died in the Shenzhen accidents.[184] Various officials were sent to prison, and, following an inspection tour by President Jiang Zemin and Foreign Minister Qian Qichen, measures were taken to improve working conditions, such as monitoring the payment of the minimum wage. This concerned mainly small and medium-sized Japanese, Taiwanese, Hong Kong and South Korean factories. The workers in Western joint-ventures are reported to have had better conditions.[185] In its campaign the Toy Coalition campaign was joined by other such groups, including the World Development Movement (United Kingdom), ICFTU, AFL-CIO (United States), Trocaire (Ireland), Italian organisations, Workers Party (France), Asia Pacific Workers Solidarity Links, PSPD (Korea), Japan Citizens' Liaison Committee for the Safe Production of Toys (Japan), Indonesian groups, and the Maquila Solidarity Network (Canada).[186] These NGOs thus constitute worldwide networks linking NGOs in Europe, the United States, Asia and other parts of the world, thus mirroring, to some extent, multinational corporations and affecting, conditioning, and helping to create the norms which are imposed by them.[187]

Despite their political origins, these codes of conduct reflect the organisation of power in the global toy commodity chain in three diferent respects. First, precisely because the dominant buyers are few in number, they are unusually susceptible to political pressure. NGOs from various countries have successfully put pressure on the small number of powerful US buyers, and the national and international trade associations they control, to elaborate codes of conduct with regard to their mainly Asian workforce. Secondly, the dominant buyers, whose power rests on their control of brands and marketing, are able in effect to determine the content of industry-wide codes of conduct and then to impose them on

---

[183] The reasons for the establishment of the Coalition and its demands for a Charter on the Safe Production of Toys are described in: Human Rights for Workers: Special Campaigns, "Our Children Don't Need Blood-Stained Toys", available at http://www-senser.com/campaign.htm.

[184] In the Zhili case, workers choked to death because all exits were locked to prevent theft by workers. Safetey regulations had been ignored, the electrician was not qualified, and the factory permit had been issued in exchange for a bribe: see W. van Kemenade, *China, Hong Kong, Taiwan, Inc.* (Alfred A. Knopf, 1997), 179 (translated by Diane Webb).

[185] Ibid.

[186] Asian Labour Update, 19 February 1999, home page http://www.freeway.org.hk/amrc/alu.html. For example, the Maquila Solidarity Network, based in Toronto, Canada, promotes solidarity with groups in Mexico, Central America and Asia organising in maquiladora factories and export processing zones to improve working conditions. Its campaigns include The International Toy Campaign. See its website at http://www.web.net/~msn.

[187] For further discussion, see David M. Trubek, J. Mosher, and J.S. Rothstein, "Transnationalism in the Regulation of Labor Relations: International Regimes and Transnational Advocacy Networks" (Labor and the Global Economy Research Circle, The International Institute, University of Wisconsin-Madison, January 1999).

their suppliers, at least contractually if not always in practice. Codes of conduct thus are analogous to multilaterally negotiated treaties which are then applied as standard-form contracts laid down by the leading firms in a particular market.[188] Thirdly, power struggles within the chain occur latently and sometimes overtly between buyers and original equipment manufacturers. The main US buyers use soft law codes, essentially outside the legal system, as a way of ensuring their dominance over Hong Kong OEM and Chinese producers, while the latter struggle to develop their own ideas and designs in order to break out of their dependence on foreign buyers and foreign market niches.[189]

Based partly on the ICTI example, the Hong Kong Toys Council (HKTC) introduced a Code of Practice for the Toy Industry in July 1997. Although not legally binding, it serves as a reference, educational and promotional device for its members.[190] In fact, however, it is not clear whether it (or another such code) is widely adopted; if adopted, whether it is enforced; or even what enforcement and compliance might mean given that the code is not legally binding and sanctions for non-compliance are inadequate. It may be hypothesised that such codes have been adopted by and apply more effectively in practice in joint venture between Chinese and western companies or in factories which produce for multinational buyers. It may also be hypothesised that codes of conduct may have little, if any, effect in factories which are wholly locally owned or produce entirely for local markets. But such a simple hypothesis, that the market for norms reflects the market for toys, is given the lie by the fact that even some companies which produce for multinational buyers evaluate the code of conduct recommended by the HKTC and the US buyer as a cost of doing business and decide not to adopt it. They consider that the items specified in a code of conduct are already dealt with by the US buyer in its specifications to the extent that they are required for marketing the product in the United States.[191]

---

[188] P.T Muchlinski, " 'Global Bukowina' Examined: Viewing the Multinational Enterprise as a Transnational Law-making Community", in G. Teubner (ed.), *Global Law Without a State* (Dartmouth, 1997), 79, 86. See also L.E. Preston, "The Evolution of Multinational Public Policy towards Business", in C.R. Lehman and R.M. Moore (eds), *Multinational Culture: Social Impacts of a Global Economy* (Greenwood, 1992), 11–22.

[189] Cf. *Journal of Commerce*, 13 January 1995. Conflicts are inherent in this relationship: see *Kader Industrial Co. Ltd.* v. *Galco International Toys NV* [1992] 1 HKC 36; *Galco International Toys NV* v. *Kader Industrial Co. Ltd.*, [1996] HKLY 260. Nor is the relationship free from abuse: in 1996 a senior manager with Mattel Toy Vendor Operations Ltd. was convicted in Hong Kong for soliciting and accepting rewards based on the value of turnover between his employer and a Taiwan textile manufacturer: see *Attorney-General* v. *Leung Kin Wai* [1996] HKC 588. Even apparently straightforward international transactions are not free from risk: see *Toymax (HK) Ltd.* v. *Redsmith International Ltd.* [1994] 1 HKC 714 (holding that signing an order form by adding the words "as agent for overseas buyer" was sufficient to indicate that no personal liability was assumed by the agent and dismissing the plaintiff's claim that the defendant was liable for the contractual default by an associated company).

[190] "Hong Kong's Toy Industry", *Hong Kong & China Economics*, on the Internet homepage of the Hong Kong Trade Development Council, available at http://www.tdc.org.hk/main/industries/t2-2-39.htm, last updated 2 July 1998.

[191] Interviews, Guangzhou and Shenzhen.

Even if a factory has a code of conduct, effective implementation and monitoring thus remain crucial issues.[192] At least in certain industries, pressure from critics and labour rights groups for effective enforcement of codes of conduct can prove effective. The Nike case is instructive. A Vietnam factory of Nike Inc. was criticised in 1997 for unsafe working conditions. By 1998 the company had improved its working conditions, and its earlier critic issued a report noting substantial improvements. In March 1999 the chairman of Nike announced that the company, based in Beaverton, Oregon, United States, would disclose the location of all its foreign factories and open them to independent monitors if competitors would agree to do the same. He also sent letters to universities with Nike contracts to enlist them to "ensure that licensed products bearing the names and logos of schools are manufacturered under fair conditions".[193] Even the structure of the athletic footwear industry differs somewhat from that of the toy sector, both are buyer-driven commodity chains so this example may be instructive in demonstrating that action by independent researchers or labour rights groups can have an effect.[194]

It also illustrates the way in which codes of conduct can be enforced through two complementary mechanisms. The first is the market, in which competing firms co-operate in mutually enforcing norms which impose costs on them all, even though one might expect these costs not to be equal and thus not to bear equally on all the affected firms. The second refers to institutions, such as universities, which are linked to manufacturers, by contract or otherwise, thus spreading the costs of effective enforcement to bodies outside the specific economic sector in question. Both of these devices transform an intra-firm code of

---

[192] A 1996 case study of a Chinese toy manufacturer's code of conduct concluded that the code did not provide for effective implementation, failed to reflect basic international labour standards, in particular concerning freedom of association, and lacked an independent monitoring device: see J. Murray, "Corporate Codes of Conduct and Labour Standards" (International Labour Organization, Bureau for Workers' Activities [ACTRAV], Working Paper 1996) available on the Internet at http://www.ilo.org/public/english/230actra/publ/codes.htm. See also J. Porges, "Codes of Conduct", on the home page of Asian Labour Update at http://www.[insert address] as of 19 February 1999. See also various issues of the *Human Rights for Workers Bulletin*, at http://www. senser.com/b21.htm. As of 1998, the Irish NGO, Trocaire, concluded that child labour was not a significant issue in China because of the existence of a large pool of unemployed workers and low wages for women. In its view, the main problem was the working conditions of women. See Trocaire, "Conditions for Toy Workers", available at http://www.trocaire.org/toy3.html. On the extent of child labour in Chinese toy factories in the mid-1990s, see "By the Sweat and Toil of Children: A Report to Congress" (Bureau of International Affairs, US Department of Labor, 15 July 1994) (available at http://www.dol.gov/dol/ilab/public/media/reports/sweat/main.htm; "Statistics on Child Workers in China", *China Labour Bulletin*, n. 25, April 1996, at http://www.citinv.it/asso ciazioni/CNMS/archivio/paesi/statistisc.html; and C. K. Wai, "Child Labor in China (Change HKCIC June 1996)", at http://www.citinv.it/associazioni/CNMS/archivio/lavoro/childlab.html.

[193] "Nike Set to Open Plants to Monitors: Firm's Offer Follows Critic's Report on Safety Gains at Vietnam Site", *International Herald Tribune*, 13–14 March 1999, 21.

[194] See also *HKSAR* v. *Wong Ying Yu* [1997] 3 HKC 452 (dismissing an appeal against conviction of disorderly conduct while staging a protest against the poor working conditions of labourers in the toy industry).

conduct into multilateral sets of norms.[195] Whether such a transformation is necessary depends in part on the structure of the sector concerned, including the buyers as well as the producers.[196] In the toy sector, a similar multilateralisation may result from the adoption of codes of conduct by international (ICTI) and local (Hong Kong) trade associations, together with effective economic and legal constraints imposed by the buyers on their factories. A third method of enforcement, which might potentially be used in conjunction with the others, is by means of international institutions such as the ILO, which has been critical of privately negotiated codes of conduct and has promoted the complementarity of private initiatives and international labour standards.[197]

Links Within a Chain

Sixth, *links* between the boxes within a commodity chain. How are the boxes within a particular commodity chain linked to each other? Which specific institutions, norms and processes create, sustain or transform these links? What role do different sites of global legal pluralism play in linking different boxes? Is there any overall co-ordination of the boxes, for example by means of vertical integration, ownership of intellectual property, or control of distribution or retail markets? How is the discreteness of a particular commodity chain maintained, and what role does global legal pluralism play in this respect?

In buyer-driven commodity chains, such as that for toys, it is the downstream service activities of marketing and distribution which co-ordinate and drive the chain as a whole.[198] Hence the importance of the Internet, both as a tool for

---

[195] On the distinction between intra-firm and industry-wide codes of conduct, see Muchlinski, above at n. 42, 85.

[196] As to the apparel industry, see *The Apparel Industry and Codes of Conduct: A Solution to the International Child Labor Problem?* (US Department of Labor, Bureau of International Labor Affairs, 1996), also available on the Internet at http://www.dol.gov/ialb/public/media/reports/apparel/main.htm. See also J. P. Sajhau, "Business ethics in the textile, clothing and footwear (TCF) industries: Codes of conduct" (International Labour Organization, Sectoral Activities Programme, Working Paper SAP 2.60/WP.110, 1998), available on the Internet at http://www.ilo.org/public/english/100secto/papers/bzethics/index.htm; and Benedicto Ernesto R. Bitonio, Jr. (Director, Bureau of Labour Relations, Department of Labor and Employment, Government of the Philippines), "Toward a Code of Conduct in the Textile, Clothing and Footwear Industries: Laws and Possibilities" (International Labour Organization, Sectoral Activities Programme, Workshop Background Paper, 1998), available on the Internet at http://www.ilo.org./public/english/100secto/papers/tcfcode/index.htm. On the apparel industry, see E. Bonacich, L. Cheng, N. Chinchilla, Nora Hamilton, and P. Ong (eds), *Global Production:The Apparel Industry in the Pacific Rim* (Temple University Press, 1994).

[197] See International Labour Office, Working Party on the Social Dimensions of the Liberalization of International Trade, "Overview of global developments and Office activities concerning codes of conduct, social labelling and other private sector initiatives addressing labour issues" (GB.273/WP/SDL/1(Add.1) and GB.273/WP/SDL/1(Rev.1), both 273rd session (Geneva, November 1998), available on the Internet at http://www.ilo.org/public/english/20gb/docs/gb273/sdl-1a1.htm and http://www.ilo.org/public/english/20bg/docs/gb273/sdl-1.htm, respectively.

[198] E. Rabach and E. M. Kim, "Where is the Chain in Commodity Chains? The Service Sector Nexus", in G. Gereffi and M. Korzeniewicz (eds), *Commodity Chains and Global Capitalism* (Greenwood, 1994), 137.

managing and co-ordinating the different sites and also as a form of retailing. Invention, design and marketing tend to be more easily integrated in buyer-driven commodity chains than in producer-driven commodity chains.[199] The conception of toys, intellectual property in brands, and control of marketing and distribution, now particularly via the Internet, are therefore boxes of the chain in which competition is most fierce and attention to law most acute.[200] In other words, the international commodity chain in toys, as with other goods, now depends fundamentally on intellectual property, contract and the provision of services, including legal services.

Connections Between Economic Relations and Specific Sites

A seventh set of questions concerns specifically the *connections between particular sets of economic relations (boxes) and specific sites* of global legal pluralism. Do specific sites concern particular aspects of specific boxes? For example, do certain sites deal with labour control, others with financial arrangements, others with marketing, others with dispute resolution, and so on? How, and why? To what extent are particular sites important in governing the social organisation of the constituent units of a box even when the sites are not geographically proximate to the box, in other words when governance, economic processes and territory are not congruent?

The lack of congruence between governance, economic processes and territory can be illustrated by two examples. The first concerns EC environmental and health legislation. Greenpeace put pressure on EU institutions and national governments to ban all toys containing phthalates, an additive used to soften PVC products. As yet, however, no such EU legislation has been enacted. Nevertheless, the risk that such legislation might be enacted in the future has already changed the practices of some toy factories in China. Some factories consider it the major issue confronting Chinese exports of toys to the EU. Their international buyers instructed them to substitute hard plastic for PVC.[201] Some individual EU Member States have already banned imports of toys containing PVC or certain other substances, and these measures have affected toy production in Hong Kong and China.[202] In the United States, the main buyers stopped using phthalates in certain baby products in early 1999, even though, as in the

---

[199] Ibid.

[200] On the growing importance of the Internet for toy distribution, see, e.g. Anders/Bannon, "EToys to Join Web-Retailer Parade with IPO", *The Wall Street Journal*, 6 April 1999, B1; Davidson, "Net retailer eToys faces big risks as its star rises", *USA Today*, 8 April 1999, B.1; Pollack, "Makeover at Barbie's: Mattel Sheds Jobs and Looks to the Internet", *International Herald Tribune*, 17–18 April 1999, 9; Edgecliffe-Johnson, "Net gains take precedence over bricks and mortar", *Financial Times*, 28–29 August 1999, 25.

[201] Interviews in Guangzhou and Shenzhen Special Economic Zone, China.

[202] See Hong Kong Trade Development Council, *Practical Guide to Exporting Toys for Hong Kong Traders* (Hong Kong Trade Development Council, Research Department, March 1999), 51.

EU, there is no legislation prohibiting it; these business decisions will inevitably affect toy production in China.[203]

A second example refers to toy safety. It exemplifies the interaction and potential incompatibility of norms, institutions and processes from two geographically discrete sites. The EC "Toys Directive"[204] provides that all toys sold in the EU must meet essential safety requirements and bear a "CE" mark indicating conformity. It was revised in 1996 to be similar to current US requirements,[205] perhaps indicating progress towards mutual recognition and standardisation on toy safety requirements.[206] Such requirements condition Chinese production of toys for export to Europe and the conduct of inspections in Hong Kong. But EU and US safety standards are not the only ones which apply to the marketing of toys produced in Hong Kong and China. In May 1998 the Swedish company Ikea was reported to be facing prosecution in Hong Kong for selling in Hong Kong a toy that caused the death of a boy in Europe; the toy met EU safety requirements but did not meet the more stringent specifications of the Hong Kong Toys and Children's Products Safety Ordinance.[207]

A third example concerns the ECJ. In 1998 the ECJ decided the cases brought by the United Kingdom and Spain in 1994 against quotas on imports of toys from China. I focus here on the UK case.[208] The point of departure of the ECJ's analysis was the principle of liberalisation of trade; the introduction of quotas was, in its view, an exception. The ECJ noted, however, that the abolition of quotas on imports was "not a rule of law which the Council is required in principle to observe, but rather the result of a decision made by that institution in the exercise of its discretion".[209] It remarked that more than 98 per cent of the imports in question were liberalised before the contested regulation was adopted,[210] and that the quotas introduced by the regulation reduced the level of Community trade by almost 50 per cent for some of the toys in question.[211] It followed its previous case-law, however, in concluding that when assessing complex economic situations the Council enjoyed substantial discretion, including making findings of fact,[212] and that the exercise of this discretion was

---

[203] See Hong Kong Trade Development Council, Research Department, "Review and Outlook of Hong Kong's Toy Exports", *Trade Watch*, April 1999, 6.

[204] Council Directive 88/378/EEC (OJ 1988 L187/1), as amended.

[205] EN 71 (OJ 1997 C190). A complete list of European standards concerning toy safety is available at http://www2.echo.lu/nasd/dckbl-3.html. See also Hong Kong Industry Department, Quality Services Division, "Health and Safety Standards Circular No. 1/97: International: Toy Safety Standards", 20 January 1997, available at http://www.info.gov.hk/id/psis/hssc/hssc0197.htm.

[206] See Hong Kong Trade Development Council, above at n. 203, 7.

[207] Pegg, "Ikea faces threat of illegal toy charges", *South China Morning Post*, 12 May 1999, 3. On the Ordinance, enacted in 1992 as "a substantial departure from the previous reluctance of government to become involved in this area", see Cottrell, "Product Liability", in Shane Nossal (ed.), *Law Lectures for Practitioners 1993* (Hong Kong Law Journal Limited, 1993), 72–85.

[208] Case C-150/94 *United Kingdom* v. *Council* [1998] ECR I-7235.

[209] Ibid., para. 34.

[210] Ibid., para. 44.

[211] Ibid., para. 40.

[212] Ibid., para. 55.

subject only to limited judicial review.[213] Similarly, in adopting new Community rules, the Council was required to take account only of the general interests of the Community as a whole.[214] The Court also held, following its Advocate-General on this point also, that the Council was entitled to do so by basing its evaluation on "the mere risk of disturbance", and this could be deduced from the increase in Chinese toy imports.[215] In other words, the judiciary will not substitute its evaluation of the facts for that of the legislator unless the legislator's assessment appears manifestly incorrect in the light of the information available to it at the time of the adoption of the rules.[216] The ECJ therefore dismissed the UK's application for annulment.

This decision, and that in the case brought by Spain, were taken more than four years after the cases were brought, and more than two years after the Advocate-General's Opinion in both cases.[217] In accordance with ECJ practice, the judgment was unanimous, but the length of time taken to reach it suggests that the form of unanimity masked the substance of deep disagreement. The ECJ judgment was a delicate compromise, as was the Council regulation which had provoked the litigation.

The judgment represented a judicial compromise, articulated in the form of a unanimous judgment, which protected the integrity of a prior legislative compromise that was expressed in the form of a complex regulation. The compromise in this second-order sense, achieved by judicial deliberation, served to ensure the discreteness and integrity of the EC political process and to insulate it to some extent from the judicial process. A Member State, or other strategic actor, could not use litigation to upset or revise a complex political compromise.

This double-order compromise was intimately bound up with the definition of EU rules for the globalisation game. These rules potentially concerned relations between market actors, relations between market actors and governance structures, and relations between different governance structures. But the ECJ did not address these issues directly. Instead, its judgment dealt with them indirectly, by emphasising the importance of judicial restraint in the face of politically sensitive Council legislation. Nevertheless, it had wider consequences. It ensured to some extent the integrity of the EU political process, insulating it from collateral attack by means of judicial review. It maintained a political space, structured to some extent by objective interests, populated by conflicts among subjective interests, and involving Member States, firms, trade associations and EU institutions. This

---

[213] Case C-150/94 *United Kingdom* v. *Council* [1998] ECR I-7235, para. 54.
[214] Ibid., para. 62.
[215] Ibid., para. 65.
[216] Ibid., para. 87.
[217] The Opinion of the Advocate-General was heard at the sitting of the Court on 26 September 1996: see Case C-150/94 *United Kingdom of Great Britain and Northern Ireland* v. *Council of the European Union* [1998] ECR I-7235; Case C-284/94 *Kingdom of Spain* v. *Council of the European Union* [1998] ECR I-7309. The Council was supported by the Commission.

space was a political market, in which the EU economic market for toys, structured by the global toy commodity chain, was interpenetrated with the EU political market, with a supply of, and demand for, economic regulation and regulatory law. Both of these markets, at least in the UK case, were characterised by what Weber called the factual "autonomy" of the propertied classes,[218] that is, an asymmetry of property, information, power and influence upon the Member States and thus the EU legislator. The double-order compromise of the ECJ judgment tended to insulate and enhance the integrity of this political space and strengthen its market-oriented normative order.

The ECJ judgment thus occurred in a highly political context, and was in fact highly political. Its main importance did not lie in a short-term economic impact. A judgment either way would probably have had only marginal financial effects on the distribution of resources among EU importers, producers, retailers or others that lost or gained as a result of the existence of quotas between the adoption of the regulation and the date of the judgment. The primary significance of the judgment lay in articulating legal principles for the future and in its broader implications for the relationship between EU law and other institutional, normative and processual sites.

The legal principles concerned the role of the EC legislator in dealing with foreign trade and inter-institutional relations within the EU, in particular between the Council and the ECJ. Their broader implications referred to how much impact the international commodity chain could have in influencing EC legislation, both by means of its structural position and by direct and indirect pressure on national governments, the Commission and the Council. They also concerned the role played by EU law as part of global legal pluralism. The ECJ judgment sanctioned the integrity of the EU political process and thus the political and law-creating salience of market structure. It thus inserted global legal pluralism into EU law and EU law into global legal pluralism. On the one hand, it imported into EU law the institutions, norms and processes of other global sites, for example regarding US intellectual property law or the organisation of toy production in the Chinese SEZ of Shenzhen. The latter were incorporated into EU economic, political and legal relations, not just as costs of international or local firms in the EU toy sector, but also as elements which contribute to create, consolidate or structure these relations and thus are an integral part of them. The ECJ judgment incorporated into the realm of EU law the norms produced by institutions and processes in other sites of global legal pluralism, in the manner of invisible legal transplants. On the other hand, the norms produced by the Council and the ECJ in EU legislative and judicial processes became part of the structure of the global commodity chain in toys. They conditioned, shaped and were integral to the decision-making calculus of strategic actors, including governments and firms, in this specific global economic network.

---

[218] Max Rheinstein (ed.), *Max Weber on Law in Economy and Society* (Harvard University Press, 1966), 146 (translated by Edward Shils).

Relations Between Sites and the Chain as a Whole

Eighth, relations between *sites and the chain as a whole*. What types of relationships, for example horizontal or vertical, competitive or co-operative, marked-based or state-based or convention-based, exist between the different sites that are relevant to a specific global commodity chain? Does any specific site concern the global commodity chain as a whole? To what extent does the plurality of sites provide an effective way of managing the chain as a whole? Would a single site or a small number of sites be more effective? What does "effective" mean in this context? In other words, what are our criteria for evaluating the effectiveness of specific sites, and of the totality of sites which we call global legal pluralism, in the organisation and management of the chain as a whole?

Certain sites concern several parts of the chain or the chain as a whole. The most well-known example is the Uruguay Round agreements associated with the World Trade Organisation (WTO). This includes the General Agreement on Tariffs and Trade (GATT), the General Agreement on Trade in Services (GATS), and the Agreement on Trade-Related Aspects of Intellectual Property (TRIPS). For some time they have been important in regard to the international commodity chain in toys, even though the main producer, China, is not yet a WTO member.[219]

The GATT/WTO was a crucial conditioning element in the negotiation of the EU quota on toys from China in 1993–1994 and the related litigation between 1994–1998.[220] It also cast a long shadow with regard to future disputes, notably by holding out, to China and multinational companies "located" there, the promise of new institutions, norms and processes which would be available on eventual Chinese accession. When China joins the GATT, the firms located there will benefit from Article XI of GATT concerning the general elimination of quantitative restrictions. The provision of services and the protection of intellectual property in brand names are likely to be affected by the eventual application of GATS and TRIPS. It may also be argued that the impact of GATT on China is already real, even if China has not yet acceded to the WTO. Companies are already positioning themselves in anticipating of further opening-up of China's domestic market to imported toys and foreign toy retailers. One has only to note that in 1997, the same year it purchased a major competitor Tyco, Mattel launched Barbie in China.[221]

---

[219] See, most recently, S. Leonard, *The Dragon Awakes: China's Long March to Geneva* (Cameron May, 1999); see also F.M. Abbott (ed.), *China in the World Trading System: Defining the Principles of Engagement* (Kluwer, 1998). On China's integration into the world system generally, see E. Economy and M. Oksenberg (eds), *China Joins the World: Progress and Prospects* (Council on Foreign Relations Press, 1999).

[220] For detailed analysis, see Snyder, "Chinese Toys" above at n. 2.

[221] See the history of Mattel on the company Internet homepage at http://www.snc.edu/baad/ba485/spr1998/group8/history.htm.

These examples do not of course mean that the WTO is the only site governing international trade. Nor does it necessarily mean that, from a sociological as
distinct from a positivist law standpoint, international trade law norms are
arranged in a hierarchical fashion, or that the WTO stands at the apex of an
institutional and normative hierarchy. The examples do indicate, however, that
the WTO affects many aspects of the global commodity chain in toys, perhaps
more aspects than any other site. This, in turn, provides a social, economic,
political and cultural basis for the WTO's claim *qua* institution to have a dominant position in international trade law, though not necessarily global law generally. It also tends to aliment institutional and often individual support for the
argument that international trade law is hierarchical in nature, with the WTO
site at the top. Seen sociologically, such developments are processes, not yet
acquired positions or states of affairs.

V CONCLUSION

I have argued here that global economic networks are governed by the totality
of strategically determined, situationally specific, and often episodic conjunctions of a multiplicity of institutional, normative and processual sites throughout the world. The totality of such sites represents a new global form of legal
pluralism.

The development of the global economic relations involved in the
international toy industry owes much to corporate strategies. Such a view is
consistent with the approach taken here, which privileges the perspective of
strategic actors. But these strategies themselves have been pursued taking
account of the framework of the law and other normative frameworks and have
been elaborated by using them. They take place within, are conditioned by, and
have contributed to the development of global legal pluralism. To put it more
accurately, the development of global networks in the toy industry has occurred
in conjunction with the development of a variety of structural sites throughout
the world, each of which comprises institutions, norms and dispute-resolution
processes.

One facet of this argument deserves special emphasis. Not only have strategic
actors used the law and been shaped by it, they have also been absolutely fundamental in determining which institutional, normative and processual sites have
seen the light of day, which have flourished and developed, and which have with-
ered and even died for lack of clients. They have also influenced profoundly the
development of sites, so that some have taken on more or less judicial and legal
characteristics, while others have not.[222] These strategic actors include governments, businesses and other organisations, and sometimes even individuals. It is

---

[222] Though of course these strategic actors are not the only cause of judicialisation and legalisation.

surprising, therefore, that the standpoint of strategic actors is often given such short shrift.[223] Legal scholarship often focuses exclusively on institutions and seeks to reconstruct the system, if any, in which these institutions are, or are assumed to be, embedded. Such a perspective is useful in tracing the elaboration of legal doctrine. I would argue, however, that it is not the most fruitful if our aim is to understand how legal institutions and other institutional, normative and processual sites are created, develop and operate in practice.

This scenario embraces, but is not limited to, EU law. Using the example of the international toy industry, I have tried to show how the EU site, with its own specific characteristics, fits into this broader picture, drawing on and contributing to the life of the other sites of global legal pluralism. Before the more detailed analysis, I sketched the relationship between global legal pluralism and legal economic networks. This order of presentation was intentional: it was intended to jolt us out of our usual way of seeing the EU institutions, including the ECJ, solely in their own terms, in the EU framework, and without placing them in any wider context. Our preconceptions, based on previous knowledge and limited experience, frequently prevent us from seeing precisely how the EU fits into this broader picture, or from grasping the implications of EU institutions, norms and processes for other parts of a complex system of global legal pluralism. I have tried to use the organisation as well as the content of this chapter to some extent to correct our otherwise limited vision. Viewed from the standpoint of economic actors, that is from the standpoint of decision-makers in economic organisations, EU law appears not as a discrete, bounded and isolated legal system, but rather as a bunch of elements in (or on) the global legal playing field. Consequently, it is not possible any longer to grasp how it operates in practice, or to understand it theoretically, without situating it within the sets of relationships that constitute this broader arena. [224]

Taken together, these different but interwoven sets of norms which comprise global legal pluralism amount to a novel regime for governing global economic networks. They are, however, less a structure of multi-level governance, than a conjunction of distinctive institutional and normative sites for the production, implementation and sanctioning of rules. In the specific case of the toy industry, they testify, in part, to the structure of authority and power within these inter-firm and intra-firm networks, which are characterised by a buyer-driven, rather than a producer-driven, governance structure. These new normative forms for governing global economic networks are among the reasons why US, EU and Chinese firms and economies are so intimately linked in the internationalised production and distribution relations which are characteristic of globalisation.

---

[223] Except, perhaps, in legal anthropology: see F. Snyder, "Anthropology, Dispute Processes and Law: A Critical Introduction" (1981) 8 *British Journal of Law and Society* 141; reprinted in revised and slightly different form in P. A. Thomas (ed.), *Legal Frontiers* (Dartmouth, 1996), 135–79. See also E. Le Roy, *Le jeu des lois: Une anthropologie "dynamique" du Droit* (LGDJ, 1999).

[224] For an analogous plea with regard to US law, see A.C. Aman, "The Globalizing State: A Future-Oriented Perspective on the Public/Private Distinction, Federalism, and Democracy", (1998) 31 *Vanderbilt Journal of Transnational Law* 769.

From this discussion we can derive several more specific hypotheses.

First, global legal pluralism is a way of describing the structure of the sites taken as a whole. Seen from the perspective of a specific global commodity chain, global legal pluralism may be described as a network, even if some segments of the network may be occuped alternatively by two or more possible sites.

Second, the sites of global legal pluralism may be classified provisionally into two rough categories. Some sites are market-based, being generated by economic actors as part of economic processes. Some are polity-based, in that they form a part of established political structures; this includes sites which are convention-based, deriving from agreements between governments. This classification scheme distinguishes between different types of sites according to their mode of creation.

Third, the various sites differ in decision-making structure, that is, in their institutions, norms and processes. They vary in the extent to which their institutions, norms and processes are inserted in a hierarchy. They may differ in their reliance on case-law, the use of precedent, and the binding force of norms and decisions: in other words, in in respect of those characteristics which are often associated with law. These factors affect the outcomes of the various sites, including the different ways in which they allocate risk. At the same time, however, it is important not to overlook the extent to which sites are interrelated, for example in relation to institutional arrangements such as jurisdiction, copying or borrowing of norms, and the interconnection of their dispute-resolution processes.

Fourth, the sites are not all equally vulnerable to economic or political pressures. It is going too far to say that the network of global legal pluralism which is put into play by the economic processes of any specific global commodity chain reflects the structure of authority and power in the global commodity chain in question. Some types of institutions, processes and norms are more permeable to economic processes than others. It should also be noted that in cases of political conflict, for example between NGOs and multinational buyers in the international commodity chain in toys, the struggle between the competing groups is not limited to a single site. Each of the groups may invoke institutions, norms and processes of different sites. This may lead to a wider conflicts between different sites, including conflicts of effectiveness and even of legitimacy.

Fifth, it has been argued recently that the world economic system is entering a new polycentric phase, and that there is no reason to assume that Western business practices and Western law, for example concepts of rule of law, will remain dominant.[225] This contrasts with Garth and Dezalay's view that, while

---

[225] R.P. Appelbaum, "The Future of Law in a Global Economy" (1998) 7(2) *Social and Legal Studies* 171. Appelbaum studied the apparel industry, where "Even the largest European or North American retailers and manufacturers cannot ordinarily directly access Chinese factories: typically they must work through Hong Kong and Taiwanese intermediaries' (ibid., 186; citing interview with S.R. Walton, Managing Director, Innova Ltd., Hong Kong, 2 May 1993).

guanxi still flourishes, formal law is playing an increasingly important role in Hong Kong and throughout China, especially because trade has fostered more relations between Chinese and non-Chinese.[226] The material presented in the present chapter does not really support Appelbaum's thesis. It suggests instead that different sites may involve different legal cultures and sets of social relations, sometimes in relative isolation from historically different ones, but sometimes in complex hybrid forms.[227]

Sixth, specific sites are affected by conflicts between economic organisations occupying the same box in a global commodity chain. For example, conflicts over markets may pit foreign producers, exporters and importers, on one hand, against domestic producers, on the other hand. Conflicts over markets also occur between companies occupying similar positions in the chain. The occupants of each of these segments try to enlist the norms, institutions and processes of the various sites of global legal pluralism to improve their position, not only *vis-à-vis* their direct competitors, but also in relation to the occupants of other segments of the global commodity chain. These conflicts involve and have important implications for sites. The most well-known example is the production of case-law and the development of legal doctrine. We need to pay more attention to how such conflicts arise, unfold, and are resolved because they are often crucial determinants of the developmental paths of the institutions, norms and processes of various sites.

Seventh, these sites are not always, or even usually, alternatives in dispute-resolution, as might be expected if one presumes that the norms governing global economic networks are ordered in a hierarchical arrangement. Instead, each site deals with, governs, or seeks to govern a discrete part of the global commodity chain. Once a chain is established, its activities are governed by a given set of rules, emanating from a variety of linked sites, except to the extent that normal conflicts of law rules, that is, private international law, allow firms a choice of governing legislation or a choice of dispute-resolution.

Eighth, taken as a whole, the various sites are not all necessarily hierarchically ordered in relation to each other. Instead, they demonstrate many other types of interrelationships, sometimes hierarchical, sometimes not, sometimes competing, sometimes collaborative. In other words, even when viewed very broadly,

---

[226] Dezalay and Garth, above at n. 51, 261–6.

[227] Jones, "Capitalism, Globalization and Rule of Law: An Alternative Trajectory of Legal Change in China" (1994) 3 *Social and Legal Studies* 195. For a useful *caveat*, see Clarke, "Methodologies for Research in Chinese Law" (1996) 30 *University of British Columbia Law Review* 201. Differences in sites are likely to be influenced also by the fact that national structures remain very important for both trade policy and multinational corporate behaviour. On trade policy, see C. Garcia Molyneux, *Domestic Structures and International Trade: The Unfair Trade Instruments of the United States and the European Union* (Hart Publishing, 2001) and his article in this book. On corporate behaviour, see Pauly/Reich, "National Structures and Multinational Corporate Behaviour: Enduring Differences in the Age of Globalization" (1997) 5 *International Organization* 1. Social and cultural differences will also certainly influence the practical implementation of any international competition rules: *cf.* Pape, "Socio-Cultural Differences and International Competiton Law", 5 *ELJ* (1999).

they do not make up a legal system. This contrasts strongly with the usual lawyer's view of the multi-level governance of international economic relations. The latter is a normative view. Here I have tried to develop a more sociological perspective.

These broad hypotheses need to be tested. In addition, numerous questions remain to be addressed by future research. For example, how are sites created?[228] How are they constituted, developed and legitimated as sites? Which sites have a specific geographical location and, if so, why? What determines the modes and organisation of dispute-resolution? What decision processes are involved? Do sites vary in their resemblance to state law (insertion in a hierarchy, reliance on case-law, binding decisions, use of precedent, etc.), and why? To what extent do the norms of a particular site combine hard law and soft law? To what extent are sites interconnected, and how are they connected? How are groups, hierarchies and networks of sites created, and how, if at all, are such processes connected to economic and political relations? Do certain sites tend to converge or become more uniform in their institutional characteristics, norms or dispute-settlement processes, and why? How do conflicts between sites arise, what are the consequences of such competition, and how are conflicting institutional, normative and processual claims handled? The answers to these questions will help us to understand further how economic globalisation is governed.

---

[228] For example, it has been argued that "the construction of international issue networks and global policy arenas does not constitute a reduction of the scope of interstate politics but rather its pursuit by other means": Picciotto, "Networks in International Economic Integration: Fragmented States and the Dilemmas of Neo-Liberalism", (1996–97) 17 *Northwestern Journal of International Law and Business* 1014, 1037.

2

The Constitution of the Global Market

MIGUEL POIARES MADURO

I INTRODUCTION

The processes of legal and economic integration at a regional and global scale have created powerful legal and economic dilemmas. They challenge the paradigms of constitutionalism, including the state's monopoly of constitutionalism, the autonomy of national political communities and the traditional forms of participation and representation. They also require profound changes in the way in which we think and teach the law. The phenomenon of globalisation has promoted the interdependence of national political communities and destroyed the artificial boundaries upon which national constitutional democracies are found and from which derive their legitimacy. Many argue for the need to regulate such process of globalisation and subject the forces that command it to some form of democratic control.[1] Some conceive the developing forms of regional integration as new forms of governance, which attempt to provide a regulatory and constitutional forum capable of controlling and legitimising the process of economic integration and globalisation. They can even be conceived as intermediary steps on the way to a global polity that may take the constitutional form tested in these regional systems. There are also those who propose far reaching models of democratisation of the global community to be undertaken, for example, through profound short- and long-term reforms of the UN system.[2] Finally, there are those who conceive the process of globalisation itself as an instrument of constitutional development and entrust to principles such as free trade and non-discrimination the leading role in developing such global or international constitutionalism.[3]

International trade law has taken a pivotal role in the discussions surrounding the legal and political form of the international society and in expressing the challenges brought by globalisation to the state and its constitutionalism. Economic integration and free trade generate competition between the different

---

[1] A Tita, "Globalization: A New Political and Economic Space requiring Supernational Governance" (1998) 32 *Journal of World Trade: Law, Economics, Public Policy* 47 at 51.

[2] David Held, *Democracy and Global Order* (Polity, Cambridge, 1995).

[3] E.U. Petersmann, "How to Reform the UN System? Constitutionalism, International Law and International Organizations" (1997) 10 *LJIL* 421, 463.

national economic and legal systems. The free circulation of companies, capital, products and services generates a process of regulatory competition among states: companies will move to where the regulatory environment is more favourable to their objectives (deregulation, lower taxes, financial incentives, etc.); consumers, in turn, can choose among goods and services conforming to different states' regulations. As a consequence, regulations themselves will also be competing in the market. There are different economic and legal analyses praising or criticising such strategy of trade liberalisation and its accompanying regulatory competition. Some stress the efficiency gains derived from a better allocation of resources and the higher freedom of choice and lower prices available for consumers. Others point to the threat to the welfare state and the risks of a regulatory "race to the bottom": companies will move to states with lower environmental, social, health or consumer protection because they can; other states must, according to the rules of free trade, accept products whose incorporated characteristics or producing rules endanger those states' conception of the right level of social, environmental or other public interest regulation. I will not be reviewing these analyses in detail.

There may be no doubt that, overall, free trade promotes efficiency and wealth maximisation. But, it is also not clear that all steps favouring free trade will produce more efficient or equitable solutions on the basis of existing alternatives. My assumption, at this point, is that whatever the final balance between regulatory and deregulatory approaches for international trade, global economic integration will develop interactions among the different national political communities and individuals leading to common interests but also to claims of interdependence and shared social decisions. In other words, whatever the final framework for international trade, it will be decided in an emerging global political arena. One of the aims of this chapter is to identify this political arena, who governs it, and according to which rules. A second aim will be to highlight the different institutional alternatives in that global political arena. It is also worth noting that the development of international trade and economic integration will raise claims for some form of global distributive justice to complement the wealth maximisation arising from free trade. The extent to which such claims will be satisfied and whether a criterion of distributive justice will dominate a new understanding of international law is an open question. The gradual outcome, however, will be the developing of global forms of political discourse and law-making, challenging state constitutionalism, and requiring some of the instruments and theories of constitutionalism.

In this chapter I will review some of these issues while focusing on the constitutional impact of economic integration and globalisation. In Part II, I will note briefly how the regulation of international trade is assuming weak constitutional forms. In Part III, I will review some of the challenges posed by free trade and globalisation to national constitutionalism. Part IV is devoted to the review of some of the different constitutional paths to which globalisation may lead.

II REGULATION OF INTERNATIONAL TRADE AS AN EMERGING CONSTITUTION

International law and mainly international trade law is starting to reflect the constitutional transformation of international society. Global constitutionalism may be the future result of the process of globalisation and, in part, it is already emerging. Petersmann speaks of a developing international constitutionalism, the contours of which are still unclear.[4] In this, international organisations can be conceived of as "a fourth branch of government for the collective supply of international public goods which neither citizens nor individual governments can secure without international cooperation".[5] As in regional forms of integration, trade law is conceived as the engine of global integration and its emerging constitutionalism.[6] The World Trade Organisation (WTO) and the agreements derived from the Uruguay Round are the primary tool of global constitutionalism. The set of rights which it protects, its emerging rule of law, the role which individuals and other non-state actors may be called to play in its development and its impact on the domestic policies of states, all have the potential gradually to help free trade law to assume a constitutional form. Nevertheless, I will argue in this chapter that it is still too early to talk of a global constitution, and the emerging elements of constitutionalism in the international arena must find a broader variety of sources of participation than those favoured by the WTO system.

International organisations have been understood as forms of reducing information and transaction costs among states, in order to promote international co-operation. Underlying this idea is the concept that is rational for states to co-operate, and what prevents it are the transaction and information costs usually involved in relations among states. In a world without transaction and information costs the net benefits arising from free trade are normally foreseen as sufficient to guarantee that states would co-operate and achieve free trade.[7] Even if a state could lose in a specific case, it would be compensated by the states whose benefit will be higher than the cost of trade liberalisation for the state. Unfortunately, reality is not a world without transaction and information costs. Information costs may determine that states are not able to perceive or calculate the benefits of free trade, and high transaction costs in the negotiation process may make co-operation difficult. States may also attempt to "free ride" (protecting their market but expecting that others will liberalise theirs). Classical international law, which confers to the state the predominant and

---

[4] E.U. Petersmann, "How to Reform the UN System? Constitutionalism, International Law and International Organizations" (1997) 10 *LJIL* 421, 463.

[5] Ibid., 464.

[6] Ibid., 445.

[7] This is, however, an assumption with departs from a unitary conception of the state which, as I will argue below, is false. It also ignores that cost/benefit analyses may vary greatly from state to state. In my view, even in a world without transaction and information costs, there would be instances of non-co-operation among states.

almost exclusive role in the international system, has predominantly conceived international organisations as forums of negotiation among states whose institutional rules are destined to reduce information and transaction costs. International organisations are set up mainly to provide the necessary framework for viable co-operation among states since this would be difficult to achieve without the institutionalised processes provided for by those international organisations. Instances of majoritarian voting or the development of mandatory dispute-resolution systems could still be explained under the same rationale and taking account of the functional nature of institutional organisations. Mandatory dispute-resolution would provide all parties involved the guarantee that none will be allowed to evade the application of the rules accepted as good for all in the co-operation process. The function of a quasi-jurisdictional system would be the prevention of free riders. That states would not be subject to rules and decisions, to which they did not intend to subject themselves, was safeguarded by the pure functional nature of those international organisations deprived of law-making power and strictly limited in their competencies.

This classical conception of international organisations is highly problematic. The functional view does not fit well with the indeterminacy and frequent lack of consensus regarding the goals attributed to international organisations. Such institutions often do much more than simply enforcing previously agreed policies. In some cases, they are forums of negotiation and exchange of information among states in which these attempt to reach more specific goals and policies to implement the initial broad and open goals. In other cases (such as the WTO) these institutions have an independent, normative authority, which leads them autonomously to determine new international policies and objectives. In this case, the classical paradigm is reversed "with nation-states serving more as agents of international bodies than as their principals".[8] As a consequence, such international organisations become much more than forums of co-operation or functional entities. They are emerging forms of power which require the normative control of constitutionalism. There is an important additional factor in this process: once international organisations are perceived by the different social sectors as emerging forms of independent power, they will attempt to profit from these organisations to pursue their different agendas. As a result, international organisations will tend to develop political and social goals which may diverge from those of their initial masters (the states). These goals will further promote a debate of constitutional character (already visible in many of the current debates surrounding the Millennium Round).

Is international law only about co-operation among states to solve collective problems which they cannot deal with on their own, or does it aim at achieving independent political and social goals (which can either be traced back to the idealised values attributed to an underlying international community, or to an

---

[8] Paul Stephan, "The New International Law—Legitimacy, Accountability, Authority and Freedom in the New Global Order" (1999) 70 *University of Colorado Law Review* 1555, 1557.

overarching consensus among all individuals of the international society)? Whatever vision taken will deeply influence how we conceive what international law is and what it ought to be. My argument at this point is that the present paths of international law lead us in the second direction. The WTO is the best example of an international organisation which, more than simply co-ordinating states, pursues independent political and social goals which are determined by a constituency of social sectors which goes well beyond the states. Furthermore, the WTO legal system is not simply a framework of rules intended to reduce free riders and transaction and information costs in the settlement of trade conflicts. As we will see, it is increasingly conceived as a minimum legal order necessary to support and protect the activity of economic sectors in a global market, while safeguarding other global interests. The objective of the WTO is not only to settle trade disputes between states, but to establish an international rule of law providing the certainty and stability needed by economic sectors to enter into international transactions and promote trade and investment.[9] Furthermore, it is the material content of the WTO legal order, and not only its original quasi-judicial system, which reinforces the idea of international trade as an area subject to the rule of law.

There are three classical principles in the WTO legal order: free trade, transparency (of trade restrictions) and non-discrimination. The development of these principles and institutions set up by the Uruguai Round appear to promote a constitutionalisation of the WTO legal order founded on the ideas of freedom, non-discrimination and the rule of law. This is Petersmann's constitutional conception of the WTO legal framework, which leads him to identify in it the basis of an international constitutionalism.[10] According to this vision, free trade requires more than non-discrimination and anti-protectionism. It requires the protection of the freedom of economic initiative from state interference with or without protectionism intent. The recent case-law of the panels and WTO Appellate Body has elements which can, in part, support such a constitutional conception of the WTO legal order. The WTO dispute-settlement bodies have invalidated national rules which did not discriminate against imported products. In the *Turtles* case, for example, a US rule prohibiting the sale (and import) of shrimp captured with nets which could harm turtles was considered as violating Article XI and not justified under Article XX. A reader familiar with international trade law will note, however, that the US rule regarding a non-incorporated standard, where the extraterritorial effects of the national rules[11] have usually been assumed, is unacceptable.[12] But the same was not the case in the *Beef Hormones* case opposing the United States with the EU. The United

---

[9] John Jackson, *The World Trade Organization—Constitution and Jurisprudence* (Chatham House Papers, London, 1998), 10.

[10] See Petersmann, above at n. 4.

[11] The US rule would regulate how Philippines' fishermen should fish in their own waters and the potential effects that could have on turtles in the Philippines.

[12] There is a good case to support that the difference between incorporated and non-incorporated standards is highly formalised, but I will not address this issue here.

States complained against an EU ban on hormone-grown beef (where the external consequence was a prohibition on the imports of such type of beef). The European Union claimed that the restriction imposed on the imports of beef was non-discriminatory and deprived of any protectionist intent. Furthermore, it was a precautionary measure justified to protect the health of its consumers in view of the scientific uncertainty regarding the effects on human health of such type of artificial increases of hormones. Both the panel and (more importantly but also more limitedly) the Appellate Body, considered the EU measure as invalid in light of the WTO rules (in particular Article XI and the SPS Agreement). The first important conclusion to be drawn from this conclusion is that the WTO has finally decided to awaken the "sleeping beauty" of Article XI. In effect, the *Beef Hormones* decision appears to indicate that, from now on, the judicial bodies of the WTO will review both national measures, which restrict trade by discriminating against imports, and non-discriminatory measures which, in any case, prevent the access of imports into the national market (even if equally restricting domestic products).[13]

Forthcoming cases already in the case-load of the WTO jurisdictional system will help to clarify the extent to which the SPS and TBT will be interpreted, together with Article XI, to challenge national non-discriminatory regulatory policies.[14] It will also be important to see what its impact on Article XX (mainly the "necessary" condition) will be. At this point, it is too early to assume that the interpretation to be given to those rules will go as far as to transform the law of international trade into a set of rights intended to balance the benefits of a state regulation with the burden it imposes on freedom of trade. There are those who argue that there is no cost-benefit or balancing rule in the WTO and that even the *Beef Hormones* case can be understood as the prevention of a form of regulatory protectionism.[15] In this case, the strict scrutiny involved in the assessment of risk and equivalence under the SIPS or the necessity of the restriction on trade under Article XX would serve to uncover more subtle forms of regulatory protectionism (it is not necessary if it therefore aims at protecting the national market from outside competition). One way or the other, however, if the *Beef Hormones* decision is to be taken seriously, it means that the Appellate Body is ready to review non-discriminatory measures under a test of necessity in the light of the SPS rules and as (we will see), possibly Article XX. Such test of necessity of a non-discriminatory restriction on trade in the light of the public interests protected under WTO exceptions will involve some form of cost-

---

[13] See the analysis by JHH Weiler, "The Transformation of Europe" (1991) 100 *Yale Law Journal* 2403.

[14] See, for example, the complaint of "regarding the prohibition of import of goods including Asbestos".

[15] See Alan Sykes, "Regulatory Protectionism and the Law of International Trade" (1999) 66 *University of Chicago Law Review* 1, arguing that the WTO law (and its "judicial" interpretation) does not reflect in any way any type of balancing or cost-benefit analysis (at 7, 31). He interprets the *Beef Hormones* decisions as preventing a measure which albeit facially non-discriminatory, constituted a form of regulatory protectionism (at 4).

benefit analysis. The reality is that once courts or quasi-judicial entities are called in to assess the justification of regulatory burdens which are not openly protectionist, that judgment will inevitably involve a cost-benefit analysis. Whether that cost-benefit analysis will be legitimised in view of the protection of economic freedom rights, or as necessary to uncover hidden protectionism, will not make much difference in the end. Substantively, there is no relevant difference in the process of conducting cost-benefit analysis as a means to uncover protectionist measures or as a means to measure the efficiency of the measure. The overall result will be an extension of the degree of control of domestic public regulation by the WTO dispute-resolution system under its free trade rules.

The expansion of the scope of action of WTO rules will result in a spill-over of international trade law into many areas of states' domestic policies. The institutional and legal framework of the WTO will interact in a manner that will erode national sovereignty. John Jackson has remarked that the implications for state sovereignty of the Uruguay Round Agreement creating the WTO system have not yet been fully understood by any government that has accepted them. This impact, at the moment, is still not sufficient to collapse the regulatory identity of the states. At the same time, the transfer of powers to international institutions which this process entails is also still not sufficient to claim for a constitutional form of control and allocation of that power. However, this development of international trade law is part of a broader context of erosion of the political autonomy of the states which questions the concept of state sovereignty itself. Whatever the policy areas on which one focuses (exchange rates, monetary and fiscal policies, environmental or consumer protection, public health, justice, crime, human rights, etc.), it is clear that the policy powers of states are increasingly constrained both in practice (by international inter-dependence and competition) and in law (by the growing international law provisions which affect, directly or indirectly, the domestic policies of states).[16] This erosion of the public powers of the state and national political communities (in which international trade law assumes a dominant role) will generate both a challenge to national constitutionalism and a claim for such power to be reintroduced at the global level. Free trade and its accompanying deregulation at state level have already given rise to increased attempts for the setting-up of international standards capable of controlling those deregulatory consequences and reinstatement of political control over the market. The new forms of power and social interaction arising from this overall process will require some form of constitutional framework.

At this point, the reader may have noticed that there is an element of constitutionalism which is still largely irrelevant in international society, namely the individual. True, much of the development of a global constitutionalism will depend on the role to be attributed to individuals in the international political and economic arena. International law is increasingly providing a set of

---

[16] See, in this sense, for example Philip Alston, "The Myopia of Handmaidens: International Lawyers and Globalization" (1997) 8 *European Journal of International Law*; Internet version available at http://www.ejil.org/journal/Vol8/No3/art4.html.

rights and obligations addressed directly to individuals. Once such processes reach a certain degree of development, the constitutional transformation of international law will be unavoidable. Any normative authority raises a claim for democratic and constitutional legitimacy once it stops being mediated by the state and starts to govern individuals directly.

At present, strong limits remain to individual and other non-state actors' participation in the international society, such as lack of judicial standing, weak forms of enforcing international human rights and the low level of participation in the institutions and processes of international law-making. Even if in economic areas individuals are recognised as having an increasingly important role, it is noted that their framework of action is still determined by the states which, to a large extent, remain the decisive factor in international law.[17] The dispute-settlement mechanism set up by the Uruguay Round reflects this overall picture and still does not recognise a full legal status to individuals. However, even in this regard, the dynamic elements of the WTO system are bound to give to individuals a stronger role than what could be simply deduced from a formal analysis of its legal rules. The Appellate Body has already recognised the right of non-state actors to be heard in WTO proceedings which may affect their legitimate interests.[18] Generally, individuals will play an important role in the promotion of litigation through their states. The lower information and organisation costs involved in the knowledge of the new WTO system and its form of rule of law (where harmonised jurisprudence increases transparency, security and certainty), the repeated litigation it is generating (already more than 200 complaints), which will increase information and decrease the marginal costs of a process, and the enhanced effectiveness of its decisions, all contribute to reduce the costs and risks involved in individuals lobbying their governments to bring forward complaints against other WTO parties and, at the same time, make states more available partners for such litigation.

The role of individuals and other non-state actors is not necessarily dependent upon the granting of legal standing in an international forum. This role may be performed on an informal basis through lobbying and other forms of alternative participation, either through their home states or directly in the international decision-making forums. Moreover, the national participation of different individuals and groups is assuming an increasing international dimension. First, there is an increased awareness by individuals and other sectors of the domestic impact of the state's exercise of foreign policy. Secondly, there is a growing awareness of the importance of the state as a vehicle for the defence and promotion of individual and group interests in the international arena and the means available for such effect. Thirdly, the international dimension of domestic forms of participation is often linked with the development of inter-

---

[17] See, for example, Bruno Simma and Andreas Paulus, "The 'International Community': Facing the Challenge of Globalization" (1998) 9 *European Journal of International Law* 266, 273.

[18] *United States–Import Prohibitions of Certain Shrimps and Shrimp Products, Report of the Appellate Body* WT/DS58/AB/R, 12 October 1998.

national strategies by individuals and non-state sectors which are planned at an international level, but executed through different domestic forums. Benvenisti recently described how "domestic interest groups often cooperate with similarly situated foreign interest groups in order to impose externalities on rival domestic groups".[19] A further international dimension arises in the context of national legal and political processes through the increased recourse to arguments derived from international legal and political sources. This is not only the case with the often-referred-to strategies of multinational companies benefiting from their large scope of action and access to information. The Internet, for example, is a powerful tool for other individuals and non-state actors both to organise common actions or to acquire legal and political information which shapes and strengthens their participation in the domestic arena.[20]

This international dimension of domestic policies, which occurs simultaneously with a growing awareness of the domestic dimension of international politics, is the best reflection of the current relation between international law and constitutional law: a contamination of influences related to the transnational character of domestic conflicts and the instrumentalisation and shaping of domestic politics in the light of international conflicts. Legally, the effects are visible. On the one hand, the expansion of the scope of international law and its growing transversal effect on state legal orders, the application of the principles of non-discrimination and economic freedom, the type of conflicts it is called upon to adjudicate, and the development of judicial systems and a direct relation with individuals, lead to the development of an emerging function of judicial review similar to that of constitutionalism and to the introduction of constitutional concepts in the dominating discourse of international law (mainly international trade law). On the other hand, international law is also being used increasingly in the context of national constitutional debates and to regulate domestic conflicts. Legal and economic sectors use both international and national constitutional arguments at the service of strategies that also have a domestic and international dimension (as the "Banana" saga in the United States and the EU clearly demonstrates). In conclusion, therefore, while international law (with international trade law in the forefront) is being constitutionalised, constitutional law is internationalised, with international institutions and rules being used to correct national constitutional malfunctions. This is nothing more than a logical consequence of the fact that internal and international policies are no longer divisible and that economic integration blurs the artificial boundaries between national political communities. The emergence of global constitutionalism is, in this way, both a consequence and an answer to the challenge brought by globalisation and economic integration to national constitutionalism. This issue will be addressed next.

[19] Eyal Benvenisti, "Exit and Voice in the Age of Globalization" (1999) 98 *Michigan Law Review* 167, 169 ff.

[20] See Henry Perritt, "The Internet Is Changing International Law" (1998) 73 *Chicago Kent Law Review* 997.

III INTERNATIONAL CHALLENGE TO NATIONAL CONSTITUTIONALISM

Constitutional law has usually been considered as the higher degree and ulti-mate source of legitimacy of the legal system and its rules. Constitutional law is conceived as the higher law of the legal system, the criterion of legitimacy and the validity of other sources of law. At the same time, the paradigm of constitu-tional law is associated with the state, which is assumed to maintain the mono-poly of power. Globalisation questions these paradigms of constitutionalism, but much of the challenges it raises serve only to demonstrate how artificial has been our understanding of the paradigms of national constitutionalism. To a great extent, national constitutionalism is still conceived as the single form of constitutionalism,[21] addressing the source and monopoly of power still being in the hands of nation states. Instead, national constitutionalism has been subject to a pluralist revolution and can no longer be conceived in those terms.[22] There is a plurality of power sources and there is a massification of the conflicts between equally valid constitutional principles. Consequently, the conception of national constitutionalism centred in the power of the state and organising a society towards pre-defined (or pre-agreed) social goals entered into a crisis. This conception has hidden, under an idealised construction of a fictional "com-mon good", the true nature of constitutionalism: that of balancing among diverse and often conflicting interests and fears.[23] At the same time, that ide-alised perception of constitutionalism has hidden the transnational character of many domestic political conflicts and the transfer of power to institutions and processes located beyond the national political borders.

Liberalisation of trade generates competition among products and services of different states which, in turn, leads to competition between different regulatory frameworks to which those products and services are subject. National polities have to determine their policies not only on the basis of their internal prefer-ences but also taking into account the need for their products and services to be competitive in the global market. The consequence is a transfer of power from the national political process to the market where decisions are taken through voluntary market transactions. A similar process will take place if, instead of trusting the regulation of international trade to the market, we decide to subject it to international standards set by international technocratic bodies. Both the markets and these technocratic bodies have an inherent rationality and a set of

---

[21] J. Shaw talks about "the unexamined conventions and traditions of modern constitutionalism, which crucially include an assumption that there is a single comprehensive form of constitutional dialogue", in "Postnational Constitutionalism in the European Union" (1999) 6 *Journal of European Public Policy*.

[22] See Gustavo Zagrebelsky, *Il diritto mite* (Einaudi, Torino, 1992, notably 4–11, 45–50.

[23] See Michele Everson, "Beyond the Bundesverfassungsgericht: On the Necessary Cunning of Constitutional Reasoning" (1998) 4 *European Law Journal* 389, 390; Josephine Shaw, *Postnational Constitutionalism*, n. 21; Cohen and Sabel, "Directly-Deliberative Poliarchy" (1997) 3 *European Law Journal* 313.

normative values which is not subject to any form of discourse; or, to put it another way, they "decide" embodied with a set of values and assumptions that are excluded from democratic decision-making. This can also be conceived as a form of democratic deficit whereby decisions previously controlled by national democracies are now subject to other forums of decision-making which do not take place according to the same democratic standards of traditional representative democracy.

Similarly, the recognition of the heterogeneity of the state and of the illusion of the uniform national interest also affect our democratic understanding of the states and the profound consequences for their role and status in international law. The image of international law focused on the promotion of peace and co-operation among states does not explain many of the failures of international law in an institutional framework favourable to co-operation. In fact, at least in instances of collective problems affecting a small number of states, the reduced number of actors and their long-term common interest should make co-operation possible between those states, as game theory explains,[24] The circumstance that that is not the usual result can only be explained by the heterogeneous character of the state.[25] Furthermore, the democratic problems of national constitutionalism may legitimate new forms of intervention of international law, not to replace but to correct the malfunctions of national constitutionalism. Naturally, these interventions will require some form of constitutional legitimacy.

Many of the problems of national constitutionalism can be included in the notion of the deterritorialisation of constitutionalism. The deterritorialisation of constitutionalism occurs in parallel with the weakening of the role of the state in international law. To a great extent, they are the cause and effect of each other. International competition and the cross-national effect of the different national policies determines that the citizens of national polities both affect and are affected by decisions taken in other political communities, creating a disparity between the polities of which we are members and the polities that regulate our interests. Current developments in international law can be seen as reinforcing this process or as an answer to it.

David Held has highlighted this global challenge to nation state democracy and the need for a new model of democracy (which can be extended to constitutionalism). In his words:

"the problem, for defenders and critics alike of modern democracy systems, is that regional and global inter-connectedness contests the traditional national resolutions of key questions of democratic theory and practice. The very process of governance can escape the reach of the nation-state. National communities by no means exclusively make and determine decisions and policies for themselves, and governments by no means determine what is appropriate exclusively for their own citizens."[26]

[24] Eyal Benvenisti, "Exit and Voice in the Age of Globalization" (1999) 98 *Michigan Law Review* 167, 197–8.
[25] Ibid., 199.
[26] David Held, *Democracy and the Global Order*, n. 2 above, 16–17 (footnote omitted).

There are thus both pragmatic and normative arguments in favour of a broader form of constitutionalism and democracy "overseeing" national constitutional democracies.[27] First, nation states can no longer (and perhaps never could) contain the impact of outside policies inside their borders, and therefore need to acquire forms of constitutional control over decision-making taking place outside those national borders. Secondly, nation states never fully fulfilled the democratic and constitutional ideals of full representation and participation. It is no longer possible to sustain the illusion of a symmetric relationship between national political decision-makers and the recipients of political decisions.[28]

Two important consequences should be taken from the discussion made so far: first, state constitutionalism is no longer a sufficient forum to secure our representation in the decision-making processes which affect us; secondly, this has an impact both in the traditional legitimacy of international law and the shaping of its future role. It also becomes clear that if international law is to play a positive role in supplementing and correcting state constitutional failures, it must, itself, develop some form of constitutional legitimacy, even if not assuming the form of a global constitution. The constitutional facets of international law and its role in the correction of state constitutional malfunctions can already be detected in international trade law. As stated before, we are increasingly being affected by polities upon which we have no control or democratic participation. Those polities, which may be organised internally in a democratic manner, affect us both within the borders of our national polities or as "wish-to-be citizens" who would like to conduct our lives outside our original polities. Trade law can (and has done so, to a certain extent) increase democracy in national polities by requiring these polities to have some form of representation of the foreign interests affected by its decisions. Paradoxically, trade law and the obligation it imposes to reconstruct and open the national regulatory and political processes may also improve the level and scope of domestic representation in the national political process. The heterogeneity of the state made clear by the way globalization and transnational strategies dispute the myth of the unitary state, and the single national interest demonstrates that what is often put forward as the national interest is nothing more than an artificial construction of the national interest in light of the interests of some special interests, which dominate the national political process. Most instances of discrimination against (or under-representation of) foreign nationals in national political processes are, at the same time, instances of capture of the national political process by an interest group against the interests of a dormant national majority. In most cases of trade protectionism, we do not really have a homogeneous national interest opposed to foreign interests; instances of trade protectionism tend to occur where concentrated national interests try to conserve their eco-

---

[27] The use of the word "overseeing" is not to be understood as defining a form of hierarchical control and supremacy as will be clearer below.

[28] Held, above at n. 26, 224.

nomic privileges at the cost of foreign competitors and national consumers. Because of the concentrated interests and high stakes of the small minority they can easily dominate the national political process even against the interests of the dispersed majority of consumers whose low per capita stakes and high transaction and information costs prevent them from being aware of their interests and exercising pressure in the political process. In these cases, international trade law can increase the scope and degree of representation of the national political processes with regard to both domestic and foreign interests.

In turn, there is a transfer of power generated by international trade law to new forms of decision-making such as the market, international standard-setting institutions and supranational judicial bodies. These institutions bring forward new problems of representation and participation, highlighting the remaining virtues of the state and the primordial role that it is to continue to play as the default form of representation and participation. How to co-ordinate these conflicting trends and develop a constitutional theory capable of legitimating the emerging forms of international law is the challenge currently facing both international lawyers and constitutionalists alike. Next, I will address the role and status of international trade law in this process.

IV GLOBAL CONSTITUTIONALISM AND THE FUTURE OF INTERNATIONAL TRADE LAW

Globalisation is often perceived as an inevitability. Even those who challenge it attempt to undermine it, at the same time that they note its ideological consequences and contest its inevitability, by using the rethoric and symbolism of the perceived inevitability to present globalisation as a kind of dark, secretive and dangerously inhumane project. As one author put it, "globalisation is universalism minus a conscience".[29] Globalisation is not inevitable (states could still reinstate many of their protectionism policies effectively). If it is assumed to be this is because, no matter how much some people criticise the consequences of globalisation, there is a large consensus that the benefits of globalisation for the large majority (if not the totality) of human beings are clearly superior to its costs. Nevertheless, such social costs are important and must be dealt with. At the same time, there is a generalised perception that globalisation and trade liberalisation give a higher voice to some interests while excluding many individuals from their processes of social decision-making. These are legitimate concerns which must be addressed. What is feared by many is that the instruments of globalisation and international trade (free trade rights) will become more than the tools for an emergent international society, to be transformed into the constitutional principles of that society. Whether and the extent to

---

[29] Pierre-Marie Dupuy, "International Law: Torn between Coexistence, Cooperation and Globalization—General Conclusions" (1998) 9 *European Journal of International Law* 278, 282.

which free trade rights should be given such constitutional status must be the object of a public discourse addressing different normative proposals for the organisation of international society and its relation with national political communities.

There are also good arguments in favour of a constitutionalisation of international trade law which would serve as the core of global constitutionalism. Petersmann argues for a "rights-based" constitutional development from the ground up, through individual litigants and courts (such as occur in the EU):[30] this will require a further development of the international recognition of the legal status of individuals and of the rights of freedom and non-discrimination that they can promote through litigation.[31] Under this view, international human rights and international trade law are not in opposition but, on the contrary, in the words of another author "they are topologically similar: both international trade law and international human rights are largely deregulatory—they declare what the State should not do. In each regime, the problem to be solved is the overbearing State which wants to control voluntary activity".[32] But, of course, this entails a particular notion of both human rights and international trade law. Human rights (even in their exclusive liberal political rights conception) may also require strong government intervention (to enforce transactions and guarantee security, for example). In the same way, international trade law may be developed by enacting international regulatory standards to which all economic operators would have to conform instead of focusing on the liberalisation of trade through the elimination of the different regulatory standards with which economic operators have to comply.

The real question to be faced is the choice of the process determining what human rights and international trade rules will be. There may actually be a world consensus on the protection of human rights and the promotion of free trade but there is no overall consensus on the content of those rights and the rules of international trade. In a broader essay defending the remaining value of statehood in international law, Koskenniemi has argued that, in spite of the generalised international agreement on a human rights discourse, the lack of a true international consensus on the number and content of human rights entails that these cannot form the basis for an alternative source of legitimacy of a new international social order.[33] For this author, the best method to prevent an authoritarian definition of what those rights and other principles of international law are is the intermediation of the state "because its formal-bureaucratic rationality provides a safeguard against the totalitarianism inher-

---

[30] Above at n. 4, 423.

[31] Ibid., e.g. 422, 425.

[32] Steve Charnovitz, "The Globalization of Economic Human Rights" (1999) 25 *Brooklyn Journal of International Law* 113.

[33] Martti Koskenniemi, "The Future of Statehood" (1991) 32 *Harvard International Law Journal* 397, 399: "The protection of human rights, however, cannot form a meaningful basis for social order. If we are to define our polity in terms of human rights, we must ascertain the number and content of such rights".

ent in a commitment to substantive values, which forces those values on people not sharing them".[34] Following this view, the definition of international trade law rights should result from co-operation and institutionalised debate among states which will remain the main actors and legitimating sources of the international society.[35] The problem with this view in the context of the WTO system is that, as the same author recognises, international organisations, more than simply enforcing pre-existing agreements, establish and define priorities and policies.[36] Although in some cases states are still the absolute masters in international organisations, that is no longer the case with the WTO, whose "policies" have much more diverse sources of input and can be defined independently of some states' agreements. Therefore, it becomes difficult to legitimate the rights defined by international trade law exclusively on the basis of state indirect legitimation.

Petersmann, in his conception of the "new international law", also departs from a liberal perspective opposing any international authoritarian definition of the prevailing values and goals. But in his case, he also abdicates, to a large extent, from the rational formality of the states' political process, and establishes a direct legitimating link between individuals and the international society. It is the voluntary agreement between individuals in the emerging international market which will define the predominating values of the international society. The role of international trade law is that of guaranteeing the freedom of individuals in the international arena so that they can fully enjoy their personal autonomy. For Petersmann there is an emerging process of global constitutionalism where democracies will operate "in a constitutional framework of national and international guarantees of freedom, non-discrimination, rule of law and institutional 'checks and balances' ".[37] In his view, the way to promote global constitutionalism is by extending the scope and application of international trade law, human rights documents and dispute-settlement mechanisms. These will be the "avant-garde" of global constitutionalism. The focus is then on a minimal notion of constitutionalism: non-discrimination, individual rights (mainly economic rights) and dispute-settlement mechanisms. The expectation is that these instances will develop into a set of individual constitutional rights protected from any form of power. The dynamics of international trade will fuel the development of an international rule of law through these economic rights and dispute-settlement mechanisms. Such dynamics will result, however, in a particular form of constitutionalism. The fundamental idea is that of constitutionalism as limited government. The fundamental fear is that it could become unlimited. The fundamental suspicion lies within the political process. In reality, behind such a conception lies a deep distrust of the political process

---

[34] Ibid., 407.
[35] People still disagree about the political good. In normal circumstances, states still provide the means to direct substantive disagreement into institutionalised debate: ibid., 410.
[36] Ibid., 403.
[37] Above at n. 4, 447, 448.

and the way it organises and exercises power. However, the alternative institutions to which power is transferred "through general rules of a higher legal rank" are generally assumed in an idealised form in Petersmann's discourse. Those institutions tend to be either the courts or the market, which are not themselves insulated from suspicion and potential malfunctions.

Free trade generates competition between the national economic and legal systems subject to the goal of efficiency. It can be disputed as to the extent to which the WTO case-law already embodies a notion of free trade rights as protecting the freedom of economic actors to choose among different regulatory systems. But, even if legally it is not imposed on states to lower their social, environmental and consumer standards, economic competition opens the national legal systems to competition and efficiency criteria, *de facto* subjecting normative ideals to economic reasoning.

The consequences of this process are deregulation at the national level and a reduction in the political control over the economic sphere. Many have conceived regional integration systems as an attempt to respond to global market competition and reinstate political control over the market in a new forum where common regulatory policies can be agreed. The long-term aim would be to develop mechanisms at global level which can regulate the global market and set minimum common standards. The failure to agree on the well-known "social clause" at the level of the WTO shows how far we are from any possibility of that kind. Others have also conceived regional integration systems as simply a step in a global process aimed at promoting the freedom and economic gains derived from economic integration and recognise, in the limits that such process imposes on public power, its great advantage.

Although the answers will probably be different, there is a common dilemma facing regional integration systems and global economic integration which is highlighted by the "instrumental" visions of regional integration systems: should free trade and economic liberalisation be pursued as an end in itself, aimed at promoting competition among states?; or does free trade require the setting-up of institutions responsible for adopting a "level playing field" and common policies with regard to certain public interests. In reality, both systems of managing economic and regulatory competition in integrated markets generate harmonisation of social rights and policies. The difference lies in the institutional framework through which each such harmonisation arises, and its impact on the final outcome of harmonisation. As stated by Trubek:[38]

> "Once economic interdependence reaches a certain point, and borders no longer serve as major barriers to economic movement, there is a pressure towards uniformity in economic policies. These pressures may come about to ensure fair competition and the smooth functioning of economic enterprises that span national borders ('level playing field'), or they may be the result of 'regulatory competition' among sovereignties in a unified space."

[38] *Social Justice "After" Globalization—The Case of Social Europe* (Typescript, November 1996), 5.

What these two policies actually entail is a different institutional choice as to the forms of decision-making responsible for balancing free trade and regulation in the global market. One argues for the allocation of such responsibility to the market; the other advocates for the setting-up of some form of global political process responsible for the regulation of the global market. There are two different constitutional choices (in reality, there are many more constitutional choices involved, depending on the shaping of that global political process). The present state of affairs appears to favour the first constitutional choice. The development of a global political process will be, at most, a long-term project difficult to achieve and with many potential risks and costs which must be taken into account. If the market is acquiring a predominant role in the current regulation of the global market, the following constitutional question regards how and who can participate in decision-making by the market.

Much of the economic debates on regulatory competition and "race to the bottom" are, in reality, over democratic questions. One can speak in this regard of the options of "voice" and "exit" which have originally been crafted by Hirschman.[39] My use of these concepts in the present context, however, does not fully coincide with the original definition given by Hirschman: "voice" refers to situations where choices are made or stances taken which express a preference for a certain regulation but do not involve leaving the jurisdiction (this includes voting and lobbying, market transactions within that jurisdiction but also, for example, workers' participation and strikes); "exit" refers to situations where preferences for a certain regulation over another are expressed by moving to a different jurisdiction (and thus the relocation of factors of production, but also consumers, taxpayers and the unemployed). In the global market, the mobility granted to companies and capital by free trade enhances their forms of exit in participating and determining the decisions of that market. Companies and capital will move to where the regulatory and economic context is more favourable to their interests (less regulation, lower taxes, more jobs, etc.). When the market is assessed, under a constitutional analysis, in order to balance free trade with regulation, the possibilities of exit and voice in the market and in the political process should be taken into account for all the different interests affected by the regulation. One of the problems of the current global market is that the participation it grants to certain interest is clearly to that of other interests (such as workers, the self-employed, the unemployed and consumers) as a result of the current available options of exit and voice. Social standards would not necessarily "race to the bottom" if labour would have the same mobility as companies and capital. Under the current constraints, the results of the competitive process among regulations subject to market choice is often perceived as reflecting the higher participation (through voice and exit) of large companies

---

[39] These concepts have been crafted by Hirschman in his well-known book, *Exit, Voice and Loyalty—Responses to Decline in Firms, Organizations and States* (Harvard University Press, 1970).

and capital. This is not to say that the market is a bad constitutional choice. It may be a bad choice, but still not as bad as the alternatives.[40]

David Kennedy presents a recent view of public international trade law as supportive and supplemental to private international trade law. The latter is a dominion of the traders which will shape and determine its applicable rules:[41]

> "The dominant players are private traders, and to a far greater extent than in even the most laissez-faire national system, they legislate the rules that govern their trade through contract. And when governments do participate, they operate 'commercially'—as private actors".

According to Kennedy the paradigmatic conception of international trade law (notably WTO law) is devoted to the protection of that dominion from state intervention.[42] This notion means that the shift of the regulatory arena from the state to the international level entails a transfer of power from all the interests represented at the state level to the interests of traders which dominate the international arena (through their forms of voice and exit in the global market). The change in the level of decision-making determines a change in the patterns and scope of participation, determining the dominance of decision-making by anti-regulatory actors. However, it could well be that representation would be even more distorted at state level. This has to do with the nature of many of trade-related or regulatory decisions. The high concentrated benefits of regulatory decisions in some economic sectors and the dispersion of the costs by consumers, competitors and foreigners, often determines that those state policies will be biased by some concentrated interests.[43] In this light, the transference of decision-making to either the market or international institutions may be a better alternative in terms of participation and representation of both domestic and foreign interests affected.

Anne-Marie Slaughter presents a different view from that of Kennedy regarding the interests that dominate the emerging international arena. She talks of a trans-governmental order in which the primary role is not envisaged to belong to international institutions and non-governmental organisations (NGOs) but to individuals which create transnational networks of action which, however, will continue to operate through the different states (but using a variety of institutions and processes within those states).[44] Slaughter's perspective sees a broad

---

[40] See *We The Court*, (Oxford, Hart Publishing, 1997) 103–149. See, also, Neil Komesar, *Imperfect Alternatives—Choosing Institutions in Law, Economics and Public Policy* (Chicago University Press, Chicago and London, 1994).

[41] David Kennedy, "Turning to Market Democracy: A Tale of Two Architectures" (1991) 32 *Harvard International Law Journal* 373, 380.

[42] Ibid.

[43] See, e.g. the report by *Time Magazine* on how the US political process operated and was dominated by special interests in bringing forward the Banana Saga.

[44] Slaughter, "The Real New World Order" (1997) 76 *Foreign Affairs* 183; cited by Alston, above at n. 16, at htpp://www.ejil.org/journal/vol18/No3/art4–02.html. In a similar sense, see Eyal Benvenisti, "Exit and Voice in the Age of Globalization" (1999) 98 *Michigan Law Review* 167, 169 *ff.*

plurality of actors participating in the agenda of international law but, at the same time, as noted by Alston reveals some disturbing elements: "It implies the marginalisation of governments as such and their replacement by special interest groups, which might sometimes include the relevant governmental bureaucrats".[45] In a recent article, Paul Stephan presents four avenues in which reforms should be made to increase accountability in the "new international law":[46]

"At the international level, we might reform the international law-making process to introduce greater transparency and to strengthen the accountability of law-makers. Domestically, we should re-examine the means by which nation-states incorporate and enforce international norms. With respect to private law, we can explore ways to give commercial actors greater freedom to contract into or out of the national legal system. Finally, the academic community must consider new perspectives on international law and reconsider some of its fundamental assumptions about the subject."

These are all valid points which only stress the need to abandon any proposals which focus on a particular idealised institution, be it the state, the global market, an international political process or other institutional alternatives. Different proposals can and have been put forward to democratise the new international order and raise the accountability of its law-making institutions. They must depart from a constitutional analysis of the different available institutional alternatives in the light of the criteria of voice and exit mentioned above. Phenomena such as globalisation and regulatory competition imply institutional choices between the market and alternative institutions (such as the courts and different forms of political processes). These choices should not be based on a false opposition between ideal normative commands (associated with the political process or the courts) and market forces. But it should also not arise as a simple functional effect on free trade. Whatever the perspective taken on the constitutional and democratic value of the market, there is an added value to be gained from subjecting such process to constitutional analysis. It subjects the decision-making powers which have evaded the states through globalisation and market competition to a new form of constitutional assessment. This will not mean that constitutionalisation and democratisation of the market will occur through its replacement by a global political process. Other alternative forms may be conceived such as the constitutionalisation of global competition law and an extended application of human rights. International trade law may also play an important role in this, even in its current form. The success of the WTO in reducing state barriers to free trade will raise the awareness of the importance of private barriers. Claims for an enhanced control of private barriers to trade and a generalised application of a global competition law will grow,[47] and encourage the voice of other actors, in particular consumers. In this respect, future plans of global competition rules should predict

---

[45] Above at n. 16, at htpp://www.ejil.org/journal/Vol18/No3/art4–04.html.
[46] Above at n. 8, 1580.
[47] See Friedl Weiss, "From World Trade Law to World Competition Law" (2000) 23 *Fordham International Law Journal* 250, 264.

the possibility of complaints being brought forward by consumers which are generally harmed by competition problems in a specific sector. Consumers should be given standing with regard to competition rules, even when no individual rights are directly affected.

The WTO will probably be the front runner of global constitutionalism. Should the development of global constitutionalism be founded on the ideals of free trade and economic freedom? Should we aim instead at developing a global democracy responsible for the regulation of cross-national affairs and conceive the WTO as a forum for the adoption of global regulatory policies? Perhaps neither. At the moment, my proposal is that the states should still be considered the default form of constitutionalism and arena in international society. After all the talk about constitutionalism and the role and rights of individuals, I have to recognise that states remain the primary actors in international society, but also the primary form of expressing our individual interests and participating both in domestic and international decision-making. The WTO still reflects that high constitutional legitimacy recognised to states though different forms of voice and exit. The WTO system attempts to reflect both this constitutional normative legitimacy of the states in the international system and, at the same time, the need to correct the growing constitutional malfunctions which I have portrayed in the second section of this chapter.

In spite of all the rhetoric of the rule of law, states still have the possibility of exit from the WTO (albeit with some conditions). They also have several forms of selective exit: the most obvious will be non-compliance with the decisions of panels and/or the Appellate Body and/or lack of direct effect of WTO provisions and decisions in their domestic legal orders. The alternative to selective exit is voice (being able to influence and co-determine the decision or rule to be applied to the state). Of course, the primary form of voice continues to be the participation of states in the multilateral negotiation process which resulted in the WTO agreements. In international law, states, as a rule, continue to be bonded only to the agreements to which they subscribe. But an important innovation of the WTO is the all-or-nothing system of agreement which denies to WTO parties the possibility to accede to only some of the multilateral agreements which compose the WTO system.[48] This linking of the different agreements composing the WTO reduces the bargaining power of individual states and their degree of voice in the overall negotiation process. Moreover, the fact that states still dominate the multilateral negotiation process does not mean that they have previously accented to the decisions and rules, which will be applicable to them. As we have seen, WTO judicial institutions have considerable law-making powers in interpreting the broad and largely undetermined provisions of the Agreements. States do, however, have forms of voice in this judicial process which are not restricted to legal standing as complaining or defendant parties. They may try to influence the composition of panels or the Appellate Body

[48] Art. II, para. 2.

(something that the DSU also limits)[49] or they may focus their input in other international bodies which, according to some of the agreements, provide the basis for the standards to be used by the WTO dispute-settlement bodies. Still, it is to be expected that the growth of the WTO law-making by its judicial system, to the extent that it is not controlled by states and other parties, will be compensated by forms of selective exit on the part of the states. As Weiler has demonstrated in the more supranational context of the EU,[50] when the possibilities for exit decrease, there is an increased need for voice, and vice versa. A reader knowledgeable of the EU will note that the judicial law-making was even much more creative and important in the EU context and that did not correspond to a large extent of selective exit. The European Court of Justice (ECJ) decisions are largely enforced and effective in the national legal spheres. There are legal and institutional peculiarities which can explain how that was possible even in the early years of European integration (when the European Community could still be conceived as merely an international organisation). But, more importantly, there is a structural and social element which explains why, in spite of its emerging judicial and legally enforceable system, the WTO will be faced with forms of selective exit. That element is related to a third concept which was also present in Hirschman's theory: that of loyalty. In the socio-political terms of the present context, I will define loyalty as the willingness to abdicate from exit or accept a short-term reduction of voice in exchange for a belief in, and adherence to, the long-term political goals (and forms of voice) of an organisation. The degree of adherence to the political goals of the WTO by the states and their constituencies is still low and, as a consequence, they are not ready to accept a short-term reduction of their forms of voice or exit in exchange for a long-term commitment to the political goals of the WTO. In other words, where loyalty is low, the cycle between voice and exit presented by Weiler will continue to occur. Loyalty, in its core form, is linked to the existence of a political community which clearly is not the case in the international arena.

A true global constitutionalism will be viable only when there is a weak form of loyalty determined by some form of political contract among all the participants of the global community. In addressing various concepts of what they call the international community, Simma and Paulus have reviewed the classical "normative" proposals for that international community. The key elements of differentiation are either the definition of who ought to provide the legitimacy of that international community (the international civil society or the states) or (for those conceiving the states as a natural form of legitimation) the nature of the relationship among states.[51] In descriptive terms they conceive the contemporary international community as albeit still dominated by states, but being

---

[49] See Arts 8 and 17.

[50] Joseph Weiler, "The Community System: The Dual Character of Supranationalism" (1981) 1 *Yearbook of European Law* 267; and "The Transformation of Europe" (1990) 100 *Yale Law Journal* 2403.

[51] Above at n. 17, 269–70.

increasingly permeated by Kantian elements which stress the role and importance of individuals in international law.[52] I will complement this idea in normative terms by arguing that the constitutional elements which need to be integrated in international law must be done so in dialogue with the state default form of constitutionalism. There is no need as yet for a global constitution, but there is a need for a constitutionalism which can embrace international law in correcting current constitutional malfunctions of the state. The point of departure of legitimation will still be the national political communities, but new forms of international law must develop normative criteria of participation and representation and apply such criteria to the institutional choices facing it.

I wish to conclude by challenging international lawyers to adopt such constitutional perspective, and take seriously the institutional choices facing them. The current obsessive debate opposing free trade to human rights is artificial and will not provide any answers until international lawyers make the right questions. The most critical views of trade liberalisation and globalization oppose what they foresee as the subjection of regulatory ideals and human rights values to the market forces. As one author puts it:[53]

"The human rights movement could thus find in market globalization the ultimate victory of the regulatory system that, by nature and operation, cannot properly take into account what the human rights movement holds most dear: that underlying positive human rights are moral entitlements that ground moral, political and legal claims which must be morally and legally prior to society and the state".

The paradox is that a defender of trade liberalisation and globalisation may well be in complete agreement with that notion of human rights, and will argue that free trade is precisely about preventing the state from interfering with those aprioristic human rights. The key to reveal the reasons for such a paradox lies in the fact that the notion of human rights is not enforceable in itself and requires a definition of the content of those rights. Where free trade advocates and free trade opponents disagree is on the definition of who should define what those rights are: the former leave that definition to the market, while the latter entrust it to the state. Therein lies the real reason for the dispute. It will be more useful, if instead of focusing on a largely inoperative rhetoric of human rights and globalisation, the debate focusses on the normative constitutional criteria that ought to be followed in making those difficult institutional choices.

"There is an urgent need to re-evaluate the extent to which the emerging shape of the international system reflects the principles of transparency, participation and accountability that are being so strongly promoted in the names of democracy and good governance in relation to domestic processes."[54]

---

[52] Above at n. 17, 276–7.
[53] Frank Garcia, "Market and Human Rights: Trading Away the Human Rights Principle" (1999) *Brooklyn Journal of International Law* 51, 52.
[54] Alston, above at n. 16, at htpp://www.ejil.org/journal/Vol18/No3/art4–06.html.

3

North American Economic Integration: Implications for the WTO, the EU and Asia

FREDERICK M. ABBOTT

This chapter will focus on five themes in respect of the North American Free Trade Association (NAFTA), the World Trade Organisation (WTO), the European Union (EU) and Asia. The first is that the legalisation of trade relations serves important economic and social welfare purposes, and that a regional integration structure such as the NAFTA or the EU is a useful legal complement to the WTO multilateral trade structure. Secondly, the NAFTA has succeeded in maintaining and accelerating economic growth and social welfare on the North American continent during an extremely turbulent period for the international economic system. This success, coupled with the comparative success of the EU relative to the rest of the world during this turbulent period, provides support for the continuing pursuit of regional economic integration. Thirdly, the NAFTA does not present a material threat to the WTO system, the EU or East Asia. Fourthly, the countries of East Asia may be well served by moving away from the Asia-Pacific Economic Co-operation (APEC) model of non-legalised soft regional integration toward a more robust legalised integration model such as that of the NAFTA. Finally, the NAFTA model of regional economic integration may be better suited to the countries of East Asia than the EU model, at least in the near-to-medium term.

I LEGALISATION OF TRADE RELATIONS

The legalisation of international trade relations serves valuable economic and social welfare purposes for the countries which participate in the legalisation

This chapter builds on and incorporates the author's prior work, including *The North American Integration Regime and Its Implications for the World Trading System* (EUI 1998) and *The NAFTA and Legalization of International Relations: A Case Study* (IO, 1999).

process. The NAFTA is a hard to moderately hard agreement in a legal sense, in that it precisely spells out the obligations of its parties (Canada, Mexico and the United States), among which there is a high level of expectation that the terms of the agreement will be complied with, and there is at least a moderate level of delegation of decision-making authority by the parties to regional institutions, principally in the field of dispute resolution. The NAFTA may be compared with the EU and APEC. The EC Treaty establishes a hard legal arrangement like the NAFTA; harder in the sense that the regional institutions of the EU are accorded substantially greater decision-making authority than those of the NAFTA institutions. APEC, on the other hand, is a soft legal arrangement. It has no legal charter, but rather operates through the mechanism of periodic meetings of heads of state, which result in the issuance of "declarations". While the countries of APEC express themselves in terms suggesting legal obligation, it is clear that there is no mechanism by which parties may be compelled to comply with APEC declarations. The APEC countries have not delegated dispute-settlement authority to regional institutions.

The basis for legalisation in the NAFTA

Using the NAFTA as an example, why did its parties choose to express their commitments in hard to moderately hard legal terms?

Most trade specialists would argue that unilateral action to eliminate trade and investment barriers is in the interests of national economic welfare,[1] so that action to eliminate such barriers should be undertaken in the absence of reciprocal conduct by other governments. The Government of the United States has long followed a policy of maintaining minimal barriers to trade and investment, notwithstanding that such barriers are common to many of its trading partners. If the Government of Mexico, for example, had decided to change its economic course and open up to trade and investment, it would not have needed to enter into an agreement with the United States and Canada obligating it to do so. It could well have undertaken these actions unilaterally (within the most favored nation (MFN) treatment constraints imposed by the WTO Agreement).[2]

Although trade specialists would make the case for unilateral action, and while there is an alternative regional trade liberalisation model that relies on "voluntary" unilateral action, Canadian, Mexican and US government officials chose to eliminate trade barriers as among the three countries on the basis of a binding written agreement. Some of the reasons for choosing a written agreement include the following.

---

[1] Remarks of Gordon Tullock and other economists at the meeting of the International Agricultural Trade Research Consortium, Tucson, Arizona, January 1997, papers from which are published in David Orden and Donna Roberts (eds), *Understanding Technical Barriers to Agricultural Trade* 33 (1997) (notes of Tullock remarks in author's files).

[2] See text at n. 30 below regarding constraints imposed by the GATT/WTO Agreement.

1. Reducing risks through commitments against backsliding

The Government of Mexico had the most compelling reason to legalise the decisions embodied in the NAFTA. Since Mexico had for a long time pursued economic policies that discouraged foreign participation in the economy, and since the Government had decided that it was in the national interest to change its economic strategy, a binding written commitment to maintain that change would have been helpful in accomplishing the goal of attracting foreign investment. In the absence of such a binding written commitment, the Government would appear to have more freedom to change course to the detriment of foreign investors. By reducing perceived risks to foreign investors, the Government would attract a higher level of investment and thereby improve the chances that its new economic strategy would be successful.[3]

2. Reducing transaction costs of default

The Governments of the United States and Canada would perceive a reciprocal advantage from a binding written commitment by Mexico. The property interests of US and Canadian investors would be more secure as a consequence of the commitment, and the transaction costs of recovering investments in the event of a Mexican decision to confiscate them would be reduced as a consequence of more certain rules. This should not obscure the fact that the United States and Canada would have a range of options for action against the Government of Mexico to recover investments in the absence of the NAFTA.[4]

3. Providing a plan for administration

Assuming that the NAFTA Governments determined that they would not undertake the elimination of trade and investment barriers in the absence of reciprocal commitments by the other parties, a written agreement would provide the mechanical framework for implementation of these commitments. In the absence of an agreement, government administrators would be required to make numerous implementation-related decisions with limited guidance.

The implementation of modern international trade arrangements involves a very high level of detailed decision-making. The recent experience of governments is that the absence of specificity is likely to lead to conflict in

---

[3] Of course, prospective investors would not entirely discount the potential risk of a change in government strategy based on a written agreement. The agreement would, however, be a factor in investor decision-making. Success of the new economic strategy would be expected to improve the position of the political party in power.

[4] The United States and Canada might rely on pure political power, or they might invoke rules of customary international law which protect foreign investors.

implementation.[5] It would be difficult to implement a modern international trade agreement in the absence of specific rules.

4. *Alleviating political pressure from formerly protected industries*

Although the United States maintained relatively modest tariff and non-tariff barriers to trade prior to the NAFTA, it did provide protection for certain industries which would be adversely affected by reducing trade barriers in favour of Canada and Mexico. The elimination of such protection would face political objection from the affected industries. The US Government could diffuse these objections by reference to the reciprocal granting of trade concessions by the Governments of Canada and Mexico as evidenced in a binding written agreement. This same rationale would apply to Canada and Mexico.[6]

5. *Facilitating business planning*

A written agreement would increase the transparency of the arrangement, allowing business enterprises to make investment plans under more certain conditions. This would reduce the effective cost of investments.

6. *Securing a GATT Article XXIV waiver*

Canada, Mexico and the United States were (and are) each parties to the General Agreement on Tariffs and Trade (GATT 1947)(now the WTO and GATT 1994). Article XXIV of GATT permitted them to enter into an agreement substantially eliminating trade barriers among themselves without extending those benefits to third countries (as is generally required by the GATT most favored nation treatment obligation).[7] Because the granting of an Article XXIV-based waiver of the MFN rule is predicated on a free trade area or customs union plan that meets specified criteria, it is doubtful that Canada, Mexico and the United States would be entitled to remove trade barriers among themselves in the absence of a binding written agreement embodying such a plan.[8]

---

[5] The GATT Uruguay Round negotiations were in substantial measure an exercise in adding detail to the GATT General Agreement and related agreements. The absence of specificity had resulted in a continuing stream of disputes concerning the proper interpretation of those agreements. See F.M. Abbott, "The Intersection of Law and Trade in the WTO System: Economics and the Transition to a Hard Law System", in *Understanding Technical Barriers to Agricultural Trade*, above at n. 2.

[6] Note that protected Mexican domestic industries would be substantially more adversely affected by competition from Canadian and the US enterprises than would protected industries in Canada and the United States be adversely affected by competition from Mexican enterprises.

[7] On Art. XXIV and the review process, see F.M. Abbott, *Law and Policy of Regional Integration* (1995), ch. 3.

[8] Plans for customs unions and free trade areas must be notified to GATT (now WTO) members, and are reviewed by a working party. Though the question has not arisen (and is unlikely to arise) in practice, the absence of a written agreement embodying the plans of GATT/WTO members to

7. *Assuaging concerns of third countries through transparency*

In addition to providing the basis for a GATT/WTO waiver, a written NAFTA would allow third countries to examine the terms of the arrangement, and to determine the extent to which it would affect their interests. An unwritten political undertaking would be likely to raise third country concerns about the intention of the parties to the undertaking. If these concerns were not adequately addressed, retaliatory action by third countries might ensue, thereby reducing the net benefits of the free trade area arrangement.

8. *Allowing transparency and co-ordination among government branches*

The nature of the political process in the NAFTA parties is that ratification of international agreements is subject to approval by the legislature or parliament. In the United States, the legislature has primary authority in the field of trade relations, and the executive acts in this area under delegated authority.[9] It would be difficult for the President of the United States, for example, to obtain legislative assent to a large-scale arrangement to eliminate trade and investment barriers in the absence of submitting a written agreement to Congress. The written agreement also allows for review and comment by non-governmental actors, i.e. it is essential to the functioning of democratic institutions within a country. The degree to which a trade and investment agreement is democratically legitimised may ultimately affect the extent to which a government is able to fulfill its obligations in the face of difficulties.

The foregoing, non-exhaustive list should help to explain why the parties to the NAFTA elected to set their agreement down in a binding legal instrument. It is theoretically possible that the NAFTA parties might have undertaken to implement a series of political decisions regarding the progressive elimination of barriers to trade and investment in the absence of a binding legal instrument.[10] As noted earlier, APEC is an existing model of regional trade liberalisation undertaken largely through a series of national government political decisions in the absence of a formal legal text.[11] In fact, all three NAFTA parties are today participants in the alternative APEC regional trade liberalisation exercise.

form a customs union or free trade area would appear to make its review impracticable, and its absence would otherwise raise potentially insurmountable issues regarding the intention of the subject parties to carry out their plan.

[9] See Stefan Riesenfeld and F.M. Abbott, *The Scope of US Senate Control Over the Conclusion and Operation of Treaties*, in S.A. Riesenfeld and F.M. Abbott (eds), *Parliamentary Participation in the Making and Operation of Treaties* (1993).

[10] The US Trade Representative has stressed the importance of high level political decision in the trade liberalisation process, and suggested that such high level decision is the key component of integration arrangements. See Remarks of Charlene Barshefsky (USTR), The American Society of International Law, Proceedings of the 90th Annual Meeting, "Are International Institutions Doing Their Job?", Washington DC, 27–30 March 1996; (1996) 90 *ASIL Proc.* 508.

[11] See J.T. Fried, "APEC as the Asia-Pacific Model for Regional Economic Cooperation", in F.M. Abbott (ed.), *China in the World Trading System* (1998) 183.

II INTRA-REGIONAL ECONOMIC EFFECTS OF THE NAFTA

The economic terms of the NAFTA have been implemented substantially in accordance with its terms.[12] As a consequence, tariff and non-tariff barriers to trade in goods and services among NAFTA countries have fallen, and cross-border flows of capital and investment have been facilitated.

Economic analysis of the NAFTA's effect is complicated by the Peso Crisis of 1994/1995, which dramatically affected the terms of trade between the NAFTA parties. Regardless of the NAFTA's effect in reducing trade barriers, the sharp drop in the value of the peso would have resulted in a short-term increase in Mexican exports to the Unoted States and Canada, and a short-term decline in Mexican imports from the United States and Canada.[13] Nevertheless, in light of large gains in Mexico's exports dominated in dollars, and the robust pattern of trade among Canada, Mexico and the United States (which included substantial gains in US exports to Mexico), it seems reasonable to attribute a positive effect of the NAFTA on increasing cross-border economic activity among its parties. At of the end of 1998, Mexico had supplanted Japan as the United States' second leading trade partner (behind Canada), and as of March 1999 Mexico was exporting (worldwide) at a rate of US $9.66 billion USD per month (US $9.2 billion non-petroleum), and importing at a US $10 billion/monthly rate.[14]

Mexico has recently experienced heavy inflows and commitments of inflow of foreign direct investment (FDI). Accumulated FDI has risen from US $14.9 billion in 1995, to US $57 billion in 1998.[15] During the period since the inception of

---

[12] This author has reviewed the implementation history of the NAFTA from a legal standpoint in two papers, F.M. Abbott, *The NAFTA as Architecture for Political Decision* (May 1997) and *The NAFTA and Legalization of International Relations: A Case Study* (August 1998), each prepared for a Project on Legalization and World Politics. The second of these papers will be published in an edited volume of collected works resulting from the project. See generally US Executive Branch, *Study on the Operation and Effect of the North American Free Trade Agreement (NAFTA)*, prepared and transmitted to Congress as required by s. 512 of the NAFTA Implementation Act 1997, at www.ustr.gov (hereafter US Executive Branch Study). In the first three years of the NAFTA operation, Mexican-applied tariffs on US goods declined from an average of 10% to 2.9%. During the same time period, Mexican-applied tariffs on goods of non-NAFTA origin increased to an average 12.5% (ibid., ii, 7). US-applied tariffs on Mexican origin goods declined from 2.07% to 0.65% in the comparable time frame, while US-applied tariffs on Canadian origin goods declined from 0.37% to 0.22% (ibid., ii, 7–8).

[13] The US Executive Branch Study confirms that it is difficult to isolate the effects of the NAFTA on regional trade or investment flows during the first three years of its operation because the Peso Crisis overwhelms NAFTA-specified changes. The US economy was exceptionally strong during the measurement period, and this alone might account for changes in import-export trends. (ibid., 12–14).

[14] The US Executive Branch Study reported only a modest increase in the level of US foreign direct investment (FDI) in Mexico in the 1994–1996 period. (ibid., 22–4). A later Mexican government report indicates a significant acceleration of FDI inflows: "Mexico Economic Update" (1999) 4 *NAFTA Works* 1, 1.

[15] See "Private Sector Shows Confidence in Mexico's Economy" (1999) 4 *NAFTA Works* 1, 1.

the NAFTA, Mexico has ranked second to China among developing country recipients of FDI.[16]

A US Executive Branch Study emphasised the positive influences of the NAFTA in Mexico's relatively rapid recovery (in aggregate terms) from the effects of the Peso Crisis.[17] After a 1982 financial crisis, it took five years for Mexican economic output to reach pre-crisis levels. Following the late-1994 Peso Crisis (in which output dropped more quickly), Mexican economic output reached pre-crisis levels in two years. Mexico's return to international capital markets was far more rapid following the 1994 crisis than following the 1982 crisis.

On the whole, it appears reasonable to conclude that the NAFTA had a net positive economic welfare effect on its three parties during its first years of operation.[18] The Mexican economy has substantially recovered from the Peso Crisis, and its economic outlook today is reasonably promising.[19]

III GLOBAL WELFARE EFFECTS OF THE NAFTA

NAFTA effects on third country trade

The classical model of regional integration economics generally posits that the global welfare effects of such arrangements may be determined by examining whether they are net trade-creating or trade-diverting.[20] If there is an increase of trade among members which exceeds the level of trade lost with non-members,[21] then there is a net positive global economic welfare effect. If the level of lost trade with non-members exceeds the increase in trade among RIA members, then there is a net negative global welfare effect. The trade statistics compiled by the United States for its three-year study do not permit a complete evaluation of the NAFTA's net effect on trade creation and trade diversion. The US Executive Branch Study indicates that diversion of trade occurred during the first three years following NAFTA's entry into force. It states, for example, that Mexico's market share gains in the US apparel sector displaced imports from

---

[16] Ibid.

[17] For example, the US Executive Branch Study, iii–iv.

[18] If we were to attribute at least partial responsibility for the 1994 Peso Crisis to the NAFTA, because the NAFTA may have encouraged over-investment of short term capital in the Mexican market, the economic picture is more mixed.

[19] A useful source of current data on the Mexican economy is *NAFTA Works*, published on a monthly basis by the Government of Mexico, SECOFI office.

[20] The classical approach was developed in Jacob Viner, *The Customs Union Issue* (1950). For discussion, including critique on grounds that trade creation/trade diversion analysis does not adequately capture welfare effects attributable, *inter alia*, to accelerated growth within customs unions and free trade areas, see WTO Secretariat, *Regionalism and the World Trading System* (1995).

[21] Trade will be lost with non-members as tariffs are reduced among members, and as these tariff reductions are not extended to non-members.

China, Hong Kong, Taiwan and Korea, the US import market share of which fell by nine percentage points in the relevant period.[22] The fact that the NAFTA has diverted trade is consistent with the expectations of NAFTA policy planners.[23]

The results of the GATT Uruguay Round were implemented after entry into force of the NAFTA. Since the substantial trade barrier reductions following the Uruguay Round should in any case have resulted in substantial increases in levels of worldwide trade,[24] it is unlikely that NAFTA party trade with non-parties has been diverted in aggregate terms, even if the market share of some non-parties has declined in relation to NAFTA parties. Over the past several years, the United States has maintained substantial trade imbalances in favour of the countries of East Asia, including China, and in light of these large imbalances it seems doubtful that a significant negative trade effect on East Asian exports to the United States could be attributed to the NAFTA.

The principal positive effect of the NAFTA appears to be its stabilising effect on the Mexican economy. Without doubt, the Peso Crisis hurt the Mexican economy and has resulted in significant social hardship. Nevertheless, Mexico has largely been spared from the effects of the 1997–1998 global economic crisis which has had an enormously destabilising effect on many developing economies, and which has resulted in substantially lower economic growth throughout Latin America. Mexico's economy and capital markets performed well during the 1997–1998 period, and the Mexican Government has publicly attributed this to its NAFTA commitment.[25]

NAFTA and the WTO legal system

Customs unions and free trade areas within the WTO system

The General Agreement on Tariffs and Trade (GATT) of 1947 was part of the Bretton Woods complex of international economic institutions established to reconstitute the international economy following the Second World War. The GATT 1947 embodied several foundational principles of international trade relations. The most important of these was the unconditional most favored nation (MFN) principle embodied in Article I. The MFN rule obligated each GATT member to extend any tariff (or related) concession granted to one GATT member to all other GATT members.

---

[22]   US Executive Branch Study, vi, 39.

[23]   Trade economists were aware of the potential for trade diversion arising from creation of the NAFTA. See C.A. Primo Braga, Raed Safadi and Alexander Yeats, *Implications of NAFTA for East Asian Exports,* draft by members of the International Economics Department, The World Bank (1994).

[24]   For predictive comparison of the NAFTA and Uruguay Round trade creation/trade diversion effects, see C.A. Primo Braga *et al.*, ibid.

[25]   See, e.g., "Private Sector Shows Confidence in Mexico's Economy" (1999) 4 *NAFTA Works* 1.

The MFN rule should have the effect of accelerating the process of trade barrier elimination since it requires a wide dispersion of concessions among GATT members.[26] However, there was a core political motive for adoption of an unconditional MFN rule. In the pre-War environment, trade concessions were widely used as an instrument of diplomacy. Political alliances were created and maintained through economic preferences. Since diplomatic decisions were often made for reasons apart from improving world prosperity, an economic system in which trade concessions were used as political instruments would be unlikely to generate a global welfare-optimising result. The MFN principle is intended to de-politicise the trading system so as to reduce the chances of breakdown into a system of diplomacy-based alliances. The net effect should be to distribute the benefits of trade widely. The MFN principle was the key "multilateralism" provision in the GATT 1947.

When the GATT 1947 was drafted, it was recognised that some form of accommodation would be necessary for customs unions (CUs) and free trade areas (FTAs). The concept of a European Economic Union was already under consideration, and the political and economic advantages of creating a pan-European market were apparent. The GATT incorporated in Article XXIV a mechanism for relieving the members of CUs and FTAs from the obligation to extend the preferential treatment granted within the CU or FTA to non-members.[27] The central criterion used by Article XXIV to determine whether a CU or FTA should be allowed to maintain its preferential character is whether its members have agreed to eliminate substantially all tariffs and other restrictive regulations of commerce on trade between its members.[28] This criterion was intended as a mechanism for limiting the number of CUs/FTAs since it precluded GATT members from using Article XXIV as a cover for eliminating tariffs on a limited number of goods. The "substantially all" criterion demanded a seriousness of purpose.

The Article XXIV mechanism for evaluating CUs/FTAs under the GATT is much criticised. The main ground of critique is that it does not subject CUs/FTAs to a meaningful review even in respect to its own defined criteria, since the outcome of the review process is controlled by members of the CU/FTA.[29] Customary practice of GATT was that decisions on matters such as Article XXIV review were made by consensus, and the members of the CU/FTA

---

[26] A counter-argument can be made that trade barrier reductions will be faster under bilateral or minilateral negotiating strategies, since governments may be more willing to grant concessions to a limited number of countries for particularised reasons. This counter-argument in part provides the theoretical basis for the customs union/free trade area exception to the MFN principle.

[27] For details on Art. XXIV, see F.M. Abbott, *Law and Policy of Regional Integration: The NAFTA and Western Hemispheric Integration in the World Trade Organization System* (1995) (hereafter *Law and Policy*), ch. 3.

[28] The additional main criteria are that the members of a CU do not "on the whole" establish external tariffs higher than those in place in each member prior to the formation of the CU, and that the members of an FTA do not individually raise their external tariffs.

[29] See, e.g. Frieder Roessler, "The Relationship Between Regional Integration Agreements and the Multilateral Trade Order", in Kym Andersen and Richard Blackhurst (eds), *Regional Integration and the Global Trading System* (1993), 311, 323.

under review had the right to block a decision that might have required them to effect a change to their implementation plan. Just as agricultural trade barriers have been a weak point in GATT–WTO liberalisation efforts on the whole, so agriculture has been a weak spot in the regional integration process. A number of important regional groups have made liberalisation commitments in the agriculture area which might be problematic under a rigorous application of the requirement that such groups eliminate substantially all tariffs and other restrictive measures of commerce.

The WTO Agreement adds an Understanding[30] that clarifies elements of the GATT 1994 Article XXIV review, but none that affects the right of members to control the outcome of the mandatory review process.[31] The Understanding makes clear that a non-member of a CU/FTA may bring a dispute-settlement action in respect to the application of Article XXIV, and this clarification may lead to increased attention to the CU/FTA phenomenon from the WTO dispute-settlement organs.[32]

The Uruguay Round brought trade in services within the purview of the WTO, and the General Agreement on Trade in Services (GATS) establishes an additional mechanism for review of regional services arrangements (RSAs). GATS, Article V permits members of RSAs to eliminate barriers on trade in services as among themselves without extending these concessions to non-members, provided that such RSAs involve substantial "sectoral" coverage, involve the elimination of substantially all discrimination in covered sectors, and do not raise barriers to non-members within covered sectors.[33] The inclusion of a provision requiring that the benefits of an RSA be extended to businesses with commercial presence within the RSA significantly ameliorates the potential discriminatory impact of these arrangements on non-party national service providers.[34]

The NAFTA clearly meets the criteria prescribed by the WTO Agreement for a free trade area (under GATT, Article XXIV) and a regional services arrangement (under GATS, Article V). By any reasonable measure, the NAFTA eliminates substantially all tariffs and other restrictive regulations of commerce on trade between Canada, Mexico and the United States, and eliminates substantially all barriers on trade in services in a substantial number of sectors.[35]

The number of CUs/FTAs among WTO members is proliferating rapidly, and this trend has raised serious concern among WTO members and in the

---

[30] Understanding on the Interpretation of Article XXIV of the General Agreement on Tariffs and Trade 1994 (hereafter Understanding on Article XXIV).

[31] These amendments include a presumption that a reasonable time for implementing the reduction of tariff and related barriers is ten years (ibid., para. 3), and a mechanism for calculation of "on the whole" tariff rates of customs unions (ibid., para. 2).

[32] Ibid., para. 12.

[33] GATS, Art. V:1. For details on GATS, Art. V, see *Law and Policy*, ch. 3.

[34] GATS, Art. V:4.

[35] The commitments of the parties in the areas of goods and services are reviewed for their GATT Art. XXIV and GATS Art. V compatibility in *Law and Policy*, chs 4 and 5.

WTO Secretariat.[36] It is widely acknowledged, however, that if the subject of this proliferation is to be concretely addressed, then reform of the existing review mechanisms is required. The existing review mechanisms are not designed or applied to significantly inhibit regionalisation of the world trading system. A working group has been established to consider this situation. This group has yet to reach any conclusions. Since many WTO members are party to one or more regional integration arrangements, perhaps it is not surprising that WTO members as a body have not aggressively pursued additional methods to exercise control over these arrangements.

CUs and FTAs such as the EU and NAFTA are derogations from a purely multilateral trading system. They are systems of preference, and they are political alliances. The founders of the GATT 1947 were concerned with preventing the international trading system from breaking down into a system of preferential political and economic alliances. The proliferation of regional integration arrangements appears to carry with it a heightened risk that the multilateral trading system will break down into a world economic system characterised by a series of regional alliances with inter-linkages of varying types.

CUs/FTAs as WTO members

The NAFTA does not possess international legal personality, and is not a member of the WTO. As a general matter, CUs/FTAs are regulated by the WTO through the participation of their nation state members.[37] Members of CUs/FTAs are obliged to assure that these arrangements are implemented in a manner which is WTO-consistent. The Understanding on Article XXIV provides that CU/FTA members are responsible for measures of regional bodies taken within their territory,[38] thereby appearing to apportion responsibility for operation of CUs/FTAs on a territorial basis.[39]

The EC has international legal personality and is a member of the WTO. The Member States of the EC also are members of the WTO. If the EC votes in the WTO, it does so on behalf of all its Member States which are members of the WTO.[40] If a Member State votes individually, then each Member State votes, and there is no separate vote for the EC. This mixed situation of the EC

---

[36] See Renato Ruggiero (WTO Director-General), "Regional Initiatives, Global Impact: Cooperation and the Multilateral System", speech to the Third Conference of the Transatlantic Business Dialogue, Rome, 7 November 1997 (www.wto.org, visited 5 July 1998).

[37] WTO membership is not limited to nation states, but may include autonomous customs territories (WTO Agreement, Art. XII).

[38] Understanding on Article XXIV, paras 13, 14.

[39] Alternative bases for attributing responsibility to CU/FTA members, such as joint liability for measures taken pursuant to mandatory provisions of a CU/FTA agreement, are a conceptual possibility.

[40] Stefan Riesenfeld has pointed out that difficulties will arise if the EC admits new Member States which are not also members of the WTO. So far this has not happened. See S.A. Riesenfeld, "The Changing Face of Globalism", in F.M. Abbott and D.J. Gerber (eds), *Public Policy and Global Technological Integration* (1997) 67.

in the WTO creates a complex internal governance situation for the EC, and a complex legal situation for WTO members outside the EC which seek to determine responsibility for EC and Member State compliance with the WTO Agreement.[41]

The juridical interface of the NAFTA and WTO

The juridical relationship between the NAFTA and WTO Agreement is of considerable interest from the standpoints of policy and technical analysis of legal norms. As a matter of policy, a decision by NAFTA negotiators whether to accord legal priority to the NAFTA or WTO would appear to involve a choice of whether to accord a greater degree of attention and concern to more narrow regional economic and political interests, or to broader multilateral interests. In light of the importance that trade policy makers have ascribed to the potential for conflict between the regional and multilateral integration models, NAFTA negotiators might have been expected to make a clear choice in this hierarchy of interests. Evidence from the text of the NAFTA and from the early NAFTA dispute-settlement panel reports, suggests that no such overarching policy determination was made or that, if it was made, the determination was implemented in an uncertain manner.

The fact that the NAFTA negotiations took place in the midst of the GATT Uruguay Round negotiations may at least in part be responsible for the unsettled state of affairs. Yet each set of international trade negotiations is a process that rarely occurs in isolation from other such processes. The uncertainty surrounding the relationship between the NAFTA and WTO Agreement may reflect the dynamic political tensions faced by the NAFTA negotiators, tensions which continue to influence the formation and implementation of policy in the NAFTA parties.[42] On one side, the NAFTA was and is portrayed by its proponents as a means of accelerating integration on the North American continent in a way which is consistent with the political and social interests of a variety of disparate groups, including the business community, labour unions and environmentalists. The NAFTA is politically justified by its attention to interests which are more difficult to address at the WTO multilateral level. If the results of the NAFTA negotiations are placed beneath WTO Agreement norms, then in theory this attention to regionally specific interests might be jeopardised by the superiority of more generalised WTO norms. There are, therefore, political and social motivations for advocating priority for the NAFTA.

On the other hand, NAFTA negotiators were and remain well aware of concerns among GATT–WTO members about efforts by particular countries and

---

[41] The ECJ has acknowledged some of the difficulties inherent in "mixed" EU/Member State treaties in its advisory opinion on EC-Member State adherence to the WTO Agreement. See *Re The Uruguay Round Treaties (Opinion 1/94)* [1995] 1 CMLR 205.

[42] See, generally, F.M. Abbott, "Foundation-Building for Western Hemispheric Integration" (1997) 17 *Northwestern JILB* 900 (hereinafter "Foundation-Building").

regions to gain advantages by extending regional preferences.[43] NAFTA negotiators would be hesitant to make a clear statement of regional legal preference
that might galvanise opposition to the agreement, or that might jeopardise
future multilateral negotiations. NAFTA negotiators may well have maintained
a preference for multilateralism among themselves, yet nevertheless have been
reluctant clearly to express such preference in the NAFTA because this might be
found objectionable by interest groups within the region whose support was
required to assure successful conclusion of the agreement.

Although the NAFTA–WTO hierarchy of norms is uncertain, and while such
uncertainty is bound to lead to or exacerbate future NAFTA disputes,[44] the
political and social forces which impelled the initial state of ambiguity have not
dissipated. While interests in political stability and economic efficiency might be
enhanced through the clarification of this matter by the NAFTA parties through
the adoption of a clarifying amendment or an intergovernmental understanding, the parties may be in no more favourable position to agree on such a
clarification in the year 2000 than they were in 1993.[45]

NAFTA norms on priority

The legal relationship between the NAFTA and the WTO Agreement is determined by examining the text of the treaties, the context in which the treaties
were made, and the rules of international law that govern the relationship
between treaties concerning the same or similar subject matter.[46] Both the
NAFTA and the WTO Agreement are written agreements between states

---

[43] The Canada–United States Free Trade Agreement (CUSFTA) which entered into force in 1989
was reviewed by a GATT Art. XXIV Working Party. The Working Party did not make any recommendations in respect of the CUSFTA, but rather limited itself to preparing a summary of members'
observations. A concern expressed by a number of members of the Working Party was that the
CUSFTA was given legal priority over GATT in trade relations between Canada and the United
States. No Art. XXIV working party prior to the CUSFTA review had made any recommendation—
affirmative or negative—with respect to a CU/FTA. Subsequent to the CUSFTA review, a working
party recommended approval without condition of the free trade area between the Czech and
Slovak Republics. See *Law and Policy*, 41–2.

[44] Interestingly, the first two cases brought before the NAFTA Chapter 20 dispute-settlement
panels have involved questions of defining the NAFTA-WTO legal relationship. The first—the
Canadian Agricultural products case (Canada/US)—is largely devoted to resolving a NAFTA/WTO
relational issue. The second case—Broom Corn Brooms (Mexico/US)—saw a NAFTA/WTO relational issue extensively argued, but the panel found it unnecessary to resolve the issue in its disposition of the case.

[45] In *Law and Policy*, 107, this author identified some aspects of this legal relationship, and suggested that it might be some time before definitive pronouncements could be made, saying:

"Because of the number of contextual factors involved in defining this relationship, it may be
some years before an authoritative definition of the relationship emerges, whether through action
taken by the NAFTA Parties to expressly establish the relationship, or through an accumulation
of dispute settlement panel opinions that may establish a common law of interpretation."

[46] On the relationship among treaty norms, see, generally, S.A. Riesenfeld and F.M. Abbott (eds),
Parliamentary Participation in the Making and Operation of Treaties: A Comparative Study (1992).

governed by international law, and therefore are "treaties" within the definition prescribed by the Vienna Convention on the Law of Treaties (VCLT).[47]

The VCLT provides that when states are parties to treaties governing the same subject matter, the latter-in-time treaty takes precedence over the earlier in time.[48] The NAFTA entered into force on 1 January 1994 and the WTO Agreement entered into force on 1 January 1995. The NAFTA parties are each original members of the WTO. Although this temporal sequence might suggest that the WTO Agreement prevails over the NAFTA, there are a number of factors involving the express text of the NAFTA and the context in which the two Agreements were made that raise doubts about this general proposition.

The NAFTA text incorporates a general principle regarding its relationship to other international agreements. It also incorporates a number of specific provisions concerning its relationship to other international agreements.

The NAFTA provides in Article 103:

> "1. The parties affirm their existing rights and obligations with respect to each other under the *General Agreement on Tariffs and Trade* and other agreements to which such parties are subject.
> 2. In the event of any inconsistency between this Agreement and such other agreements, this Agreement shall prevail to the extent of the inconsistency, except as otherwise provided by this Agreement".

Article 104 of the NAFTA provides an exception from the general rule of Article 103(2). Obligations in certain environment and conservation agreements (such as the Basel Convention on Transboundary Movement of Hazardous Waste) as listed in Article 104 of the NAFTA, expressly prevail over the NAFTA rules in the event of inconsistency.

Article 301(1) of the NAFTA, as example, is a specific NAFTA rule that defines a relationship with the GATT–WTO Agreement. It states:

> "1. Each Party shall accord national treatment to the goods of another Party in accordance with Article III of the *General Agreement on Tariffs and Trade* (GATT), including its interpretative notes, and to this end Article III of the GATT and its interpretative notes, or any equivalent provision of a successor agreement to which all Parties are subject, are incorporated into and made part of this Agreement".

There are various other provisions of the NAFTA which are directed to defining relations with the GATT.[49]

---

[47] Although the United States has not ratified the VCLT, it accepts that the VCLT substantially reflects customary international law applicable to treaty relations. Canada and Mexico are parties to the VCLT.

[48] VCLT, Art. 30(3). The parties to successive treaties may elect to vary this general rule by agreement.

[49] Art. 710 of the NAFTA, sets forth a rule displacing Art. 301, and its incorporation of Art. III of the GATT (as just stated above), in regard to NAFTA sanitary and phytosanitary measures. NAFTA sanitary and phytosanitary rules are not governed by Art. III (or Art. XX(b)) of the GATT, notwithstanding the terms of Art. 301(1) of the NAFTA.

The express text of Article 103(1) of the NAFTA affirms existing obligations among NAFTA parties under the GATT and provides that the NAFTA prevails over the GATT to the extent of any inconsistencies. Article 103(2) does not expressly provide that the NAFTA prevails over any later-in-time agreements. By way of contrast, for example, Article 301(1) expressly refers to a "successor agreement" to the GATT.[50] If NAFTA negotiators had intended that the NAFTA would in general take priority over the agreements resulting from the Uruguay Round negotiations (i.e. the WTO Agreement and related agreements), they might have referred to such "successor agreement(s)" in Article 103.

Consider, however, that reference to "successor agreement(s)" to the GATT may have a broader meaning than reference to the GATT standing alone. GATT 1994 is incorporated as a multilateral trade agreement binding on all WTO Members in the WTO Agreement. GATT 1994 is identical to GATT 1947, which was an agreement existing among the NAFTA parties when the NAFTA was concluded. The WTO Agreement specifically incorporates the *acquis* of interpretations and understandings with respect to GATT 1947 into its legal framework, and signals an intention that there be a continuity between GATT 1947 and GATT 1994.[51] GATT 1994, as incorporated into the WTO Agreement, is effectively an agreement to which the NAFTA parties were subject when they entered into the NAFTA. This provides a basis for concluding that the NAFTA continues to prevail over GATT 1994 within the meaning of NAFTA, Article 103.

However, this conclusion may be undercut by specific language in the WTO Agreement which states that GATT 1947 and GATT 1994 are "legally distinct".[52] If GATT 1994 is a new agreement only considered to have entered into force on 1 January 1995 (as part of the WTO Agreement), then it would not fall under the express priority rule of NAFTA, Article 103 with respect to existing agreements. Yet the reason why the WTO Agreement creates a legal distinction between GATT 1947 and GATT 1994 was not to create a break in continuity between the rights and obligations of the parties to the two agreements. The legal distinction was provided for with the specific intention of facilitating the institutional transition between the GATT and the WTO by allowing some members of the old GATT to delay their entry into the WTO by remaining members of the former institution, at least for a transition period.[53] Outside of

---

[50] The NAFTA refers to GATT successor agreement(s) in a number of provisions, included in the dispute-settlement chapter.

[51] WTO Agreement, Art. XVI:1.

[52] Ibid., Art. II:4.

[53] When the Uruguay Round was concluded, it was not clear that all former GATT contracting parties would choose to join the new WTO. At least for a transition period, it was contemplated that some states might remain parties to GATT 1947, and that relations between them, and relations between them and members of the new WTO, would need to be defined. It was foreseen that for an interim period two legally distinct agreements might be needed. See *First Report of the Committee on International Trade Law*, International Law Association, 66th Conference, Buenos Aires, August 1994 (E.U. Petersmann and F.M. Abbott, Rapporteurs). As it happens, they were not needed. All GATT contracting parties became original members of the WTO.

facilitating this transition, the negotiators clearly signaled an intention not to break continuity between GATT 1947 and GATT 1994.

Whether the "General Agreement on Tariffs and Trade" referred to in the NAFTA, Article 103 rule of priority is limited to GATT 1947, or whether it encompasses also GATT 1994, is not susceptible to a categorical answer. If the NAFTA Article 103 reference to the GATT is understood to encompass GATT 1994, the resulting priority rule is ambiguous because the WTO Agreement incorporates significantly more than GATT 1994, including the new area agreements of the GATS and TRIPS, and a number of supplemental agreements in areas such as technical standards and agriculture. The NAFTA might take priority over GATT 1994 and a limited number of supplemental agreements, and yet not take priority over other WTO agreements.[54] The full panoply of WTO agreements might constitute the "successor agreement(s)" to the GATT referred to elsewhere in the NAFTA.

The use of the term "successor agreement(s)" to the GATT in contexts outside the Article 103 rules of priority does not neatly resolve the uncertainty. Consider Article 301(1) of the NAFTA as an illustration. In that article the parties incorporate GATT, Article III and its interpretative notes. This express incorporation encompasses the comparable provision of a GATT "successor agreement". Yet if the negotiators of the NAFTA thought that the results of the Uruguay Round would take priority over the NAFTA by way of Article 103, the reference to a GATT successor agreement in Article 301(1) would be superfluous. The new GATT or WTO article would, by operation of international law, take priority over the old NAFTA and/or GATT rule. We might conclude that the reference to "successor agreement" was included in NAFTA, Article 301(1) because its drafters assumed that the NAFTA would otherwise take priority over the GATT resulting from the Uruguay Round. Article 301(1) of the NAFTA may have been drafted to add clarity to a particular part of the NAFTA, but it does not resolve ambiguity surrounding the meaning of Article 103.

NAFTA rules on forum

Determining as a matter of international law which obligation should prevail in relations between states is different from determining what authority should decide a dispute between these states. It is possible for a dispute-settlement authority to be limited in regard to which rules it may apply in a dispute by the terms of its charter. Ultimately, states are bound in their relations by the superior norms to which they have agreed, even if they have not conferred on a particular dispute-settlement body the authority to make a determination

---

[54] The subject matter of these new area agreements is generally outside the scope of GATT 1947 and does not appear to fall within the GATT continuum. There may be a gray area surrounding certain of the WTO agreements that supplement GATT 1994, since these supplemental agreements in some cases embody GATT 1947 practices and in others largely embody Tokyo Round Agreement rules.

concerning their rights and obligations. The question whether NAFTA or WTO rules will take priority in a particular case involving Canada, Mexico and the United States is distinct from the question as to which dispute-settlement authority will decide the case.

The NAFTA, Chapter 20 dispute-settlement rules generally permit a complaining party to elect either NAFTA or GATT–WTO dispute-settlement in cases arising under both agreements.[55] An exception is made in respect of claims involving environmental, SPS and technical standards matters, as to which the responding party may demand that the matter be settled by a NAFTA panel.[56] NAFTA, Chapter 20 provides that once a dispute-settlement procedure is initiated in either the NAFTA or GATT forum, and subject to the right of a responding party to demand NAFTA dispute-settlement on environment-related claims, "the forum selected shall be used to the exclusion of the other".[57] The default terms of reference for a NAFTA panel are:

"To examine, in the light of the relevant provisions of the Agreement, the matter referred to the Commission (as set out in the request for a Commission meeting) and to make findings, determinations and recommendations as provided in Article 2016(2)".

The report of a panel is adopted by a majority of panelists. Panels are not empowered to issue orders to the parties. The determinations of the panels are instead referred to the parties for implementation. Article 2018 of the NAFTA provides:

"1. On receipt of the final report of the panel, the disputing parties shall agree on the resolution of the dispute, which normally shall conform with the determinations and recommendations of the panel, and shall notify their Sections of the Secretariat of any agreed resolution of any dispute.
2. Wherever possible, the resolution shall be non-implementation or removal of a measure not conforming with the Agreement or causing nullification or impairment . . . or, failing such a resolution, compensation".

Failure by the party in default to implement an adequate solution entitles the aggrieved party to withdraw concessions.

Just as there is ambiguity surrounding the question whether NAFTA or WTO rules prevail in the event of inconsistency, so there is ambiguity surrounding the question whether NAFTA panels may apply the law of the WTO in cases before them. On the one hand, since the NAFTA expressly contemplates that claims arising under both agreements may be brought under NAFTA, Chapter 20, it can be argued that the NAFTA implicitly allows the panelists to consider the law of the WTO. The NAFTA accepts that cases involving the parties may involve overlapping rules and overlapping jurisdiction. If NAFTA panels are precluded from examining both sets of rules, it cannot completely adjudicate a claim, and

[55] NAFTA, Art. 2005(1) refers to cases arising under the GATT or "any successor agreement".
[56] NAFTA, Art. 2005(3), (4).
[57] Ibid., Art. 2005(6).

the parties might be required to pursue a second proceeding in the WTO before a case is resolved. Since the NAFTA demands that the first selected forum be used to the exclusion of the other, it is clear that such dispute-settlement procedures should, at least, take place in sequence.

On the other hand, Article 2004 of the NAFTA expressly provides that Chapter 20 procedures shall apply with respect to interpretation or application of "this Agreement". Similarly, the NAFTA default terms of reference for panels refer to determinations under "this Agreement". On the basis of this language which identifies a specific legal instrument, it might be argued that only NAFTA rules may be applied in a proceeding, at least as to matters in which the parties do not agree on alternative terms of reference incorporating WTO rules.[58]

If the parties accept that a case arises under both the NAFTA and WTO, and yet a NAFTA panel may not consider and apply WTO rules, a party found in default which considers that WTO issues were not adequately addressed may argue that it should not resolve the claim (by withdrawing offending measures, etc.) until its WTO claim is considered at the WTO. Although the NAFTA provisions on implementation may authorise the NAFTA complainant to withdraw concessions based on the NAFTA panel determination, a conflicting WTO result could authorise an offsetting suspension of concessions.

WTO norms and forum

WTO norms and their relationship to outside norms

The WTO Agreement does not directly address the issue of its relationship with other international agreements as does the NAFTA, although it does address the interrelationship of its own component agreements, and the status of its predecessor agreements. The WTO Agreement provides that it is binding on all WTO members,[59] and it provides that each member "shall ensure the conformity of its laws, regulations and administrative procedures with its obligations as provided in the annexed Agreements". The absence of a clearly defined relationship between the WTO Agreement and other international agreements has been a source of concern and controversy, particularly in relation to environmental agreements and measures, and the WTO Committee on Trade and Environment has had this issue under consideration for a number of years.[60] GATT

---

[58] Such difficulties might be avoided if the parties are able to agree on terms of reference which authorise a NAFTA panel to consider both agreements, although this might indeed lead to difficulties in the WTO if a NAFTA party suspended concessions based solely on a NAFTA panel determination. Difficult questions are also raised when considering whether the WTO Dispute Settlement Body (DSB) may consider NAFTA rules in the context of claims also arising under the WTO Agreement. The WTO Dispute Settlement Understanding (DSU) does not make reference to agreements outside the WTO Agreement, and a WTO panel may be presented with a claim in which conflicting NAFTA and WTO rules might yield different results. This is considered below.

[59] WTO Agreement, Art. II:2.

[60] See Abbott's reports to the *Yearbook of International Environmental Law*, (Oxford University Press, Oxford, 1991–97).

dispute-settlement panels, and more recently the WTO Appellate Body, have rendered several decisions in which the issue of the relationship between the WTO Agreement and other international agreements is considered.

Until very recently, GATT–WTO panels have shown considerable hesitancy in considering legal rules from outside the GATT–WTO, although the possibility has not been excluded.[61] In adjudication of claims under the TRIPS Agreement, the WTO Dispute Settlement Body (DSB) will necessarily consider legal claims outside the narrow confines of the WTO Agreement since the TRIPS Agreement incorporates by reference terms, *inter alia*, from the Paris and Berne Conventions.[62] However, because terms of these agreements are incorporated by reference in the TRIPS Agreement, such consideration may not necessarily provide a foundation for adjudicating rights under non-incorporated agreements, for example regional agreements.

A potentially far-reaching development in GATT–WTO jurisprudence is evidenced in the recent *Shrimp-Turtles* decision of the WTO Appellate Body. In the *Shrimp-Turtles* case the WTO Appellate Body extensively consulted agreements and context outside the WTO Agreement as an aid in interpretation of key provisions of the GATT 1994.[63] Although the *Shrimp-Turtles* decision does not directly involve the application of treaty norms outside the WTO Agreement to resolve a WTO dispute, the Appellate Body's extensive consultation of non-WTO sources of law in aid of interpretation suggests a willingness on the part of the Appellate Body to put an end to the view of the GATT–WTO as a self-contained legal regime.

[61] In the *Tuna II* GATT panel decision, the panel accepted that GATT members might be subject to rules of international agreements outside GATT, which agreements might provide the basis for GATT, Art. XX exception from compliance with otherwise applicable GATT rules. However, the panel did not find such agreements to be pertinent to the case under consideration: United States—Restrictions on Imports of Tuna (*Tuna II*), Report of the Panel (1994) 33 *ILM* 842. In the January 1994 GATT *Banana* decision, the panel rejected a claim by the EC that certain actions could be justified because the Lomé Agreement constituted a free trade agreement which provided an Art. XXIV waiver. In doing so, the panel construed the terms of the Lomé Agreement. However, this determination was limited to whether an agreement constituted a measure justifying an exception from otherwise applicable GATT rules, and so might be viewed more in the context of a determination of GATT law than a determination of Lomé Agreement law: General Agreement on Tariffs and Trade: Dispute Settlement Panel Report on the *European Economic Community—Import Regime for Bananas*, January 18, 1994 (Not Adopted) (1995) 34 *ILM* 177.

[62] F.M. Abbott, "WTO Dispute Settlement and the Agreement on Trade-Related Aspects of Intellectual Property Rights", in E.U. Petersmann (ed.), *International Trade Law and the GATT/WTO Dispute Settlement System* (1997) 415.

[63] *United States—Import Prohibition of Certain Shrimp and Shrimp Products*, AB-1998-4, WT/DS58/AB/R, 12 October 1998 (98–3899). For example, the Appellate Body referred to a number of environment-related treaties, such as the Convention on Biological Diversity, for aid in interpreting the meaning of arbitrary discrimination in the adoption of measures relating to the conservation of exhaustible natural resources under GATT, Art. XX(g) (at para. 173). The Appellate Body also considered the Rio Declaration on Environment and Development, referred to in a WTO Ministerial Decision on trade and environment, to illustrate international support for a multilateral approach to adoption of environmental measures within the WTO (ibid.).

If the Appellate Body is prepared to construe GATT 1994 norms in the context of multilateral environmental agreements, then it may also be prepared to construe the WTO rights and obligations of WTO members in the context of their regional treaty commitments. For example, assume that NAFTA parties agreed to require compliance with certain health and safety-related labour standards in the production of goods. One NAFTA party then prohibited the import of goods produced in another NAFTA party in breach of this obligation. If the NAFTA party whose imports were blocked sought relief under the WTO Dispute Settlement Understanding (DSU) because of an alleged breach of GATT, Article XI (prohibition of quotas), the Appellate Body might consider whether the express agreement by the NAFTA parties to enforce labour standards by trade measures might—as between those specific parties—provide a justification under GATT, Article XX(b) for the protection of human health, even if it would not otherwise justify a multilateral exception to Article XI applicable to other WTO members.

The prospective problem that arises regarding application of non-WTO norms among parties to specialised agreements is that the WTO would develop separate bodies of jurisprudence applicable to limited numbers of its members. Conceptually, this may not appear a significant problem to the lawyer trained to deal with court decisions limited in application among the parties to specific disputes. However, the "single undertaking" characteristic of the Uruguay Round result was a major achievement for the new WTO that eliminated the balkanized legal system that prevailed following the Tokyo Round. WTO Members (and the Appellate Body) may be reluctant to introduce a system of jurisprudence that might appear to create different tiers of obligation.[64] This reluctance might be overcome by careful attention to compartmentalising specialised rules, but it is important to call attention to the issues involved.

There appears to be a trend in WTO jurisprudence toward willingness to apply agreements outside the WTO Agreement to disputes among members, and this willingness might extend to the application of regional integration agreements. There are prospective problems raised by the development of specialised jurisprudence within the WTO legal system which deserve careful study.

WTO Forum

There is no provision of the WTO DSU that specifically contemplates the adjudication of legal claims outside the WTO agreements. Just as the NAFTA default terms of reference refer to consideration of the NAFTA, the default

---

[64] Concern has been expressed by some judges of the International Court of Justice regarding the jurisprudentially divisive potential of the Chambers procedure in which disputing parties effectively select the panel of judges. See dissenting opinion of Judge Shahabuddeen in *Case Concerning the Land, Sea and Maritime Frontier Dispute (El Sal. v. Hond.)*, Order Regarding Application for Permission to Intervene (1990) ICJ 3.

WTO DSU terms of reference for panels refer to examination of WTO agreements.[65] Although there is little precedent under which a WTO panel might adjudicate a NAFTA claim as between the NAFTA parties, the WTO text does not appear to preclude such adjudication. There are policy arguments which might favour such action. As with respect to the NAFTA, there is a basic issue of adjudicatory and political economy. If the NAFTA parties have claims arising under both the NAFTA and WTO Agreement, there may be no point in requiring two adjudications. WTO panelists and the Appellate Body would certainly be competent to review NAFTA rules. A more expeditious resolution of a dispute seems likely to mitigate political conflict. In those cases in which the NAFTA parties to a WTO dispute agree on terms of reference which authorise the WTO DSB to consider NAFTA rules, there would appear to be constructive reasons to allow this.

Complementary and Competing Legal Frameworks

Despite the complex nature of the juridical interface between the WTO and the NAFTA, there is only limited reason to believe that conflicts between these legal systems will lead to long-term difficulties. GATT 1947 and EU legal systems have operated in tandem since the inception of the EU. Although there have been conflicts between EU rules and WTO rules—notably in the ongoing Banana dispute—these conflicts have not so far threatened to undermine the GATT–WTO legal system. It is, nevertheless, important to bear in mind the potential for such threat when considering the advantages and disadvantages of regional integration mechanisms.

IV APEC AND THE LEGALISED REGIONAL INTEGRATION MECHANISM

The underlying theme of this chapter is that a legalised regional integration mechanism such as the NAFTA or EU is preferable to a soft consensus-based arrangement such as APEC. In times of financial and political stress, governments come under severe pressure to assert national interests over regional and multilateral interests. A soft consensus-based arrangement such as APEC provides only a weak basis for government adherence to particular policies, e.g. market liberalising policies. Since the obligations imposed on governments are imprecise, it is more difficult for government policy makers to use those obligations as a basis for defending their economic decision-making. During the 1994/1995 Peso Crisis, the Mexican Government pointed to its NAFTA obligations as a compelling reason to avoid the imposition of protectionist measures. During the 1997/1998 Asian financial crisis, governments could not point to similar obligations.

---

[65] WTO DSU, Art. 7:1.

In addition, harder legal regimes are better designed to survive changes in government, even when such changes result in substantial changes in market philosophy. By assuring local and foreign investors that changes in government will not readily result in changes in market access policies, harder agreements provide a more secure foundation for local and foreign investment, and reduce risk premiums otherwise paid by the local economy to offset insecurity.

Reaching a hard integration agreement requires government policy makers to confront difficult issues *ex ante*. While APEC leaders assert that governments will get together and work things out when problems in implementation arise, it is generally easier to reach agreement in advance of problems than to address them after they have arisen. Governments will not be able to foresee all contingencies, nor will they reach agreement on all points of potential dispute. Nevertheless, it is better to develop a hard blueprint for construction than to make up a blueprint as workers proceed.

Binding dispute-settlement is an important part of a hard regional arrangement, and reaching agreement on a binding dispute-settlement mechanism is perhaps the most sensitive area in which governments will negotiate. Nevertheless, it is essential to a hard legal arrangement that some reasonably effective enforcement mechanism be implemented, otherwise disputes will remain settled by power politics.

This chapter recommends that the process of regional integration in East Asia focus on a harder legal form of agreement than that embodied in APEC, recognising that the ASEAN arrangement involves at least a partial move toward such an agreement.

V   NAFTA AS A PREFERABLE MODEL FOR EAST ASIA

NAFTA and EU models compared

The NAFTA is a significantly different model of regional economic integration than the EU.[66] The EU is loosely based on the concept of a federal polity with an allocation of power between EU organs—the Council, Commission, Parliament and ECJ—on one side, and Member State governments on the other.[67] The NAFTA is in the nature of a confederation among independent sovereigns, each maintaining autonomous political decision-making authority within constraints defined by agreement.[68] The political decision-making appa-

---

[66] See, generally, by F.M. Abbott, *Law and Policy*; *Integration Without Institutions: The NAFTA Mutation of the EC Model and the Future of the GATT Regime* (1992) 40 *AJCL* 917; and "Foundation-Building", above at n. 45.

[67] Each Member State government allocates internal political power according to its own constitutional structure.

[68] On the constitutive differences between the EU and the NAFTA from the standpoint of US constitutional law, see F.M. Abbott, "The Maastricht Judgment, the Democracy Principle, and US Participation in Western Hemispheric Integration" (1994) 37 *Germ YBIL* 137.

ratus of the NAFTA is closely circumscribed to roughly include within the boundaries of its central authority (the Free Trade Commission) the powers traditionally conferred upon trade ministers by their governments. The ECJ has referred to the EC Treaty as a constitutional charter, and the Court has viewed its role as the guardian of that constitution.[69] The NAFTA does not purport to serve as a constitution in the sense of altering the distribution of powers among its parties.

The EC Treaty provides for the adoption of directives, regulations and decisions by the EU political organs. These enactments are customarily referred to as "secondary legislation" reflecting their status underneath the "primary legislation" of the EC Treaty. The relationship between primary and secondary EU legislation is similar to the traditional relationship between the constitution and parliamentary enactments of a national federal government. The EC Treaty and secondary legislation may have direct effect in the EU Member States, meaning that this legislation may be relied on by individuals in the courts of the Member States in appropriate circumstances.

The NAFTA political institutions are not empowered to enact secondary legislation except in very limited circumstances prescribed by the Agreement (such as in adopting rules of procedure for NAFTA dispute-settlement panels). There is no general legislative power allocated to the NAFTA political institutions. The NAFTA is in theory capable of direct effect within the national courts of its parties. The United States has by legislation deprived the NAFTA of potential direct effect in US courts.[70]

The economic undertakings of the parties were negotiated in detail. The results of these negotiations were expressed in the NAFTA text. The parties have so far carried out the economic undertakings of the NAFTA substantially in accordance with its terms. Although a few matters are disputed, in the context of the overall undertaking, these disputes are modest.

The NAFTA prescribes mechanisms for the resolution of disputes between its parties, and in limited circumstances for the resolution of disputes between the nationals of its parties and party governments. The general dispute-settlement mechanism of the NAFTA is an arbitral procedure that refers determinations to party governments for political resolution. This is consistent with the NAFTA's limited design in respect to intrusion on party autonomy. The NAFTA's anti-dumping and countervailing duty dispute-settlement apparatus directly binds party governments.[71] Party nationals are entitled to pursue third party

---

[69] See, generally, J.H.H. Weiler, *The Transformation of Europe* (1991) 100 *Yale LJ* 2403; and for a review of EC governance preceding the Single European Act and subsequent reforms, S.A. Riesenfeld, "Legal Systems of Regional Economic Integration" (1974) 22 *AJCL* 415.

[70] Regarding the non-self-executing character of the NAFTA in the United States, see F.M. Abbott, "Regional Integration Mechanisms in the Law of the United States: Starting Over" (1993) 1 *Indiana J Glob. Leg Stud* 155.

[71] The NAFTA includes a separate dispute-settlement mechanism in respect to anti-dumping and countervailing duty (AD/CVD)-related complaints (NAFTA, Chapter 19). The NAFTA contains no rules regarding the substance of the AD/CVD laws of the parties, requiring only that each party act

arbitration of investment-related claims at International Centre for the Settlement of Investment Disputes (ICSID) or under UNCITRAL rules.[72] Each of these dispute-settlement mechanisms is operational.

The EU is a customs union. The EC Treaty prescribes the elimination of tariffs and other restrictive regulations of commerce on trade between its Member States, and prescribes the establishment of common tariffs applicable to goods originating outside EU territory. The EC Treaty prescribes that goods originating outside its territory are in free circulation within its territory following the payment of the applicable common tariff upon entry into any Member State. The EC Treaty prescribes a common commercial policy which binds its Member States to follow a co-ordinated trade policy program. The EC Treaty prescribes the free movement of services, capital and persons between its Member States.

The NAFTA is a free trade area. It prescribes the elimination of tariffs and other restrictive regulations of commerce between its parties, but does not prescribe common tariffs applicable to goods originating outside NAFTA territory. Except in so far as goods originating outside the NAFTA are transformed within a party(s) so as to assume a regional character, such third country goods are subject to the payment of tariffs upon entry into each NAFTA party.[73] The NAFTA prescribes the free movement of services and capital, and limited free movement of business persons, between its members. Except in so far as the parties are limited in their relations with third countries by its terms, the NAFTA does not mandate that the parties pursue a common commercial policy.

NAFTA and East Asia

The EU was formed in a rather unique historical context. In the late 1940s and 1950s the governments of Europe, which had a long history of conflict, were willing to cede significant levels of sovereign prerogative to regional political institutions. On the institutional side, it seems doubtful that East Asian governments starting from a non-legalised tradition of trade relations would be willing

in domestic AD/CVD actions in compliance with its own laws. In the AD/CVD dispute-settlement system, arbitral panels constituted on a case-by-case basis make decisions as to whether a country party has complied with its own AD/CVD laws in a particular action. The decisions of AD/CVD panels are directly binding on the country parties. There are approximately 30 completed or active Chapter 19 panels reviewing AD/CVD decisions of Canadian, Mexican and US administrative authorities: NAFTA Secretariat, www.nafta-sec-alena.org, 13 August 1998.

[72] The NAFTA also permits investors of parties to pursue third party arbitration against a host government in the International Centre for the Settlement of Investment Disputes (ICSID) or under UNCITRAL rules. NAFTA, Arts 1115 *et seq.* See *Law and Policy*, 102. The NAFTA obligates the parties to make adequate provision for the enforcement of resulting arbitral awards. Several proceedings based on NAFTA investment rules have been initiated in the ICSID by US nationals against the Government of Mexico, and claims both by US nationals against the Government of Canada and by Canadian nationals against the Government of the United States have been initiated or threatened.

[73] The parties may each elect to limit applicable tariffs to the single highest tariff payable in any NAFTA party (so as to avoid double tariffing).

to make the kinds of political concessions necessary to create a EU-model regional institutional arrangement, at least in the near-to-medium term. The NAFTA model, by way of contrast, involves substantially more modest concessions of sovereignty, and thus may provide at least a starting point for a harder East Asian regional institutional regime.

The free trade area tariff structure of the NAFTA also demands a lower level of political accommodation than the EU customs union model. NAFTA governments did not need to reach agreement on common external tariffs, which may have proved difficult in light of the substantial differences in levels of economic development between Canada, Mexico and the United States. The free trade area model of the NAFTA presents drawbacks from the standpoint of third country exporters, and requires a more complex, intra-regional customs bureaucracy than the EU model. For this reason, the EU model may well be preferable both from an internal and external trade standpoint. Whether it would be worthwhile to attempt to pursue the customs union form of regional tariff arrangement in East Asia would depend on an *ex ante* analysis of existing regional tariffs, and a determination of the political feasibility of reaching an accommodation. While the EU model may be preferable, it may not be politically feasible.

The NAFTA and EU are substantially similar regarding the general basis of treatment of services, investment and capital movement. However, while the NAFTA and EU each provide for national treatment, only the EU makes express provision for the promulgation of secondary legislation by which potentially trade distorting rules may be harmonised or approximated. While granting regional institutions the power to approximate rules is a very useful component of a comprehensive regional integration arrangement, it is not vitally necessary, particularly at the earlier phases of integration. Granting to regional institutions the power to adopt mandatory legislation is a major step in the concession of state sovereignty, and again might better be envisioned at later stages of the integration process.

The EU provides for the free movement of workers, while the NAFTA provides limited free movement for professional and managerial personnel. At the present time, it is doubtful that complete labour market integration is a necessary or practicable option for East Asia, and thus a more limited NAFTA model opening of the labour market might be more appropriate.

On the whole, a comparison of the NAFTA and EU integration models in respect of the circumstances of East Asia suggests that most elements of the NAFTA model would be preferable, at least for the near-to-medium term. There are of course variations of these models in the Andean Pact, Mercosur and elsewhere, which models provide additional sources for comparison and consideration.

VI NAFTA, EAST ASIA AND THE WTO SYSTEM

Inherent in regional integration are risks to the WTO system. The EU has become such an important political and economic force that this exercise in regionalism may have diminished the importance of maintaining an open multilateral trading system from a European standpoint. Similarly, the NAFTA has brought added economic security to the North American region, and it can be argued that this, too, potentially undermines the role of the WTO and multilateralism.

Yet the threats remain largely in the domain of theory. The EU has enjoyed political stability and sustained economic growth, despite the very costly reunification of Germany and a major world monetary crisis. It was predictable that Mexico would suffer social and political dislocation as its economy was privatised and liberalised, and this prediction has borne fruit. However, in comparison with other countries at comparable levels of economic development and political transition, Mexico is doing fairly well. The North American economy has been strong in the face of economic crisis. The political and economic strength and resiliency of the EU and NAFTA have provided an extremely important anchor for the global economy over the past several years.

There is no proof that regionalisation of the EU and North American economies has been responsible for their success. Strong US, British, French and German economies may alone have provided the necessary engines for economic growth in North America and Europe. However, on the historical record, it is difficult to make the case that regional integration has harmed the global economy, or that there is any near-to-medium-term threat present. The NAFTA is so far a healthy complementary institution to the WTO.

The critical element in regional integration planning in East Asia is the maintenance of WTO compatibility and complementarity. As with the NAFTA and EU, attention must be paid to the longer-term process of building and maintaining a strong multilateral trading system which assures that the benefits of global economic integration are taken advantage of fully, and that the fruits of integration will be distributed widely.

4

Establishing the Rules of the Game: Domestic Structures and Unfair Trade Instruments[1]

CANDIDO GARCIA MOLYNEUX

I INTRODUCTION

This chapter tries to make the following points. First, despite globalisation, individual countries continue to have market economies embedded in different domestic socio-economic structures. These diverse domestic structures exist at a world, as well as at a regional level, such as the European Union (EU). Neoliberalism as reflected in the WTO or the Single Market Initiative, fails to create a uniform worldwide market. Thus, coping with globalisation requires dealing with this diversity. Secondly, globalisation is not simply an economic, technological nor neutral phenomenon, but is instead, to a certain extent, also the result of political will and law. Globalisation implies establishing the rules under which international trade can take place. Thirdly, unfair trade instruments such as anti-dumping, countervailing laws and market access instruments like the US section 301 of the 1974 Trade Act or the EU's Trade Barriers Regulation, play an important role in defining the rules of the system. I argue that making a distinction between defensive and offensive instruments is limited, as they both attempt either directly or indirectly to establish the rules of the international trade game. Fourthly, the different domestic structures, and not only the trading partner's comparative economic power, affect the ability to influence the international system. In this sense, the persistence of a variety of market economies within the EU lead the Common Commercial Policy to second best outcomes.

With the purpose of arguing the previous points, this chapter is divided into two main parts. I start with a theoretical section where I argue (a) the existence of different market economies both at a world and EU level and (b) the use of trade instruments to attempt to win the globalisation game by imposing the domestic standards on foreign countries. Thereafter, I present a case study

---

[1] I am grateful to Professors Francis Snyder and Mary Volcansek (see chap. 6 below) for their useful comments.

which tries to explain how the EU used its anti-dumping law to target the domestic structures of Japan. In Part IV, I make some conclusions.

II THEORETICAL FRAMEWORK

Globalisation and diversity

Despite globalisation, the world is divided into a variety of market economies embedded in different domestic structures.[2] The concept of structure referred to in this chapter describes the stress in the relations between business and the state as well as the contradiction between organised capital and organised labour.[3] This approach analyses not only the strength or weakness of the government but also the organisation or plurality of the market. It focuses first on how the market is organised. It takes into account how industry is organised in a specific country, the relationship between export-led and domestic industry, the relationship between industry and finance and the relation between business and labour. Hence, it looks at whether the market is characterised by the existence of strong trade unions, strong or weak industrial trade associations, the capacity of banks to control the system, and the capacity of the economic actors to reach a consensus, etc. Secondly, it looks at the interaction between the state and the market. Thus, it looks at the state and its ability to interfere with business. It analyses whether a given state has a "government intervention" or "hands off" tradition, and whether or not it has a strong government capable of influencing the market, etc. States differ in terms of the reigning political beliefs that render legitimate particular types of state involvement in the market.[4] All states intervene in the market but they do so in very different ways. Indeed, states may influence, regulate, mediate, distribute, redistribute, produce and plan the market.[5] Furthermore, some countries will have stronger states than others and thus government intervention will be both more likely and easier. This will depend both on the market and the state.[6]

[2] See Suzanne Berger, "Introduction", in *S. Berger and R. Dore (eds), National Diversity and Global Capitalism* (Cornell University Press, 1996). See also Robert Boyer, "The Convergence Hypothesis Revisited: Globalization but Still the Century of Nations?", in ibid., 29–59; L.W. Pauly and Simon Reich, "National Structures and Multinational Corporate Behaviour: Enduring Differences in the Age of Globalization" (1997) 51(1) *International Organisation* 1; Neil Fligstein and Robert Freeland, "Theoretical and Comparative Perspectives on Corporate Organisation", 21 *Annual Rev Sociology* (1995) 21.

[3] See P.J. Katzenstein, "Conclusion: Domestic Structures and Strategies of Foreign Economic Policy, in P. Katzenstein (ed.), *Between Power and Plenty: Foreign Economic Policies of Advanced Industrial States* (University of Wisconsin Press, 1978), 295, 333.

[4] See G.J. Ikenberry, "Conclusion: An Institutional Approach to American Foreign Economic Policy" (1988) 42(1) *International Organisation* 219, 228.

[5] See T.J. Biersteker, "Reducing the Role of the State in the Economy: A Conceptual Exploration of IMF and World Bank Prescriptions" (1990) 34 *International Studies Quarterly* 477, 480.

[6] A good example of the different ways through which a government can influence the market is the practice of administrative guidelines as used in Japan. Such guidelines are not considered to be

A structuralist point of view implies a critical approach to the normative idea of free trade by rejecting historical and structure-blind assumptions and asserting the primacy of social, economic and political structures.[7]

Free trade is an extension of the regime of free markets to the international sector. It proscribes that all countries will gain economically if each first specialises in the production of those goods and materials in which it has a comparative or absolute advantage.[8] In the absence of distorting constraints, individuals will engage only in economic exchange if it brings them benefit. Under the theory of free trade, the market is considered to be a device through which individuals voluntarily interact in their capacities as producers and consumers to exchange goods and services. Price is the mechanism which transmits information to both consumers and producers, enabling them, through demand and supply, to determine exactly what is produced and in what quantity. Thus, without central direction, millions of individual economic decisions are

law in force and are not legally binding. This practice has been examined under different GATT dispute-settlement panels. In *Japan—Restrictions on Imports of Certain Agricultural Products*, L/6253, 22 March 1988, BISD 35 S/163, Japan argued that, to the extent that governmental measures were effective, it was irrelevant whether or not the measures were mandatory and statutory. The governmental measures "were effectively enforced by detailed directives and instructions to local governments and/or farmers' organisations and such centralised and mutually collaborative structure of policy implementation was the crux of government enforcement in Japan". In that case, the panel upheld Japan's argument. It noted that "the practice of administrative guidance played an important role" in the enforcement of the Japanese supply restrictions, that this practice was "a traditional tool of Japanese government policy based on consensus and peer pressure" and that the administrative guidance in the special circumstances could therefore be regarded as a governmental measure enforcing supply restrictions. This interpretation was followed in *Japan, Trade in Semi-Conductors*, L/6309, 24 March 1988, BISD 35 S/116. In that case, where Japan argued to the contrary, that its administrative guidelines could in no way be considered as government action, the panel held that these administrative guidelines could be considered to violate Art. XI of GATT. The panel noted that Art. XI:1 of GATT "unlike other provisions of the General Agreement, did not refer to laws or regulations but more broadly to measures. This wording indicated clearly that any measure instituted or maintained by a contracting party which restricted the exportation or sale for export of products was covered by this provision, irrespective of the legal status of the measures". Furthermore, "the panel recognised that not all mandatory requests could be regarded as measures within the meaning of Article XI:1. Government industry relations varied from country to country, from industry to industry, and from case to case and were influenced by many factors. There were thus a wide spectrum of government involvement ranging from, for instance, direct government orders to occasional government consultations with advisory committees. The task of the panel was to determine whether the measures taken in this case would be such as to constitute a contravention of Article XI". Thus, "In order to determine this, the panel considered that it needed to be satisfied on two essential criteria. First, there were reasonable grounds to believe that sufficient incentives or disincentives existed for non-mandatory measures to take effect. Second the operation of the measures to restrict export of semi-conductors at prices below company specific costs was essentially dependent on Government action or intervention. . . .The panel considered that if these two criteria were met, the measures would be operating in a manner equivalent to mandatory requirements such that the difference between measures and mandatory requirements was only one of form and not of substance, and that there could be therefore no doubt that they fell within the range of measures covered by Article XI:1".

[7] See Simon Hix, "The Study of the European Community: The Challenge of Comparative Politics" (1994) 17 *West European Politics* 1, 9.

[8] See David Ricardo, *The Principles of Political Economy and Taxation* (I. M. Dent & Sons, 1973), 77–93.

co-ordinated to utilise resources in the most efficient manner possible to determine optimum production.[9]

Hence, the idea of free trade requires the separation of economics from politics. No politics should interfere in the market process. However, the extent to
which such classical economic theory is really apolitical is doubtful.[10] The norm
of the free market tries to submit the whole society to its own principles. The
free market economy tries to subject everything to the rule of profit and considers labour, land and money as nothing more than a commodity. What distinguishes the self-regulating market from any other economic system is that it
subjects the whole society to its own rules. The economy does not adapt to the
society but rather the society must adapt to the rule of the market.[11]

Yet, in fact, markets are neither neutral nor exist in isolation. First, markets
are a source of political power, and thus affect political life. Political life is
entangled with the workings of markets and market institutions.[12] Secondly,
markets are embedded in political and social institutions. Thus, a global market
does not result from the elimination of barriers. The systematic elimination of
tariffs and non-tariff trade barriers, known as negative integration, ruled by
neoliberal ideology does not create a unified economic space because it fails to
address the importance of the political and social peculiarities in which market
exchange takes place.[13]

Capitalism may be defined by the existence of free markets and private property rights. However, economic action is shaped not just by markets and private
property but also by a wide range of institutions. The market is just one institutional device among others co-ordinating the governance of a society.[14] There is
not a single and unique method of organising capitalist economies. Markets and
property rights are always part of, and modified by, local institutional contexts
which are not economic. These social and political institutions surrounding markets and property rights are the sources of differences amongst capitalist
economies.[15] Thus, it is not clear that the globalisation process brings uniformity

[9] See R. D. McKinlay and R. Little, *Global Problems and World Order* (Frances Printer, 1986), 29.

[10] See Gunnar Myrdal, *The Political Element in the Development of Economic Theory*
(Routledge & Kegan Paul, 2nd ed. 1955); See also C.B. Macpherson, *The Political Theory of
Possessive Individualism: Hobbes to Locke* (Oxford University Press, 1964).

[11] See Karl Polanyi, *The Great Transformation: The Political and Economic Origins of Our
Time* (Beacon Press, 1957). On the different visions of market society see A.O. Hirshman, "Rival
Views of Market Society", in *Rival Views of Market Society and Other Recent Essays* (Elisabeth
Sifton Books, Viking, 1986), 105.

[12] See John Zysman, *Government, Markets and Growth: Financial Systems and the Politics of
Industrial Change* (Cornell University Press, 1983), 17.

[13] See John Grahl and Paul Teague, "The Cost of Neo-Liberal Europe" (1989) *New Left Review*
33, 41.

[14] See J. Rogers Hollingsworth and Robert Boyer, "Coordination of Economic Actors and Social
Systems of Production", in J. Rogers Hollingsworth and R. Boyer (eds), *Contemporary Capitalism:
The Embeddedness of Institutions* (Cambridge University Press, 1997), 1.

[15] See J. Rogers Hollingsworth, Philippe Schmitter and Wolfgang Streeck, "Capitalism, Sectors,
Institutions and Performance", in J. Rogers Hollingsworth, P. Schmitter and W. Streeck (eds),
Governing Capitalist Economies: Performance & Control of Economic Sectors (Oxford University
Press, 1994), 3, 5.

among nations.[16] Production methods, industrial relations, technology processes, taxation and economic policy styles remain very specific to each state.[17] In fact, increased interdependence implies the growing significance of domestic structural differences.[18] The reduction of barriers in the form of tariffs or different government interventions in the market has highlighted the importance of the different socio-economic structures in which national markets are rooted.

Following Katzenstein, it is possible to divide countries into four types with regard to their socio-economic structures:[19]

		MARKET	
		ORGANISED	PLURAL
G		1	3
O			
V	STRONG	STRONG	STRONG
E		ORGANISED	PLURAL
R			
N			
M	WEAK		
E		WEAK	WEAK
N		ORGANISED	PLURAL
T		2	4

This model is very abstract. Countries cannot deliberately be placed in one category. However, for the sake of clarity it is useful to classify countries into four categories.

---

[16] See Robert Boyer and Daniel Drache, "Introduction", in R. Boyer and D. Drache (eds), *States Against Markets: The Limits of Globalization* (Routledge, 1996), 1.

[17] In this sense, the existence of different economic models and the controversy of which one should be followed was strongly highlighted by the press which reported on the G8 Economic Summit held in Denver in June 1997. See Emanuel Todd, "The French Exception", *Newsweek*, 23 June 1997, 26; see also Michael Hirsh, "Looking Upward", *Newsweek*, 23 June 1997, 12; Christopher Dickey, "Sun and Synapses", *Newsweek*, 23 June 1997, 24; Louis Uchitelle, "America's Economy: Could a Model for the World Be Oversold?", *International Herald Tribune*, 23 June 1997.

[18] See J.G. Ruggie, "Trade, Protectionism and the Future of Welfare Capitalism", (1994) 48 *Journal of International Affairs* 1, 7.

[19] See Peter Katzenstein, above at n. 3, 324; see also Wolfgang Streeck and Philippe Schmitter, *Community, Market, State—and Associations: The Prospective Contribution of Interest Governance to Social Order*, European University Institute Working Paper No. 94 (1984). Another way of understanding market diversity is by focussing on the three elements which are necessary for the existence of a market economy: property rights, governance structures and rules of exchange. Property rights refer to the legal definitions of ownership. They define the limits between the public and the private. Governance structures refer to laws and informal practices that set the boundaries of competition and co-operation between the different market actors. Finally, rules of exchange facilitate trade by establishing the rules under which transactions are undertaken. In this sense, uniformity has only taken place at the level of rules of exchange and slightly at that of property rights but not at the level of governance. See Neil Fligstein and Iona Mara-Drita, "How to Make a Market: Reflections on the Attempt to Create a Single Market in the European Union" (1996) *American Journal of Sociology* 1; see also Neil Fligstein and Robert Freeland, "Theoretical and Comparative Perspectives on Corporate Organisation" (1995) 21 *Annually Rev Sociology* 21.

Models 1 and 2 are countries which tend towards a corporativist system characterised by the existence of a highly organised market. These countries are likely to have strong and highly organised trade unions, strong trade and industrial associations, a very strong banking system, itself capable of financing and controlling industry, a strong tendency towards consensus within industrial relations, the reliance on technically correct solutions, a strong and fluid dialogue between government and industry, etc. Models 1 and 2 differ from each other with regard to the strength of their governments. Under model 1, the government will be strongly interventionist. It will tend to develop an industrial planning policy. An example of model 1 would be Japan.[20] A good example of model 2 could be Germany which, as the result of the Nazi tragedy, has developed a tradition of non-intervention and governmental division of power.[21] However, the difference between countries of models 1 and 2 is not so important. Often, it matters less whether or not a government is interventionist, but rather within which market it has to intervene. Generally, examples of countries falling under models 1 and 2 are small European countries such as the Netherlands, Denmark, Sweden, Finland, Austria or Belgium.[22]

Model 3 is characterised by the existence of a strong government, by strong government intervention in the economy, and the authoritative imposition of such, but also by a pluralist society. These countries, such as France, Spain and Italy, are countries with a strong government intervention tradition but which have a market characterised by the existence of weak trade unions, or trade unions which are not taken into account, by a weak banking system, by weak trade associations and by an incapacity of industrial actors to reach solutions through consensus. They will be characterised by strong government intervention in forms such as subsidies but much less effectively than in countries falling under models 1 and 2.[23]

[20] See P.J. Katzenstein, "Japan, Switzerland of the Far East?", in Inoguchi and Okimoto (eds), *The Political Economy of Japan. Volume II: The Changing International Context* (Stanford University Press, 1988), 275. See also Jonathan Steele, "Yeltsin fails to Win Japanese Hearts or Trust", *Guardian International*, 8 July 1993, 8 (reporting how Japanese scholars consider the Japanese market to be very different from that of the West. In this sense, the article argues that in the same way that Japan has its own economic model, Russia will have one of its own); nn. 64–71 below and accompanying text.

[21] On the domestic structures of Germany, see Kenneth Dyson, "The State, Banks and Industry: The West German Case", in Andrew Cox (ed.), *The State, Finance and Industry* (Wheatsheaf, 1986), 118; see also T.R. Howell and G.I. Hume, "Germany", in Thomas Howell, Alan Wolff, Brent Bartlett and Michael Gadbaw (eds), *Conflict Among Nations: Trade Policies in the 1990s* (Westview Press, 1992), 145; Wolfgang Streeck, "German Capitalism: Does it Exist? Can it Survive?", in C. Crouch and W. Streeck (eds), *Political Economy of Modern Capitalism: Mapping Convergence and Diversity* (Sage Publications, 1997), 33; Paulette Kurzer and C.S. Allen, "United Europe and Social Democracy: The EC, West Germany and its Three Small Neighbours", in C.F. Lankovski (ed.) *Germany and the European Community: Beyond Hegemony and Containment?* (Martin Press, 1993), 102.

[22] See P.J. Katzenstein, *Small States in World Markets: Industrial Policy in Europe* (Cornell University Press, 1985).

[23] On the domestic structures of France, see Andrea Boltho, "Has France Converged on Germany? Policies and Institutions since 1958", in Suzzane Berger and Ronald Dore (eds), *National*

Pluralist Anglo-Saxon countries like the United Kingdom and the United States fall under model 4. These countries are characterised by the weakness of their governments and by a plural, disorganised market. Trade unions tend to be very weak. There is a constant lack of strong trade associations because of the weakness of the banking system industry tending to finance itself through the stock market; there are difficult relations between industry and government and, in general, industrial actors are unlikely to reach a consensus.[24]

These different socio-economic structures, of which national markets are part, result from different historical experiences. Societies' economic organisations and arrangements are interdependent. The way in which the state and society are actually linked is historically conditioned. Different national traditions conceive of the public–private dichotomy in different ways and thus their different national traditions allow different access to regulatory space.[25] The capacity of the state in a capitalist economy to mobilise and use resources effectively is conditioned by ideologies and institutions and, at a deeper level, by the historical and structural factors that have shaped the development of these ideologies and institutions.[26] Social institutions are rooted in local, regional or national political communities and their shared beliefs, experiences and traditions. The way the market actors interact with each other even without the intervention of the state depends on their expectations. Such expectations, however, are rooted in their past experiences. Thus, although identical technologies and market conditions make for similarities in the industrial organisation and

Diversity and Global Capitalism)Cornell University Press, 1996), 89; see also Robert Boyer, "French Statism at a Crossroads", in *Political Economy of Modern Capitalism: Mapping Convergence and Diversity* (1997), 71; Jack Hayward, *The State and the Market Economy: Industrial Patriotism and Economic Internvetion in France* (Wheatsheaf Books, 1986); Chris Howell, "French Socialism and the Transformation of Industrial Relations since 1981", in A. Daley (ed.), *The Miterrand Era: Policy Alternatives and Political Mobilization in France* (New York University Press, 1996), 141; W.J. Adams, *Restructuring the French Economy: Government and the Rise of Market Competitition since World War II* (The Brookings Institution, 1989).

[24] On the domestic structures of the United States, see Henry Farber and A.B Krueger, *Union Membership in the United States: The Decline Continues*, National Bureau of Economic Research, Working Paper No. 4216 (1992); see also James Fallows, *More Like Us: Making America Great Again* (Houghton Mifflin Company, 1989); J.A. Hart, *Rival Capitalists: International Competitiveness in the United States, Japan and Western Europe* (Cornell University Press, 1992); S.M. Lipset, *American Exceptionalism: A Double-Edge Sword* (W.W. Norton & Company, 1996); S.B. Hansen, "Industrial Policy and Corporativism in the American States" (1989) 2(2) *Governance* 172; Alan Wolf, "The Failure of American Trade Policy", in Howell, Wolf and Gadbow (eds), *Conflict Among Nation: Trade Policies in the 1990s* (Westview Press, 1992), 469.

[25] See Leigh Hancher and Michael Moran, *Organizing Regulatory Space*, in L. Hancher and M. Moran (eds), *Capitalism, Culture and Economic Regulation* (Clarendon Press, 1989), 271, 280.

[26] See Kenneth Dyson, *The State Tradition in Western Europe* (Martin Robertson, 1980); see also Kenneth Dyson, "The Cultural, Ideological and Structural Context", in Dyson and Wilks (eds) *Industrial Crisis: A Comparative Study of State and Industry* (Martin Robertson, 1983), 66; John Zysman, "How Institutions Create Historically Rooted Trajectories of Growth" (1994) 3(1) *Industrial & Corporate Change* 243, 245.

the governance of sectors across countries, there are still significant differences due to different past experiences.[27]

It is important to distinguish between governmental policies and socio-economic structures. While it will be possible to change and control the different policies of a state from the external sphere, it will be much more difficult to change the structures of such a country that are firmly historically rooted. The structures which rule the organisation of the market and strongly condition the role of the state in the market will have to undergo a much slower erosion process. Although it is possible that some models will be better off than others, countries will not be able to adapt themselves smoothly to different domestic structures.[28] Thus, globalisation is characterised both by homogeneity and diversity. Globalisation does not create a completely homogenous worldwide market place, but instead, while enforcing a thin Anglo-Saxon market uniformity, it puts together different market frameworks.[29] Globalisation makes possible the interaction between different systems.[30]

Unfair trade instruments in the global diversity

The persistence of different domestic socio-economic structures within the globalisation process results in a constant exchange of goods, services and capital

[27] See Colin Crouch, "Sharing Public Space: States and Organized Interests in Western Europe", in J. Hall (ed.), *States in History* (Basil Blackwell, 1986), 177; see also Louis Hartz, *The Liberal Tradition in America* (Harcourt, Brace & World, 1955) (where the author analyses the US' liberal economic system as a result of its historical process of development).

[28] But see Michel Albert, *Capitalism versus Capitalism: How America's Obsession with Individual Achievement and Short Term Profit Had Led it to the Brink of Collapse*, Four Wall Eight Windows (1993); see also Michael Hodges and Stephen Woolcock, "Atlantic Capitalism versus Rhine Capitalism in the European Community" (1993) 16 *West Euro Pol'y* 329, (arguing the existence of a competition between different capitalist models in which one model will finally impose itself).

[29] Thin globalisation refers to the idea of a superficial uniformity underneath which different national characteristics subsist. Professor David Trubeck, "Social Justice After Globalization: The Case of Social Europe", paper presented at the Seminar *Globalization and the Law*, European University Institute, November 1996; see also C.A.G. Jones, "Capitalism, Globalization and Rule of Law: An Alternative Trajectory of Legal Change in China" (1994) 3 *Social & Legal Studies* 195, 202–203. Thin Anglo-Saxon uniformity prevails for two reasons. First, in building an international trade regime negative integration (the reduction of trade barriers), is always easier than positive integration (the adoption of common market structures). The Anglo-Saxon model, characterised by government decentralisation and market pluralism, is the minimum common denominator of all market systems. Secondly, the United States has been the only trading partner with both the economic muscle and the ability to act efficiently in the international trading system so as to impose the rules of the game; though even for the United States this has been to a limited extent only.

[30] See P.G. Cerny, "Globalization and Other Stories: The Search for a New Paradigm for International Relations" (1996) *International Journal* 617, 625; see also Robert Boyer, "The Convergence Hypothesis Revisited: Globalization but Still the Century of Nations?", in S. Berger and R. Dore (eds), *National Diversity and Global Capitalism* (Cornell University Press, 1996), 29, 51. In this sense, multinational corporations, considered to be by many authors as main actors in the globalisation process, continue to have their patterns of internal governance and financing determined by their background nationalities. See L.W. Pauly and Simon Reich, "National Structures and Multinational Corporate Behaviour: Enduring Differences in the Age of Globalization" (1997) *International Organisation* 1, 4.

between different market frameworks. Although the flow of trade and invest-ment has a great impact on the domestic life of each trading partner, yet domes-tic socio-economic structures are not easily subject to change, so states try to protect their domestic spheres by means of participating in bilateral and multi-lateral negotiations and unilateral unfair trade instruments, in order to influence the rules of the market. Globalisation becomes a cut-throat struggle in which the trading partners try to protect themselves by imposing policies on others which accord with their own domestic structures.[31] In this sense, to a certain extent, unfair trade instruments reflect, in their conceptions of fairness, the different socio-economic frameworks in which markets are embedded.

Unfair trade instruments are rationalised on grounds of fairness. The trading system in place since the end of the World War II is not based on the idea of uni-lateral free trade, but rather on a cosmopolitan free trade idea.[32] Free trade must be reciprocal and subject to certain rules. Free trade is argued not to mean free for all, but rather free and fair trade.[33] Fair trade is supposed to be concerned with the equitable treatment of all participants in international trade.[34] All trade participants should be treated in the same way. Thus it is related to the notion of a level playing field. Competition in international trade should be played according to a set of rules which all participants must share.

However, societies and their economic systems differ so much that what seems to be unfair for one state may seem perfectly reasonable to another.[35] Hence, it is difficult to agree on a uniform set of market rules. In this sense, the agreements of the multilateral trading system can only succeed to a limited extent. International rules can change domestic governmental policies, but less so the deep socio-economic structures which condition the expectations and behaviour of market actors. Rules can control to a limited extent the role of the government, but rarely how the market and its actors are organised.[36] This interdependence between different economic systems may cause harm and eco-nomic dislocations to some. Unfair trade instruments can thus be seen as buffer mechanisms, as interface instruments to share the burden of the adjusting costs between different systems.[37]

---

[31] In this sense, de Sousa Santos considers that one of the processes of globalism is globalised localism whereby a local phenomenon is successfully globalised. Globalised localism is paralleled by localised globalisation which is the restructuring and adjustment of the local sphere as a result of globalisation. See de Sousa Santos, "Globalisation, Nation-States and the Legal Field: From Legal Diaspora to Legal Ecumenism?", in *Toward a New Common Sense: Law, Science and Politics in the Paradigmatic Transition* (1995) 250, 263.

[32] See Jagdish Bhagwati, *The World Trading System at Risk* (Harvester Wheatsheaf, 1991), 50–51.

[33] See Alan Tondson, "Beating Back Predatory Trade" (1994) 73(4) *Foreign Affairs* 123.

[34] See Phendon Nicolaides, "How Fair is Fair Trade?" (1994) 21 *Journal of World Trade Law* 147.

[35] See J.H. Jackson, *The World Trading System: Law and Policy of International Economic Relations* (The MIT Press, 1989), 218.

[36] In this sense, there are many who believe that the WTO agreements will have very little effect on the behaviour of governments. Interview with John Greenwald (Washington DC, June 1995).

[37] See J.H. Jackson, above at n. 35, 249; see also Ronald Dore, "Convergence in Whose Interest?", in S. Berger and R. Dore (eds), *National Diversity and Global Capitalism* (Cornell University Press, 1996), 366–371.

States will use unfair trade instruments in order to limit the dislocation costs caused by goods and services coming from different economic systems. States will impose as their fairness benchmarks their own domestic socio-economic standards. The fair trade notion will extend to any foreign government policy or institution that is different from one's own.[38] In this sense globalisation, instead of a process of tolerance and mutual acceptance, is simply one of *campanillismo*. The relationship between one state and its private industry and those between its market actors will be the model used to evaluate the trade practices of other nations.[39] No country may assist its home industry or interfere with consumer market preferences to a greater extent than is done in the targeting country. Likewise, foreign market actors may not organise to a greater extent than what is already being done in the targeting country.

Furthermore, unfair trade instruments can be misused and result in competing struggles between different market economies. Because the elimination of tariff and non-tariff barriers does not lead *per se* to a neutral and global market economy, but rather to the interaction between a variety of market systems, each with its own peculiarities, states will compete in the establishment of an international trade legal system which reflects their own domestic sphere. Thus, trade instruments can be understood not only as buffer mechanisms between markets with different socio-economic frameworks but also as states' means of protecting their own structures by trying to change the policies and structures of others. This is especially the case because as international trade rules establish loose constitutional frameworks for the interaction between different market economies, they are not always clear.

In the world of globalisation all states are sensitive to interdependence. However, some states are more vulnerable than others.[40] States may have bigger export or import markets or they may be more import or export dependent than others. This creates an asymmetrical relationship which will imply the existence of power of one state over another. Power can be defined as the ability of one actor to get others do something they otherwise would not do.[41] In this sense, trade instruments may be seen as examples of both relational and structural power. Relational power would be the power of state A to get state B to do something it would not otherwise do. Structural power is the power to

---

[38] See Jagdish Bhagwati, "Fair Trade, Reciprocity and Harmonization: The New Challenge to the Theory and Policy of Free Trade", in Deardorff and Stern (eds), *Analytical and Negotiating Issues in the Global Trading System* (The University of Michigan Press, 1994), 547, 584.

[39] See Judith Goldstein, "Ideas, Institutions and America's Trade Policy" (1988) 42 *International Organisation* 179, 198; see also D.K. Tarullo, "Beyond Normalcy in the Regulation of International Trade" (1987) 100 *Harvard L Rev*. 547.

[40] See R.O. Keohane and J.S. Nye, *Power and Interdependence* (Little Brown and Co., 4th ed., 1977), 11–13. Sensitivity implies degrees of responsiveness within a policy framework. It assumes that the framework remains unchanged. Vulnerability, however, defines the relative availability and cost of the alternatives that various actors face.

[41] Ibid., 11.

shape and determine structures of the global economy within which other states, their political institutions and economic enterprises have to operate.[42]

By using unfair trade instruments a state may use its power to intervene in a foreign country's domestic structure in order to undo the latter's institutional advantages or to impose the same socio-economic framework that it itself has.[43] By simply using the power of its import market a state may impose the conditions of trade and thus alter the policies and structures of a foreign country.[44] Trade instruments are nothing more than the old strategy of "the carrot and the stick".[45] Reverse convergence—the adaptation to its own domestic structures— may be demanded as a condition for free trade when access to the market of a larger country is made conditional on the smaller country accepting foreign intervention in its domestic structures.[46] However, reverse convergence will be much more successful when addressing government policies rather than when dealing with those practices affecting trade which are deeply embedded in a market's industrial organisation and society.[47]

---

[42] See Susan Strange, *States and Markets* (Pinter Publishers, 1988), 24.

[43] See J. Rogers Hollingsworth and Wolfgang Streeck, "Countries and Sectors: Concluding Remarks on Performance, Convergence and Competitiveness", in Hollingsworth, Schmitter & Streeck (eds), *Governing Capitalist Economies: Performance & Control of Economic Sectors* (Oxford University Press, 1994), 270, 282–283.

[44] See J.H. Jackson, "Perspectives on Countervailing Duties" (1989) 21 *L & Pol'y Int'l Bus* 739.

[45] A way of understanding this is through game theory. See Hans Rieger, "Game Theory and the Analysis of Protectionist Trends" (19867) 9 *World Econ* 171; see *also* William Mock, "Game Theory, Signalling and International Legal Relations" (1992) 26 *Geo Wash J Int'l L & Econ* 33; K.W. Abbot, "Modern International Relations Theory: A Prospectus for International Lawyers" (1989) 14 *Yale J Int'l L* 335; Robert Axelrod and R.O. Keohane, "Achieving Cooperation under Anarchy: Strategies and Institutions' (1985) 38 *World Pol'y* 226; John Conybear, "Trade Wars: A Comparative Study of Anglo-Hanse, Franco-Italian and Hawley-Smoot Conflicts" (1985) 38 *World Pol'y* 147; Kenneth Oye, "Explaining Cooperation Under Anarchy" (1985) 38 *World Pol'y* 1; A.O. Sykes, "Constructive Unilateral Threats in International Commercial Relations: The Limited Case for Section 301" (1992) 23(2) *L & Pol'y Int'l Bus* 263; Robert Axelrod, *The Evolution of Cooperation* (Basic Books, 1984); Robert O. Keohane, "Reciprocity in International Relations" (1986) 40(1) *Int'l Org* 1; Richard Diamond, "Changes in the Game: Understanding the Relationship Between Section 301 and U.S. Trade Strategies" (1990) 8(2) *BU Int'l J* 351; S.A. Coffield, "Using Section 301 of the Trade Act as a Response to Foreign Government Trade Actions: When, Why and How" (1981) 6 *NCJ Int'l L & Com Reg* 381; R.E. Hudec, "Thinking About the New Section 301: Beyond Good and Evil", in J. Bhagwati and H.T. Patrick (eds), *Aggressive Unilateralism: America's 301 Trade Policy and the World Trading System* (Harvester Wheatsheaf, 1991), 113.

[46] See G.R. Saxonhouse, "A Short Summary of the Long History of Unfair Trade Allegations against Japan", in J.N. Bhagwati and R.E. Hudec (eds), *Fair Trade and Harmonization: Prerequisites for Free Trade?* (The MIT Press, 1996), 472, 501 (analysing the US Super 301 and the Structural Impediments Initiative against Japan. But the author considers that the U.S. initiative was successful because in Japan there were some domestic calls, such as the Maekawa Commission Report, for such changes); Nayyar Zuberi, "Disregard for EU Laws Would Mean Ouster from World Market", *Business Recorder*, 12 March 1997, 8.

[47] See John McMillan, "Why Does Japan Resist Foreign Market-Opening Pressure?", in J.N. Bhagwati and R.E. Hudec (eds), *Fair Trade and Harmonization: Prerequisites for Free Trade?* (The MIT Press, 1996), Vol. I, 515.

Unfair trade instruments may also be used to build up an international trade regime which is compatible with a state's own domestic structures.[48] By using trade instruments against foreign countries, states may create precedent and establish the standards of the future international regime. An international regime may be defined as a set of explicit or implicit principles, norms, rules and decision-making procedures around which actor expectations converge in a given area of international relations.[49] International regimes are not simply neutral. Regimes reflect the underlying power and interests of the dominant hegemonic states. International trade regimes should thus be seen as institutions that establish the standards for the socio-economic world market framework. Powerful states will try to impose regimes which reflect their own market economy's framework. The construction of international economic regimes is thus exactly analogous to domestic regime building in that both, by defining the cultural, social and political rules under which economic transactions may take place, determine which firms' strategies and capacities will have competitive advantage over others.[50]

One way of understanding this is to focus on subsidies. A state can impose countervailing duties to restrain the use of subsidies and influence the future agenda of negotiations on subsidies. However, despite its possible economic rationale, limiting subsidies is not neutral. Restraining the use of subsidies implies limiting a way of government intervention in the economy. Such limitation most benefits those countries which have traditionally had a weak government and thus, even if international rules allowed for subsidies, it would not be so easy for it to grant them. On the other hand, limiting subsidies will seriously handicap countries which traditionally have had a strong and interventionist government.

In this sense, distinguishing between defensive and offensive trade instruments is somewhat limited. Arguably, anti-dumping and countervailing duties would protect domestic producers from the unfair trade of a foreign producer, whereas market access instruments would try to open up unfair foreign markets for domestic producers. But this is only to a certain extent. In practice, defensive instruments may also indirectly (and therefore less efficiently) be offensive. It all depends on the magnitude of the asymmetrical relationship between the different trading partners. Indeed, unfair trade laws seem to benefit countries with big import and export markets in contrast to countries with small markets.[51]

---

[48] See D.W. Leebron, "Lying Down with Procrustes: An Analysis of Harmonization Claims", in ibid., 41 (arguing that instruments such as section 301 could be attempts of unilateral harmonisation. The author considers, however, that such efforts are only partially successful and are, for the most part, aimed at bilateral harmonisation rather than multilateral harmonisation.)

[49] See J.A. Finlayson and M.W. Zacher, "The GATT and the Regulation of Trade Barriers: Regime Dynamics and Functions" (1981) 35 *International Organisation* 561; see also B.M. Hoekman, "Multilateral Trade Negotiations and Coordination of Commercial Policies", in R. Stern (ed.), *The Multilateral Trading System—Analysis and Options for Change* (Harvester Wheatsheaf, 1993), 29.

[50] See Hollingsworth and Streeck, above at n. 43, 282.

[51] See J.H. Jackson, *Restructuring the GATT System* (Chatham House Papers, 1990).

The possibility of anti-dumping and countervailing duties being offensive in an indirect manner can be illustrated by the following example. Think of country A which, because of a long-standing political and economic closeness, has a domestic economic system which is different to that of most of the biggest world trading partners.[52] Imagine that, as many countries, country A is desperate to obtain foreign income in order to import new technologies and improve its economy. One of the most important means of country A to obtain foreign income is an intensive export policy.[53] Thus, it decides to massively export steel or chemical products in which it is most competitive. Yet, imagine that the countries with the biggest export markets for steel and chemical products develop a countervailing or anti-dumping methodology which severely punishes products coming from domestic economic systems such as that of country A. As a result of this, its products are systematically subject to duties and thus partially lose their original competitiveness. What can country A do? It can keep its domestic economic system and thus its export products, or it can start to change its economy, play by the rules of its biggest export markets, and improve its anti-dumping profile.[54]

However, country A may still have a third way, which, while not necessarily providing a complete solution, may smooth its transformation process. Country A may try to play with the domestic structures of its targeting country. Indeed, the ability to impose the rules of the game does not rely exclusively on economic power. It depends also on the domestic structures which affect the taking of trade policy decisions. To influence the international regime for their benefit, states have to act rationally and as monoliths. States are required to act efficiently and with one voice as if there were no internal domestic differences. But globalisation itself creates the paradox. Due to the increasing effects of globalisation in the internal sphere, trade relations can no longer be considered to be an issue for a reduced number of experts. Rather, all different constitutional units of power within a state will want to have a voice.[55] Thus, states will need to develop constitutional procedures which will provide the necessary domestic legitimacy to act effectively in a global system characterised by diversity. Through constitutional procedures, states will try to solve the paradox by creating mechanisms for co-operation which allow a voice to the different powers, while at the same time permitting the state to have a uniform voice in the external sphere.

[52] An illustration of this example could be Spain in its transition period from a Franquist system to its full political and economic integration in the EC.

[53] It could also do so by attracting foreign investment.

[54] A few years ago I had a great discussion with an American room-mate. I argued that we Spaniards had the right to subsidise our industries as a way of improving our economy and keeping our social welfare state. He said: "Sure, you can subsidise but we do not want your subsidised products. If you subsidise we will impose countervailing duties against your exports". But then I thought: "If we cannot sell our products to the United States, who is going to buy them? So either we stop subsidising or we do not export".

[55] See G.R. Winham, "Robert Strauss, the MTN, and the Control of Faction" (1980) 14 *J World Trade L* 377.

However, political action prescribed by formal constitutions is part of a much wider socio-economic context.[56] Because countries have diverse market frameworks, they respond differently to globalisation.[57] To understand why constitutional political actors behave as they do it is important to consider their socio-economic context. Thus, not all trading partners can solve the paradox of globalisation to the same extent. In this sense, the EU shows the extent to which domestic structures can seriously affect a trade policy outcome. The persistence of different domestic structures and thus of different market economies within the EU leads the Member States to a constant conflict regarding trade policy and thus to second best outcomes. The Single Market Initiative has not created a single Community market economy framework. Instead, while allowing for a thin Anglo-Saxon homogenisation, it has failed to remove the different national socio-economic frameworks in which the fifteen market economies are rooted.[58] As a result, the EU Member States continue to be divided between those which are characterised by a tradition of strong intervention, such as France, Greece, Italy, Spain and Portugal, and those which are characterised by market corporativism which replaces the need for state intervention, such as Germany, the Netherlands, Denmark and Sweden. Because Member States have different market structures, they perceive differently globalisation and, thus, they are in a constant conflict with regard to international trade. This in turn implies the lack of a uniform and efficient strategy in the international trading system to impose the rules of the game. Indeed, the great challenge for the EU is to deal efficiently with global diversity by creating legitimacy procedures on the basis of domestic heterogeneity.

III THE EU'S ANTI-DUMPING METHODOLOGY AGAINST JAPAN

The Background

Between 1980 and 1996 the Community imposed massive anti-dumping duties against Japanese exports of electronic products, which radically changed the economic and political relations between the two partners.[59] One of the most

---

[56] See Tony Prosser, "The State, Constitutions and Implementing Economic Policy: Privatization and the U.K., France and the U.S.A" (1995) 4 *Social and Legal Studies* 507.

[57] See R.O. Keohane, "The World Political Economy and the Crisis of Embedded Liberalism", in J.H. Goldthorpe (ed.), *Order and Conflict in Contemporary Capitalism: Studies in the Political Economy of Western European Nations* (Clarendon Press, 1984), 15.

[58] See Martin Rhodes and Bastian van Apeldoorn, "Capital Unbound? The Transformation of European Corporate Governance" (1998) 5(3) *European Public Pol'y* 406; see also Kenneth Dyson, "Cultural Issues and the European Single Market: Barriers to Trade and Shifting Attitudes" (1993) 64 *Political Quarterly* 84; Stephen Wilks, "Regulatory Compliance and Capitalist Diversity in Europe" (1996) 3(4) *J European Public Policy* 536.

[59] See Norio Komuro, "EC Antidumping Measures Vis-A-Vis Japan", in *The European Union in a Changing World*, Third ECSA-WORLD Conference, Brussels, 19–20 September 1996, 107.

important legal issues within the dumping determinations of these proceedings was the "asymmetry" issue when comparing normal value and export price.

In order to understand the "asymmetry" dispute it is necessary to take into account several background issues.

The concept of dumping

First, it is important to revise the concept of dumping. Article VI of GATT defines dumping as the process "by which products of one country are introduced into the commerce of another country at less than the normal value of the products".[60] Due allowance must be made in each case for differences in conditions and terms of sale, for differences in taxation and for other differences affecting price comparability. However, the 1979 GATT Antidumping Code considered:

> "a product as being dumped, i.e. introduced into the commerce of another country at less than its normal value, if the export price of the product exported from one country to another, is less than the comparable price, in the ordinary course of trade, for the like product when destined for consumption in the exporting country".[61]

As we shall see, a main issue in the definition of dumping is whether it is profit discrimination, i.e. selling at lower profits abroad than in the home market, or price discrimination, i.e. charging a higher price in one country than in another. While considering dumping as profit discrimination would imply taking into account all the differences in costs in each market and, thus, would equalise both markets, price discrimination would take account only of different costs of different markets as long as it can be proved that such costs clearly affect the different prices and, thus, would penalise the existence of different markets.[62] The idea of dumping as price discrimination would be based on the asymmetrical access of markets, i.e. dumping would be possible because the domestic markets are closed and, thus, the costs do not necessarily affect the price.[63] The fact is that the international rules do not provide a clear definition.

[60] Under Art. VI(1) of GATT, "a product is to be considered as being introduced into the commerce of an importing country at less than its normal value if the product exported from country to another is less than the comparable price in the ordinary course of trade, for the like product when destined for consumption in the exporting country, or, in the absence of such domestic price, is less than either the highest comparable price for the like product for export to any third country in the ordinary course of trade or the cost of production in the country of origin plus a reasonable amount for selling cost and profit".

[61] See Art. 2(1) of *Agreement on Implementation of Article VI of the General Agreement on Tariffs and Trade* (GATT, 1979); 26th Supp. BISD 171 (1980). Article 2(1) of the WTO Antidumping Code repeats the 1979 Antidumping Code. See Art. 2(1) of the *Agreement on the Implementation of Article VI of GATT 1994*.

[62] For the argument that dumping can only be defined as profit discrimination see Paul Waer and Edwin Vermulst, "The GATT Panel Report on the EC Anti-Dumping Proceedings Concerning Audio Tapes in Cassettes: Back to Basics in the Concept of Dumping?" (1995) 29(6) *J World Trade* 31, 44; compare with Wolfgang Muller, Nicholas Khan and Hans-Adolf Neumann, *EC Anti-Dumping Law—A Commentary on Regulation 384/96* (John Wiley & Sons, 1998), 3–8.

[63] Interview at the Commission, Brussels, May 1997.

The structure of market distribution

Secondly, it is important to understand how the market distribution of a product works. Usually, the producer does not sell directly to the consumer.[64] Instead, the producer sells to the distributor, who in turn sells to the wholesaler, who in turn sells to the dealer, who finally sells to the end-user. This is important because each market actor will have its costs and will wish to make a profit. Furthermore, if the producer can control the distribution chain of its products it might control its market sector.

Direct and indirect costs

Thirdly, we must understand the difference between direct costs and indirect costs (variable/fixed costs). Direct costs (variable costs) would be all those costs which directly influence making an economic transaction. Thus, they would include transport, production, handling, taxes, etc. Indirect costs (fixed costs) are all those expenses which the economic agent has, independently of whether or not it makes the transaction. Indirect costs are the general, selling and administrative expenses of the producer.[65]

Japan's diversity

Finally, we should be aware of the market organisation of Japan. Indeed, the Japanese market illustrates the extent to which international trade is based not only on exchange rates set by capital markets and legal barriers set by governments, but also by concrete relationships among the different market actors that actually make the buying and selling decisions.[66] The pattern of Japan as a cohesive market based on consensual ordering has reflected itself in the existence of complex networks of long-term contractual relationships and the persuasive reliance on relational contracting, the *keiretsu*.[67]

---

[64] Though this is increasingly changing with Internet.

[65] However, to a certain extent, whether costs are variable or fixed depends on the market economy of the economic agent. See J.H. Jackson, *The World Trading System: Law and Policy of International Economic Relations* (The MIT Press, 1989), 218–223.

[66] See Michael Gerlach, "Keiretsu Organization in the Japanese Economy: Analysis and Trade Implications", in C. Johnson *et al.* (eds), *Politics and Productiviety: How Japan's Development Strategy Works* (Harper Business, 1989), 141.

[67] See J.O. Haley, "Luck, Law, Culture and Trade: The Intractability of United States-Japan Trade Conflict" (1989) 22 *Cornell Int'l LJ* 403, 416; see also T.J. Pempel, "Japanese Economic Policy, The Domestic Bases for International Behaviour", in *Between Power and Plenty: Foreign Economic Policies of Advanced Industrial States* (The University of Wisconsin Press, 1978), 139; see also John McMillan, "Why Does Japan Resist Foreign Market-Opening Pressure?", in J.N. Bhagwati and R.E. Hudec (eds), *Fair Trade and Harmonization: Prerequisites for Free Trade?* (The MIT Press, 1996), Vol. I, 515; Nobuyuki Yasuda, "Social Clause, Human Rights and East Asian Legal Culture", paper presented in the seminar *Globalisation and European Union Law*, European University Institute, Spring 1996.

The word *keiretsu* literally means "affiliated chain".[68] They are not formal organisations in the legal sense, but instead are loosely organised alliances within the social world of the Japanese business community.[69] The relevance of these social and economic networks is highlighted by the fact that they take place in a system where the Japanese Government delegates most of its regulation power to private market actors.[70]

There are basically two types of *keiretsu*: horizontal *keiretsu* and vertical *keiretsu*. An horizontal *keiretsu* is like a corporate convoy where large groups of companies travel together and keep an eye on each other around an identity enterprise, usually a large city bank, next to a trading company and a few giant insurance and industrial firms.[71] There are no formal structures within the groups; instead, they are organised by two processes. Whereas the core members of the group meet in informal councils to define the overall interests of the group, the flow of resources affecting ownership, finance and trade are the manifestation of such defined interests.

The vertical *keiretsu* overlap usually with the horizontal groups. Most of the big companies of the horizontal group are heads of their own vertical *keiretsu*. These may be production *keiretsu*, consisting in a pyramid of suppliers and assemblers providing goods to the parent company, and distribution *keiretsu*, a pyramid of enterprises that market the goods of the main firm. Many times, the vertical groups are composed of production and distribution *keiretsu* so that they look like two pyramids put together by their main points, with the main firm in the intersection.

Because the *keiretsu* developed as heterogeneous networks with a stake in all sectors of the Japanese economy, they are compelled to compete ferociously between themselves to survive in the Japanese market.[72] *Keiretsu* are not sector wide cartels which guarantee short-term profits. Instead, the overall benefit of the *keiretsu* is security and long-term economic viability. However, while the *keiretsu* compete between themselves, such a set of cohesive structures is a strong barrier to the entrance of newcomers. Only those companies which are part of a group are able to survive economically. For our purposes the most problematic *keiretsu* are the vertical distribution *keiretsu*. During the 1960s the

[68] See Toby Myerson, "Barriers to Trade in Japan: The Keiretsu System-Problems and Prospects" (1992) 24 *Int'l L & Politics* 1107, 1108.

[69] See G.K. Bader, "The Keiretsu System of Japan; Its Steadfast Existence Despite Heightened Foreign and Domestic Pressure for Dissolution", (1994) 27 *Cornell Int' LJ* 365. As to the historical roots of the *keiretsu*, see Kenichi Miyashita and David Russell, *Keiretsu: Inside the Hidden Japanese Conglomerates* (McGraw-Hill, 1994), 21–33; see also James Fallows, *Looking at the Sun: The Rise of the New East Asian Economic and Political System* (Pantheon Books, 1994), 72–116.

[70] See F.K. Upham, "Privatized Regulation: Japanese Regulatory Style in Comparative and International Perspective" (1996) 20(2) *Fordham Int'l LJ* 396. The great difference between Japan and the European corporativist systems is that while in the latter the role of market actors has a public sanction, in Japan regulation is privatised and many times secret (ibid., 495).

[71] There are six big horizontal *keiretsu* in the Japanese economy. These are Mitsubishi, Mitsui, Sumitono, Fuji, Sanwa and Dai-Ichi Kangyo. See Gerlach, above at n. 66, 144.

[72] See John Zysman, "How Institutions Create Historically Rooted Trajectories of Growth" (1994) 3(1) *Industrial & Corporate Change* 243, 249–251.

electronic and auto industries developed huge networks of affiliated distributors. The producers supplied the goods, the marketing tools and most of all the prestige, while the small dealers provided the shop and labour. Thus, the producer bore most of the marketing costs but in return the small dealer had to be loyal to its brand names. The main advantage of the system was savings for the parent firm, as the affiliated firms forming part of the vertical *keiretsu* and distributing the goods to the dealers shared in the marketing costs. Because the producers controlled the entire retail network, they could control the price of the products and the entrance of newcomers. Therefore, competition by cheaper alien products became limited and thus the competition between the different *keiretsu* focused on the quality of the goods and on developing even larger distribution networks as close as possible to the consumers.

The result of this process is that while it is extremely difficult for foreigners to enter the Japanese market, Japanese producers have the necessary domestic economic support to compete in foreign markets. Indeed, for years the European institutions have claimed that the Japanese distribution systems are the main barriers to market access which allow Japanese firms to dump in foreign markets.[73] However, whether this issue is fair or unfair depends on whether we consider fairness as strict market share reciprocity, and thus to a certain extent similar market organisation, or we take fairness to mean national treatment, i.e. treating foreigners in the same way that Japanese are treated. Because Japanese producers face themselves with equally severe restrictions in the access to distribution networks and other prerequisites for new entry in their home Japanese market as foreign entrants, to ensure reciprocity of market share to foreign producers would in fact imply special favours for foreigners.[74] Indeed, the entire distribution structure does not necessarily provide more profits to the overall entity but rather a security which is the result of a very long-term investment and a sense of mutual loyalty between firms. The entire distribution network implies huge costs which are in fact met by the producer or its subsidiaries.

EU's asymmetry methodology

The eagerness of the Community institutions to gain credibility and authority led them to develop an "asymmetrical" comparison methodology with the purpose of dealing with what was considered to be the "Japanese problem".[75] This concern was two-sided. On the one hand, despite tariff reduction and govern-

---

[73] See Hiroko Yamane, "E.U. Efforts to Open the Japanese Market: Government, Market, Structure and Private Practices" (1998) *EFA Rev* 481, 501; see also Ron Schiran, *Dumping by Japanese Companies*, 553–556; *Communication from the European Communities, Japan— Nullification or Impairment of the benefits Accruing to the EEC under the General Agreement and Impediment to the Attainment of GATT Objectives*, L/5479, 8 April 1983.

[74] See Haley, above at n. 67, 420.

[75] See Christopher Norall, "New Trends in Anti-Dumping Practice in Brussels" (1987) *World Economy* 97, 98; see also Brian Hindley, "Dumping and the Far East Trade of the European Community" (1988) 11 *World Economy* 445, 446.

ment liberalisation, the Japanese electronic market continued to be closed to European and third country products. On the other hand, and for many as a result of this, Japan continued to gain market share and to drive out European producers from the electronic sector. The panic concerned both the loss of employment opportunities and the technology race as European industries were losing out in the "sun-rising products". Thus, the EC institutions took advantage of the looseness of the Antidumping Code and the EC Antidumping Regulation and developed a series of methodologies, the result of which clearly discriminated against Japanese electronic producers.[76] The purpose was twofold. First, it attempted to stop the flow of Japanese products into the European market. Secondly, to a certain extent, the Community used its anti-dumping measures as a second-best instrument to punish and break into what it considered to be the Japanese closed market system. However, as we shall see, not only the results of the approach were limited but, in the process, the Community as a whole would lose its international credibility and frictions would arise between Member States. The Community would be trapped in the paradox of globalisation.

A determination of dumping consists in a comparison between the price of the product exported to the Community and the normal value of the identical or closely similar product. Hence, to asses whether dumping exists it will be necessary to make three basic calculations: (a) the determination of normal value, (b) the calculation of export price and (c) a fair comparison between the export price and the normal value.[77] The Community would fashion each of these calculations in such a way as to discriminate products from Japan and other Asian countries.

The concept of "economic single entity"

First, in determining the normal value, the Community developed the striking concept of "economic single entity". In general, normal value is established on the basis of the comparable price actually paid or payable for the like product in the ordinary course of trade in the exporting country. However, for the purposes of establishing the normal value, "prices between parties which appear to be associated or to have a compensatory arrangement with each other may not be considered to be in the ordinary course of trade unless it is determined that they are unaffected by the relationship".[78] In the context of market distribution networks, the sales between the producers and distributors with which they have an association or compensatory agreement are not used and, instead, the Community takes as the domestic price that charged to the first independent

---

[76] See Edwin Vermulst and Paul Waer, *EC Anti-Dumping Law and Practice* (Sweet & Maxwell, 1996), 182.

[77] See Francis Snyder, *International Trade and Customs Law of the European Union* (Butterworths, 1998), 214–229.

[78] Art. 2(1) of Council Regulation No. 384/96 (OJ 1996 L56/1), as amended.

buyer.[79] The normal value calculated at the level of the price charged to the independent buyer will normally be higher than that charged by the producer to the related distributor since the resale price charged by the related distributor will have to cover the extra cost which it has incurred.[80] The extra costs of the related distributor will in practice be both direct and indirect.

The Community interprets the term "associated" in a functional manner by focusing on the existence of a single economic unit as opposed to a legal entity.[81] For the purpose of determining the existence of a "single economic entity", the Community will not focus on the legal structure of such entity but instead will make: (a) a functional analysis, i.e. whether the function of the sales companies is to sell or facilitate the selling of the producer's goods; (b) an equity analysis, i.e. whether the producer controls the equity of the distributor; and (c) a management analysis, i.e. whether there are strong links between the companies with respect to management personnel and staff. In practice, the Community will treat parties as associated where there is at least 5 per cent of common shareholding.[82] Thus, in *Certain Electronic Scales Originating in Japan*, the Commission stated with regard to the producer Tokyo Electronic Co.:[83]

> "On further investigation of the case, however, the Commission arrived at the conclusion that, within the framework of the Tokyo Electronic Co.'s organisation, both manufacturing firm and sales company formed parts of the one corporate structure, the sales company fulfilling functions substantially similar to those of sales branch or sales department. The fact that the sales company in law constitutes an independent undertaking does not alter the fact that one is dealing here with a single economic entity. What is of relevance in this case is not the legal structure but the fact that the main function of the sales company is to sell, or promote the sale of, the corporate product and that it is controlled by the corporate parent company whether because of majority share ownership or otherwise.
>
> In the case of the Tokyo Electric Co., its sales company is controlled by the corporate parent company and its exclusive function is to sell the corporate products on the

---

[79] The GATT basis for this approach would be the emphasis of Art. 2(1) of the Antidumping Code on "the ordinary course of trade" when determining the normal value. The Commission argues that sales between associated firms or those which have compensatory arrangements cannot be considered to be in the ordinary course of trade. See *Certain Thermal Paper Originating in Japan* (OJ 1991 L270/15); see also *Certain Compact Disc Players Originating in Japan* (OJ 1990 L12/21); *Drams from Japan* (OJ 1990 L193/1); *Plain Paper Photocopies Originating in Japan* (OJ 1986 L239/5) (recital 7) (where the Commission argued: "Despite certain exporters' claims to the contrary, the Commission considered that it would be inappropriate to take account of any transfer price between related companies or branches of any exporter when establishing normal value by means of domestic prices, these prices not being those paid or payable in the ordinary course of trade for the like product. Accordingly, only prices to independent purchasers were used for the determination of normal value"); Paul Waer, "Constructed Normal Values in EC Dumping Margin Calculations—Fiction or Realistic Approach? (1993) 27(4) *J World Trade* 5.

[80] See Ivo Van Bael and Jean-Francois Bellis, *Anti-Dumping and other Trade Protection Laws of the EC* (CCH, 3rd ed. 1996), 66.

[81] See Vermulst and Waer, above at n. 76, 179.

[82] Ibid., 182.

[83] *Certain Electronic Scales Originating in Japan* (OJ 1985 L275/5) (recital 15); see also *Electronic Weighing Scales Originating in Japan* (OJ 1993 L104/4).

domestic market. The sales company is therefore to be seen as part of its corporate structure and only selling prices charged by this company to clients independent of it can be regarded as occurring in the ordinary course of trade and therefore be taken to reflect the product's true normal value".

The Commission's rationale has been that only by taking into account the prices charged by the subsidiaries is it possible to ensure that costs which would be an integral part of the selling price were the same made by the exporter's internal sales department, are taken into account in cases where the selling activity is carried out by the company which, although a legal entity, is controlled by the manufacturer.[84] All costs (both direct and indirect) should be included because all such costs would be included in the selling price if the marketing had been carried out by the producer.

The ECJ has upheld this approach in determining the normal value. Thus, in *Silver Seiko* v. *Council*,[85] the Court held:

"The division of production and sales activities within a group made up of legally distinct companies can in no way alter the fact that the group is a single economic entity which carries out in that way activities that are in other cases carried out by what is in legal terms as well a single entity. By taking into consideration the sales subsidiary's prices it is possible to ensure that costs which manifestly form part of the selling price of a product where the sale is made by an internal sales department of the manufacturing organisation are not left out of account where the same selling activity is carried out by a company which, despite being financially controlled by the manufacturer, is a legally distinct entity".

If the normal value must be constructed, the Community institutions will include all costs from both the producer and the related subsidiaries. The Community will include the direct expenses as well as the selling, general and administrative expenses of both firms.[86] As the aim of constructing the normal

---

[84] See Muller, Khan and Neumann, above at n. 62, 69.

[85] Joined Cases 273/85 and 107/86 [1988] ECR 5927; see also Joined Cases 277 and 300/85 *Canon* v. *Council*, [1988] ECR 5731; Case 250/85 *Brother Industries* v. *Council* [1988] ECR 5683; Case 301/85 *Sharp* v. *Council* [1988] ECR 5813; Case C-179/87 *Sharp Corporation* v. *Council* [1992] ECR I-1635. The Court's single economic entity argument seems to be applied inconsistently, however. In *Gao Yao* v. *Council* where the Court, having to decide whether a firm in Hong Kong which was basically owned by a Chinese firm, thus, in practice, both being the same economic entity, should have legal standing as representing the whole entity, simply stated that both firms were separate legal entities (Case C-75/92 *Gao Yao (Hong Kong) Hua Fa Industrial Co. Ltd.* v. *Council of the European Union* [1994] ECR I-3141). The Advocate-General argued instead that both firms should be considered as a single economic entity and thus Gao Yao should be granted legal standing.

[86] See *Certain Types of Electronic Microcircuits known as DRAMs Originating in Japan* (OJ 1990 L20/5) (recitals 48–50) (where: "Constructed values were determined by adding cost of production and a reasonable margin of profit. The cost of production was computed on the basis of all costs both fixed and variable, incurred in Japan, of materials and manufacturer to which was added a reasonable amount for selling, administrative and other general expenses and profit. . . Cost of production was established by examining the economic entity of the exporter with regard to its activities on the Japanese market. They were computed on the basis of the full costs of the parent/manufacturer company and the full costs of any sales subsidiary or related companies performing the function of a sales department for the parent company. In this sense, transactions between the parent/manufacturing company and its sales company were disregarded and transactions by the

value is to determine the selling price of the product as if it were sold in the country of origin, the Community considers that all the expenses (direct and indirect plus their related profits) of the related subsidiary should be taken into account.

Determination of export price

The Community has developed an export price methodology which assumes that the European market is and should be a perfect, plural market. Thus, it has considered that the rules for the establishment of the export price are completely different from those of the normal value. The export price is the price actually paid or payable for the product when sold for export from the exporting country to the Community.[87] The export price is the price at which the product leaves the country of exportation, not the price at which it enters the Community market. It is the price of the product before entering the Community frontier. Where there is no export price or where it appears that the export price is unreliable because of an association or a compensatory arrangement between the exporter and the importer or a third party, the export price may be constructed on the basis of the price at which the imported products are first resold to an independent buyer, or are not resold in the condition in which they were imported, on any reasonable basis.[88] Unreliability is assumed from the mere fact that there is, or it appears that there is, an association or compensatory arrangement.[89] Importers and exporters are usually considered to be associated if there are links between them other than those which exist in a straight arm's-length, buyer–seller relationship. In such cases, the Community institutions will take the price to the first independent buyer and then deduct all the expenses which have been incurred between the importation of the product and the final sale to the independent buyer. The purpose of this construction is to enable a price at the Community frontier which is not influenced by the relationship between the producer/exporter and its associated importer.[90] Thus in *Electronic Weighing Scales Originating in Singapore and the Republic of Korea*,[91] the Council held:

"... the Commission came to the conclusion that this price could not be regarded as the export price since it became clear, from the limited information made available to the Commission, that the related company in the Community was concerned with

sales company to independent customers were taken into consideration for normal value purposes").

[87] Art. 2(8) of Council Regulation 384/96, as amended.

[88] Ibid., Art. 2(8). This provision basically follows Art. 2(5) of the Agreement on Implementation of Art. VI of GATT, 26th Supp BISD 171 (1980), as well as Art. 2(3) of the Agreement on Implementation of Article VI of GATT 1994.

[89] See Van Bael and Bellis, above at n. 80, 107.

[90] See *Housed Bearing Units Originating in Japan* (OJ 1987 L35/32) (recital 13); *Compare with Electronic Weighing Scales Originating in Japan* (OJ 1993 L104/4) (recital 21); see also *Certain Compact Disc Players Originating in Japan and South Korea* (OJ 1989 L205/5) (recital 13) (where, as sales were made to independent importers in the Community, export prices were determined on the basis of the prices actually paid or payable for the product sold for export to the Community).

[91] OJ 1993 L263/1 (recital 6).

sales to unrelated customers by virtue of processing orders, performing marketing functions, invoicing these customers in the Community and receiving payment.

This related company therefore incurred costs normally born by an importer. In these circumstances, the export price was constructed on the basis of the price to the first independent buyer...

Consequently, the price actually paid to the related company in the Community by the first independent customer was adjusted by the costs of this related company".

The Community will make adjustments for all costs, including duties and taxes, incurred between importation and resale, and for profits accruing to establish a reliable price at the Community frontier level.[92] The Community will reduce from the price to the first independent buyer all the costs which would have normally been borne by an independent importer.[93] It will actually deduct both the direct and indirect costs (selling, general and administrative expenses) of the related importer plus profit.[94]

The asymmetric comparison

Finally, the Community implemented an asymmetry methodology in comparing export price and normal value. Once the export price and the normal value have been determined it is necessary to compare both prices. The problem with regard to Japanese imports was that whereas the normal value was at the level of the sale from the related distributor to the first independent buyer, the export price was at a level corresponding to prior importation. Thus, whereas the normal value included all costs (direct and indirect plus their related profits) of the related distributor and producer, the export price included only the cost of the producer.

A fair comparison would require adjustments to be made so that both prices reflected the same level of trade and the same product.[95] Thus, Article VI of GATT required due allowance for differences in conditions and terms of sale, for differences in taxation, and for other differences affecting price comparability. Prior to the 1979 Anti-dumping Regulation, the Community maintained a flexible approach towards the possibility of making adjustments.[96] However, in

---

[92] See Art. 2(9)(b) of Council Regulation 384/96, as amended.

[93] Note that under Community law, it is the importer who is supposed to pay all import duties and taxes.

[94] The items for which adjustment is made are *inter alia* usual transport, insurance, handling, loading and ancillary costs, customs duties, any anti-dumping duties, any other taxes payable in the importing country by reason of the importation or sale of the goods, as well as a reasonable margin for selling, general administrative costs and profit. See Art. 2(9)(c) Council Regulation 384/96, as amended. In this sense, the Community takes as profit that of an independent importer and not that of the related importer. See *Certain Hydraulic Excavators Originating in Japan* (OJ 1985 L68/13) (recital 11); see also *Certain magnetic disks from the United States, Mexico and Malaysia* (OJ 1985 L249/3); Joined Cases 273/85 and 107/86 *Silver Seiko* v. *Council* [1988] ECR 5927.

[95] Sometimes, the constructed value and the export price could be based on like products which had some differences.

[96] See Van Bael and Bellis, above at n. 80, 114.

1979, in implementing the Tokyo Antidumping Code, the Community changed its approach radically and adopted the principle that no adjustments should be made for indirect costs.[97] Council Regulation No. 2423/88 established an exhaustive list of adjustments which, again, excluded indirect costs of the domestic selling subsidiaries.[98]

The adjustment process, netting back, implied that the export price was established at the ex-factory level, whereas the normal value included the indirect costs, i.e. selling, general and administrative expenses, of the related subsidiaries, plus the amount of profit which was supposed to correspond to such expenses.[99] The Community put forward an economic and a legal argument for this approach. First, it argued that only those adjustments which clearly affected price comparability could be made. It argued that the definition of dumping was based on price comparability and, thus, only those costs which affected price could adjusted. In an open market, prices were influenced by buyers, who were not concerned with the costs of selling overheads, and possibly by other suppliers, whose selling overheads could be different.[100] Only if the producer were able to set the price without constraint, and thus in practice held a monopoly which the Community considered to be the basis of dumping, would the indirect costs affect the final price. From a legal point of view, the Community argued that both the EC and the GATT established different rules for the calculation of the normal value, the export price and the comparison. There was no reason to deviate from this principle merely because of formal structures such as the delegation of certain functions to one or more companies, the corporate structure of the group under company law or the handling of sales by the integrated company department or independent subsidiary.[101] In practice, the Community was comparing markets.

---

[97] See Art. 2(10)(c) and (d) of Council Regulation No. 3017/79 (OJ 1979 L339/1).

[98] The Regulation allowed adjustments for differences in physical characteristics, import charges and indirect taxes, selling expenses resulting from sales made at different levels of trade or in different quantities or under different conditions, and terms of sale. But the selling expenses which could be adjusted were limited to: transport, insurance, handling, and ancillary costs; packing; credit; warranties, guarantees, technical assistance and other after-sales services; and personnel engaged in direct selling activities. See Art. 2(9) of Council Regulation No. 2423/88 (OJ 1988 L209/1). The Court upheld the principle that such list was exhaustive: see Case 204/84 *Toyo Bearing* v. *Council* [1987] ECR 1809; see also Joined Cases 294/86 and 77/87 *Technointorg* v. *Commission and Council* [1988] ECR 6077.

[99] See E.A. Vermulst and Folkert Gaafsma, "A Decade of European Community Anti-Dumping Law and Practice Applicable to Imports from China" (1992) 26 *J World Trade* 5, 24; see also Jean Francois Bellis, "The EEC Antidumping System", in J. Jackson and E. Vermulst (eds), *Antidumping Law and Practice: A Comparative Study* (Harvester Wheatsheaf, 1990), 41.

[100] See J. F. Beseler and A. N. Williams, *Anti-Dumping and Anti-Subsidy Law: The European Communities* (Sweet & Maxwell, 1986), 105.

[101] See *Certain Electronic Scales Originating in Japan* (OJ 1985 L275/5) (recital 25); see also *Certain Compact Disc Players Originating in Japan and South Korea* (OJ 1989 L205/5) (recital 59); *Electronic Typewriters from Japan* (OJ 1985 L163/1); Case 204/84 *Toyo Bearing* v. *Council* [1987] ECR 1809; Case 258/84 *Nippon Seiko* v. *Council* [1987] ECR 1923; Case 260/84 *Minebea* v. *Council* [1987] ECR 1975; Case 250/85 *Brother Industries* v. *Council* [1988] ECR 5683; Joined Cases 277 and 300/85 *Canon Inc.* v. *Council* [1988] ECR 5731; Joined Cases 273/85 and 107/86 *Silver Seiko* v. *Council* [1988] ECR 5927.

By considering that the export price should be established on an arm's-length basis, it was punishing those markets which were different from the ideal perfect market, which the Community was supposed to be. The Japanese producers were being punished because their market was not a plural market characterised by transactions between producers and the chain of distributors on an arm's-length basis, but instead consisted of cohesive groups which expanded from the manufacturer of the product's components to the final sale to the consumer.

The Community limited this approach somewhat by introducing the concept of "selective normal value".[102] If the producer could show that it sold both to related distributors as well as to unrelated distributors, the Community would take as normal value the price of sale to the independent distributor. However, the application of this exception was restricted in practice as the producer had to show that it sold in its domestic market to both related and independent distributors.[103]

One of the most contentious issues of the Uruguay Round of the anti-dumping negotiations was the problem of fair comparison. Japan and other Asian countries pressed for an adjustment for indirect costs when making a fair comparison. The Community, on the other hand, refused such approach, as it considered that a systematic adjustment would imply a redefinition of dumping from price discrimination to profit discrimination.[104] In the end, the contracting parties reached a loose compromise which, while maintaining the requirement of price comparability being affected, required a fair comparison to be made, i.e. that where the export price had been constructed the normal value should be established at the same level of trade and that authorities should indicate to the parties what information is necessary to ensure a fair comparison and shall not impose an unreasonable burden of proof on those parties.[105] Thus, the new Code does not preclude making adjustments for indirect costs and related profits but it does not say that such adjustment should be made *per se* as it always includes the requirement of affecting price comparability.

The Community implemented the new Code by inserting an adjustment for level of trade where, in relation to the distribution chain in both markets, its is shown that the export price is at a different level of trade than the normal value, and the difference has affected price comparability which is demonstrated by consistent and distinct differences in functions and prices of the seller for the different levels of trade in the domestic market of the exporting country.[106] The

---

[102] See Pierre Didier, "EEC Antidumping: The Level of Trade Issue After the Definitive CD Player Regulation; Japanese Proposal to GATT on the Level of Trade Issue" (1990) 24(2) *J World Trade* 103, 104.

[103] See *Electronic Weighing Scales Originating in Japan* (OJ 1993 L104/4) (recital 30); see also *Certain Compact Disc Players Originating in Japan* (OJ 1990 L12/21) (recitals 24–7).

[104] See Muller, Khan and Neumann, above at n. 62, 125.

[105] See Art. 2(4) of the Agreement on Implementation of Article VI of GATT 1994; see also Paul Waer and Edwin Vermulst, "EC Anti-Dumping Law and Practice after the Uruguay Round: A New Lease of Life?" (1994) 28(2) *J World Trade* 5.

[106] See Art. 2(10)(d) of Council Regulation 384/96, as amended.

Community keeps insisting on defining dumping as price discrimination and to consider that not all costs affect price *per se*. As with the selective normal value methodology, the main obstacle is the fact that this provision presupposes that the producer sells at different levels of trade in its domestic market. Furthermore, it is very difficult to prove that prices at the several levels of trade are different from each other on a transaction-by-transaction basis as there may always be specific instances in which sales prices charged at one level of trade overlap with specific sales price at one or more other levels of trade.[107]

Audio tapes in cassettes panel

The asymmetry issue ended up in a GATT dispute-settlement panel.[108] Once again, the GATT dispute-settlement body had to deal with conflicts derived from the existence of different market structures in the international trading system.[109] Japan had brought a complaint against the Community's imposition of anti-dumping duties on audio-cassettes originating in Japan in 1991.[110]

[107] See Paulette Vander Schueren, "New Anti-Dumping Rules and Practice: Wide Discretion Held on a Tight Leash?" (1996) 33 *CML Rev* 271, 284; see also Edwin Vermulst and Paul Waer, "The Post Uruguay Round EC Anti-Dumping Regulation- After a Pit Stop, Back in the Race" (1995) 29(2) *J World Trade* 53, 59; E.R. McClafferty, "Identifying Level of Trade in U.S. Antidumping Law" (1996) 36(4) *Virginia J Int'l L* 1021, 1064; *Stainless Steel Fasteners and Parts Thereof Originating in the People's Republic of China, India, the Republic of Korea, Malaysia, Taiwan and Thailand* (OJ 1998 L50/1) (recital 38) (where a claim for adjustment was granted because the companies provided sufficient evidence showing that a part of domestic sales was made at a level of trade different to export sales and that this difference affected price comparability. The Community considered that there were consistent and distinct differences in the functions and prices of the two companies for the different levels of trade. Consequently, the claim was granted and the calculation based on a comparison of the domestic and export sales to traders only where they were made in sufficient quantities to be representative); compare with *Advertising Matches Originating in Japan* (OJ 1997 L158/8) (recital 20) (where the Community rejected a claim for adjustment because it was established that for sales on the domestic market to the different categories of unrelated customers no discernible differences could be established, either in the quantities sold or in the pattern of prices charged. In most cases, it could also not be demonstrated that the different categories of customer on the domestic market would de facto have different functions in the distribution channel between producers and end users); see also *Personal Fax Machines Originating in the People's Republic of China, Japan, Republic of Korea, Malaysia, Singapore, Taiwan and Thailand* (OJ 1998 L128/1) (recital 33); *Bicycles Originating in Taiwan* (OJ 1998 L10/26) (recital 36) (where the company failed to show any consistent and distinct differences in functions and prices of the seller for the different levels of trade in the domestic market).

[108] *EC—Anti-Duties on Audio Tapes in Cassettes Originating in Japan*, ASP/136, 8 April 1995. Although the panel report was delivered in 1995, Japan had brought the case in 1993 and its claims referred to the Tokyo Anti-dumping Code. Thus, the dispute-settlement procedure was governed by that of the Tokyo Agreements and not by the new WTO dispute-settlement agreement.

[109] Among other GATT panels dealing with the issue of different domestic structures are *Japan—Restrictions on Imports of Certain Agricultural Products*, L/6253, 22 March 1988, BISD 35 Supp 163; *Japan, Trade in Semi-Conductors*, L/6309, 24 March 1988, BISD 35 Supp 116; *United States—Imposition of Countervailing Duties on Certain Hot-Rolled Lead and Bismuth Carbon Steel Products Originating in France, Germany and the United Kingdom*, SCM/185, 15 November 1994. Of course the most recent and famous one is *Japan—Measures Affecting Consumer Photographic Film and Paper*, WTO/DS44/R, 31 March 1998.

[110] See *Audio Tapes in Cassettes Originating in Japan, the Republic of Korea and Hong Kong* (OJ 1990 L313/5) (provisional); see also *Audio Tapes in Cassettes Originating in Japan, the*

Amongst the several claims brought by Japan the most important one was the Community's asymmetric methodology.[111]

The arguments of the parties were those which had been put forward for more than a decade.[112] Japan insisted on the Antidumping Code's requirement of fairness when comparing normal value and export price.[113] Thus, Article 2 of the Code had to be read as a whole requiring a fair determination of dumping. Fairness implied comparing like with like. If adjustments were made on the export price, the same adjustments should be made on the domestic price used for normal value.

The Community argued that there was no such symmetry requirement in the Code. The Agreement only established rules concerning the determination of normal value, export price and a comparison where adjustments should be made if these affected price comparability. The rules on the determination of export price and the determination of normal value had a different rationale. One set of rules was intended to establish the export price as if it had been based on an arm's-length basis, the other set aimed at determining the price of the product destined for consumption in the domestic market. In making the comparison there could be no allowance for the indirect costs of the related subsidiaries because these in an open market did not affect price comparability.

In fact, the main argument was the definition of dumping. Thus, the parties' main difference laid on whether anti-dumping should be used as an instrument to compare markets and punish those which were different from a ideal perfect one based on an arm's-length basis; whether determining dumping implied comparing markets and thus was based on price discrimination, or whether an adjustment should be made for all the differences in market structures so that dumping would only mean profit discrimination. In this sense, the Community argued in one of its submissions to the panel:[114]

"The purpose of dumping investigations is not to determine what economic conditions allow differential pricing between import and export price, but merely to establish that price discrimination exists. The differential costs (if any) may form part of the

---

Republic of Korea and Hong Kong (OJ 1991 L119/35) (definitive). These measures had been taken under Council Regulation No. 2423/88.

[111] Other claims concerned zeroing, calculation of constructed normal value and the determination of injury.

[112] The arguments of the parties concerning asymmetry can be found in para. 80-112 of the panel report.

[113] In this sense, Art. 2(6) of the Antidumping Code read: "In order to effect a fair comparison between the export price and the domestic price in the exporting country (or the country of origin), or, if applicable, the price established pursuant to the provisions of Article VI:1(b) of the General Agreement [determination of normal value other than on the basis of ordinary sales in the domestic market], the two prices shall be compared at the same level of trade, normally at the ex-factory level, and in respect of sales made at as nearly as possible at the same time. Due allowances shall be made in each case, on its merits, for the differences affecting price comparability. In the cases referred to in paragraph 5 of Article 2 [construction of export price] allowance for costs, including duties and taxes, incurred between importation and resale, and for profits accruing, should also be made".

[114] Interview at the Commission, Brussels, May 1997.

structure which allows market separation and dumping to be practised. If dumping is found to exist, any allowance granted on the basis of indirect cost comparison would inevitably be flawed because the cost structure would be a reflection of two different markets with two different price structures. The basic purpose of anti-dumping actions which is recognized and permitted by the Code, would be nullified".

The panel's reasoning with regard to the asymmetry issue was extremely confusing as a result of the fact that there has never been an agreement between the different contracting parties on both the definition of dumping, and which allowances to make when comparing normal value with export price.[115] Still, its main conclusion was that differences in costs and profit could affect price comparability. As the Community Regulation allowed only for an exhaustive list of adjustment items which did not include the indirect costs of the distribution subsidiaries, such Regulation was not in compliance with the Antidumping Code.

However, the panel report could be interpreted in two ways. On the one hand, it could be interpreted as establishing an obligation on the investigating party to make adjustments for indirect costs without requiring the exporter to demonstrate that such costs affected the price. On the other hand, it could be interpreted that the report only considered that the Community was wrong in excluding *per se* indirect costs as an adjustment item. The panel report should only be interpreted as allowing for the possibility of adjustments for indirect costs to be made; otherwise, it would be establishing a definition of dumping as profit discrimination for which there has never been consensus between the contracting parties.

Implementation of the panel report in the Community

The panel's report was a shock for the Community even though it ruled against the Community only in regard to the asymmetry issue. This was so due to two reasons which illustrate the paradox of globalisation. First, the panel threatened one of the main strategies of the Community to deal with what it considered to be the "Japanese problem". Secondly, the report increased the tensions between the different Member States concerning the Community's anti-dumping policy. The way the Community reacted to the report reflected a balance between its intent to preserve anti-dumping as a trade weapon, the divisions between the different Member States and the Community's official commitment to the new international trading system.[116]

The first factor the Commission took into consideration when making its proposal to the Council for a Community reaction to the report was the division between the Member States concerning anti-dumping. In the anti-dumping and Article 113 committees it became clear that the Member States' differences

---

[115] The panel's reasoning with regard to asymmetry can be found in paras 367–388 of the report. Indeed, the Community and other anti-dumping users alleged the confusion of the report as one of the arguments not to implement it.

[116] Interview at the Commission, Brussels, May 1997.

which had always been typical concerning their approach towards anti-dumping re-emerged with regard to the report. While Spain, Belgium, Italy, Portugal, Greece and France preferred the rejection of the panel, the United Kingdom, the Netherlands and Sweden were positive about adoption. Germany kept its options open, and Austria was inclined towards adoption, insisting that the whole issue should be seen within the context of the EC–Japanese relations.[117] Again, the different domestic structures of the different Member States affected their division.[118] Whereas the plural markets and traditional reliance on the state in the southern countries pushed them towards protection in order to cope with globalisation, the countries with markets characterised by concertation and co-operation preferred a full commitment towards the international trading system.[119]

Thus, the Commission officials realised that there were four possible basic alternatives. First, the Community could adopt the panel report and implement the Regulation accordingly. On the one hand, this would prove the Community's commitment towards the new WTO rules and, thus, would enhance its prestige in the international trading system. On the other hand, such approach implied too many shortcomings. (a) The Community would risk the panel report being interpreted as always requiring an adjustment for indirect costs and therefore adopting the definition of dumping as profit discrimination. The Community would then lose a fundamental interface instrument to deal with different market economies. (b) Most importantly, there was no way the Commission would obtain the necessary votes in the Council to adopt such proposal since the southern Member States strongly opposed the panel report. (c) It was unlikely that other contracting parties which were traditional users of anti-dumping law would support the Community.

---

[117] Ibid.

[118] A similar pattern of positions has been taken in other EC anti-dumping feuds. See "Anti-Dumping: Bed Linen Imports Slapped with Duties Up to 27%", *European Reports* No. 2233, 19 June 1997, 2; see also "EU/Anti-Dumping: Council Decides by Small Majority to Introduce Definitive Anti-Dumping Duties on Certain Outdoor Shoes in Textiles Originating from China and Indonesia (With Some Exceptions)", *Agence Europe* No. 7041, 31 October 1997, 6–7; "Commission Losses Controversial Vote on Duties", *Financial Times*, 17 September 1998, 3; "EU Ministers Reject Cotton Duties Again", *Financial Times*, 6 October 1998, 4; Neil Buckley, "Business Balks at Dumping Duties", *Financial Times*, 17 July 1997, 2; Emma Tucker, "French Fury at Cotton Duties Threat", *Financial Times*, 19 May 1997, 3; Jenny Luesby, "EU Split on Cotton Dumping Action", *Financial Times*, 21 March 1997, 5; Guy Jonquieres, "French Clash with Brittan on Dumping", *Financial Times*, 30 January 1997, 7; "EU Refines Dumping Regulations", *Financial Times*, 1 October 1996, 5; Emma Tucker, "EU Split Over Dumping Duties", *Financial Times*, 15 September 1995, 5; "Council Regulation Establishes Definitive Anti-Dumping Duties on Leather Bags Originating in China, Giving Up Duties on Synthetic Bags, in Response to Criticism by Importers and Traders", *Agence Europe*, 1 September 1997, 5. As to the division amongst Member States and its impact on the development of the Community interest clause in its Anti-dumping Regulation, see R.M. Maclean and R.J. Eccles, "A Change of Style not Substance: The Community's New Approach Towards the Community Interest Test in Anti-Dumping and Anti-Subsidy Law" (1999) 36 *CML Rev* 123.

[119] The exception to this was the United Kingdom.

Secondly, the Community could simply refuse to accept the panel report and make no changes to its basic Regulation. This was possible since the panel had decided under the old GATT dispute-settlement rules. By not adopting the panel report, the Community would be sure to safeguard its anti-dumping strategy. But this met the very strong opposition of the northern states as it would diminish the prestige of the Community in the multilateral trading system.

Thirdly, the Commission considered proposing the adoption of the report but with a reservation concerning the asymmetry issue and thereafter make some amendments to the Regulation. However, while basically saving the commitment of the EC to the new trade rules, the reservation could not ensure that the panel report would not threaten the Community's long-standing position on anti-dumping. Furthermore, Commission officials realised that not even this proposal would obtain the necessary votes in the Council.

Finally, the Commission decided to make a proposal which was based mainly on its possibility of obtaining the necessary votes in the Council. The formula was to refuse to adopt the panel report but to make some amendments to the basic Regulation which would reflect the Community's interpretation of the panel's reasoning. By taking this approach, the Community would not lose its prestige completely, while being sure of preserving its anti-dumping strategy. Most importantly of all, this proposal would be a balance between the different Member States' positions. Whereas the southern Member States were reassured that the Community would basically keep its methodology, the free trade states foresaw more restraint in the Community's anti-dumping practice.[120]

In amending the Regulation, the Council first introduced an additional paragraph to Article 2(10)(d) whereby when an existing difference in level of trade cannot be quantified because of the absence of the relevant levels on the domestic market of the exporting countries, or where certain functions are shown clearly to relate to levels of trade other than the one which is to be used in the comparison, a special adjustment can be granted.[121] This amendment is a recog-

---

[120] As to the Commission's official proposal, see Commission of the European Communities, *Proposal for a Council Regulation (EC) Amending Regulation (EC) No 384/96 on protectionist against dumped imports from countries not members of the European Community*, COM (96) 145 final (April 1996). See also "Japan in EU Cassette Row", *Financial Times*, 20 September 1996, 4.

[121] Art. 2(10)(d) thus now reads:

"(i) An adjustment for differences in levels of trade, including any difference which may arise in OEM (Original Equipment Manufactuer) sales, shall be granted where, in relation to the distribution chain in both markets, it is shown that the export price, including a constructed export price, is at a different level of trade to the normal value and the difference has affected price comparability which is demonstrated by consistent and distinct differences in functions and prices of the seller for the different levels of trade in the domestic market of the exporting country. The amount of the adjustment shall be based on the market value of the difference.

(ii) However, in circumstances not envisaged under (i), when an existing difference in level of trade cannot be quantified because of the absence of the relevant levels on the domestic market of the exporting countries, or where certain functions are shown clearly to relate to levels of trade other than the one which is to be used in the comparison, a special adjustment may be granted."   *cont./*

nition that a level of trade cannot be refused simply on the grounds that the exporter is not in a position to quantify its claim.[122] However, the producer must show that it is performing certain functions which refer to levels of trade other than the one which is to be used in the comparison.[123]

With the purpose of not being criticised for having an exhaustive list of possible adjustments, the Community introduced a new Article 2(10)(k) whereby an adjustment may be made for differences in other factors not provided for under subparagraphs (a)–(j) if it is demonstrated that they affect price comparability, in particular that the customers consistently pay different prices on the

See Art. 2(10)(d) of Council Regulation No. 384/96 (OJ 1996 L56/6), as amended by Council Regulation No. 2331/96 (OJ 1996 L317/1). The wording of the final amendment is in fact different from that of the proposal which reads: "An adjustment for differences in levels of trade, including any difference which may arise in OEM (Original Equipment Manufacturer) sales, shall be granted where, in relation to the distribution chain in both markets, it is shown that the export price, including a constructed export price, is at a different level of trade to the normal value. An effect on price comparability must be demonstrated by evidence which confirms as clear distinction between the prices for the different levels of trade on the domestic market of the exporting country. However, where information relating to such price effects does not exist for that market, or where certain functions are shown to relate to levels of trade other than those which are to be compared, a special adjustment may be granted". In contrast with the proposal, the amendment keeps the principle that the adjustment must be based on the market value of the difference. Furthermore, in contrast with the proposal, the amendment says that the functions must relate *clearly* to levels of trade other than the one which is to be used in the comparison. Thus, the amendment seems to be a bit more restrictive than the proposal. See COM(96)145 final.

[122] See Muller, Khan and Neumann, above at n. 62, 132. See *Personal Fax Machines Originating in the People's Republic of China, Japan, Republic of Korea, Malaysia, Singapore, Taiwan and Thailand* (OJ 1998 L128/1) (recital 39) (where the Council held: "Nevertheless, in circumstances not covered by an adjustment for differences in levels of trade as defined by Art. 2(10)(d)(i) of the Basic Regulation, Art. 2(10)(d)(ii) allows the granting of a special adjustment when certain functions are shown to relate to a level of trade other than the one used for the comparison. In the present case, the investigation revealed that while the adjustment for differences in levels of trade could not be granted, the functions of advertising should receive a special consideration in the light of Art. 2(10)(d)(ii). The Commission examined, in particular, whether the companies concerned incurred advertising expenses to encourage sales at levels of trade other than the one used for the comparison. It was found indeed that, for the companies concerned, certain advertising expenses related, in the present case, to a level of trade other than the one used in the comparison. In consequence it was decided pursuant to Art. 2(10)(d)(ii) of the Basic Regulation, to exclude from the computation of the normal value those advertising expenses incurred in domestic sales which relate to level of trade other than distributors").

[123] See Edwin Vermulst and Bart Driessen, "New Battle Lines in the Anti-Dumping War: Recent Developments on the European Front" (1997) 31(3) *J World Trade* 135, 138; see also *Stainless Steel Wires with a Diameter of Less than 1 mm Originating in the Republic of Korea* (OJ 1999 L1/12) (recital 19) (where the Commission held: one company requested an adjustment in the level of trade on the grounds that on the domestic market all its sales were made directly to customers whereas on the Community market part of its sales were made through a related importer. It was argued that since all expenses incurred by the related importer would be deduced from the export price for the comparison, the indirect selling expenses incurred for the domestic sales should be deducted from the domestic price as well. This claim could provisionally not be accepted because the exporting producer concerned was not able to demonstrate that the constructed export price was at different level of trade than the normal value and that this differences affected price comparability as required by Art. 2(10(d) of the Basic Regulation); *Stainless Steel Wires with a Diameter of 1mm or more Originating in India* (OJ 1999 L13/24) (recital 17).

domestic market because of the difference in such factors.[124] The new provision, however, makes an attempt to preserve the effectiveness of the Antidumping Regulation against the Japanese and other Asian markets, and insists on the principle that the different costs must affect price comparability. It must be shown that the customers consistently pay higher prices because of the difference in the other factors.[125]

IV CONCLUSION

By developing a methodology concerning normal value, export price and the comparison for its anti-dumping procedures, the Community attempted to manage what it considered the "Japanese problem". Through its anti-dumping practice the Community attempted to deal with the diversity of the Japanese market system. The European institutions tried to limit the impact which a different market economy could have in their domestic markets. Furthermore, by using the anti-dumping law, they aimed both to establish a precedence in the international trading system and, to a certain extent, to discourage Japanese distribution networks.

However, the Community's policy was determined by the persistence of different market economies within the European boundaries. From an institutional perspective, as the implementation of the audio tapes in cassettes panel report highlights, the Community's policy was strongly determined by the conflict of interests between the different Member States. In the aftershock of the panel's report, Member States realigned again according to their trade interests. The European states were prisoners of their diverse domestic market structures and, hence, the Commission had to broker between these diverse interests to preserve, as much as possible, the prestige and effectiveness of the Community in the international trading system. Indeed, despite the differences, the Commission was capable of promoting what it considered as the Community's interest.

From a substantial point of view the obvious question is why the Community used its anti-dumping law as an aggressive instrument to target the Japanese

---

[124] See Art. 2(10)(k) of Council Regulation No. 384/96 (OJ 1996 L56/6), as amended by Council Regulation No. 2331/96 (OJ 1996 L317/1).

[125] See *Personal Fax Machines Originating in the People's Republic of China, Japan, Republic of Korea, Malaysia, Singapore, Taiwan and Thailand* (OJ 1998 L128/1) (recital 54) (where the Council held: "All companies which made the claim under Article 2(10)(k) of the Basic Regulation, failed to provide evidence of significant and consistent price differences as required by that provision. To show only a difference in costs between the export and the domestic sales departments of the same company is an insufficient basis for a claim for differences in price comparability, let alone to demonstrate an impact of prices. Furthermore, the assumption that the request for a difference in prices is given as an example is incorrect, since subparagraph (k) reinforces the two requirements set in the general part of Article 2(10) of the Basic Regulation, i.e. that the adjustments listed in (a) to (k) can only be granted if it is claimed and demonstrated that they affect prices and price comparability. In the absence of any evidence showing that these conditions were met in this specific case, the claim had to be rejected").

market. After all, anti-dumping duties only indirectly put pressure for changes in foreign markets.[126] If the Community intended to open the Japanese market, the best and preferable option would have been to do so by offensive means and not by imposing duties on imports into the Community.[127] The obvious answer is that the Community, unlike the United States which has section 301 of the Trade Act 1974, did not have, nor has, such an offensive instrument to attempt to break into the Japanese market.[128] Indeed, neither the New Commercial Policy Instrument,[129] which was clearly handicapped as it required a complaint from an entire Community industry, nor the new Trade Barriers Regulation, which is strongly committed to the rules of the international trading system, provide much chance for the Community to target Japan. Within the framework of the Trade Barriers Regulation, the balance of interests between the different Members States, the Commission, the Council and the European Parliament led to a strict commitment to the standard of international trade law as reflected in the WTO or other multilateral trade agreements.[130] And as the *Kodak* case illustrates, WTO rules provide for limited space to target the organisation of private market actors.[131]

From a defensive point of view, the international trading system prevented the Community from making a discriminatory use of safeguard measures which would have been much more effective and probably domestically less polemical. But as the Member States which had traditionally relied on government intervention claimed some form of protection to compensate from the changes resulting from integration, the Community institutions developed instead an "asymmetry" methodology which would guarantee a high level of dumping and thus protection in the form of anti-dumping duties or harassment. Yet, by taking an instrument allowed in the GATT agreements and developing its methodology at a maximum, they would achieve the Community's interest only to a certain extent. While distinguishing the Japanese market system could be argued to be in the interests of the Community in safeguarding the European markets from an alien system, the irony is that such approach implied promoting an international trading system characterised by a plural market which the Community has traditionally lacked. By playing the GATT game, the Community would be granting protection on the basis of a liberal instrument

---

[126] See B.M. Hoekman and P.C. Mavroidis, "Dumping, Antidumping and Antitrust" (1996) 30(1) *J World Trade* 27, 30.

[127] See Frans Engering, Hans De Brabander and Edwin Vermulst, "EC Antidumping Policy in a Globalized World: A Dutch Perspective" (1998) 32(6) *J World Trade* 115, 117.

[128] I use the word "attempt" because section 301 itself can succeed in changing the socio-economic structures of Japan only to a very limited extent. Yet, section 301 can be useful to establish the agenda on future negotiations on competition and can improve the individual US access to the Japanese market.

[129] See Council Regulation No. 2641/84 (OJ 1984 L252/7), as amended by Council Regulation No. 522/94 (OJ 1994 L66/10).

[130] See Art. 2 of Council Regulation No. 3286/94 (OJ 1996 L349/71), as amended.

[131] See Norio Komuro, "Kodak-Fuji Film Dispute and the WTO Panel Ruling" (1998) 32(5) *J World Trade* 161.

which reflects its domestic system only partly. Indeed, the Community's policy reflected the thin Anglo-Saxon homogenisation of the Community's market. In doing this, the Community authorities were overseeing the persistence of market differences within the Community and thus allowing the controversies of the Common Commercial Policy, and the anti-dumping practice in particular, to continue.

5

Indian Foreign Policy on the Threshold of the Twenty-first Century

RAJENDRA K. JAIN

With the end of the Cold War, multipolarity, the economic regionalisation of the globe and the disintegration of the former Soviet Union, many of the familiar moorings of Indian foreign policy have been lost. The new world order in the 1990s has put an end to the comforting familiarity of bipolarity and rendered many of the old geopolitical assumptions invalid. The more uncertain and complex global environment has increased Indian vulnerabilities, but, at the same time, also offers challenges and opportunities. If India is to play a role commensurate with its size and economic potential, its leaders will have to demonstrate considerable dexterity in tackling the challenges on the domestic front and exploiting the opportunities opening up in the new world order.

This chapter examines the impact of the end of the Cold War on Indian foreign policy. It looks at the elements of continuity and change in Indian foreign policy towards the United States, China, the former Soviet Union, Southeast Asia, and its role and profile in Southern Asia. It concludes with an examination of whether India is a regional power or a global power.

I IMPACT OF THE END OF THE COLD WAR

The end of the Cold War has compelled India to ponder over its international position and basic strategy probably more profoundly than at any time since the end of the Second World War. Non-alignment has lost its *raison d'être* with the collapse of the Soviet Union.[1] In the post-Cold War world, Indian foreign policy confronted a dilemma: choosing between joining the *Pax Americana* and the charting of an independent Nehruvian course.[2] The reorientation of Indian

---

[1] There are those who contend that the essentials of non-alignment are still relevant in the changed circumstances. See Muchkund Dubey, "India's Foreign Policy in the Evolving Global Order" (1993) (30(2) *International Studies* 117; M.S. Rajan, "Indian Foreign Policy: The Continuing Relevance of Nonalignment" (1993) 30(2) *International Studies* (New Delhi) 141.

[2] D.S. Kamtekar in *The Telegraph* (Calcutta), 8 January 1991.

foreign policy has, to a considerable extent, been facilitated by the improvement in the regional and global security situation. India has shed its tendency to play high politics and concentrate on economic diplomacy as markets, finance, technologies and foreign collaborations have assumed greater importance. A new division of economic co-ordination was created in the Ministry of External Affairs.[3]

India was slow to adapt to the momentous changes in Europe, partly because these changes came at a time of political transition in India. The twenty months between November 1989 and June 1991 witnessed three governments and two General Elections. The P.V. Narasimha Rao Government (June 1991) inherited a serious balance of payments crisis and a foreign policy which was in shambles because of the preoccupation of the minority governments of V.P. Singh (December 1989) and Chandra Shekhar (November 1990) with domestic issues and relations with neighbours, which precluded rapid responses to external challenges. India had to adopt the policies of liberalisation, free markets and prudent budgeting because of its precarious fiscal situation, which was the result of large, scale commercial borrowings in the 1980s as a result of which foreign debts rose to $40.77 billion by the end of 1989, with a high debt servicing ratio of 27.7 per cent.

A major change in Indian foreign policy was the metamorphosis towards Israel. India's vote in December 1991 in support of Israel by rescinding an earlier UN resolution equating Zionism with racism was an indication of the complete change in the approach towards Israel. It also liberated India from the constraints imposed by the Islamic voting bloc in the United Nations, which had so far prevented India from judging the question of relations with Israel on its own merits. Since the establishment of diplomatic relations in January 1992,[4] trade and defence co-operation with Israel has increased.

The world's largest democracy has been variously described as either a "caged tiger"[5] or a rambling elephant, renowned for its "Hindu rate of growth". Both descriptions were partially true because the Indian Government's inward-looking policies for over three decades fostered inertia, which hindered economic growth, preventing it from growing at a pace consistent with both the existing and potential size of the economy. Having embarked on a process of economic liberalisation since 1991 and by radically reorienting its economic

---

[3] During his visit to Germany in September 1991, Prime Minister P.V. Narasimha Rao stated: "foreign policy from now on will have a larger component of economics and culture. The Ministry of External Affairs has to prepare itself for this reorientation". Cited in Sumit Chakravarty, "Sowing the Seeds of New Partnership," *Mainstream* (New Delhi), 14 September 1991, 2–5, 34.

[4] See Fahmida Ashraf, "Indo-Israeli Relations" (1993) 16(12) *Strategic Studies* 99; Bansidhar Pradhan, "India's Policy towards the PLO", in Riyaz Punjabi and A.K. Pasha (eds), *India and the Islamic World* (New Delhi, 1997), 65–84.

[5] Abid Husain, former Indian Ambassador to the United States, remarked: "One economist described India as a tiger in a cage. When the cage is opened, the tiger would show its real strength. The cage is now open but the tiger refuses to come into the cage," *India Today* (New Delhi), 15 March 1993, 19. See also Joe Rogaly, "The Tiger Refuses to Leave the Cage", *Financial Times*, 23 June 1992.

policies, dismantling the license *raj* (which both protected and stunted growth of the private sector) and a heavily interventionist state, India is becoming increasingly attractive for investors.

II THE MAJOR POWERS

United States

A major catalyst in the improvement of Indo–US relations in the late 1980s[6] has been greater US flexibility in permitting the supply of dual-use technology, such as permission to export a highly sensitive, dual-use super computer, sale of GE 404 jet aircraft engines and fly-by-wire avionics for use in India's indigenous light combat aircraft (LAC) project.

One of the beneficial impacts of the disintegration of the Soviet Union was that India was compelled to reassess its priorities and strive rapidly to improve relations with both China and the United States. Washington showed greater appreciation for Indian concern about policies regarding Punjab and Kashmir, and Pakistani support to terrorism. The end of the Cold War raised hopes that the military aspect of the US's special relationship with Pakistan was likely to abate and diminish the political and security burdens it placed upon India, because Pakistan would lose its strategic value to the United States. Washington's support of India in the World Bank and International Monetary Fund (IMF) had rescued India from "a very trying situation".[7] The end of the Cold War also led to the closing of Indo–US military links and the conduct of joint military exercises in 1992, 1993 and 1996. However, by mid-1992, the initial optimism began to wane as a result of the unilateral invocation of "Super 301" and US pressure on the Russians to cancel the Indo-Russian cryogenic engine contract.[8]

Major sources of frictions with the United States have been, and are likely to be, acrimony over bilateral commerce, transfer of technology,[9] and nuclear and missile non-proliferation. The United States and other Western powers are pursuing a policy of "carrots and sticks" *vis-à-vis* India: gaining market access

---

[6] For a background study, see Rajendra K. Jain (ed.), *US-South Asian Relations, 1947–1982* (New Jersey, 1983); Dennis Kux, *Estranged Democracies: India and the United States, 1941–1991* (New Delhi, 1994).

[7] Foreign Minister Gujral's address at the Bandaranaike Centre for International Studies, Colombo, 10 August 1992, as reproduced in *Mainstream*, 12 September 1992, 12.

[8] See B.K. Shrivastava, "Indo-American Relations: Search for a New Equation" (1993) 30(2) *International Studies* 215; Nalini Kant Jha, "Reviving US-India Friendship in a Changing International Order" (1994) 34(2) *Asian Survey* 1035; Ramesh Thakur, "India and the United States: A Triumph of Hope over Experience?" (1996) *Asian Survey*, 574; Francine R. Frankel, "Indo-US Relations: The Future is Now", *The Washington Quarterly*, Autumn 1996, 129.

[9] See Brahma Chellaney, "Non-proliferation: An Indian Critique of U.S. Export Controls", *Orbis*, Summer 1994, 439.

through investments and trade preferences, but disciplining/punishing India through instruments like the "Super 301" and technology denials.

For India, the United States is India's largest trading partner, the largest foreign investor, and the largest technology exchange partner. The post-Cold War era has led to a sharp decline in US bilateral assistance from a peak of $902 million in 1966 to a paltry $127 million in 1991, of which only $22 million was for developmental aid.[10]

A recent Council on Foreign Relations study urged a more extensive economic and trade relationship with India and Pakistan, supply of conventional arms to both countries, loosening of restrictions on dual-use technology, and the development of a strategic relationship with India.[11] A vigorous attempt is needed to persuade the US strategic community that a secular and democratic India is an obvious ally in a volatile region, and that as an ally India needs to be encouraged rather than curbed.[12]

Relations with Russia

Even before its disintegration, the Soviet Union's perceptions of economic and strategic interests with India began to be influenced by radical changes in Moscow's policies towards the Third World.[13] Domestic economic needs compelled the former Soviet Union to shed its old euphoria and adopt more viable economic policies in trade and aid towards developing countries.[14]

The disintegration of the Soviet Union compelled India to undertake the task of "disaggregating Republic-wise, Indo-Soviet ties"[15] and deprived India of a reliable source of trade, diplomatic support and military supplies.[16] Politically, the changed geopolitical milieu of the 1990s and the improvement in Moscow's relations with the United States and China diluted the geostrategic imperatives that cemented the Indo–Soviet relationship. No longer can India rely on the veto

[10] Cited in Surjit Mansingh, "Indo-American Relations in the Post-Cold War Period", *Research-in-Progress Papers, History and Society*, Second Series, No. 82 (New Delhi: Centre for Contemporary Studies, Nehru Memorial Museum and Library, November 1993), 15, 18.

[11] N.C. Menon, "Washington to Give More Emphasis on South Asia", *Hindustan Times*, 24 January 1997.

[12] "Good Move", *Hindustan Times*, 8 January 1997.

[13] See e.g. Andrei Kozyrev, "A Transformed Russia in a New World", *Izvestiya*, 2 January 1993, as translated in the *Current Digest of the Soviet Press*, 5 February 1993, 23.

[14] W. Ramond Duncan and C.M. Ekedahl, *Moscow and the Third World under Gorbachev* (Boulder, CO, 1990), 84, 222–3; Margot Light, "Soviet Policy in the Third World", *International Affairs*, April 1991, 265–7, 274; Rajendra K. Jain, "European Development Aid Policies in the 1990s: Implications for India", (52(3) *India Quarterly* (New Delhi) 31.

[15] Government of India, Ministry of External Affairs, *Annual Report 1991–92* (New Delhi, 1992), 37.

[16] See Rajendra K. Jain (ed.), *Soviet-South Asian Relations, 1947–1978* (New Jersey, 1979); Surjit Mansingh, "Is there a Soviet-Indian Strategic Partnership?", in Hafeez Malik (ed.), *Domestic Determinants of Soviet Foreign Policy toward South Asia and the Middle East* (Macmillan Press, London, 1990), 141. For a more recent study, see Bhupinder Brar (ed.), *Soviet Collapse: Implications for India* (Ajanta, Delhi, 1993).

of a former superpower on hostile resolutions at the United Nations, and on its continued support on the Kashmir question. The pillar of Indo–Soviet relationship now needs to be balanced by a wider network of relationships.

India was relatively slow in reacting to the collapse of the former Soviet Union, and its inept handling of its reaction to the abortive August 1991 coup annoyed the new Soviet leadership of Boris Yeltsin. Moscow's endorsement in November 1991 of Pakistan's resolution on declaring Southern Asia as a nuclear weapon-free zone in the UN General Assembly, a proposal which India had consistently and strongly opposed led to considerable annoyance and consternation in India. Despite the renewal of the Indo–Soviet Treaty just before the coup and the conclusion of a new Treaty of Friendship and Co-operation in January 1993, the commonality of strategic interests is no longer evident.

With Soviet hardware constituting about 70 per cent of India's weaponry, the end of the communist regime marked the end of the major source of defence supplies at concessional prices. Delivery schedules of spares had slipped because of production problems in armament firms spread throughout the successor Republics and their insistence on immediate payment in hard currency. However, concern about losing the biggest market for Russian military hardware in the Third World and fears that competitors would quickly fill the vacuum soon led to a keen desire in Moscow to prop-up declining arms exports. Defence Minister Sharad Pawar's visits to Russia in September 1992 and December 1992, followed by Boris Yeltsin's visit to India in January 1993, cleared the way for the resumption of military spares and equipment and the conclusion of a deal for the purchase of ten MiG-29 combat and training fighters worth about $320 million.[17] The end of the Cold War also opened the possibility of re-export by India of Moscow-sourced weapons produced in Indian factories and offered good prospects for a new major base from which to export jointly manufactured equipment to other Asian-Pacific countries.[18]

In October 1996, India gave its assent to the long-pending deal for the purchase of forty SU-30 MK combat aircraft worth around $2 billion, for which it had already paid an advance of Rs 5 billion. This demonstrated to the Russians that India remained the biggest buyer in a shrinking armaments market. India also showed sustained interest in the Mikoyan MiG-AT trainer aircraft. Russia reportedly intends to sell approximately $8 billion worth of weapons to India till the year 2000.[19]

---

[17] See Ramesh Thakur, "The Impact of the Soviet Collapse on Military Relations with India" (1993) 45(5) *Europe-Asia Studies* 841; Fred Weir, "$600 m Russian Arms for India", *Hindustan Times*, 29 July 1995.

[18] In July 1994 India and Russia agreed to set up a joint venture (Indo–Russian Aviation Private Ltd.) with an equity base of $400 million to manufacture spare parts for military aircraft of Russian origin and to offer maintenance facilities for Russian aircraft.

[19] *Pioneer* (New Delhi), 31 March 1996; "The Sukhoi Advantage", *Hindustan Times*, 16 November 1996; Pushpinder Singh, "Fighters in the Sky: IAF Returns to Russia", *Times of India*, 27 January 1994.

India's trade declined substantially as a result of the economic and political disruptions in the former Soviet Union. The introduction of trade in convertible currency and the shift towards more competitive, alternative sources of supply also put an end to a large portion of trade which was conducted on the basis of bilateral balancing of trade and payments, or through countertrade. The collapse of the Russian and some of the Eastern European trading arrangements led to a collapse of Indian exports to Russia and East European countries—a 45.2 per cent decline in 1990–1991 and 1991–1992, followed by a 62 per cent decline in 1992–1993 to the Rupee Payment Area.[20] But Indo-Russian trade has gone up from Rs 28.14 billion in 1993–1994 to Rs 41.13 billion in 1994–1995, a 44 per cent hike, and to Rs 63.56 billion in 1995–1996, which marks a 54 per cent increase.[21] Indo–Russian trade turnover is expected to increase by two-and-a-half times to reach $5 billion by the year 2000.[22] Commerce Secretary, Tejindra Khanna, predicted that India's exports to the Commonwealth of Independent States (CIS) would rise to 10 per cent of India's global trade by the end of the century. Indian exports, which had fallen to 1.5 per cent in 1992–1993 from 10 per cent prior to the disintegration of the USSR, rose to 4 per cent of India's total exports, amounting to $6.8 billion in 1995–1996.[23] About 320 Indian companies maintain registered representative offices in Russia, mostly in Moscow and St. Petersburg. However, Indo–Russian trade declined from Rs 63,600 million in 1995–1996 to Rs 49,950 million in 1996–1997. The major impediment to boosting bilateral trade is that nearly 85 per cent of Indian exports to Russia comprise of rupee payments worth $1 billion every year under the Indo–Russian rupee-rouble agreement (January 1993).[24] Other major problems have included the lack of an effective and transparent mechanism for utilisation of rupee funds,

[20] The USSR accounted for 95% of the total trade turnover betweeen India and the three countries under the Rupee Payment Area (RPA), *viz.* the USSR, Czechoslovakia and Romania. The decline in exports was mostly in exports of agricultural products to RPA. The decline in imports was mainly in imports of crude oil and petroleum products from Russia. Exports to Russia (former Soviet Union) which accounted for as much as 16.1% of India's total exports in 1990–1991, came down to 9.2% in 1991–1992 and further to 3.2% in 1992–1993: Government of India, Ministry of Finance, Economic Division, *Economic Survey 1992–93* (New Delhi, 1993), 103; *Economic Survey 1993–94* (New Delhi, 1994), 72, 81.

[21] Mahindra Ved, "Many Indo-Russian Projects on Anvil", *The Times of India* (New Delhi), 13 January 1997.

[22] "India Asked to Diversify Export Basket to Russia", *Economic Times*, 18 September 1996.

[23] "Exports to CIS Set to Touch 10% of India's Trade", *Hindustan Times*, 18 September 1996. However, the share of India in Russian trade with Asia was only 9.3% and the Indian share in total Russian trade turnover was approximately 1.5%. Speech by Russian Deputy Prime Minister and Minister of Foreign Trade, Oleg Davyodv, at the plenary session on "A New Era of Business and Economic Partnership between India and Russia", at the India Economic Summit organised by the World Economic Forum and Confederation of Indian Industry, New Delhi, 29 October 1996. "Need to Revitalise Indo-Russian Trade", *Hindustan Times*, 30 October 1996.

[24] For details, see Anita Inder Singh, "India's Relations with Russia and Central Asia" (1995) 71(1) *International Affairs* 75; Government of India, Ministry of Finance, Economic Division, *Economic Survey 1993–94* (New Delhi, 1994), 74. Almost 78% of all Indian exports to Russia are financed through the repayment of Delhi's debt to the former USSR, and only 22% represent independent deals made freely between Indian and Russian companies. Fred Weir, "Gujral Visit Likely to Boost Indo-Russian Cooperation", *Hindustan Times*, 10 February 1997.

procedural problems resulting from lack of reliable banking channels, and the establishment of proper shipping channels.[25]

Under US pressure, Russia, in July 1992, suspended the $250 million cryogenic rocket engine contract (signed in January 1991) in the wake of the imposition (11 May 1992) of a two-year sale and technology-transfer embargo on space-related materials on both Glavkosmos, the Russian space agency, and the Indian Space Research Organisation (ISRO) on the plea that the technology being dual-use was violating the Missile Technology Control Regime (MTCR). US arm-twisting was largely motivated by commercial compulsions: to push Russia out of the Indian market for these types of services and prevent India from emerging as a potential competitor. The cancellation of the deal in July 1993 led to a renewed agreement whereby Moscow agreed to sell seven cryogenic rocket engines to India, five more than originally agreed.[26] There was renewed US pressure on the Russians to cancel the projected sale of two 1,000 MW nuclear power reactors for the Kundakulum atomic power station worth $2.5–$3 billion. But this time the Russians argued that the sale was an economic necessity, and criticised the United States for seeking to oust Russia from the Indian and other Asian markets in the nuclear energy field. Subsequently, talks did not apparently make much headway as the Russians insisted that the entire project should be paid for in dollars. The Russians have also not welcomed President Clinton's unsolicited advice to stall defence co-operation with India.

The visit of Russian Prime Minister, Yevgerny Primakov, to India (20–22 December 1998) led to the signing of seven agreements. Especially significant were those dealing with military, technical co-operation until 2010, the development of trade, economic, industrial, finance, science and technological co-operation and co-operation in the field of communication in civil aviation, underling that Russia is likely to remain an important source of defence equipment and advanced technology. However, the visit led to unwarranted speculation in the press about an emerging strategic partnership between China, India and Russia in order to counterbalance US domination of world politics.[27]

European Union

In its search for new markets, sources of collaborative ventures, investment, and advanced technology, India, in the 1990s, has increasingly turned towards the West. Harsh economic realities, the loss of assured markets in the former Soviet Union and Eastern Europe, and the increasingly competitive and hostile international economic environment has moved the West much higher in the scale of

---

[25] See G. Ganapathy Subramaniam, "India Keen on Trade Pact with Russia during Yeltsin Visit", *Hindustan Times*, 16 March 1998; "Indo-Russian Trade Talks Begin Today", *Hindustan Times*, 26 November 1998.

[26] On this, see Jyotirmoy Banerjee, "Indo-Russian Rocket Deal" (1994) 34(6) *Asian Survey* 544; R.P. Goel, "Sky's the Limit for India's Space Plans", *Times of India*, 23 August 1994.

[27] See J.N. Dixt, "The Primakov Visit", *Hindustan Times*, 20 January 1999; Amitabh Mattoo, "Triangle of Vision", *Hindustan Times*, 3 January 1999.

priorities of Indian foreign policy. The European Union (EU) has been, and remains, India's largest trading partner and a leading source of credit, technology and industrial collaboration.[28]

In the early 1990s, India urged an overhaul of its co-operation agreement with the EU and an upgraded political dialogue, since the EU was not merely another trading area, but increasingly the collective diplomatic centre for Western Europe. A "third generation" agreement on partnership and development was signed between India and the EU on 20 December 1993 (in force since August 1994). Annual "troika" meetings, having been held since 1984, are now taking place under the 1994 "Joint Statement on Political Dialogue" to reinforce and intensify their mutual relations on political, economic, technological and cultural fields.

Apart from being the largest beneficiary of EU development assistance, the EU is the single most important trade entity for India—currently absorbing 26 per cent of Indian exports and a source of one-quarter of Indian imports. Indo–EU trade in the first four years of the 1990s recorded an annual rate of growth in the region of 20 per cent. Sixty per cent of Indian exports, however, is accounted for by the United Kingdom, Germany and France. However, there is essentially an asymmetric trade relationship between India and the EU. In the context of the EU's global transactions, India's share is marginal.[29] While total two-way trade between the two sides is around $20 billion and has grown significantly, the trade balance with the EU, which is crucial to India's current account balance, continues to be negative for India. There has been a sharp and sudden rise in India's trade deficit with EU-15, which widened to ECU 1,600 million (about $2 billion) in 1995 from ECU 230 million in 1994.[30] Other major irritants in Indo–EU relations have included the repeated use of trade protection instruments like anti-export subisidy duties, frequent anti-dumping actions on specific items like textiles, and inadequate market access for marine and agricultural products and textiles, which hurt bilateral trade in a big way. The EU's complaints include India's automobile policy and quantitative restrictions on imports (against which it has initiated several disputes in the WTO).[31]

In its recent discussion paper on India (June 1996), the EU took a long-term perspective of India as an increasingly key element of the EU's Asia strategy. It called for a stronger partnership between India and the EU. Outlining the path to a deeper and more dynamic partnership, the paper urges more frequent and

---

[28] See Rajendra K. Jain, "India and the European Union", in India, Ministry of External Affairs, *Indian Foreign Policy—Agenda for the 21st Century* (Foreign Service Institute, New Delhi, 1998), Vol. 2, 44.

[29] In 1990 EC exports to India constituted only 0.5% of its total exports, and India's share in the Community's overall imports was a meagre 0.4%.

[30] Malcolm Subhan, "Ramaiah Pushes Leon to Cap Trade Deficit", *Economic Times*, 28 November 1996.

[31] See Swapan K. Bhattacharya, "India-EU Trade Relations in the 1990s: Role of the World Trading Organization", in H.S. Chopra (ed.), *India and the European Union into the 21st Century* (New Delhi, 1998), 93.

numerous contacts at all levels, leading to the setting-up of working groups, producing sectoral agreements and arrangements.[32]

India reached an agreement in November 1997 with the EU for a six-year phase-out of quantitative restrictions on imports of about 2,400 items. This agreement reflects India's willingness to come to an early understanding on the vexed Quantitative Restrictions (QR) issue within the framework of the WTO.

A major problem in the Indo–EU economic relationship is that it is essentially four of the fifteen Member States which are major players (i.e. Germany, the United Kingdom, France and Italy) in foreign direct investment, joint ventures or industrial collaborations. The other Member States are less interested in India partly because of their growing preference for Eastern European economies.

The EU is and will remain the pivot of Europe's politico-economic future. As the largest integrated market, its policies and perspectives on diverse international issues are and will continue to be of considerable importance for the rest of the world. Indian policy makers will have to take the EU more seriously as the main interlocutor in Europe, not just on economic, but also on political and security issues. There is growing realisation that Germany—the largest foreign investor and trading partner of India in the EU and the richest and strongest democracy in Europe—will exercise greater influence in shaping the course and policy of the EU in the future.

China

The end of the Cold War engendered greater pragmatism in India's relations with the People's Republic of China, a process which had begun since the late 1980s.[33] Since Prime Minister Rajiv Gandhi's December 1988 China visit, after a gap of 26 years, marked the normalisation of Sino–Indian relations, the two countries moving in a cautious and deliberate fashion to establish a reasonably normal relationship. In December 1991, Premier Li Peng's return visit was the first visit by a Chinese Prime Minister in 31 years. There has been an exchange of many high level visits and confidence-building measures, but agreement is not yet near to the disputed border treaty totalling almost 125,000 square kilometres. No Indian leader can concede Indian territory to China without risking accusations of a sell-out and jeopardising his or her own political position.[34] The two countries have agreed to resolve the dispute gradually. India and China are in agreement that the border dispute should not continue to remain an

[32] Malcolm Subhan, "Commission Calls for Greater EU-India Political Dialogue", *Economic Times*, 27 June 1996.
[33] For a background study, see Rajendra K. Jain (ed.), *China-South Asian Relations, 1947–1980* (New Jersey, 1981).
[34] See Sumit Ganguly, "The Sino-Indian Border Talks, 1981–1989" (1989) 24(2) *Asian Survey* 1123.

impediment to an overall improvement in relations.[35] China's nuclear status also poses a challenge. India–China trade has grown eight-fold from $200 million in 1990 to $1.6 billion in 1995, and $1.83 billion in 1997, but it remains confined to low-value items.

Although there is a toning-down of the potential military threat posed by China, it continues to be the main external power with sufficient political and military capability to meddle in Southern Asian affairs to India's disadvantage, for example by provision of military assistance to India's neighbours (apart from Pakistan, to Nepal, Bangladesh, and Myanmar).

India's nuclear explosion of May 1998 pushed other issues to the backburner. China perceives India as a potential rival in Asia. The India–China Joint Working Group has not met and there has been no structural dialogue with China since the Pokharan II tests. China's policy has sought to prop up India's smaller neighbours to keep Delhi tied down to the Southern Asian region, and continuing the process of rapprochement by accepting an extremely slow-moving process of confidence-building measures.[36] Jaswant Singh, at his first conference after taking over as Foreign Minister, reiterated India's commitment to "further improving" ties with China and he urged Chinese leaders to help India "untie the knots" through frequent consultations and dialogue.[37]

Japan

India has also targeted Japan as a major source of trade, investment, and technology. Since 1991, more than seventy Japanese companies have established manufacturing bases in India. Nearly 100 Japanese trade and industry delegations visited India between November 1995 and March 1996, apart from 250 others who made individual forays.

Japanese investment in India has almost quadrupled since 1994, from an initial trickle. In the calendar year 1995, the Indian Government approved $436 million worth of Japanese investments, up four times compared with $112 million the previous year.[38] Total Japanese investment during the six years since the beginning of economic reform was Rs 37 billion, or over $1 billion, a 62-fold increase as compared to merely Rs 600 million during the six-year period before

[35] See G.P. Deshpande, "Looking into the Next Millennium: India and China" (1993) 30(2) *International Studies* 207; Abu Taher Salahuddin Ahmed, "India-China Relations in the 1990s" (1996) 26(1) *Journal of Contemporary Asia* 100; Sujit Dutta, "India-China Relations in the post-Cold War Era" (1994) 16(11) *Strategic Analysis* 1411; Nancy Jetley, "Sino-Indian Relations: Old Legacies and Vistas" (1994) 30(2) *China Report* 215.

[36] Swaran Singh, "Sino-Indian Ties: Need for Bold Initiatives" (1999) 22(1) *Strategic Analysis* 1729.

[37] "India Ready for Talks with China: Jaswant", *The Hindu* (New Delhi), 25 December 1998.

[38] "Japanese Investment in India up Four-Fold", *Business Standard*, 23 September 1996. See also Japan Economic Research Institute, *The Liberalization of India's Economy and Japan's Contribution* (Tokyo, 1993); Horimoto Takemori, "Synchronizing Japan-India Relations" (1993) 40(1) *Japan Quarterly* 34.

reforms began. Moreover, two-thirds of this investment took place during 1995 and 1996.[39]

Japan has also been India's largest bilateral donor, a position it has maintained for the last nine years. During 1996–1997, Japan will provide India with an amount of 132.746 billion yen (approximately Rs 41.15 billion) as Official Development Assistance (ODA).[40] Until 1996, India received Japanese ODA, mostly in the form of soft loans, totalling nearly US $470 million. The share of Japan in India's total external assistance increased from 4.7 per cent in 1985–1986, to nearly 33 per cent in 1994–1995.[41] Japan is also one of India's largest trading partners, but lags behind the United States and the EU. In 1995, India's bilateral trade with Japan increased by 16 per cent, to reach $5.5 billion.

Eastern Europe

The transformation of the geopolitical milieu and foreign policy priorities and perspectives of Central and East European countries (CEECs) had significant repercussions on Indian foreign policy.[42] The East European revolutions destroyed many impressions and delusions. The logic of India–East European relations had changed considerably. India was a little slow to make an overall politico-economic assessment of the changing landscape in Eastern Europe and the Soviet Union and assess implications for itself.[43] The lesson, Foreign Minister Inder Kumar Gujral concluded, was that "successful socialism needs democratic party participation".[44] With the failure of state socialism in the former Soviet Union and Eastern Europe, the state socialist model had ceased to be a realistic option for the South. The lesson, the Foreign Minister concluded, was that "successful socialism needs democratic party participation".[45]

Unlike the past, when the CEECs perceived India with Moscow's eyes, the 1990s have witnessed changes in how they view Indian domestic and foreign policy. No longer can India rely on them for continued political support on

---

[39] Address by JETRO's Chairman at the Indian Engineering Trade Fair Japan Day Ceremony, New Delhi, 10 February 1997, mimeographed, 5.

[40] "Japan to Give Rs4115 cr ODA", *Hindustan Times*, 14 January 1997.

[41] Confederation of Indian Industry, India-Japan Symposium, Background Paper, *"Vision 2000 and Beyond . . .",* 10 February 1997, New Delhi, 1–3, 9.

[42] See Rajendra K. Jain, "India, Hungary, and the European Union", paper presented at a seminar organised by the Hungarian Institute of International Affairs, Budapest, 18 November 1998.

[43] Minister of State for External Affairs, K. Natwar Singh, who visited East Germany, Hungary and Poland when these changes occurred, recounts a discussion with Solidarity leader Lech Walesa, who asked: ". . . tell me where was India all these ten years?"—a reminder of India's neglect of the region during the Cold War era. The Indian Minister replied: "Mr. Walesa, I want to talk to you about the future, not the past". As a former Ambassador to Poland, Singh admitted: "I knew we had absolutely no contacts in these countries, and frankly, because we did not expect those changes". Cited in Maharajkrishna Rasgotra (ed.), *Rajiv Gandhi's India: A Golden Jubilee Retrospective, Volume 3: Foreign Policy: Ending the Quest for Dominance* (New Delhi, 1998), 154.

[44] Cited in Barbara Crossette, "Shock Waves from Eastern Europe Rattle 'Nonaligned' India", *International Herald Tribune*, 15 March 1990.

[45] Ibid.

various international issues (e.g. Kashmir). They are less appreciative of India's stand towards the Non-Proliferation Treaty, human rights violations in Punjab and Kashmir, and policies towards neighbours. It was expected that Eastern European countries would evaluate the cost and efficacy of their joint ventures in India and was likely to abandon those which were found to be inefficient or ineffective.[46]

Since the traditional *bonhomie* had virtually disappeared, Foreign Minister Gujral urged Indian missions in Eastern Europe to look for opportunities for fostering closer links at higher levels and to take full advantage of Indian "contacts with the people in these countries which predate the establishment of [the] Communist regime".[47]

There was exchange of high-level visits. President Shankar Dayal Sharma visited Bulgaria and Romania in May–June 1994. The visit led to the signing of various agreements with the two countries. Relations with Bulgaria and Romania were described as providing "a role model" for interaction with other Eastern European countries.[48] This was followed by visits to the Czech Republic and Slovakia in October 1996 by President Sharma. The visit resulted in two agreements on investment protection and co-operation in the fields of culture, education and science and a protocol on foreign office consultations with the Czech Republic, India's largest trading partner in Central Europe.

The crumbling of the familiar old order in the centrally planned economies took away the earlier tidiness provided by annual trade plans for exports and imports, the mechanism for balancing them over a five-year period, and the identification of items in bilateral trade. The Eastern European markets had become increasingly competitive, especially as they switched to trading in hard currency.[49] This was on top of traditional problems in boosting exports to the CEECs because of Indian constraints in providing substantial suppliers' credits. India also has potential as the Eastern Europeans seek to expand trade and economic links with Asian growth centres. The CEECs also represent opportunities if India can restructure its export basket. Indian exports to Eastern Europe, which had witnessed its worst year in 1992–1993, have shown signs of improvement.

Eastern Europe will have greater priority for financial flows, technology transfer and market access. While it was felt that the diversion of financial

[46] Harish Chandola, "Changes in East Europe, Likely Fallout in India", *Indian Express* (New Delhi), 10 February 1990.

[47] "India to Strengthen E. European Missions", *Hindustan Times* (New Delhi), 10 March 1990.

[48] Minister of State for External Affairs, Salman Khursheed, cited in M.K. Dhar, "India, Romania to Sign Several Pacts", *Hindustan Times*, 2 June 1994.

[49] At the beginning of 1990–1991, India had bilateral clearing arrangements providing for trade on the basis of payments of a non-convertible Indian rupee and on a balanced basis with five out of eight countries in the region, *viz.* the USSR, Czechoslovakia, the German Democratic Republic (GDR), Poland and Romania. With the unification of the two Germanys, the rupee payment arrangement with the GDR ended in December 1990. An agreement with Czechoslovakia (17 January 1991) extended the bilateral trade and payments arrangement for two years, i.e. until December 1992. Trade with Poland, Hungary, Bulgaria and Yugoslavia began to be conducted on the basis of payments in any freely convertible currency.

resources on the part of the West to Eastern Europe may not be a medium- or long-term phenomenon, but in the short term, it was definitely going to affect the flow of resources to the Third World. It is likely that labour-intensive goods from middle-income least developed countries (LDCs) will suffer most from changing East–West relations. As the CEECs, especially the Visegrad Four (Poland, Hungary, the Czech Republic and Slovakia), are elevated in the EU's hierarchy of trade preferences and will reach the top of the "pyramid of privilege" sooner rather than later, India will face serious challenges because it will result in fiercer competition and severe adjustment problems in its traditional Western markets. A recent study by the Indian Institute of Foreign Trade argued that the net fallout on India's trade under the new tariff regime would be positive as a result of the eastward expansion of the EU. The Ministry of Commerce concluded that to tap the potential of an enlarged EU market, the onus would be on India and its exporters to adjust to the new industrial fabric in Europe and the ensuing changes in methods of production, commerce, and trade.[50]

III SOUTH AND SOUTH-EAST ASIA

South Asia

The end of the Cold War has resulted in the general improvement of interstate relations in Southern Asia since it has toned down the malign influence and intrusion of external powers in fostering tension in the region. Some of the traditionally contentious issues in Southern Asia have been moderated and relations have improved in general with the revival of democratic institutions and processes in Bangladesh, Nepal and Pakistan. India's recent willingness to accept a degree of asymmetry, without insisting on reciprocity, in bilateral relations with smaller neighbours, has begun to pay dividends. The United Front's "Neighborhood Policy" enjoined upon India, being a larger country, to do more than what it would expect from the smaller neighbours.

Relations with Pakistan continue to be as intractable as before. The world is getting tired of relentless, almost unending, Indo-Pak antagonism. The adversarial relationship with Pakistan has affected India's regional profile, slowed down regional economic integration efforts and created various complications in domestic politics. After several decades, Indian foreign policy has recently outgrown its obsession with what Pakistan is and is not doing. No longer is mobilisation of international support against Pakistan the cornerstone of India's foreign policy. The jettisoning of the Pakistan-centric features in India's foreign policy have enabled India to play a bigger role in subcontinental affairs and in international politics. For some time now, India has been stressing

---

[50] T.V. Satyanaranan, "EU Expansion to Benefit Indian Exporters: Study", *Economic Times*, 28 July 1998.

greater "people-to-people" ties and one-sided confidence-building measures, for example the recent "bus diplomacy" and the inauguration of the Delhi-Lahore bus service (February 1999) and the relaxation of visa requirements (March 1999). It is pursuing a deliberate policy of avoiding "any polemical interaction" or reactive rhetoric with Pakistan.[51] There is broad-based "Kashmir fatigue" around the world. India's greater transparency on human rights, allowing foreign envoys to visit Jammu and Kashmir, the conduct of elections, and restoration of the political process have produced very positive images abroad, which, in turn, have greatly diluted Pakistan's attempt to internationalise or multilateralise the dispute and continually complain about India's aggressive intentions.[52]

Relations with Nepal had considerably deteriorated as a result of India's hardened stand, partly over questions of extending the Indo–Nepal Trade and Transit Agreement, displeasure at Kathmandu's decision to purchase arms from China, and the imposition of restrictions on the entry of Indian nationals into the Himalayan Kingdom. These strains were resolved in June 1990 when the two countries signed an agreement to restore the status quo. Land-locked Nepal has also been permitted to use the Chittagong port, thereby allowing Nepal to link with Bangladesh through Indian territory. The ratification of the Mahakali River Treaty in September 1996 by a two-thirds majority in the Nepalese Parliament to harness the irrigation and power potential of the Mahakali river system marked the beginning of a new phase in economic co-operation between India and Nepal. The successful implementation of the Mahakali project is bound to have a demonstrative effect in convincing the people of Nepal as to how much more can be achieved through mutual co-operation.

Indo–Sri Lankan relations showed considerable improvement in the aftermath of India's decision to withdraw the Indian Peace Keeping Force (IPKF) from Sri Lanka in March 1990. Despite recurring tensions which impinge on bilateral relations on account of the occasional spillover of domestic problems in Sri Lanka and emotive politics in Tamil Nadu, there is broad consensus on enhancing economic co-operation. The conclusion of a landmark investment promotion and protection agreement in February 1997 gave a further boost to bilateral economic ties.

Relations with Bangladesh have considerably improved.[53] The most contentious issue, the sharing of Ganga waters, has been resolved by the signing of the historic treaty in December 1996.[54] Other bilateral irritants have also been removed, for example the transfer of the Tin Bigha corridor to Bangladesh.

---

[51] Foreign Minister Gujral's press conference in Singapore, 21 August 1996. "India Demands Honest Nuclear Test Ban Treaty", *Hindustan Times*, 22 August 1996.

[52] Aabha Dixit, "Kashmir-fatigue around the World?", *Hindustan Times*, 22 October 1996.

[53] Shyamali Ghosh, "Political Dynamics in Bangladesh: Relations between Bangladesh and India" (1995) 32(3) *International Studies* 237.

[54] See Iftekharuzzaman, "Ganges Water Sharing Issue: Diplomacy and Domestic Politics in Bangladesh" (1994) 15(3) *Bliss Journal* (Dhaka) 215; Ashok Swain, "Conflicts over Water: The Ganges Water Dispute" (1993) 24(4) *Security Dialogue* 429.

India however, continues to remain sensitive about the question of illegal Bangladeshi immigration[55] from the highly porous border between the two countries and the establishment of a number of training camps for insurgents, allegedly run by Pakistan's later Services Intelligence (ISI), which recurrently hinders better bilateral understanding and co-operation. Other bilateral issues which remain on the agenda are the question of inland water transit facility for Indian goods, and the pending task of the demarcation of the Indo–Bangla boundary in the forty-nine-kilometre stretch between Tripura and West Bengal.

India's policy towards its neighbours is based on bilateralism and resistance to external powers. This approach is criticised interference by others who argue that India, as the region's dominant power, remains "chained" to the notion that bilateral advantages outweigh any gains that may be derived from dealing with other neighbours on a multilateral basis.[56]

Regional economic co-operation in South Asia

The resolution of contentious issues between India and its neighbours have engendered greater enthusiasm among smaller member states of the South Asian Association for Regional Cooperation (SAARC) to appreciably improve the climate for fostering regional and sub-regional economic co-operation. As economic issues have come to the fore in the 1990s, all Southern Asian countries have undertaken liberalisation of their economies and actively solicited direct foreign investment.

Intra-regional trade in Southern Asia doubled from $1.089 billion in 1985 (or 2.4 per cent of world trade) to $2.919 billion in 1994 (or 3.5 per cent of world trade). But trade continues to be constrained by several factors.[57] Under the existing state of co-operation among the Southern Asian members of SAARC, intra-regional trade was estimated to rise above $3 billion by the year 2000 and to $9 billion by 2015. But if land transport, communication networks and transit facilities improved in the region, intra-regional trade, according to one estimate, could rise to over $17 billion by 2015.[58]

The balance sheet of SAARC, after completing more than a decade since its establishment, has been creditable. A major achievement has undoubtedly been

[55] There are an estimated twelve million illegal migrants from Bangladesh in various parts of India, of which 9.4 million are concentrated in Assam and West Bengal. Mohan Guruswamy, "In Search of Land?", *Hindustan Times Sunday Magazine*, 16 February 1997, 5. See also Rakesh Sinha, "Continuing Threat of Bangladesh Migrants", *Hindustan Times*, 10 September 1998.

[56] Lloyd I. Rudolph, "The Faltering Novitate: Rajiv at Home and Abroad in 1988", in Marshall M. Boulan and Philip Oldenberg (eds), *India Briefing* (Boulder, CO, 1989), 26.

[57] These are: (i) competitive export baskets; (ii) high rate of tariff and non-tariff barriers; (iii) lack of adequate transport and information links; and (iv) political differences and a lack of willingness to create trade complimentarities. Kishore C. Dash, "The Political Economy of Regional Cooperation in South Asia" (1996) 69(2) *Pacific Affairs* 203.

[58] A survey conducted in 1994 by M. Rahmatullah, Director of the Transport, Communication and Tourism Division of the Economic and Social Commission for Asia and the Pacific. "Trade in S. Asia Likely to Rise", *Hindustan Times*, 27 January 1997.

the ratification of the SAARC Preferential Trade Agreement (SAPTA) by all SAARC members in December 1995 and their decision to create an SAARC Free Trade Area (SAFTA). Significant progress has also been made in promoting greater understanding on various issues, such as terrorism and narcotics, and in fostering regional cultural and economic programmes. Given the lack of progress in Indo–Pak relations, there is greater willingness to forge sub-regional groupings within the SAARC. There is growing realisation that the SAARC activities should be concentrated on a few specific fields and that political differences among member states should be addressed to create a proper environment for collective growth and economic development.

As the pivotal power in Southern Asia, India would have to play a reasonable role based on a national understanding of rights and duties.[59] India should shed its "marwari, quick profit and reciprocal mentality and show the vision and long-term perspective in taking initiatives towards creating structures of mutually advantageous economic interdependence".[60] As the largest member state with a comparative advantage in virtually all sectors, India has been more generous in offering unilateral, non-reciprocal reduction, or elimination of barriers to imports from the region. Thus, India unilaterally announced that it would remove import restrictions on more than 2,000 products as of 1 August 1998. As the strongest economy in the region, with whom all member states of the SAARC (except Bhutan) have a big deficit in balance of payments, India took the bold initiative of lifting qualitative restrictions maintained for balance of payments on a preferential basis for SAARC countries with effect from 1 August 1998. This generous gesture by India is in keeping with the desire of all SAARC countries (except Pakistan) to hasten the birth of SAFTA from the proposed date of 2003 to 2001 and the South Asian Economic Community shortly thereafter. It is obvious that a strategy of making unilateral concessions on the economic front will have a long-term beneficial impact.

A major step in integrating Southern Asian economies and accelerating regional economic integration in the region was the signing of a free trade agreement (FTA) between India and Sri Lanka on 28 December 1998. The key provision was for India to move towards a free trade regime within three years and Sri Lanka within eight years. All duties on imports from each other are to be renewed within the stipulated period except those levied on items included on the negative lists. The agreement raised considerable criticism in the Sri Lankan media. The FTA, in fact, seemed a timid step towards economic integration because it was limited to movement of goods and not services, had no stipulation as to when the items on the negative lists of the two countries would be liberalised, and raised doubts about how preferential treatment could be

---

[59] See Shrikant Paranjape, "From State-Centrism to Transnationalism: SAARC, SAPTA and SAFTA" (1996) 52(1) and (2) *India Quarterly* 95.

[60] S.D. Muni, "Coping with Contentious Issues in South Asia", in L.L. Mehrotra, H.S. Chopra and Gert W. Kueck (eds), *SAARC 2000 and Beyond* (New Delhi, 1995), 94.

suspended.[61] During its first decade, SAARC engaged in only symbolic co-operation. It is only in recent years that it is moving towards a more "goal-oriented co-operation", especially with an emphasis on economic issues. By and large, governments of almost all member states of SAARC share Indian views that co-operation in economic, social and technical fields need not wait for the solution of political problems. However, it is very likely that the restraint in the SAARC Charter preventing the taking-up of contentious political and regional issues, especially the bilateral ones, might be overcome sooner rather than later.

India's "look East" policy

For the first time since independence, India has decided to give "a special policy thrust to its relations with the ASEAN" and sought to forge improved relations with individual countries in the Association of South-East Asian Nations (ASEAN) region and with ASEAN as a collective entity.[62] India's rediscovery of Southeast Asia, especially member states of the Association of South East Asian Nations (ASEAN), in the 1990s has been motivated by both economic compulsions and political reasons. Political dialogue and strategic interaction has been facilitated by the overcoming of earlier ASEAN fears about Indian naval expansion in the 1980s and because ASEAN governments probably saw "a Soviet halo" around New Delhi at that time. India's hasty recognition of the Heng Samrin regime was detrimental to India's relations with ASEAN, and led to no discernible advantage to India.[63] Foreign Minister Gujral described India's "look East" policy as: "an outward-looking India is gathering all forces of dynamism, domestic and regional, and is directly focusing on establishing synergies with a fast, consolidating and progressive neighbourhood to its east in the mother continent of Asia".[64] The Asia–Pacific could be "the springboard for our [Indian] leap into the global marketplace".[65] Thus India's "look East" policy seeks to gain greater access to the markets and capitals of the "tigers" and "dragons" of East and South-East Asia.

[61] See Muchkund Dubey, "On a Faster Track: Cementing Economic Links with Sri Lanka", *Times of India*, 14 January 1999.

[62] Government of India, Minstry of External Affairs, *Annual Report, 1992–93* (New Delhi, 1993), 6, 27.

[63] On this, see G.V.C. Naidu, "The Indian Navy and Southeast Asia", *Contemporary South Asia*, June 1992; Rahul Roy-Chaudhury, "Role of the Navy in Indian Security Policy" (1993) 2(2) *Contemporary South Asia* 151; Mihir K. Roy, "India's Quest for a Coherent Maritime Policy", *Strategic Analysis* (New Delhi), June 1992, 223; Alexander Gordon, "India's Security Policy: Desire and Necessity in a Changing World", in Chandran Jeshurun (ed.), *China, India and Japan and Southeast Asia* (Institute of Southeast Asian Studies, Singapore, 1993), 42; Mohammed Ayoob, *India and Southeast Asia: Perceptions and Policies* (New York, 1990); Baladas Ghoshal, *India and Southeast Asia—Challenges and Opportunities* (New Delhi, 1996).

[64] Statement by I.K. Gujral at the opening of the post-ministerial conference of ASEAN States plus 10 States, Jakarta, 24 July 1996. "Gujral Rejects Pressures over Signing CTBT", *Hindustan Times*, 25 July 1996.

[65] Prime Minster P.V. Narasimha Rao's 13th Singapore Lecture, 8 September 1994; cited in V.V. Banoji Rao, "APEC Perspectives and India", *Economic Times*, 11 October 1994.

A greater appreciation of India's maritime interests and threats by ASEAN (including India's potential role as a balancer in the region) have paved the way for joint naval exercises between India and Indonesia, Malaysia and Singapore. The most significant progress has been in forging strategic links with Singapore and Malaysia. With Malaysia, India signed a Memorandum of Understanding (MOU) in February 1993 on defence co-operation, stipulating the provision of training to Malaysian defence forces and the supply of spare parts and servicing for MiG-29 aircraft. Singapore has been permitted to use India's missile testing range for testing of guns and missiles.[66]

India's relations with ASEAN have been steadily upgraded. India became a "sectoral" dialogue partner of ASEAN in January 1992 (in the areas of trade, technical and manpower development, technology and tourism), a full dialogue partner in December 1995, and a member of the ASEAN Regional Forum (ARF) in June 1996.[67] Full dialogue partnership with ASEAN was the "manifestation of the Indian 'look East' destiny" and because India is "geographically inseparable, culturally conjoined and now more than ever before economically and strategically interdependent and complementary".[68] However, there is a growing feeling in South-East Asia that India should get involved, definitely not directly but substantially and only at an intermediate date, with strategic issues vital to the region. For its part, however, despite growing defence co-operation and joint maritime exercises, India has no intention of playing a major security role or attempting to fill the power vacuum in the region.

India now has a major and increasing economic stake in ASEAN. Indian trade patterns between 1992–1993 and 1994–1995 underwent a substantial (8 per cent) directional shift in favour of East and South-East Asia, which now takes 42 per cent of India's exports, while the share of the EU has fallen to 27 per cent.[69] Indo–ASEAN trade had doubled from $3 billion to $6 billion during 1993–1996. Even after the recent financial crisis in the region, the volume of trade remains virtually the same, although ASEAN exports outstrip those of India.

India has displayed greater dynamism in actively forging new economic links with ASEAN countries, some of which have targeted India as a key area for investment and trade. Between 1991 and May 1995 approved equity investment by ASEAN countries amounted to Rs 21.7 billion or 6.2 per cent of total approved investments.[70] Common interests are also evident in resisting Western pressure on new issues like labour standards, corruption and the social clause.

[66] See G.V.C. Naidu, "India and ASEAN" (1996) 19(1) *Strategic Analysis* (New Delhi) 65.

[67] India, according to one observer, was invited to join the ARF because most of the East and South-East Asian nations are increasingly concerned about the potentially growing Chinese hegemonism and view India as a potential counterweight to it. K. Subrahmanyam, "Hubris of the Hegemons", *Economic Times*, 21 August 1996. See also Ganganath Jha, "India's Sectoral Partnership with ASEAN" (1992) 20(3) *Indonesian Quarterly* 298.

[68] "Gujral Rejects Pressures over Signing CTBT, ,*Hindustan Times*, 25 July 1996.

[69] Interview with Commerce Secretary Tejinder Khanna in *Economic Times, Special Supplement on European Union*, 9 May 1995, iv; "India's Trade Shifts from W. Europe to Oceania, East Asia", *Times of India*, 3 May 1995.

[70] Naidu, above at n. 66, 70.

Trade declined as the recession-hit South-East Asian countries reeled under the monetary crisis. The plummeting east and South-east Asian exchange rates ate away at India's competitiveness. India has been able to successfully ward off any spill-over from the South-east Asian currency crisis because the Reserve Bank of India took a number of steps in 1998 on monetary management.

India's exclusion from the inaugural Asia–Europe Meeting (ASEM) in March 1996 was partly the result of India not being a full dialogue partner of ASEAN and partly because of the fierce opposition by Thailand and Malaysia as well as Japan, primarily because they argued that expanded membership would dilute ASEM's East Asian/Pacific orientation and make it more difficult and unwieldy for the Asian side to take initiatives within ASEM.[71] India's membership of ASEM, even at the forthcoming Soeul meeting (2000), remains uncertain, since many ASEM officials feel that it is too early to talk of new members.[72]

IV POLITICS OF ECONOMIC REFORM

The economic crisis of 1991 was a deviation from Nehru's development strategy of delivering moderate growth and maintaining economic stability through prudent fiscal management. It was the "result of breaking these three essential pillars, the subordination of longer-term economic policy to electoral exigencies, high government borrowing, most of it being used to subsidise and placate, and not for productive or infrastructural purposes".[73] To some extent, as Jagdish Bhagwati rightly observes, "changing India's uniquely damaging policy framework, nourished for over three decades, is a task akin to cleaning up after a typoon: the task is enormous and cannot be done all at once".[74]

Despite Westerners' dissatisfaction with the content and pace of reforms, a reality often missed by many is that most reforms and high economic growth have been achieved in India in times of political uncertainty and by weak coalition governments, which baulk at pushing through many politically difficult reforms (especially reducing food and fertiliser subsidies, and ending state monopolies on key sectors). Obviously, more substantial change is not possible without political will. Management of the economy has apparently been largely insulated from the inadequacies and insecurities of the political leadership, and the emerging consensus on economic reforms remained essentially unchallenged. The process of reform will continue, irrespective of governmental changes, because economic liberalisation is guided more by economic imperatives rather than political rhetoric.

[71] Amy Siratori, "Difficulties Await Asia-Europe Link", *Japan Times*, 4 March 1996.
[72] "Indian Membership in ASEM Uncertain", *Hindustan Times*, 4 February 1997.
[73] Sunil Khilnani, *The Idea of India* (Delhi, 1997), 88, 92, 98.
[74] Jagdish Bhagwati, "The Design of Indian Development", in Isher Judge Ahluwalia and I.M.D. Little (eds), *India's Economic Reforms and Development: Essays for Manmohan Singh* (Delhi, 1998), 36.

Despite its positive responses to the mantras of "liberalisation" and "globalisation", India is determined to fine-tune the reform process in the country, taking into account its ground realities. It is keen to avoid adverse impacts of unrestrained liberalisation, as exemplified in the slogan "yes to silicon chips, no to potato chips". There are many who argue that there is no third way, no alternative to complete liberalisation, deregulation, privatisation and globalisation—other than meltdown, collapse and economic ruin. But a greater majority feel that India has to address its problems by itself and focus on an agenda based on its people's needs and priorities.

The doctrine of economic liberalisation encountered ferocious resistance from that section of business which lacked the competitive edge to battle it out with global players in the market place. Consequently, there seems to be a tendency, at the first hint of an economic downturn, to exert enormous pressure on the system to invoke Indian uniqueness and exceptionalism and retreat into the settled ways of regulation and protectionism. Businessmen are now bitterly complaining about an "uneven playing field" on which they have to contend with foreign competition and seek government help to survive and fight on. Officials and politicians who have benefited from what was known as the *neta babu, or* leader-bureaucrat *raj*, are fighting to preserve at least some of the controls which gave them their power and commissions. But there are growing sections of the business community who increasingly feel that business acumen lies not in acquiring licences but in possessing entrepreneurial vision and managerial acumen. The present Indian system of corporate governance is encumbered with serious problems: conflicts of interest and lack of cohesion among many controlling families, and the adverse effects of large interlocking, inter-group investments on small shareholders from decisions with regard to corporate restructuring, mergers, disinvestments, etc.

There is a very general agreement that the poor must share the benefits of growth, and even enjoy a disproportionate share for some time, if that is possible without significantly reducing the growth rate. Those who criticise reform as being hostile to poverty show ignorance or prejudice. In fact, "reform is or should be designed not only to be good for growth, but also good for labour-intensive growth, and increasing the demand for relatively unskilled labour is the only way to reduce the massive widespread poverty that still pervades India today".[75] There is no conflict between growth and poverty alleviation. If India could achieve the spectacular growth rates of East Asia, mass structural poverty could be eliminated within a generation.[76]

Comparisons of India with countries like Singapore, Taiwan and South Korea are, on the face of it, invidious. There are obvious differences in the scale of problems confronted, the size of population and the political systems adopted (autocracy drove economic growth in all three cases, but at a price which plu-

---

[75] Isher Judge Ahluwalia and I.M. Little, "Introduction", in Ahluwalia and Little, ibid., 13.
[76] See Deepak Lal, "Economic Reform and Poverty Alleviation", in ibid., 231.

ralist India could not pay). India has not found itself to be immune from the unprecedented economic crisis in East and South-East Asia. Careful not to repeat mistakes of the Asian tigers, India is determined to fine-tune the reform process in the country, taking into account its own priorities and ground realities. It is conscious of the adverse impacts of unrestrained liberalisation, the shortcomings of the market and the pitfalls of globalisation.

Impact of economic reform

The free market reforms since 1991 have unleashed a market revolution. Consumer is king. Capitalism is already recasting India's economy and society. Economic reform has implications for social cohesion in India. The opening-up of India to foreign goods, greater opportunities and acesss to overseas travel, access to nearly fifty satellite television channels (which are going *desi* (localising) in order to be watched), and the Internet have led to shrill criticism that these foreign influences are undermining Indian civilisation and cultural values. India seeks to pursue reform to foster its economic strengths and capabilities, but this seems to be accompanied by a fear of losing its identity. Despite growing trends, especially amongst the youth in urban India, towards Westernisation and consumerism, it is incorrect to assume that Indians can somehow be accultured out of their Indianness. To globalise, it must realise that its culture must stand on its identity and its inner strengths.

The most durable achievement of the economic reform process initiated by Manmohan Singh has been the changing of the political mindset in the country. The bold beginning made in 1991—the decisive break away from the strongly inward-oriented trade policy regime in India, thereby providing an environment for efficient industrialisation and better export performance and the economy's very favourable response to it holds out the promise of further progress.

The transfer of reforms does not seem to bode well for the future of reforms since the capacity of the new political elite to deal with the complex economic and strategic issues facing the country is limited. The "agenda of the new political elite in 'Mandalised' India is dominated by caste and regional considerations. Their skills to deal with a new liberalised and globalising Indian economy are under strain. Their concern is not with development but what they call 'social justice'. Translated into plain English, it means direct sops to their electoral constituency".[77] The next fifteen years, political economy will be greatly influenced by the increasingly vocal and politially powerful Other Backward Classes (OBCs) and Scheduled Castes (SCs). But in the long run the rapidly growing middle class will be the most formidable influence on the Indian political economy for the rest of the twenty-first century, making India a major political and economic global power.[78]

---

[77] V.A. Pai Panandiker, "The Political Economy of Centre-State Relations in India", in ibid., 375.
[78] Ibid.

Economic change in the 1990s has engendered social ferment. Economic reform faces serious political obstacles in democratic India. Indian politicians are dominated by the expedient and the short term. Thus, the new national consensus on economic reform is "beset with what some see as compromise and hesitation, and others judge as political wisdom: liberalisation yes, politically painful dismissals and cuts, no".[79] Politicians also have to guarantee that liberalisation is not accompanied by short-term catastrophes for the more vulnerable sections of the population. The new consensus is on "a very muffled sort of liberalisation. All parties agree on the need for a welfare state, and in practice this translates into special dispensations such as subsidies for various interest groups". Moreover, with sectarian parties making huge electoral gains and with voters increasingly embracing religious, caste and regional loyalties, the state now seeks to promote social change not through secular development, but through quotas and reservations for different sections of the population. Aiyar therefore concludes that today the role of the state has changed from "economic commander to provider of subsidies and sectarian reservations".[80]

Liberalisation in India will not free the state from demands being made upon it. Demands, often contradictory, will increase. In fact, India's democratic politics have released "a multitude of voices and interests, which make the effort to maintain fiscal prudence and to devise and conduct strategies of economic development more complicated than ever before . . . There are now more arguments, more interests, more conceptions of what development is and what it means for India".[81] The Indian polity has been subjected to diverse pressures in recent years: the relentless logic of democratic urges and aspirations in an unequal and hierarchical society. Since the 1980s, India has witnessed growing conflicts among social groups whose identities could be activated for political ends: religious, urban or rural, caste, language, class or ethnic origin. Therefore, the "conflicts in India today are the conflicts of modern politics; they concern the state, access to it, and to whom it ultimately belongs".[82]

The Indian polity is changing and change is redefining how political power is held and wielded in India. In fact, in India the state has come to play "an extraordinary role in the economic life of the country so that competition for political power in the state has become competition for the power to control, to regulate, and to benefit through the process of appropriating, dividing, and distributing the economic resources of the state".[83]

---

[79] Shashi Tharoor, *India: From Midnight to Millennium* (New Delhi, 1997), 186.
[80] Swaminathan S. Anklesaria Aiyar, "The Changing Role of the Indian State", in Gautam Adhikari (ed.), *India: The First 50 Years* (London, 1992), 69.
[81] Khilnani, above at n. 73, 105–106.
[82] Ibid., 50, 59–60.
[83] Tharoor, above at n. 79, 271.

Foreign direct investment

Indian development strategy in the 1990s has shed the earlier stress on the import of technology on outright purchase or through licensing arrangements. In the post-Cold War era, India more clearly understands the link between direct foreign investment (FDI) and export growth. Despite resistance in some quarters to shield Indian industry from foreign competition, there is a broad consensus that India must upgrade its technological, managerial and competitive strength. European business recognises the tremendous potential of India, the second largest market in the world, with a growing, highly educated, urban, consumerist middle class numbering 150–200 million (depending on how you define it).

Liberalisation of the FDI policy regime has led to a substantial expansion of FDI approvals and flows. The total number of foreign collaborations approval went up from 950 in 1991 to 2,124 by November 1995. However, the enormous increase in approvals by the Foreign Investment Promotion Board (FIPB) or the automatic clearances given by the Reserve Bank of India are no indication of the investment actually coming in, because the mortality rate is high. Of the total approvals till 1995 for Rs 612.48 billion, less than 22 per cent (Rs 132.35 billion) was actually received. A Federation of Indian Chambers of Commerce and Industry study revealed that only 24 per cent of total FDI approvals between August 1991 and October 1994 had actually flowed into India. This has happened either because the investor may be exploring different options in other countries or because the investor does not always come to the FIPB with a neatly prepared project report.[84] From US $620 million in 1993–1994, FDI more than doubled to US $1.31 billion in 1994–1995. Total foreign investment flows, direct and portfolio, rose sharply to US $4.11 billion in 1993–1994, with a further increase to US $4.89 billion in 1994–1995.[85] Unlike the popular myth that FDI flows have primarily been in potato chips, the bulk of FDI sanctions (78 per cent) continued to concentrate on telecom, fuel, chemicals, transportation, electrical equipment and certain high-tech service sectors between August 1991 and December 1995.[86] Even though cumulative FDI inflows are estimated to have reached $3.3 billion during January and November 1998 (up from $3.2 billion in 1997), India is still far from realising the target of $10 billion set by former Finance Minister P. Chidambaram.[87]

A major hurdle in attracting greater foreign investment is poor infrastructure, which will require over $200 billion during the next five years. But many feel that planning in India should shift from a mere setting of targets to a clear demarcation of policy options associated with those targets.

[84] D.H. Pai Panandiker, "Lags in Foreign Investment", *Hindustan Times*, 1 July 1996; Rajiv Shirali, "Investment Climate: The Tortoise Trail", *Economic Times*, 24 March 1995.
[85] Government of India, Ministry of Finance, Economic Division, *Economic Survey 1995–96* (New Delhi, 1996), 12, 97.
[86] Amit Mitra, "FDI Proposals and Equity Holdings", *Hindustan Times*, 28 December 1996.
[87] "The FDI Scene", *Hindustan Times*, 29 July 1998.

The approximate share of Western European FDI in India was 20 per cent in 1993, which rose to 30 per cent a year later. By mid-1995, this had resulted in the conclusion of agreements worth $7.2 billion in all. Despite these efforts, the level of European investments in India is not very high and Europe's share in foreign investments in India had even dropped from one-third to one-fifth.[88] However, the quantum of FDI that India is able to attract is much smaller than China, which has a 13-year headstart over India.

In an increasingly integrated world, considerations of cost, quality, punctuality and reliability will determine India's competitiveness. Infrastructural constraints continue to raise the cost of production in India. Apart from infrastructure constraints, a major hindering factor in promoting FDI is that foreigners complain that little has changed since they are obliged to deal with middle and lower levels of bureaucracy at the centre and states.

Declining aid, growing debt

India has slipped from first to sixth among recipients of OECD Development Assistance Committee aid during the last twenty years and from being the largest recipient of EC aid in 1980–1981 to the tenth largest a decade later.[89] To a certain extent, the decline in aid to India is explained by India's growing capacity to access external finance on commercial terms.

An area for much-needed reform is better utilisation of concession aid. It is indeed regrettable that concessional aid lies unused while the country accumulates high-interest debt in commercial terms. Thus, in 1995–1996 net aid was negative. Utilisation was $3.5 billion, against which repayments and interest amounted to $3.8 billion.[90] During fiscal year 1996, ending 30 June, India returned to the World Bank $723 million more than it received from the institution. During 1991–1996, India received commitments of $11.989 billion and disbursements of $10.893 billion. After repayment of principal and payment of

[88] Statement by Kamalesh Sharma, Deputy Secretary, Ministry of External Affairs, at the hearings on the EU New Strategy for Asia organised by the European Parliament's Committee on External Economic Relations at the end of June 1995. *Agence Europe*, No. 6519, 10/11 July 1995, 12. The EU-15 accounted for Rs 133.48 billion of approved FDI between August 1991 and March 1996 second only to the United States. Among the EU Member States, the United Kingdom was the leading investor with £3 billion, followed by Germany £2.5 billion, Netherlands (about £2 billion), France (about $1 billion), and Sweden (about £1 billion). Sudeep Chakravarti, "India and the European Union: Looking to the Future", *India Today*, 30 June 1996, 97; see also T.S. Viswanath, "European Union may Outstrip US in FDI, *Economic Times*, 4 November 1996; "European Investment Touches Pound 6 bn", *Hindustan Times*, 27 December 1996; Man Mohan, "India Must 'Speed Up' Privatisation", *Hindustan Times*, 24 October 1996.

[89] Judith Randel and Tony German, *The Reality of Aid: An Independent Review of International Aid* (June 1993), xii; see also Rajendra K. Jain, "European Development Aid Policies in the 1990s: Implications for India" 52(3) *India Quarterly* (New Delhi) 31.

[90] "How to Use Aid", *Economic Times*, 24 September 1996. This is due to two factors: first, because state governments are bust, and unable to come up with matching rupee funds; and, secondly, because many states have failed to make policy changes they promised as part of a loan package, with the result that the World Bank and other agencies have refused to disburse money.

interest, the country was left with only $609 million.[91] Thus, as former Finance Minister Manmohan Singh put it, since the days of concessional aid were over, India should not expect it to be used like it used to do before the reform programme began in 1991.[92]

India's external debt rose from US $75.90 billion in 1990 to US $95.2 billion at the end of September 1998. Debt service payments as a percentage of current account receipts also declined significantly from 35.3 per cent in 1990–1991 to 19.5 per cent in 1997–1998. India's debt service payments as a percentage of exports of goods and services was 25.1 per cent in 1993–1994.[93]

World Trade Organisation

India is becoming increasingly conscious that major developed countries are going to use the World Trade Organisation (WTO) to their utmost advantage. In fact, the WTO is being increasingly perceived as "an instrument for aiding in the determination of the world economic power equation in the twenty-first century than as merely a negotiating forum for trade".[94]

The developed nations, including the EU, are keen that India join the Millennium Round of the WTO, which should be broadened to include other crucial subjects like investment, trade, environment and development co-operation.[95] However, India has been consistently opposing the idea, arguing that it be postponed until a later period to allow for much more prior discussion which is crucial to most countries. Finance Minister Yashwant Sinha asserted that there was a need to consolidate the gains of the Uruguay Round and ensure that all the WTO agreements are implemented before moving to the next round. India has warned that it would not participate in the new round of trade liberalisation talks unless tangible benefits are provided to developing countries and least-developed countries as specified in the Uruguay Round agreements. These issues include: the need for greater market access for movement of professionals, skilled and semi-skilled persons; a review of Articles 18B and 25 of GATT, which deals with waivers based on balance of payments considerations; a censure of unilateral action by developed countries; the proposal on the "security exception" under Article 21 of GATT 1994; a review of GATT's dispute-settlement mechanism; and a developing country perspective on food security.

[91] "India Gave $723m more than it received from IBRD in Fiscal '96", *Economic Times*, 27 September 1996.

[92] Address by Manmohan Singh at the 69th annual session of the Federation of Indian Chambers of Commerce and Industry, New Delhi, 10 December 1996. "Continue with Reforms or Miss Bus", *Hindustan Times*, 11 December 1996.

[93] Government of India, Ministry of Finance, Economic Division, *Economic Survey 1995–96* (New Delhi, 1996), 101, 122; *Economic Survey, 1998–99*, in *Economic Times* (New Delhi), 25 February 1999, 9.

[94] Bhagirath Lal Das, "India's Trade Negotiations: Past Experience and Future Challenges" (1998) 35(4) *International Studies* (New Delhi) 408.

[95] See e.g. Sir Leon Brittan, "Shared Interests in a Liberalising Agenda", *Economic Times*, 13 January 1999.

The G-15 plan to stall inclusion of new issues under the WTO purview till the existing issues are solved to their satisfaction. India is arguing that overloading the WTO agenda by holding a comprehensive Millennium Round may not be realistic unless it has implemented its obligations under the Uruguay Round in the first instance, and assessed the impact of such implementation.[96]

Instead of encouraging completely free trade, the WTO has contributed to the growth of regionalism. In order to absorb regional groupings, a blind eye was turned to members of a regional bloc offering greater concessions to each other than they were willing to offer to other members of the WTO. There is growing feeling that trade liberalisation under the WTO regime has substantially benefited the developed countries. There is a feeling that this must change and it must gear-up its trade diplomacy to extract "reciprocal concessions from an unwilling West".[97]

V   INDIA, CTBT AND NON-PROLIFERATION

Non-proliferation has become an increasingly contentious issue in India's relations with the West, especially the United States, in the 1990s. As the West has redefined its agenda of nuclear non-proliferation for India, European powers' policies on non-proliferation and more effective co-ordination of export policies on sensitive and dual-use technologies coalesce with those of the United States. The West realises that the impact of sanctions imposed under various denial regimes in the security and economic fields created by the United States on India's economic and technological potential will only be marginal.[98] It may also not be possible indefinitely to sustain unity regarding technology export control.

India maintained that its refusal for over a quarter of a century to sign the Non-Proliferation Treaty (NPT) was because of its discriminatory character and the lack of logical and universal applicability of norms (e.g. the untenable position of both Britain and France to continue as nuclear powers). Developments in Iraq, Sweden, Pakistan and North Korea are all evidence of how the NPT has failed to prevent proliferation and that International Atomic Energy Agency safeguards are inadequate to prevent cheating. The rise of the so-called "rogue states" is ample evidence that strict treaty compliance is not enough to safeguard international security. India has been genuinely concerned when Pakistan has surreptitiously been able to obtain components and technologies from both the professed European nuclear powers (such as the United

---

[96] "Time to Consolidate Gains of Uruguay Round: Sinha", *Economic Times*, 16 February 1999; "India will not Take Part in WTO Talks unless Tangible Benefits Accrue", *Economic Times*, 11 December 1998.

[97] "Advantage India", editorial in *Hindustan Times* (New Delhi), 18 November 1997.

[98] On this, see G. Balachandran, "India's Nuclear Option: Economic Implications" (1996) 19(2) *Strategic Analysis* 143.

Kingdom and France) as well as from countries which are supposedly non-nuclear (Germany, Sweden and Switzerland). This has had a destabilising effect on Southern Asia.

The end of the Cold War did not appreciably improve the security situation in Southern Asia. The easy availability of weapons of mass destruction oin the subcontinent, and the missiles to deliver them, has radically altered the region's security environment. Highlighting this disturbing situation, the 1995–1996 Annual Report of the Ministry of Defence recommended the development of Agni and other indigenous missiles, and the deployment of the proven Prithvi, as warranted by exigencies.

The CTBT was principally targeted at the three nuclear threshold states (India, Israel and Pakistan) who have never signed the NPT. The Ramaker Draft was used to politically isolate and browbeat India, which was viewed as the single biggest obstacle to the Treaty.

India's veto of the CTBT was based on two arguments; refusal to recognise legitimate national security concerns (being situated between two nuclear weapon powers with an ongoing relationship of nuclear weapon co-operation) and the lack of any linkage of the Treaty with a time-bound programme of universal nuclear disarmament. The refusal of the nuclear "have nots" to forcefully amend the entry in the article was aimed at imposing the Treaty on an unwilling India, which was being treated as a country of limited sovereignty and compelling it to forego its nuclear option.[99] The CTBT text also did not meet Indian objections to on-site inspections and the use of national technical means, that matters regarding compliance with the Treaty must be vested with the proposed executive council and must not rest with individual states and parties. It also put too much control over verification in the hands of the declared nuclear powers. The Indian refusal to sign the CTBT did not resolve its nuclear dilemma and meet its security needs. Some urged that India, as a neighbour of three nuclear weapon states (China, Pakistan and Russia), begin addressing its nuclear option's long-neglected technical demands and undertake a long-term evaluation of its genuine security needs. Many in India stressed the need for a more explicit security policy instead of the mantra of keeping options open, which was an alibi for inaction, and more clearly spelling out the aims and goals in respect of India's nuclear policy. The nuclear threat from China and Pakistan (especially after the clandestine transfer of Chinese-made, nuclear-capable M-11 missiles and ring magnets) underline the need for India to retain its nuclear option.

The United States and China (which has a special relationship with Pakistan that involves military, nuclear and missile trade) are nuclear weapon powers and NPT parties with vested interests in Southern Asia. They are not "neutral referees". The United States has, in fact, "a tainted record" of pursuing selective

---

[99] K. Subrahmanyam, "Middle Path to Nuclear Security", *Economic Times*, 27 June 1996; K. Subrahmanyam, "The Chinese Chicanery", *Economic Times*, 14 August 1996.

proliferation in relation to its friends, especially Israel, and selective non-proliferation in relationship to the Third World.[100]

The strategy of keeping options open, but stopping short of nuclearisation, indicates that while India is willing to exercise "the extreme option" in case its security is gravely jeopardised, it is not willing "to pay the price for full nuclearisation in terms of national opprobrium and sanctions". Similarly, the missile programme (with Agni, the "technology demonstrator") demonstrates India's delivery capability, yet it will resist deploying the most powerful of these missiles.[101] But a section of the Indian strategic community feel that keeping options open for over twenty years even as the nuclear and missile threats to the country steadily increase, raises, serious doubts about our understanding of the role of nuclear weapons and missiles in the current strategic milieu.

Pokharan II and after

The series of five nuclear explosions at Pokharan on 11 and 13 May 1998 proved beyond doubt the Indian technological capability to design and make nuclear bombs of different varieties, ranging from thermonuclear to sub-kiloton yields (which demonstrated its capability in tactical weaponry). The decisions to conduct these tests were taken in the context of the deteriorating security situation in the country. India had justified its nuclear tests on the grounds that China had proliferated nuclear and missile technologies to Pakistan. In fact, no other nation has faced a security situation analogous to India, being placed, as it is, within two nuclear weapon powers between whom there is an ongoing nuclear weapon technology relationship. The nature and method of finalising the CTBT had, in fact, pushed India into undertaking the tests to prove the credibility of its capability. The Indian tests violated no international treaty. India is "a nuclear weapon state. This is a reality that cannot be denied. It is not a conferment that we seek; nor is it a status for others to grant. It is an endowment to the nation by our scientists and engineers".[102]

The United States immediately imposed sanctions against a wide range of Indian private and public sector companies engaged in high technology, which was expanded in November 1998. The impact has been estimated to be close to US $500 million.[103] India's nuclear doctrine, announced on August 1998, essentially included a minimum deterrent capability, credibility of deterrence, smallness of arsenal, survivability of nuclear force and no arms controls fetters on research and development.

[100] Ashok Kapur, "Western Biases", *The Bulletin of the Atomic Scientists*, January/February 1995, 42.

[101] Shekhar Gupta, *India Refines its Role*, Adelphi Paper No. 293 (International Institute of Strategic Studies London, 1995), 45.

[102] Paper presented at the Lok Sabha on Evolution of India's Nuclear Policy, 27 May 1998.

[103] C. Fred Bergsten, Director, Institute of International Economics, Washington DC, 11 March 1999; cited in "Sanctions Impact Minimal on India", *Hindustan Times*, 12 March 1999.

After eight rounds of Indo–US talks spread over eight months—the most recent one being in Janaury 1999—there has not been much headway in resolving major differences. The talks have focused on a broad range of issues, especially the CTBT, the Fissile Missile Material Cut-off Treaty, export controls and defence posture (the minimum credible nuclear deterrent). Washington still continues to insist that India subscribe its minimum nuclear deterrence in a manner that would negate the very purpose of the Pokharan tests of May 1998. India has been reiterating that the need for minimum security was not a fixed one because the external environment was dynamic and could not be fixed. Moreover, whereas the tests were conducted primarily with a view to evolve a credible deterrent capability against China, the United States continues to assert that New Delhi accept major restraint measures in a subcontinental framework with Pakistan.

It seems that India would not join any non-proliferation regime which would tend to diminish its nuclear and missile capabilities for national defence in a constantly changing security environment. It is likely that the gradual acceptance of India as a *de facto* state with nuclear weapons would start to make accommodation more feasible. Since India is not likely to renounce its nuclear weapons, "mutual adjustment would appear to be a course of action in the best interests of all parties concerned".[104]

VI INDIA: A REGIONAL OR GLOBAL POWER?

Unlike the bipolar world, when India was a leader of the non-aligned world, in the post-Cold War era, the question remains: is India a world power or a regional power?

India's great power arguments, according to Selig S. Harrison, are rooted in the fact that it is one of the world's oldest and largest civilisations. Indians, he claims, have "what might be called 'a dated self-image'. They take their great power status for granted and expect others to treat them as if they had, in fact, already arrived".[105] Another observer argued that with the snapping of the Indo–Soviet link, the "keystone of India's pretence and power in the 1980s", India's "reach for great power status is in a shambles".[106] One commentator felt that since 1971 India has been "a preeminent power" in Southern Asia. But India's policy, given its size and aspirations, has been global in scope, without seeking a prominent role for India as a global power. Therefore it is "a middle power with regional preeminence".[107] After becoming a centre of force in Southern Asia, a regional naval power in the 1980s, India in the 1990s, according

---

[104] Jasjit Singh, "India, Europe and Non-proliferation: Pokharan II and After", address at the Europe Forum, New Delhi, 24 September 1998, 7–8.

[105] Selig S. Harrison, "Dialogue of the Deaf: Mutual Perceptions and Indo-American Relations", in S.R. Glazer and Nathan Glazer (eds), *Conflicting Images* (Riverdale, 1990); cited in Selig S. Harrison and Geoffrey Kemp, *India and America after the Cold War* (Washington DC, 1993), 20.

[106] Ross H. Munro, "The Loser: India in the Nineties" (1993) 32 *National Interest* 62.

[107] Mukund G. Untawle, "India and the World", *Conflict* (New York), April–June 1991, 126.

to two Soviet scholars, will emerge as a major regional power of Asia. Some may be irritated by the prospect of India becoming a world power, they added, but this process can "only be slowed-down a little, not stopped".[108]

India has generally seen itself as "a world power in the making"[109] and has conducted its regional and international relations accordingly. But Indian policy makers have been tempted "to indulge in high-flying diplomacy and play a political role in world affairs out of proportion to our intrinsic strength".[110] Traditionally, India has tended to inject certain moral values into *realpolitik*, assuming a moral highground much to the irritation of the western Powers. India also upheld its right to speak for the developing nations of the Third World under the non-aligned umbrella. There seems to be a unanimous agreement among the present Indian strategic elite that India "should be a global power", but no model seems appropriate. The Indian elite holds "an expanded vision of their country's destiny", but it remains to be seen whether they will turn vision into reality.[111]

With the end of the Cold War, India, according to another observer, has emerged as "a far more pragmatic power, more willing to serve its fundamental economic and trading interests, less engaged in sanctimonious moralising". It is poised to emerge in the early twenty-first century as a far more important and influential power in the Indian Ocean region, and even globally, than it was in the latter part of the twentieth century.[112] Another scholar felt that India, freed of Cold War pressures, is "a logical candidate" to assume leadership of a reinvigorated Third World campaign to regain political influence. But at a time of aid-fatigue and growing protectionism, and India's economic difficulties, its "credibility as a leader", is lacking.[113]

Given its size and resources, an India firmly integrated in the global economy has all the prerequisites of becoming a major player in world politics. Home to one-sixth of the global population, in economic terms India is the eighth largest industrial country and is poised to become the fourth largest by the year 2015. If the current trend continues, India's global ranking as the thirtieth largest importer in the world is bound to improve. India's tremendous market potential and reserves of skilled manpower have been widely recognised, but the problem has always been in transforming this potential into real market and economic strengths.[114]

[108] See M.V. Bratersky and S.I. Lunyov, "India at the End of the Century" (1990) 30(10) *Asian Survey* 927.

[109] Ramesh Thakur, "India after Nonalignment", *Foreign Affairs*, Spring 1992, 182.

[110] V.V. Paranjpe, "Global Changes: Need to Keep Pace", *Hindustan Times*, 11 July 1991.

[111] Stephen P. Cohen, "The Regional Impact of a Reforming India", in *Asia's International Role in the Post-Cold War Era, Part II, Adelphi Paper* 276 (London, 1993), 92.

[112] Sandy Gordon, "South Asia after the Cold War: Winners and Losers" (1995) 35(10) *Asian Survey* 894.

[113] Thomas P. Thornton, "India Adrift: The Search for Moorings in a New World Order" (1992) 32(11) *Asian Survey* 1067.

[114] See S.D. Muni, "India and the Post-Cold War World: Opportunities and Challenges" (1991) 31(9) *Asian Survey* 872.

Despite its political stability, technological, industrial and economic growth, and its pursuit of technological self-reliance, India's ability to play a role in the international system commensurate with its actual and potential capabilities has been hindered by two factors. First, strained relationships with neighbours have tended to "seriously lower India's leverage in playing its rightful role as a major power in the world arena. A hostile neighbourhood provides scope for outside Powers to hold India on a leash".[115] A complicating factor has been that India has been judged by the world through the "prism" of Indo–Pak relations. However, with most Western nations getting weary of persistent Indo–Pak antagonism and greater attraction for the huge Indian market, the influence of this factor will tend to decline considerably in the years to come. Secondly, stability at home and economic strength will enhance its international status and give credibility to its claims to global aspirations.

Of late, India has on several issues, displayed a more assertive diplomacy. There are many in India who increasingly argue that India should be more self-assertive and not overrate the capability of the West to intervene. For instance, Foreign Minister Jaswant Singh asserted: "We have a tendency to underrate our strengths, and to overrate international ability to intervene. We should increase self-assertiveness, born of a sense of India and economic sovereignty. Our size and potential cannot be treated offhand if we are able to stand up for ourselves". Market access to a nation of 900 million people is "a weapon" in India's armoury.[116] India has also stressed its demand for a permanent seat on the UN Security Council, in support of which it cites fairer geographical distribution, size of its population, and its contribution to UN peacekeeping operations.

The West does not share Indian aspirations for a greater profile in international affairs. Powerful countries display "a tendency to control economic and technological potentialities" of countries like India by the creation and imposition of international control and monitoring regimes affecting nuclear and space technology, environmental management, trade and investment policies.[117] But India has "a strong tradition of national pride, well-developed sensitivities to unequal treatment with deep roots that go back to its colonial experience, and a recent historic commitment to autarchy at almost any cost".[118] Thus, a policy of pressure and denial is unlikely to achieve the desired results. Technology restraint regimes have no doubt taken their toll and resulted in delay and more expensive indigenous substitutes. Indian policy makers realise

---

[115] Muchkund Dubey, "India's Foreign Policy in the Evolving Global Order" (1993) 30(2) *International Studies* 127. "[A]s long as India is at odds with its immediate neighbors and is unable to organize its region into an effective unit in an international constellation, South Asian voices will not be heard with much respect.": Thomas P. Thornton, "India Adrift: The Search for Moorings in a New World Order" (1992) 32(1) *Asian Survey* 1073.

[116] Interview with Jawant Singh; see *Economic Times*, 11 June 1996.

[117] J.N. Dixit, "India and the Post-Cold War World", *The Hindu* (Madras), 31 March 1994.

[118] M. Granger Morgan, K. Subrahmanyam, K. Sundarji, and Robert M. White, "India and the United States" (1995) 18(2) *The Washington Quarterly* 167.

that the challenge of change and progress cannot be met through the soft option of technology imports or collaborative arrangements.

Indian policy makers now realise that India "cannot hope to play the same leadership role among developing countries as in the past, and that the benefits of such a role may not be commensurate with the costs". Moreover, other developing countries may not permit "a domestically weak and internationally vulnerable India to take such a leadership". Thus, in multilateral trade negotiations, India is likely to pursue its own interests more vigorously and contribute to the negotiations in more constructive and yet less visible terms.[119] While Indian negotiators will continue to resist the bilateralisation of essentially multilateral issues, India's position in multilateral trade negotiations will henceforth be "more unambiguously inspired by clearly defined national interests" than the requirements of leadership.[120]

VII CONCLUSION

The end of the Cold War compelled India's political establishment to change its world view. It increased the manoeuvreability and flexibility of Indian foreign policy in a multipolar world. A marked feature of Indian foreign policy in the 1990s is India's conscious effort simultaneously to cultivate mutual beneficial relations with all major powers apart from the United States, such as Germany, Japan and ASEAN. Articulating the main principles and thrust areas for the new millennium, Foreign Minister Jaswant Singh asserted that economic relations would provide the bulwark of India's foreign policy. India, he said, was working towards strengthening globalisation. He stated that India would not delay the forceful entry of the CTBT and was working towards building a national consensus. While admitting that there was no question of rolling back the nuclear programme, he clarified that India's nuclear programme was not Pakistan-centred. India, he concluded, would "retain its right to articulate independent positions in international affairs".[121]

India is the world's sixth largest economy, endowed with a middle-class of around 250 million, a huge domestic market and the world's second largest pool of trained scientists and engineers; there is therefore reason to be bullish about India. As a rising Asian tiger, it is projected to emerge as the fourth largest economy by the year 2020. There have been important achievements since 1991, but India still has a long way to go and the unfinished agenda is daunting. There is an urgent need to reprofile ourselves and reorient our mindsets, which are

[119] Rajiv Kumar, "The Walk Away from Leadership: India", in Diana Tussie and David Glover (eds), *The Developing Countries in World Trade: Policies and Bargaining Strategies* (Boulder, 1993), 166–167.

[120] Ibid., 168.

[121] "Foreign Policy to Focus on Economic Relations: Jaswant", *Economic Times* (New Delhi), 25 December 1998.

changing in an increasingly competitive environment. A major challenge is of de-governmenting the nation.

In the 1990s India confronts an international trading scenario marked by increasing protectionism, the erosion of multilateralism, and the gradual consolidation of a new directorate of Northern hegemony. In an era of increasing trade warfare and the politics of exclusion actively pursued by regional economic groupings, one of the greatest potential dangers to Indian exports is the threat to use the so-called social clause relating to child labour and the environment to harm Indian exports. The industrialised states, in a bid to counteract the competitive threat from Third World exports, also insist on bringing labour-related rights into multilateral trade talks as a practical move to deprive emerging economies of their natural advantages. By also linking human rights and environmental conditions, the developing countries are being pressurised to apply environmental regulations resulting in high costs so that their exports are not able to compete in the developed countries. India confronts a hostile economic environment. Indian foreign policy suffers from several drawbacks. It is imperative for India to set up a much-needed institutional mechanism to purposefully pursue its foreign policy in a more co-ordinated manner. An urgent need is to develop integrated national security policy making and evolve a policy process that seeks to harmonise defence policy, economic policy, internal security and foreign policy with one another within an overall national strategy. It is no longer desirable for India to survive on a reactive strategy of just dealing with a Western agenda. It is high time for India to evolve its own proactive agenda and pursue a strategy of coalition-building with South and Southeast Asian nations on issues of common interest. Moreover, as India has entered an era of coalition government at a national level, diverse pressures on the making of Indian foreign policy might become more evident, which might hinder the adequate exercise of political will at the highest level.

A number of factors interfere with the expansion and effectiveness of Indian influence in the EU and other Western nations. Image-building ought to be a key foreign policy objective because, both at the popular level and in the European media, the dominant image of India is one of a backward, conflict-ridden and poverty-stricken country constantly plagued by riots, natural disasters and epidemics, despite its tremendous economic and scientific achievements. The popular attitude reflects indifference towards India. The media displays a tendency to reinforce traditional, exotic images and the old clichés of India. In fact, the Western media has generally been excited about China and has, by and large, tended to ignore India.

The Western elite, the political leadership and the business community display a political and economic preoccupation eastwards of China. To them, Asia primarily means the "tigers" and "dragons" of East Asia and South-East Asia. Even though India is becoming a more significant component of the Asian reality of growth, the image of Europeans will not appreciably change in the near future, despite growing confidence in the national consensus on economic reform. India's ability to attract foreign investment will be comparatively less since it started relatively late in the liberalisation process.

The new and open economic environment in India and its outward-looking policies will result in a dynamic growth in commercial and economic exchanges. To a certain extent, the solution to adapting Indian foreign policy seems to be less of creating new institutions, but of changing ideas. Unless and until India puts its own house in order, its international status and respect will not be significantly appreciated. As the nation moves into the twenty-first century, and if India is to play a role commensurate with its size and economic potential, its leaders will have to demonstrate considerable dexterity in tackling the challenges on the domestic front and exploiting the opportunities opening up in the new Millennium.

6

Courts and Regional Integration

MARY L. VOLCANSEK

A number of regional agreements emerged in the 1980s and 1990s in response to changing world economic and political conditions. One addressed protecting human rights,[1] but the more common were regional trade arrangements. At least 109 of the latter had been registered with the World Trade Organisation (WTO) by 1999,[2] and there is no reason to expect that the trend will reverse in the foreseeable future. The proliferation of regional agreements, whether for trade or other purposes, has potentially wide-ranging implications for both politics and economics on a global scale, but there is only one such agreement that has been available for long-term analysis. The European Union (EU) stands as the model for endurance and effectiveness. It was created half a century ago and continues to attract a long list of applicant nations. Some students of the EU attribute its success in maintaining a trajectory toward deeper economic integration to its institutions and, in particular, to its court.[3]

The EU experience has been regarded as unique,[4] and its exceptionalism as sufficient reason not to compare it with other regional arrangements. Yet, studies of the EU have generated some theoretical speculation that, although designed to explain internal dynamics of European integration, may be instructive for understanding how and why other multilateral regional organisations evolve. In this chapter, I borrow the theory of institutionalisation devised by Wayne Sandholtz and Alec Stone Sweet[5] and explore what insights it may offer for the role of courts in regional integration. The institutional arrangements of the many newly formed economic alliances vary considerably,[6] but I propose a framework for comparing their institutional characteristics. Using that guide, I argue for the desirability of some mechanism for formal dispute-resolution such as a court, if regional economic co-operation is to be stable and durable.

---

[1] Scott Davidson, *Human Rights* (Open University Press, 1993).
[2] S.-H. Park, "Regionalism, Open Regionalism and GATT, Article XXIV", unpublished paper presented at Conference on Regional and Global Regulation of International Trade, Insituto de Estudos de Macau, 1999, 1.
[3] D.M. Wood and B.A. Yesilada, *The Emerging European Union* (Longman, New York, 1996), 11.
[4] T. Risse, "Approaches to the Study of European Politics" (1999) 12 *ECSA Review* 6.
[5] W. Sandholz, and A. Stone Sweet (eds), *European Integration and Supranational Governance* (Oxford University Press, 1998).
[6] E.D. Mansfield and H.V. Milner, *The Political Economy of Regionalism* (Columbia University Press, 1997), 14.

I INSTITUTIONALISATION

The precise genesis of the new forms of regional integration is unclear, although there are a number of possible explanations for the explosion of regional customs unions, free trade areas or other co-operative ventures in the waning years of the twentieth century. The end of the Cold War and break down of a bipolar world obviously coincided with the emergence of regionalism and may have provided a space for new economic configurations. Those events alone cannot, however, explain the increased propensity to embrace market-oriented economies in both industrialised and developing nations, North and South, East and West.[7] Acceptance of free trade and its inherently liberal market underpinnings is the result of a convergence of multiple factors and is not likely to be a short-lived phenomenon. Moreover, the various regional economic arrangements vary significantly in their form and reach; they can be found across many continents: MERCOSUR, or the Common Market of the South (Argentina, Brazil, Chile, Paraguay and Uruguay); ASEAN (Association of South-East Asian Nations); APEC (Asia-Pacific Economic Co-operation); NAFTA (North American Free Trade Association); and the EU, to mention only the most prominent. Despite their obvious diversity, there may nonetheless be common trends in their development worth tracking and directions meriting informed speculation.

Regions are by definition reflective of geographic proximity, but a prior sense of belonging together is not the causal factor in the new regionalism. The regional phenomenon of the last two decades has largely been a state-led attempt to devise strategies for meeting the new exigencies of economic globalisation. The new regionalism is geographic, within an economic space, but is also dynamic, inevitably changing in response to the winds of global trade.[8] Recognising this dynamic quality of geo-economic arrangements is essential to understanding and projecting their development. Agreements that are reached between states can lead to soft or hard regionalism, with the former referring exclusively to economic ties and the latter implicating political ones.[9] Some are predicated on long-standing and natural affinities that pre-date any formal connections, as is the case of relations between Canada and the United States. Others are reactions solely to the move toward globalisation. Whereas most regional experiments of the last twenty years are intended solely as means of nurturing free trade, there is a tendency for them to harden into formal agreements and international obligations that extend well beyond the traditional goals of lowering or eliminating tariffs.[10]

[7] M. Kahler, *Regional Futures and Transatlantic Economic Relations* (Council on Foreign Relations Press, New York, 1995), 3.
[8] J. Grugel and W. Hout, "Regions, Regionalism and the South", in J. Grugel and W. Hout (eds), *Regionalism across the North-South Divide* (Routledge, 1999), 10.
[9] Kahler, above at n. 7, 8.
[10] Ibid., 9.

Mapping the progression from soft regionalism to a harder form is where experiences and conceptual models from the European experience can be helpful, since the distinction between soft and hard regionalism is equivalent to that often drawn in analyses of the EU between intergovernmental and supranational politics. Regional relations and, indeed, most interstate relationships do not fit neatly into one or the other category, for the distinction is really a matter of degrees between the two poles. As various regional arrangements mature or change, different aspects of the interstate relationships may fit more closely to one or to the other.

The framework of institutionalisation presented by Stone Sweet and Sandholtz to explain different aspects of the EU is useful not only for understanding the etiology of regional agreements, but also their progression toward or into supranational arrangements or harder forms of regionalism. Briefly, and hopefully without too much damage to their concept, let me synthesise the Stone Sweet and Sandholtz argument that is intended to explain how what began as an interstate bargain in Europe was transformed into a multidimensional, quasi-federal polity. The basis of their theory is that European society became transnational, and that economic, social and political transactions and communications regularly crossed national borders. Non-state actors soon found that national legal rules created transaction costs and inhibited the generation of wealth and other collective goods and, therefore, exerted pressure on national, that is state, decision-makers, who naturally had their own vested interests in preserving state autonomy and control. States are inclined to resist transnational agreements so as to conserve sovereignty, but in doing so, they risk blocking increased prosperity within their borders. State actors may enter into limited intergovernmental negotiations, but are thereafter in a position of reacting to pressures for increased integration.[11]

Those non-state actors engaging in cross-border transactions sought European rules to govern transaction costs and to lower the price of cross-border relationships. Transnational exchanges can flow more efficiently when a single standard for customs, health, technical standards, environmental regulations, commercial law and currency rates exists. Once the rules are in place, however, there is a need for mechanisms to enforce them. When those mechanisms are created or institutionalised, the transition to hard or supranational governance has begun. Stone Sweet and Sandholtz envision a continuum of integration that ranges from intergovernmentalism to supranational governance, with various points along that space denoting different degrees of linkages among nations and among transnational actors on different policies and in different realms. Intergovernmentalism or soft regionalism focuses on national actors, who bargain over different policies; it is a passive structure enabling more efficient state-to-state negotiations. At the opposite end is supranationalism, where centralised

---

[11] A. Stone Sweet and W. Sandholz, "Integration, Supranational Governance and the Institutionalization of the European Polity", in Sandholz and Stone Sweet, above at n. 5.

structures have some jurisdiction over the geographic area of all of the states. These supranational bodies are then institutionalised and able to affect and constrain both nation states and individuals; the institutions are also influenced in a reciprocal manner. Notably, and very importantly, Stone Sweet and Sandholtz see that even within the EU there is a highly uneven pattern of integration, where supranational politics are paramount in some policy arenas, but where intergovernmental politics dominate in others.[12]

The key elements of the Stone Sweet and Sandholtz thesis are (1) transnational society that leads to interdependency, (2) supranational rules and (3) supranational organisations. The same logic that has led to the EU as it stands at the end of the twentieth century also explains and may predict the direction of the newly emerging regional trade agreements. The interests of economic elites in various nations in reducing the costs of cross-border transactions pressure national decision-makers for formation of regional trading areas, because globalisation of trade increasingly rendered navigating multiple national trade regimes inefficient and expensive. At some point, state interests and those of other social and economic actors converged, and intergovernmental bargaining occurred to create a customs union or free trade zone within a confined geographic space. State interests are, however, not monolithic, but rather are an amalgam of competing demands by interest groups. In the area of trade, economic elites, exporters and investors are likely the ones who prevailed, usually over the wishes of other interests, to secure a reduction of cross-border transaction costs.[13]

Once initial intergovernmental negotiations forming a free trade or customs area are completed, a series of rules must follow: rules of origin, restrictive measures, anti-dumping, subsidies, countervailing duties, non-tariff discrimination, and health and environmental standards, to mention but a few. These rules are essential to insure that competition is fair to all players and to replace the earlier national trade norms. Rules imply, however, a means of enforcement. Administration of the rules is where many a regional experiment may either break down or begin the course toward supranational governance. Enforcement may be achieved through diplomacy and, when that fails, resort may be to other measures. The 1999 EU–US dispute over importation of bananas into the EU is an obvious example. When the United States believed that the EU was illegally discriminating against bananas grown by US companies, though not produced in the United States, it followed the course of diplomacy first. When that route failed, the next stop was the Dispute-Settlement Board of the WTO. Only after the US position was validated and sanctions were upheld through the WTO mechanism, did the United States escalate to threats of punitive tariffs.

Another scenario for the durability of regional trade agreements that have no mechanism to resolve disputes is simple dissolution of the agreement. Indeed,

---

[12] Ibid., 1–16.
[13] W. Hout and J. Grugel, "Regionalism across the North-South Divide", in Grugel and Hout, *Regionalism across the North-South Divide*, above at n. 8, 176.

184 regional integration agreements were at some point communicated to GATT/WTO, but some seventy-five of them are no longer in force.[14] Although the reasons for disintegration have not, to my knowledge, been systematically explored, the inability to resolve competing claims or interests is likely to explain some failures.

Without some level of institutionalisation or other means of enforcement, national commitment to a regional trade area can wax and wane with each electoral cycle and subsequent shift in national administration. Transnational trade is obviously inhibited when the validity and enforcibility of contracts, obligations and rules cannot be guaranteed beyond the term of office of an administration.

Thus, Stone Sweet and Sandholtz's framework for analysing regional organisations becomes relevant. Some means separate from nation state control must exist to produce, monitor and enforce the rules. Cross-border transactions created the need for transnational rules, but the efficacy of the rules depends on the mechanism to administer them. This is where an inclination toward supranational governance arises. The Stone Sweet and Sandholtz framework does not necessarily imply an inevitable motion toward diminution of national sovereignty and a rise of federalism. Rather, they recognise substantial variation by policy domain. Their continuum of intergovernmental politics to supranational ones acknowledges unevenness across policies within the EU and makes placement of any policy dependent on both the presence and the intensity of transactions, rules and organisations.[15] State-centered intergovernmentalism may remain the essential means of carrying out some policies, whereas supranational governance may predominate in others. The EU anticipated, from its earliest days as the European Coal and Steel Community, a mix of national primacy and supranationalism. Most of the newly emerging regional trade associations apparently were created, with the notable exception of MERCOSUR, with no larger goal than establishment of a tariff-free area, administered at the intergovernmental level.

II DISPUTE-SETTLEMENT SYSTEMS

As Enzo Grille said, however, at this stage of development of regional trade agreements few certain conclusions can be arrived at concerning the economic role and consequences of this movement. He adds that one of the potential motivating factors behind the growth of regional arrangements may be a lack of confidence in the capacity of the GATT multilateral trading system *to enforce a rule of law in trade relations.*[16] With little certain about the future of regionalism

---

[14] Park, above at n. 2, 1.

[15] Stone Sweet and Sandholz, above at n. 11, 9.

[16] E. Grille, "Multilateralism and Regionalism: A Still Difficult Coexistence", in R. Faini and E. Grille (eds), *Multilateralism and Regionalism after the Uraguay Round* (Macmillan Press, 1997), 224.

in trade, some speculation about mechanisms to authoritatively resolve disputes and interpret the rules—to enforce a rule of law in trade relations—is in order.

The need to seek a neutral third party to resolve disputes is so natural as to require almost no elaboration. Richard Abel explained that conflicts are part of the fabric of social relationships and are transformed into disputes when conflicting claims are asserted publicly. Most will never reach a judicial body, broadly defined. Some may simmer indefinitely without resolution, whereas others demand closure of some sort. Some disputes remain solely between the competing parties, whereas others gain momentum and are driven to seek a third party to intervene and apply the rules authoritatively.[17] At the interstate level, when the dispute remains between the two parties, diplomacy is the mechanism for resolution. Of course, that option holds out the potential for no conclusion to the dispute. The intervention of a third party, whether as a mediator, arbitrator or judge, carries such obvious logic that, according to Martin Shapiro, courts have become a universal political phenomenon.[18] The simple act of including a dispute-settlement device may actually force the parties to resolve their conflict without involving the outside third party.

That logic has led to some form of outside, third party intervention mechanism in a number of international and transnational arrangements: the International Court of Justice, the European Court of Human Rights, the Inter-American Court of Human Rights, the WTO's dispute-settlement bodies, and the EU's Court of Justice. Other treaty arrangements provide for less legalistic forms of enforcement, such as NAFTA's inclusion of dispute-settlement panels for different types of conflicts or mandatory use of the WTO mechanism for others. A panel of scientific experts is included, for example, to decide environmental and health issues, and some other categories of disputes are assigned directly to national courts for resolution.[19] One study of the newly emerging regional trade associations recognised the obvious need for a formal mechanism to resolve competing claims and strongly recommended that all such agreements should provide for open forum dispute-resolution mechanisms and access to the dispute-settlement boards of the WTO.[20] Notably, despite the logic of third party dispute-resolution, most of the newly formed regional trade associations rely on the presumption of self-regulation.[21] Self-regulation of interstate agreements may prove largely successful, but when it fails to achieve compliance, diplomacy is the only recourse. The General Agreement on Tariffs and Trade

---

[17] R.L. Abel, "A Comparative Theory of Dispute Institutions in Society" (1973) 8 *Law and Society Review* 217, 224–47.

[18] M. Shapiro, *Courts: A Comparative and Political Analysis* (University of Chicago Press, 1981), 1.

[19] M.F. Bognanno and K.J. Ready (eds), *The North American Free Trade Agreement* (Quorum Books, 1993), 38.

[20] J. Serra, *Reflections on Regionalism* (Carnegie Endowment for International Peace, Washington DC, 1997), 54–5.

[21] W.D. Coleman and G.R.D. Underhill (eds), *Regionalism and Global Economic Integration* (Routledge, 1998), 9–10.

(GATT) experience is instructive about the future of such a configuration: from its beginnings in 1952, it used a diplomacy-based approach, but by 1979 legal mechanisms had evolved as central to its structure.[22] The Uruguay Round of negotiations institutionalised the legal approach.

There are several problems involved in state-to-state negotiations to resolve disputes. The most obvious is, of course, that no resolution may be possible. A second is the hierarchy among nations that prevents some from bargaining or asserting their claims on an equal footing. More fundamental, though, is the absence of a single, unified state interest when issues of trade are involved. Indeed, multiple competing interests are likely. Labour and management seek different outcomes, consumers do not necessarily share the interests of producers, and importers and exporters see trade advantages from opposite viewpoints. Even though national solutions to many policy problems have lost their credibility,[23] the nation state and its concern for sovereignty and power can still, nonetheless, overshadow those of free trade economics. The tide is ebbing from state-centered solutions, however, as global interconnections are drawing states into a larger and more complex political structure that is the counterpart of the production and financial systems.[24]

Increased interdependency at social, economic and political levels implies the logic of a third party mechanism to monitor, enforce and resolve disputes that arise between trading partners, but the inevitability of institutionalising trade regimes is not typically welcomed by nation states. Resistence by national actors is hardly surprising in light of the conclusions of so many scholars' description of the European integration process as one with an immutable link between law and legal processes, and integration, conventionally if somewhat simplistically, "understood as a process leading towards greater centralisation of governmental functions".[25]

Is the apprehensiveness felt by national actors warranted? Even a casual familiarity with the EU experience would suggest that it is. The oft-told story, so familiar to European lawyers, is one in which the European Court of Justice (ECJ) transformed the treaties into a constitution and established a system of supranational governance.[26] To recall a brief version of the process, the ECJ was created by the Treaty of Paris, signed in 1951. More than a decade later the constitutionalising of the treaties commenced, first, with the decision in *Van Gend en Loos*[27] which established the doctrine of direct effect and enabled

---

[22] R.E. Hudec, *Enforcing International Trade Law: The Evolution of the Modern GATT Legal System* (Butterworths, Salam, 1993), 11–15.

[23] D. Wincott, "Political Theory, Law and European Union", in J. Shaw and G. More (eds), *New Legal Dynamics of European Union* (Clarendon Press, 1995), 308.

[24] Coleman and Underhill, above at n. 21, 6.

[25] J. Shaw, "Introduction", in J. Shaw and G. More (eds), *New Legal Dynamics of European Union*, above at n. 23, 3.

[26] M.P. Maduro, *We the Court. The European Court of Justice and the European Economic Constitution* (Hart Publishing, 1998), 7–30; J.H.H. Weiler, *The Constitution of Europe: Do the New Clothes Have an Emperor?* (Cambridge University Press, 1999), 221–4.

[27] Case 26/62 [1963] ECR 1.

citizens of the various signatories to the treaties to assert their rights in national courts. Thereby enforcement of the treaties was transferred from interstate negotiations to national courts. The following year, the doctrine of the supremacy of Community law over any conflicting national law was asserted in *Costa v. ENEL*.[28] That doctrine complemented the concept of direct effect and elevated the stature of the treaties to a supranational plane. Various decisions that followed solidified the position of European treaties as fixing the rules of the game and, thus, investing lower-order norms with authority (legitimacy).[29] Subsequently, even private law has been recognised as Europeanised,[30] and member nations can even be held financially liable for damages resulting from failure to meet their obligations under the treaties.[31] The sum of the ECJ's jurisprudence led to establishment of supranational governance in a large range of legal questions.

When state leaders became disturbed by the scope of the ECJ's rulings and its inclination to raise issues to the supranational level, agreements were reached through intergovernmental bargaining to limit the judicial reach for the future. Specifically, in the 1991 Maastricht Treaty the Court was denied any role in new policy areas of the EU, particularly those in which national sovereignty is most directly implicated, justice and home affairs.[32] That serves as a reminder that even when institutionalisation at the supranational level has occurred, state-led negotiations can still limit the scope of supranational governance.

Soft intergovernmental trade agreements are not invariably transformed into hard, political arrangements by the inclusion of a dispute-settlement system. Indeed, the European judges could not have accomplished what they have in European law without a number of accomplices. The ECJ began as a relatively weak body, as courts even in national systems usually are. Or, as Karen Alter put it, "the ECJ can *say* whatever it wants, [but] the real question is why anyone should *heed* it" (emphasis in original).[33] National courts were clearly of crucial importance in acceptance and enforcement of the European Court's pronouncements, as has been noted repeatedly. Even so, as the weak cogs in national government machinery, their compliance could also have been blunted. Rather, as Alter also noted, the ECJ employed a judicial strategy whereby it took large judicial strides by providing national policy makers with immediate material and political rewards; when the Court established a far-reaching legal doctrine, it did not apply it against the state whose action was challenged.[34] The

---

[28] Case 6/64 [1964] ECR 585.

[29] A. Stone, "What Is a Supranational Constitution? An Essay in International Relations" (1994) 54 *Review of Politics* 441, 444.

[30] C. Joerges, "The Impact of European Integration on Private Law: Reductionist Perceptions, True Conflicts and a New Constitutionalist Perspective", (1997) 3 *European Law Journal* 378.

[31] T. Tridimas, "Member State Liability in Damages for Breach of Community Law: An Assessment of the Case Law", in J. Beatson and T. Tridimas (eds), *New Directions in European Public Law* (Hart Publishing, 1998).

[32] Wood and Yesilada, above at n. 3, 111.

[33] K. Alter, "The European Court's Political Power" (1996) 19 *West European Politics* 458, 459.

[34] Ibid., 473.

different time horizons of politicians and judges worked to the advantage of the judges.[35] There was no direct loss to the state as a consequence of ECJ decisions when first announced, which diminished potential negative reaction by state actors. Compliance or acquiescence on the part of national political arms was secured.

The remaining player in solidifying the power of the ECJ was the citizenry of member nations. Without individual litigants, there would be no cases presented to national courts and thus no basis for legal integration.[36] Of course, most observers readily note that the average citizen is not likely to be knowledgeable about the legal implications of their disputes in two or more legal realms. In fact, even as recently as 1993, a half-century after its creation, most of the European electorate had no knowledge of the ECJ.[37] It is the legal profession that transmits awareness of rights and obligations to clients and seeks desirable outcomes by relying on the legal remedies available. Further, it was only through the reference procedure in Article 177 of the EC Treaty that individual litigants were granted access to the ECJ when European law was implicated in their cases. The uneven record of various national courts for making preliminary references to the ECJ is linked to the quantity of intra-Union trade in which a nation is involved.[38] In other words, the origins of regional arrangements and the mechanism for expanding judicial power at the supranational level are one and the same cross-border transactions.

III IMPLICATIONS OF DISPUTE-RESOLUTION MECHANISMS

The EU experience sends a clear message: any state actor interested in retaining sovereignty and limiting transnational incursions into domestic affairs should eschew a separate and formal mechanism for resolution of disputes in regional trade arrangements at a supranational level. Yet, the transformation of the EU in some policy realms to supranational governance was contingent on a convergence of several factors: a supranational court staffed with strategic-minded judges, compliant national judges, and a means for citizen access. At the same time, the experience of GATT's dispute-settlement system where none of those factors were present illustrates that it was nevertheless altered from one operated by the diplomats and politicians to a formal mechanism, staffed by lawyers. Is a court or court-like arrangement inevitable?

[35] K. Alter, "Who are the Masters of the Treaty?: European Governments and the European Court of Justice (1998) 52 *International Organisation* 121, 122.

[36] W. Mattli and A.-M. Slaughter, "Revisiting the European Court of Justice" (1995) 39 *American Journal of Political Science* 459.

[37] J.L. Gibson and G.A. Caldiera, "The Legitimacy of Transnational Legal Institutions: Compliance, Support, and the European Court of Justice" (1995) 39 *American Journal of Political Science* 459.

[38] A. Stone Sweet and T.L. Brunnell, "Constructing a Supranational Constitution: Dispute Resolution and Governance in the European Community" (1998) 92 *American Political Science Review* 92.

Clearly, trade and other transnational exchanges are facilitated by the presence of a dispute-resolution mechanism that is independent of national governments. The rules cannot be monitored, applied or enforced impartially without it. Yet, there are other models available than that offered by the EU. The tribunals created to monitor and enforce human rights agreements offer alternative designs that are less threatening to sovereignty. Human rights constitute, possibly more than economic issues, an area where states tend to be especially sensitive to outside intervention. Even though almost all nations give lip service to the importance of human rights, the absence of agreement on the substance of those rights is inhibiting. Culture, religion and domestic politics are all intimately interconnected in how a nation chooses in a specific situation to deal with its own citizens. External pressure to define and even sanction a state for failure to comply with treaty requirements presents a potentially larger threat to national sovereignty than the enforcement of any trade regime could. To illustrate that point, I note that the United States has not accepted the jurisdiction of the Inter-American Court of Human Rights,[39] and not all signatories to the European Convention on Human Rights accept the compulsory jurisdiction of its court.[40] In the case of the European Court of Human Rights, even if a state accepts compulsory jurisdiction, it can derogate jurisdiction through a claim of public security and still escape supranational judicial scrutiny.

Three models of regional agreements on human rights exist: the African Charter of Human and Peoples Rights, the American Convention on Human Rights, and the European Convention on Human Rights and Fundamental Freedoms. The African Charter, also known as the Banjul Charter, is a creation of the Organization for African Unity (OAU) and is the least institutionalised of the group. The Inter-American version is somewhat more capable of acting at a supranational level, but is still largely dependent on intergovernmental bargaining. The European rights arrangement has decided the most cases and had ruled against at least thirteen states in the first thirty years of its existence, 1959–1989,[41] but has still not achieved the level of supranationalism that the ECJ represents.

The OAU was created in 1963 by thirty-two independent African states, and in 1981 unanimously ratified the African Charter, which entered into force in 1986.[42] The Charter addresses the normal range of political and civil rights, as well as social and economic rights, and it lists duties. Parts of the Charter reflect peculiarly African concerns, such as the prohibition on mass expulsion of non-

---

[39] J.F. Stack, "Human Rights in the Inter-American System: The Struggle for Emerging Legitimacy", in M.L. Volcansek (ed.), *Law Above Nations: Supranational Courts and the Legalization of Politics* (University Presses of Florida, 1997), 105.

[40] D.W. Jackson, *The United Kingdom Confront the European Convention on Human Rights* (University Presses of Florida, 1997), 53.

[41] D.W. Jackson, "Prevention of Terrorism: Security, Discretionary Power and Transnational Rights", in M.L. Volcansek (ed.), *Law Above Nations: Supranational Courts and the Legalization of Politics*, above at n. 39, 17.

[42] A. Cassese, *Human Rights in a Changing World* (Polity Press, 1990).

nationals. Unlike any of the other regional human rights organisations, the African Charter includes no court. Enforcement and monitoring are handled by a Commission, which allows a focus on reconciliation and consensus as a means of settling disputes, rather than upon contentious procedures, and is thus more in keeping with African culture.[43] The first eleven members of the Commission were elected in 1987[44] and are charged with investigating and resolving disputes receives via communications. Both interstate and individual communications are possible, with the former permitting formal complaints of one state against another, with notice to the Commission, or complaints filed directly with the Commission. In either case, the Commission is to investigate allegations and report to the OAU Heads of State and Government. The Commission's report may include recommendations for disposition, but the emphasis of the entire process is on finding amicable solutions. Individuals or groups, such as non-governmental organisations, can also file communications with the Commission, but only after all local or state remedies have been exhausted. Individual is really a misnomer for the kinds of complaints accepted, since the Commission cannot act on a single alleged violation of rights, but rather on series of serious or widespread violations. Once the Commission has verified that there may exist a serious violation, it reports to the OAU Heads of State and Government, where two-thirds of the states represented must agree to any action. The political arm can authorise the Commission to undertake an indepth study of the situation, but that report remains confidential until or if the political leaders choose to make it public. During its first four years of operation, no decisions on any communications or reports were made.[45] Not only are there no stipulated sanctions, but also no publicity of alleged or even verified abuses is permitted without the concurrence of a super-majority of the states in the association. The OAU is clearly intergovernmental and an example of a soft regional arrangement.

The American Convention on Human Rights was concluded in 1969 under the auspices of the Organisation of American States, but did not come into force until 1978. It is binding on twenty states in the Americas, but not on the United States or Brazil. The Convention enumerates a number of political and civil rights and has two supervisory arms to enforce them, a Commission and Court. The Commission is empowered to consider complaints and present conclusions or recommendations and to allow allegations to be forwarded to the Court. Unlike its counter-part on the African continent, the commission may also publish reports on the human rights situation in a specific country.[46] Like the African version, complaints cannot be considered by the Commission until all internal state remedies have been completed. Notably, the Commission has never taken an action as a result of a complaint filed by an individual, and a

---

[43] Davidson, above at n. 1, 156.
[44] Cassese, above at n. 42, 203.
[45] Davidson, above at n. 1, 158–61.
[46] Cassese, above at n. 42, 201–203.

petition by an individual cannot reach the court without passing through the Commission or a state that has accepted binding jurisdiction. The Inter-American Court was a later addition to the OAS structure, established in 1980 and rendering its first decision in 1983. In fact, it had only decided nine cases as of 1997, but it can and has assessed damages to states found in violation of the charter. The other aspect of the Court's jurisdiction is its power to issue advisory opinions, through which it can determine the compatibility of a domestic law with the charter. This mechanism is seen as having a greater potential for integration than do decisions in contentious cases.[47] Though the American Convention's record at this point is modest, it remains an evolving system. Interestingly, the intention at the time that the mechanisms were created was to foster a specifically supranational competency to obstruct or at least hinder autocratic regimes, but the record of almost two decades suggests that it retains an essentially intergovernmental character.[48] That is due in part to institutional rivalries between the Commission and the Court that deter the Commission from allowing many contentious cases to reach the next level; the Commission prefers, also, to sanction recalcitrant states through public opprobrium or quiet diplomacy.[49]

The oldest of the regional human rights organisations is European, founded in 1949. The Council of Europe is composed of states (forty-one in 1999, with other applications waiting) which have accepted the European Convention for the Protection of Human Rights and Fundamental Freedoms proposed in 1950. Its structure is that of Commission and Court, with every signatory state having one judge and one commissioner. Commissioners are elected by ministers of the states from a list of three submitted by the nation whose seat is vacant. Judges are theoretically elected by the Assembly, but in actual practice each Member State names its judge. Complaints can be received by the Commission from states, from individuals and from non-governmental organisations, but those from individuals constitute the largest number. The Commission reviews complaints and dismisses about 90 per cent as inadmissible. The Commission is charged with investigating complaints and pursuing amicable solutions and reports its conclusions and recommendations to the Committee of Ministers. One recommendation may be referral to the court.[50]

The Commission serves as a filter to the court, and the record of referrals is instructive. From 1961–1982, the Commission received about 9,000 complaints and found about 200 admissible, but only thirty were referred to the court. Over the next ten years, however, 379 cases had reached the judicial body.[51] That exponential escalation continues and is not explained simply by the increased number of signatory states. Whatever inter-institutional rivalries may have at

---

[47] Stack, above at n. 39, 106–113.
[48] Cassese, above at n. 42, 201.
[49] Stack, above at n. 39, 113.
[50] Jackson, above at n. 41, 11–15.
[51] Ibid., 15.

one time characterised relations between the Court and the Commission, they seem to have abated as caseloads and delays increased. Yet, observers are quick to point out the political quality of the decisions rendered by both. The European Court of Human Rights was initially quite cautious in its treatment of complaints about UK practices for combating terrorism in Northern Ireland[52] and has been less than sympathetic to claims of discrimination brought by women.[53] Even so, what was obviously begun as an experiment as a quasi-intergovernmental and quasi-supranational dispute-settlement system has evolved into a judicial system that is approaching the ECJ in its level of supra-nationalism.

What can be gleaned from the records of these three human rights models of regional dispute-settlement mechanisms? First, there is a model, that of the Organization for African Unity, in which intergovernmentalism and a focus on reconciliation between nations is preserved. It is also the only model that is rel-atively new (in force only since 1986) and has no body charged directly with adjudicating disputes. Further, that single example has been singularly ineffec-tive in deterring wholesale human rights abuses, as the situations in Rwanda and Burundi in the 1990s demonstrate.

The other noteworthy trend among the three regional human rights organisations is one toward greater judicialisation and greater supranationalism. Judicialisation refers to the infusion of judicial decision-making and of courtlike procedures into political arenas where they did not previously reside.[54] The Council of Europe began in 1950 as a body committed to deterring human rights abuses within the region of Western Europe and included two escape clauses that preserved the option of revert-ing to intergovernmental negotiations—Member States did not have to accept the court's jurisdiction and, in specific situations, they could seek a derogation on grounds of public security. With time, however, the dispute-settlement system of Commission and Council became institutionalised at the supranational level. The sister organisation in the Americas also sought to anchor its enforcement of human rights more securely by relying on a commission of experts and a panel of judges who were not named by, nor representative of, their national governments. Inter-institutional rivalries kept monitoring of abuses at a somewhat intergovernmental level, since the Commission first sought to achieve amicable resolution of com-plaints. Nonetheless, the court has used the few cases that reached it vigorously to enforce prohibitions on disappearances and practices of torture and to impose finan-cial liabilities on offending states. The trajectory of the Inter-American system is likewise toward institutionalisation at the supranational level.

---

[52] J.F. Stack, "Judicial Policy-Making and the Evolving Protection of Human Rights: the European Court of Human Rights in Comparative Perspective" (1996) 15 *West European Politics* 137.

[53] D.M. Provine, "Women's Concerns in the European Commission and Court of Human Rights", in M.L. Volcansek (ed.), *Law Above Nations: Supranational Courts and the Legalisation of Politics*, above at n. 39.

[54] T. Vallinder, "When the Courts Go Marching In", in C.N. Tate and T. Vallinder (eds), *The Global Expansion of Judicial Power* (New York University Press, 1995), 13.

IV INSTITUTIONALISATION AND JUDICIALISATION

Almost none of the newly established regional trade arrangements have hard or institutionalised regionalism as its goal, and they aspire to do no more than foster trade and economic growth within a specified geographic sphere. So long as the rules agreed upon through state-to-state negotiations are followed to the satisfaction of the negotiating partners, there is no apparent requirement for complicating matters by introduction of any institutions. There is no necessity to contemplate contingencies until a state or the economic elite within a state believes that it is being harmed by the failure of other parties to comply with the rules. But, as the experience of the older regional trade or human rights associations demonstrate, at some point a choice must be made between effective monitoring of the rules and more genteel diplomacy. The former implicates a measure of supranationalism, while the latter retains an intergovernmental quality. The choice becomes one of how best to blend the two so as to insure the efficacy of the treaties that define the rules.

A court or other formal mechanism to resolve disputes has a number of attributes to commend it. Foremost are the assumptions of a specially trained and impartial staff that objectively applies preordained rules consistently in all disputes. The fear that nation states have of such a device is that they cannot control the outcome in any specific case and that, over time, the process of regionalism becomes judicialised. In that situation, the power of the supranational judges is enhanced at the expense of the national politicians, and judicial decisions begin to reach into more traditionally political spheres.[55] Transferring the power to settle disputes among trading partners from the negotiating table to a legal forum further institutionalises the regional system and shifts power toward a supranational plane.

In addition to the threat of supranationalism, there remains a question of compliance, even with judicial decisions. Enforcement of legal decisions is hardly automatic even within the confines of a single nation state,[56] and agreement on the substance of what a court actually decided is often elusive. In other words, guarantees of compliance with transnational rules, whether decided by a court or other formal disputes-settlement mechanism, still depends largely on the trustworthiness of the other contracting parties. The alternative is to accept that the rules are always subject to negotiation, which protects sovereignty and vested national interests, but also guarantees the sovereignty and, therefore, the impunity of neighbouring states. Even in the experience of the European Union and the European Convention on Human Rights, where the signatories to the treaties are all historically committed to the rule of law and share a common political, economic and cultural context, the movement toward supranational-

---

[55] *The Global Expansion of Judicial Power* (New York University Press, 1995), 13–14.

[56] B.C. Canon and C.A. Johnson, *Judicial Policies: Implementation and Impact* (CQ Press, Washington DC, 1999).

ism could not be stemmed. It provided the formal protection that one nation's suspicions about the intentions of its neighbours could be decided in an open forum. Compliance with decisions reached in that manner seemed more likely than the outcome of persistent renegotiation of the rules, and some external pressure to comply appears even more essential in regions where the trading partners are less homogenous.

The transformation of the General Agreement on Tariffs and Trade (GATT) into the WTO is instructive. The entire structure of the GATT was predicated upon diplomacy, and the early decades of the agreement's existence were characterised by negotiated settlements of the rules and of their application. The diplomats were eventually replaced by lawyers, and ad hoc panels were used to decide specific disputes. As the GATT was transformed into the WTO, the Dispute-Settlement Body replaced the earlier legal panels, and movement is now towards a fixed set of judges to apply and interpret the growing jurisprudence that governs the organisation.[57]

Both the positive and negative aspects of a formal dispute-settlement system for monitoring and enforcing regional trade agreements are obvious. A formal institution fixes the rules and determines when a violation has occurred; if independent from national governments, it can insure the integrity of the rules. On the other hand, it cannot insure compliance. Moreover, creation of any institution beyond the control of national governments potentially diminishes national sovereignty.

What, then, determines the necessity or desirability of a formal dispute-settlement system? The Stone Sweet and Sandholtz concept of institutionalisation is helpful. Whereas their intention was to explain variations between supranationalism and intergovernmentalism within the context of the EU, they also offer a clue to explain why different policy areas are more prone to be governed by one or the other. That is intensity: the intensity or pervasiveness of the rules, the presence and intensity of the organisation, and the intensity of the cross-border transactions.[58] A movement toward supranational and institutionalised arrangements is seemingly preconditioned by the success of the regional agreement. If a regional trade agreement succeeds in fostering more cross-border transactions, then there is a greater need for rules and regulations to govern those transactions. The proliferation of both trade and rules, in turn, requires someone to monitor, apply and enforce the rules. The more intense and pervasive the rules and the transactions become, the greater will be the authority of the organisations devised to execute the rules. The transnational trade regime may then become institutionalised at a supranational level. In other words, based on the experience of other regional agreements, whether for the purpose of fostering trade or protecting human rights, the more durable, stable and effective the agreements are, the greater the inclination to institutionalise at

---

[57] Hudec, above at n. 22.
[58] Stone Sweet and Sandholtz, above at n. 11, 9.

the supranational level. When institutionalisation is contemplated, the lessons of the EU are instructive. The reach of a court or court-like body can be enhanced or limited by the routes of access to it. When national judges are made players and when individuals are permitted access, the arms of the supranational judges can extend further. That lesson may enable state actors to design bodies that are capable of resolving trade disputes and preserving the integrity of the rules with less potential intrusion into state sovereignty.

The regional trade arrangements in place at this time are, however, new and in many ways novel experiments. Their character is hardly set in stone; changed priorities or altered alliances within states, and/or change at the global level, will probably result in a renegotiation of policy.[59] With so many regional agreements emerging, undoubtedly there will be great variety in the structures, longevity and trajectories among them, and the nation state is not likely to disappear.[60] The regional arrangements that endure and grow in intensity will likely adopt, at some point, a supranational means for settling disputes whereby judges sit beside the diplomats.

---

[59] Grugel and Hout, above at n. 8, 12.
[60] M. Horsman and A. Marshall, *After the Nation-State: Citizens, Tribalism and the New World Disorder* (Harper Collins, 1994), 264.

7

China's Economic Development and the WTO Membership Issue: Stakes and Strategies

FRANÇOIS GIPOULOUX

I INTRODUCTION

Zeno's arrow will finally reach its target. After fifteen years of a chequered history, China is very close to regaining access to the World Trade Organisation (WTO). A founding member of the General Agreement on Tariffs and Trade (GATT) in 1948, China left the international body in 1950, as the country engaged in a course of self-reliance course, or more precisely, began "leaning to one side", namely that of the Soviet Union. China's endeavour to enter the WTO for over a decade reflects the growing stature of China in the world economy. It is widely admitted that China is the most important trading nation not to be a member of the WTO. In 1997, the country was among the world's top ten for both importing commercial services and exporting merchandise. The growth in China's export volume has been impressive, while its share in some high, value-added manufacturing sectors such as telecommunications and the office equipment market has shown spectacular increase. Its share in world clothing exports has doubled since 1990, to 18 per cent in 1997. The size and weight of China's trade are not only impressive, they are also part of the problem. Moreover, multiple barriers in China's foreign trade regime prevents it from having smooth access to the WTO, derived from the unfinished process of dismantling central planning mechanisms.

This chapter focuses on three questions which assess the structural difficulties preventing China from smoothly regaining access to the WTO: the first is that of the strong control of the state over foreign trade; the second is that of over-capacity in determined sectors (textile and steel) leading to price wars and dumping; the third examines the weak implementation of tariff collection.

It then explores the thorny issue of market access for China's foreign partners. Fair market access has been a question at the centre for China's major trading partners monitoring its entry to the WTO. What does market access mean as foreign funded enterprises (FFEs) are fiercely competing with domestic enterprises on the Chinese market? To remove some of their preferential treatment could help to kill two birds with one stone, i.e. to level the playing field in order to comply with WTO requirements, and to foster the position of domestic ailing industries which feel discrimination.

Finally, special consideration is given to the reasons underlying the Chinese opposition to re-entry. The question addressed here is the complex mechanism of economic interests, political and geopolitical issues involved in an apparently purely economic process. I shall assess the effects of China's integration in the WTO on the country's economic structure. In particular, while FFEs are controlling roughly half of China's foreign trade, what role is left for an ailing state sector, the heritage of Soviet-style industrialisation? In other words, how will access to the WTO affect the increasing competition between FFEs and Chinese firms on the domestic market?

II   CHINA IN THE WTO: THE STRUCTURAL OBSTACLES

Twenty years ago, at the wake of the economic reform program, China ranked thirty-second in the world as a trading nation. The turnover of its foreign trade was barely US $20 billion. In 1998 it had reached US $323.9 billion, and ranked ninth in the world. Should these impressive figures advocate for an immediate entry of China in the WTO? What could be the benefits for China in joining an international body whose objectives are to set and enforce rules for international trade, to negotiate and monitor trade liberalisation, to settle trade disputes and to improve trade transparency?

To begin with, there are several important factors which have never been correlated, or even seldom underlined, in the apologetic literature devoted to China as a world trade power.

1. Foreign trade is heavily controlled by the state. In 1994, foreign trade enterprises and other state-owned enterprises (SOEs) still assumed the lead in China's external trade: 70.2 per cent of exports and 52.1 per cent of imports. Although this ratio has evolved recently, foreign trade enterprises and SOEs controlled 53 per cent of China's foreign trade in 1997. Moreover, there is a complex set of licences which constrain foreign trade. Roughly speaking, it is prohibited to import anything without government authorisation. This inflexibility is hidden by a profusion of goods entering China through special permits—sometimes granted by local governments, temporary import authorisations and smuggling. This situation could last for a very long time since it provides the central government with hard currencies, while tax collection is very inefficient.

2. Next, we should consider the previous ratio of control over foreign trade from a different angle. In 1997 about half of China's foreign trade was handled by state controlled companies, and half was handled by FFEs. This also means that China's capacity to export directly is weak, since its service industry is underdeveloped. Logistics are not only rudimentary, but the advanced services (testing, consulting, legal arbitration, etc.), along with

modern manufacturing, are also lacking. In Sichuan, for instance, 80 per cent of the province's foreign trade is handled by Hong Kong companies.

3. We must be actually aware of what is the Chinese content of the so-called Chinese exports. It is important to understand that China's foreign trade is made of two distinct parts: ordinary trade and processing trade (importing of processing and assembly, exporting of processed goods). The customs regimes are different for these two categories. Processing trade benefits from special duty exemptions. Generally speaking, ordinary trade is handled by foreign trade enterprises and other SOEs. At a regional level, foreign trade enterprises specialise in dealing with the exports of township and village enterprises. A study of China's foreign trade at the enterprise level indicates that in 1997, TVE generated 90 per cent of the export value of the regional foreign trade enterprises. Among Chinese exporters, these enterprises are active or predominant in Africa, developing Asia, Central and Eastern Europe and Latin America.

    Processing trade, on the other hand, registers a low added value. It taps Chinese cheap labour resources, while key functions such as marketing, design and selection of input are carried out from abroad by the buyer. FFEs are dominant in this specific form of trade. In fact, FFEs play a minor role in ordinary exports (i.e. total trade minus processing trade): 8 per cent in 1993, 6 per cent in 1994, 4 per cent in 1995. Of special interest is the fact that the retained value of the foreign trade volume is about 50 per cent. Moreover, net exports in processing trade (exports minus imports) are low: 6 per cent in the case of equity joint ventures or 12 per cent for fully foreign owned enterprises.

    The local content ratio of Chinese exports appears to be fairly low in most of the export oriented provinces of China's eastern seaboard. China seems to be a springboard for re-exporting goods which originate in Taiwan, Korea, Hong Kong, Singapore and even Japan, more than a great trading power.

4. So far, subcontracting generated trade has remained isolated from the rest of the Chinese economy, and the domestic market is relatively well protected from import competition. What could be the effect, for domestic producers, of further lowering of Chinese custom duties? Consider the evolution of duties in some industrial production sectors. While duties were very protective, an average of 35 per cent–23 per cent in 1996, and a declared further reduction to an average of 15 per cent in 2000, China claims that its import duties do not exceed 3 per cent–4 per cent of the value of its imports, since a significant amount of items are exempt from duty collection. There is also the case in which bribes are paid to avoid tariffs. Is the domestic production (i.e. the production generated by Chinese enterprises) gradually being replaced by imports? This does not seem to be the case. What about the growing competition between Chinese firms and FFEs on the domestic market? The conflict is striking in several sectors, because FFEs are increasingly oriented towards the domestic market. This obviously depends on the sectors and on the countries, but the trend is clearly perceptible.

In the food and beverage industry, FFEs are operated under an import-substitution scheme. They mainly serve the domestic market. However, for garments and leather, Chinese firms control a large share of the domestic market and exhibit a strong export orientation. As for intermediate goods (textile, basic chemicals, chemical fibres) FFEs mainly produce for the domestic market. They provide FFEs operating in the downstream sectors with intermediate goods. In the case of machinery, the competition between foreign firms and domestic firms is virtually non-existent, because all of the output is exported.

5. Yet another factor is that of overcapacity and price wars. Anti-dumping complaints (fourteen in 1994 involving US $2 billion) are generally revealing as to the level of competition between provinces, cities and corporations within China. Some sectors dump their assets in order desperately to gain some outcome from their ailing production. It also reveals the excess capacity level in some sectors, even where the penetration of foreign direct investment (FDI) is strong. While monopolies have disappeared, sharp competition has arisen between Chinese importers. Price wars have erupted in China during the last two years. Dumping practices among provinces or corporations can be traced back to the dramatic increase in export volumes, while the export value registers only a slight increase. This is ultimately linked to production overcapacity in several sectors: textiles and clothing, among others.

6. Last but not least is the enforcement of duty collection which, especially at a local level, is plagued with malpractice, if not corruption, not to mention the huge amounts of smuggling flourishing in various sectors (automobile, electronics, etc.) in which local governments are often implicated. This leads to a crucial question—that of economic sovereignty of the centre over local government. How can a member of the WTO argue that it cannot be responsible for what is carried out at local government levels—provinces, or even in China's stagnant FDI? Starting from an export structure dominated by low, added value products, China is now climbing, sometimes arduously, up the technological ladder. It is confronted with tremendous difficulties: competition stemming from Asian countries—Japan, Korea and Taiwan, on the upper end of the ladder, and Thailand and Indonesia, whose currencies have been devalued, on the lower end. The painful restructuring of its own industrial system relies on state spending at a local level, rather than the market, to create new employment. But the most worrying issues are undoubtedly the stagnation of FDI inflows. There was a decline in investment during the first two months of 1999, and in 1998 the FDI figure was less than one million over the 1997 level. Certainly, FDI has played an integrating role and has often been positively correlated with export growth, if not with growth in general. China's liberalisation of FDI absorption policies started in 1979.

However, from the beginning of the 1990s, FDI inflows in China have undergone four major changes.

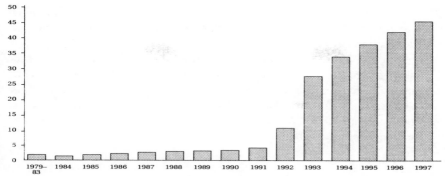

FIG. 1. FDI Actually used in China, 1979–1997 (Billion US$) (*Source*: Zhong Guo Tongji Nianjian. Various years)

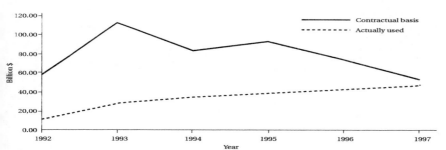

FIG. 2. FDI in China (*Source*: ZGTJNJ. Various years)

1. Steady increase in the amounts involved and decrease in the contracted amounts. This decrease in contractual investment observed since 1995 will inevitably translate into a drop in realised investment after a one-to-two-year time span. The reason behind this decline (prior to the Asian crisis) is related to growing complaints regarding the complexity of the investment climate in China, the multiplication of barriers, the predatory tax system and the difficulty in converting the yuan into profits. Since China lacks capital to revamp its industrial system with advanced technology and fresh management techniques, WTO membership should reassure investors, enforce international rule and reduce protectionism. But this view is encountering strong political opposition inside. In heavy industries, but also electronics and even in textile sectors, SOEs are not able to withstand foreign competition without the protection of high tariffs.

2. More concentration on manufacturing and decline of real estate. The first wave of FDI was concentrated on sectors such as real estate and hotels, and operated by Hong Kong and overseas Chinese firms. The second wave is more devoted to the domestic market and particularly the downstream sectors of FFEs, i.e. manufacturing and assembling. Within manufacturing

there is polarisation on more added-value sectors, as shown in the annual growth of Chinese exports (1993–1997) in computer and telecommunication equipment.

Figure 3. There is a strong correlation between FDI absorption and the steady increase in imports and exports of manufactured goods. However, FDI in high tech projects has been much more the exception than the rule. The Chinese export market share is dominant in trunks, bags, baby articles, footwear and other clothing, while it remains very low in computer and telecommunication equipment.

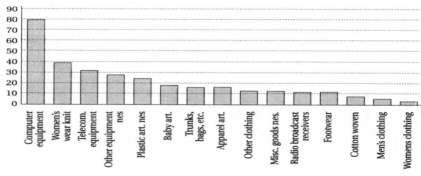

Fig. 3. Annual growth p.a. (%) 1993–1997 (*Source*: WTO. ITC. 1998)

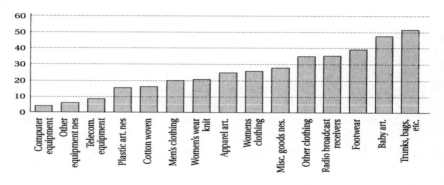

Fig. 4. Chinese exports Market share (%), 1997 (world) (*Source*: WTO–ITC 1998)

3. A prevailing preference for wholly owned foreign enterprises, and a decline in the joint venture (JV) form (both equity and co-operative JV). FDI in China falls into four large categories: equity joint venture, contractual joint venture, oil exploration contract, and fully owned foreign companies. The ratio between these four forms has considerably evolved in the last five years.

4. Evolution of geographic origin of FDI: relative decline from Hong Kong and Taiwan, increase of Nies and the United States. While the share of Hong Kong

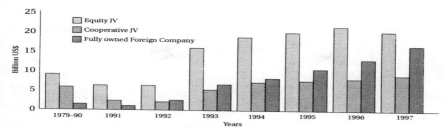

F_{IG}. 5. Forms of FDI in China (*Source*: 1979–1996: Zhongguo dwiwon Muoyi mianjian)

and Macao has been declining for the last five years, those of Japan and the Nies (Hong Kong excluded) has been continuously on the rise. Hong Kong, Taiwan and Macao, along with overseas Chinese investment in China, has focused on labour intensive, low tech sectors: garments, toys and shoes. To rely solely on FDI to modernise China's industrial system could prove to be a dangerous illusion. The process will have to go through the development of local enterprises backed by a banking system which could channel funds into it.

III   THE MARKET ACCESS ISSUE

Where are the main friction points?

1. The openness of the telecommunication market, the financial services and the agricultural sector are three sectors in which US companies are strong. The main concessions from the Chinese side (as exposed on 15 March 1999, during Zhu Rongji's press conference), are focused on the opening of the telecommunications market to foreign investors, and on a substantial liberalisation of the narrow scope of business in local currency to which foreign banks are limited.

   This first set of concessions reveals strong tension among China's economic administration. The WTO entry issue could thus be used as a powerful tool for conducting changes which domestic compromises have failed to bring so far. Telecommunications is now the fastest growing sector in China. Turnover in 1998 rose 25.4 per cent to RMB 229.5 billion. So far, a cut of 25 per cent in domestic and foreign phone tariffs has been implemented. The cost of a call from the mainland to Hong Kong and Taiwan was cut from RMB 8.1 (HK $7.54) a minute to RMB 5. However, Mr Zhu Rongji wants to break the monopoly and encourage competition. A possible consequence would be the departure of the information industry minister, Mr Wu Jichuan, a powerful advocate of China's telecom monopoly, and a staunch opponent to foreign competition in that sector. The conflict between Mr Wu and Premier Zhu is about protecting a sector considered an issue for national security, and to keep the flow of revenue it generates in the domestic operators' hands. The objective of the State Council (the plan has already been

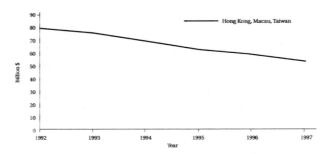

Fig. 6. FDI From Hong Kong, Macau and Taiwan in China (*Source*: ZGTJNJ. Various years)

approved) is to divide the operations of China Telecom into four separate companies: mobile telephones, fixed lines, paging and satellite. While there are more than 1,000 paging companies, only one competitor is operating in mobiles (increasing by 10 million units annually) and fixed line services, China Unicom, whose market share is negligible. So far, foreign firms have been banned from that sector.

2. Chinese SOEs in the insurance sector have five years to adjust to foreign competition, according to the deal negotiated during Shu's visit to Washington. This is very revealing of China's strong preference for bilateral agreements. So far, foreign insurers have been restricted to two Chinese cities, Shanghai and Canton. A handful of foreign insurers (eight in all) have licences to sell policies on the Chinese market, which were doled out on a country-to-country basis. Except for two of them (American International Group and Aetna), foreign insurers cannot exceed a 50 per cent stake in joint ventures.

3. With regard to the opening of the banking system to foreign operators, a substantial liberalisation of the Renminbi market for foreign banks is expected. The fear behind the openness of China's capital markets is to leave China vulnerable to huge money flows that have played a crucial role in the East Asian crisis. It will also threaten the very fragile and poorly managed banking sector.

4. Concerning access for US farm products, lifting of the ban on wheat, citrus and meat is at stake. In this sector, overall tariffs would be reduced to 17% by 2004, from the existing 40 per cent level.

5. The demand is that China enters the WTO as a developed and not a developing country. The United States maintains that it is too big to be granted the same conditions as the poorest of countries.

IV   WHAT COULD CHINA GAIN FROM MEMBERSHIP OF THE WTO?

The main argument employed by the Chinese Government is that without China and its huge markets, the WTO would not be a truly global organisation. At stake is also better access to US high technology, badly needed for China's economic modernisation, and submitted to a US Congress review every year.

China will benefit from favourable treatment in the market of other WTO members. It will also allow China to refer trade disputes to a neutral party (WTO), and, finally, entry will end the annual review of the mainland's most favoured nation status by US Congress.

At the same time, membership could accelerate the opening of sectors in which public ownership has been dominant. The WTO entry issue is used by some reformers like Zhu Rongji, who wants to exert external pressure on the state sector, while domestic reform policies have failed so far. The various purposes of China's entry have been well stated by Zhang Qiyue, an official of the Ministry of Foreign Affairs: "Entering the WTO is the demand of China's reform, and also the need of the organisation, which should adapt to the new structure of global economy and maintain its representation".

Stakes and oppositions

China's favourable trading status with the United States was rephrased from "Most Favoured Nation" to "Normal Trade Relations". The White House position concerning Congress is to unlink political issues and China's access to the world trade body. Joe Lockhart, spokesman of the White House, stated that "China enjoys much of the WTO benefits, as far as access to the US market, while American business does not enjoy access to the Chinese market that the WTO brings". In the US Congress, however, forces hostile to a WTO agreement reflect the position of the unions who fear for US labour in industries such as steel and textiles. US negotiators want to impose longer quota periods for Chinese textiles (five years) before phasing them out. The point is important because one of the benefits China hopes to retrieve from WTO entry is an increase in its textile exports.

For Beijing, the WTO is not representative without China's participation, because China is already a great trading power. The Chinese leadership, however, is divided about the schedules for a re-entry. Significantly, the main opponents to the re-accession are focusing on the premature lifting of protective barriers since China's development will require more time to be able to withstand competition with foreign firms on an equal footing. Generally speaking, ministries and state commissions are staffed with executives imbued with a neo-mercantilist view, tolerating imports of capital goods for the needs of economic modernisation, while large portions of the Chinese market—including agriculture—should be insulated from foreign competition. Indeed, the economic bureaucracy is well aware of the high degree of non-profitability of SOEs and of the weakness of its banking system. It is also undeniable that, in sectors like electronics, cosmetics and photographic film, foreign companies (Motorola, Procter and Gamble, Eastman Kodak) have obtained a prominent position in industries to which they have gained access.

Strong opposition is emerging from industries represented by the ministries of construction, the information industry, communications and agriculture, and by several industrial bureaux such as those for coal, machine-building, metallurgy and petro-chemicals. The main argument of these economic bureaucracies is that they are not prepared to face competition from efficient and cash-rich foreign companies when they are crippled with outdated equipment, overstaffed by thousands of redundant workers, and obliged to carry a state-imposed burden of pension and welfare obligations.

This compulsory market opening could translate, in their views, into a quick pace of demise for the state sector, and push up the unemployment rate. The state sector is generating less than 40 per cent of the industrial output, but still employs the lion's share of the workforce. The official unemployment rate in 1998 was 3.1 per cent, not counting the six million workers still being cared for by their state employers. The state media in China, however, recognises that the rate is closer to 11 per cent. If the rural unemployed are counted, the rate tops 17 per cent. The social consequences of a rapid break up of the state enterprises on urban unrest are not to be neglected. Last, but not least, nationalistic sentiments can be heard from voices strongly protesting against a creeping form of economic colonialism.

There is also strong opposition coming from the textile industry. Officials in that sector reject the US demand to maintain the quota for Chinese textile exports until 2010. The textile lobby exerts influence on the top leaders of the Chinese Communist Party (CCP) because Shanghai is both the power base for Jiang Zemin as well as the entire sector. Opponents to an overly wide and premature opening of the economy are also vocal in the banking and insurance industries. The fear of a devaluation of the Renminbi Yuan (RMB) will induce a lot of Chinese savers to switch to dollar denominated accounts or policies. At stake is the fate of the Chinese banking and insurance system: in 1996, 78 per cent of household financial assets were savings deposits in banks.

Finally, opponents can be found among foreign investors in China. So far the automobile industry is protected by tariffs as high as 100 per cent. They should be lowered to 25 per cent by 2005 according to the April 1999 agreement. In that case, the prospect of gaining access through joint ventures with Chinese partners will lose most of its appeal.Generally speaking, conservative views are coalescing around two major concepts.

1. Economic sovereignty: state secrets might be leaked as foreign companies gain control of strategic or sensitive sectors such a telecommunications. The openness of banking and securities to foreign fund managers could also jeopardise the country's financial security.
2. Ideological conflict: foreign capital and foreign goods are a "Trojan horse" used by "neo-imperialists" to turn China into a capitalist country through "peaceful evolution".

The final decision makers

The process of compliance with the WTO rules, which with the formal application in June 1981 began in 1986, is also highly intertwined with political issues in both China and the United States. While other members of the international body, especially the European Union (EU) and Japan, have played a significant role in promoting China's view, the final decision depends on negotiation with the United States. This bilateral exclusive relationship is by no means imposing strain on the consensus rules which characterise the WTO. Meanwhile, it reveals how much the negotiations have been intertwined with domestic policies both in China and in the United States. Finally, it is emblematic of the would-be strategic relationship which both China and the United States want to build.

Although the EU is expressing concern that the United States should not negotiate China's entry into the WTO on terms that grant special favours to Washington, the final decision will be made by the United States. This is not to say that the EU and Japanese positions are negligible. For the EU and Japan, China's membership is more a political issue than a simply commercial one. The EU as well as Japan prefer China to be in rather than out of the world trade body and for a simple reason: WTO regulation keeps moving and will never, by its evolution, allow China to adjust to those new requirements. The WTO has implemented some moves recently aimed at making the market more open and accessible to foreign competition. Such moves could make it harder for Beijing to join.

The Japanese position accords with its major interests. Japan's automobile makers for instance, could benefit from China's trade membership in order to sell more cars. The real deal, however, will be struck between China and the United States. It will involve bilateral commercial issues such as the trade deficit. Firstly according to statistical methods used by Beijing, the US deficit with China in 1997 was only US $16 billion, rather than the $50 billion recorded by the US administration. The United States claims that the deficit with China, which reached $57 billion in 1998, rose to nearly US $84 billion in 200. It is already the second largest US deficit after that with Japan. The disagreement is related to some extent to discrepancies in the way in which Hong Kong statistics are treated. Goods shipped through Hong Kong do not count in Beijing's figures. But for the United States, the question is biased by employment issues.

The China WTO entry question has also been mixed with political issues such as human right abuses and espionage claims, for example the recent case of the Los Alamos laboratory's Taiwanese-born scientist, Lee Wen-ho, allegedly passing on secrets to China which were used to produce nuclear warheads. It remains to be seen whether the problem is emblematic of "porosity" between the US and Chinese scientific systems through multiple contacts, the Hong Kong universities being one example of high level scientists of the two countries getting together. In one word, internal strife in the United States over who is to manage the global relationship with China will strongly interfere in the negotiations.

If there is no deal on membership by the end of 2001, what kind of compromise could be worked out? Different options are that China could be an "observer with privileges" status. This formula would allow China to play a special role in the WTO, in recognition of its position as a major trading nation. China could participate and be present at negotiations, but denying Beijing the right of veto, and without the possibility of blocking proposals or discussions. Its view could, however, be heard.

V   CONCLUSION

A failure in 2001s entry attempt could imply the risk of losing FOI. Companies will not have to wait too long before gaining access to the market. South-East Asia is offering many alternatives for manufacturing for exports. Dramatic reforms have been implemented, and currency remains cheap.

There are also political considerations. From the Chinese side, there seems to be conflicting strategy oscillating between two goals: the first one is of a nationalistic nature. WTO membership is seen by some Chinese leaders to provide the recognition by the world community of China's economic role. In this sense, the WTO is the last worldwide body to which China has been denied entry since its reintegration of the most prestigious international organisations (the United Nations in 1971, the World Bank and the International Monetary Fund, APEC, the Asian Development Bank, etc.). To become a member of the organisation which dictates the rules of the game will flatter China's nationalistic fibre. The second advantage is to benefit from membership or to destabilise internal opposition to reform.

Does China really need to enter the WTO? Historically it seems that Taiwan's request has triggered Chinese frustration and ultimately the Chinese demand for entry. Membership means complying to such a vast array of transparent commercial rules that one may wonder if China is really ready to enter. The disrespect of a multitude of rules will generate endless disputes with a multilateral body whose legitimacy is enshrined in international law. The benefits resulting from Chinese re-entry could be jeopardised by the eruption of a flurry of trade disputes with countries realising that greater access for Chinese products into their markets will translate into a decrease in their own access.

It would be naive to think that China will easily relinquish the right to obtain trading advantages through bilateral negotiations, in which it has so far excelled. Chinese leaders are talking about becoming the second superpower after the United States, as to that aim it would then have to be a member of all major global organisations. The WTO is the last organisation China has not been allowed to enter. The trade-off between national prestige and economic benefits is a very complex game.

Chinese development is confronted with a situation in which an integrated domestic market still does not exist, while priority has been given to the full-swing participation in international trade. What effect will regaining access to the WTO have on this situation is unclear. The high level of decentralisation of foreign trade has undoubtedly weakened the control of the central government over external trade operations, while high protectionism and price wars have broken out between provinces. The application of multilateral trade regulations will, under these conditions, be an extremely arduous and lengthy process.

8

The WTO as the Legal Foundation of International Commercial Relations: Current Status and Options for the Next Decade

RICHARD BLACKHURST

I GENERAL OVERVIEW

International economic relations are regulated by formal legal agreements (treaties) on three levels: bilateral agreements, plurilateral agreements (often among countries in a particular region), and multilateral agreements. In the area of international trade, countries often have legal obligations on more than one level. The United States, for example, has bilateral agreements with many non-World Trade Organisation (WTO) countries, participates in two regional integration agreements (one with Israel and one with Canada and Mexico), and is also a member of the WTO.

Although this chapter, in pursuing the goal of identifying changes taking place in the regulation of international economic relations at the turn of the century and what the future perspectives are, focuses on the WTO, the discussion also includes a brief overview of the interaction between WTO rules and the rules in regional integration agreements (RIAs).

A brief look at the GATT/WTO system

Created in 1947 as an interim arrangement pending the ratification of the International Trade Organisation, the General Agreement on Tariffs and Trade (GATT) had two fundamental goals or functions which were, with certain additions (indicated by italics), carried over to the WTO:[1]

---

[1] See R. Blackhurst, "The Capacity of the WTO to Fulfill Its Mandate", in A. Krueger (ed.), *The WTO as an International Organization* (University fo Chicago Press, 1998), for a more detailed discussion of these and related points.

- to reduce policy-related uncertainty surrounding the exchange of goods *and services* across national frontiers, by providing a set of rules and procedures governing selected trade-related policies;
- to provide a forum for dispute-settlement, for negotiations both to strengthen and extend the rules and procedures and to further liberalise trade-related policies, *for the review of national trade policies, and for co-operation with the International Monetary Fund (IMF) and World Bank with a view to achieving greater coherence in global economic policy making.*

Petersmann, an academic lawyer, sees the GATT/WTO system as having a "constitutional" function designed to protect freedom, non-discrimination and the rule of law in international commercial relations.[2] Goldstein, a political scientist, starts from the well-known argument that because (i) the gains from freer trade are spread throughout society, whereas (ii) the adjustment costs tend to be focused on certain groups, interest group pressures are biased in favour of those who lose from freer trade. The resulting chronic over-representation of protectionist interests means that without the kind of institutional support provided by the GATT/WTO, it is difficult for a country—especially a democracy—to sustain a liberal trade policy.[3]

The GATT/WTO moves inside the border

Over the past 30 years, the ongoing integration of the world economy has caused a growing number of ostensibly "domestic" policies to become trade-related policies. Up to and including the Kennedy Round, GATT rules and negotiations were about measures applied at the border, primarily tariffs. In the Tokyo Round (1973–1979), the GATT moved "inside the border" to consider production subsidies, technical barriers and government procurement. This process continued unabated in the Uruguay Round, with expansion of the newly created WTO mandate to include rules governing national policies on services (where the barriers to trade are primarily domestic regulations), the protection of intellectual property, sanitary and phytosanitary regulations, and pre-shipment inspection.

As will be evident from the discussion of "options for the next decade" later in the chapter, there is considerable pressure, particularly from many of the

---

[2] E.U. Petersmann, *The GATT/WTO Dispute Settlement System: International Law, International Organisations and Dispute Settlement* (Kluwer Law International, 1997). See also F. Roessler, "The Constitutional Function of the Multilateral Trade Order", in M. Hill and E.U. Petersmann (eds), *National Constitutions and International Economic Law* (Kluwer, Boston, 1993).

[3] J. Goldstein, "International Institutions and Domestic Politics: GATT, WTO and the Liberalization of International Trade", in A. Krueger (ed.), *The WTO as an International Organisation* (University of Chicago Press, 1998). Goldstein identifies four ways in which international institutions affect domestic politics: by acting as agenda setters, thereby tying the hands of domestic policy makers and undercutting the influence of protectionist interest groups; by bundling or linking different issues, thereby making it easier to put together a majority in favour of further trade liberalisation; by changing the status of domestic courts and legal institutions; and by altering the domestic normative discourse.

OECD countries, to further expand WTO rules to cover other policy areas which traditionally have been thought of as being entirely within the realm of domestic politics.

Drawing on the work of Douglass North

The work for which Douglass North shared (with Robert Fogel, another economic historian) the 1993 Nobel Prize in Economics, offers perhaps the best framework for understanding these institutional/legal developments. His work, which fills a large gap in traditional economic analysis by explicitly introducing such factors as transactions costs, property rights, rules of the economic game and, more broadly, the role of institutions, combines modern economic theory and extensive empirical analysis of economic growth, particularly in the United States before 1860 and in Western Europe from the Middle Ages to the eighteenth century.

Specialisation based on comparative advantage drives the gains from trade, be it trade between neighbours, tribes, villages, cities, provinces or countries. Those gains from trade, in turn, play a central role in economic growth. The tone of North's analysis, as well as one important aspect of that analysis, is evident in the following quotation from his 1990 study[4] of why some countries are rich and others are poor:

"The institutions necessary to accomplish economic exchange vary in their complexity, from those that solve simple exchange problems to ones that extend across space and time and numerous individuals. The degree of complexity in economic exchange is a function of the level of contracts necessary to undertake exchange in economies of various degrees of specialization. Non-specialization is a form of insurance when the costs and uncertainties of transacting are high. *The greater the specialization and the number and variability of valuable attributes [of commodities, services and the performance of agents], the more weight must be put on reliable institutions that allow individuals to engage in complex contracting with a minimum of uncertainly about whether the terms of the contract can be realized.* Exchange in modern economies consisting of many variable attributes extending over long periods of time necessitates institutional reliability, which has only gradually emerged in Western economies. There is nothing automatic about the evolution of cooperation from simple forms of contracting and exchange to complex forms that have characterized the successful economies of modern times". (emphasis added)

The Press Release from the Royal Swedish Academy of Sciences announcing the award noted:

"According to North, new institutions arise when groups in society perceive a possibility of availing themselves of profits that cannot be realized under prevailing institutional conditions. If external conditions permit an increase in income, but it is prevented by institutional factors, then new institutional arrangements are likely to

[4] D.C. North, *Institutions, Institutional Change and Economic Performance* (Cambridge University Press, 1990), 34.

develop. . . . North does not regard innovations, technical changes and other generally accepted factors as sufficient explanations [of differences in the rate of economic growth between countries and over time]. These factors themselves are part of the growth process and cannot explain it".

These quotations are an excellent starting point for understanding (1) the creation of the rules-based GATT system in 1948 and its subsequent evolution and activities, culminating in the establishment of the WTO on 1 January 1995, (2) the proliferation of RIAs in the post-war period, and especially since the beginning of the 1990s, and (3) the expanding coverage, in terms of policy areas covered by the rules of both the GATT/WTO and the RIAs. In other words, as the world economy becomes progressively more integrated, North's conclusions about the central role of *domestic* institutions become increasingly applicable at the *multilateral* level. Countries clearly believe that internationalised economic activity requires *effective* rules-based plurilateral and multilateral institutions.

A costly lesson

It is worth taking a moment to recall that this lesson was learned the hard way. It is now commonplace to observe that the degree of globalisation—as measured, for example, by countries' ratios of trade to GDP or international capital flows—was quite high on the eve of the First World War. Although it is difficult to be precise, it appears that the world's ratio of trade to GDP did not regain its 1913 level until sometime in the late 1970s or early 1980s.[5] Thus, globalisation is not a new phenomenon, but rather a process that has been underway for a long time, and that it particularly gathered steam with the signing of the Cobden-Chevalier Treaty of 1860, with its justifiably famous most favoured nation (MFN) clause between England and France. As every major European country except Russia signed bilateral commercial treaties with France and England and with one another, the MFN clauses in those treaties generalised the tariff concessions, creating "a network of commercial treaties which severely reduced the level of protection throughout Europe".[6]

The "dis-integration" of the world economy between 1914 and 1945 was the result of two world wars, the economic disorder of the 1920s and the economic chaos of the 1930s. With respect to developments in the 1920s and—especially—the 1930s, there is little doubt that the absence of legally binding commitments, in the form of bilateral commercial treaties (or an effective multilateral institution dealing with commercial relations), was a major factor. The lesson for policy makers with first-hand experience of the 1920s and 1930s was clear. Establishing and maintaining a liberal world trading system required *legally binding constraints on national trade policies*, based on the MFN principle and coupled with an effective procedure for resolving disputes. The great innovation of the drafters of the Havana Charter (out of which came the GATT by default)

---

[5] See A. Maddison, *The World Economy in the 20th Century* (OECD, Paris, 1989).
[6] G. Curzon, *Multilateral Commercial Diplomacy* (Michael Joseph, 1965), 16.

was to base the new system not on a large number of bilateral treaties, but on a single set of multilateral rules and disciplines.

Winham, a political scientist, commenting on the success of the GATT/WTO system, notes that "The WTO places more emphasis on trade rules than on collective action"[7] and later concludes:[8]

> "In the relatively brief history of international organisation, states have made greater efforts to establish strong organisations than to establish strong rules. The success of the GATT/WTO 'contract' regime is a reminder that in an international system with sovereign actors, rules rather than formal organisation may be a better basis on which to promote international cooperation".

The perception in Geneva is that the WTO system, now in its fifth year, is functioning well. Dispute-settlement is often singled out as both the most important success so far and the area which is currently posing the greatest challenges (the banana case now apparently settled, the US/EU dispute over beef growth hormones is in the spotlight, with genetically modified foods looming ominously on the horizon).

The sovereignty issue (in brief)

For many countries—even those which attach great importance to "rule of law"—discussions of the need for effective multilateral rules often turn quickly to the complex and sensitive issue of "loss of sovereignty". It is true, of course, that submitting one's trade (or other) policies to multilateral rules involves some loss of discretion over those policies—or what has been termed "the right of unfettered decision-making in the future.[9]

But this is by no means necessarily a bad development. There are at least three important sources of gain: other countries' policies become more predictable and your own policies become more predictable—both of which benefit your own domestic investors and consumers—and the government gains a tool which can be used to control domestic special interest groups. (Regarding the third source of gain, it is evident from the literature on the political economy of trade policy, as well as from the more broadly applicable public choice theory, that a person would have to be unbelievably naive to believe that government economic policies are motivated solely, or even most of the time, by what is best for the country as a whole.)

It is important to stress that while the WTO's multilaterally agreed rules limit the amount of discretion over a range of trade-related policies, this is not the same as an institution with legislative or policy-setting powers. Setting limits on what governments can do—limits defined by rules they themselves have written

---

[7] G.R. Winham, "The World Trade Organization: Institution-Building in the Multilateral Trade System", *The World Economy*, May 1998, 358.

[8] Ibid., 366.

[9] Ibid.

and accepted—is generally different from telling them what they should or must do (as is so often true of generaliations about the WTO, the Agreement in Trade-Related Aspects of Intellectual Property (TRIPs) being an exception).[10]

Country coverage

When discussing the coverage of the WTO rules, it is important not only to enumerate the policy areas covered by the rules, but also the country coverage, in other words to consider the degree of "universality" of the WTO membership. The facts are well-known: there are currently 134 members (sixteen from the European Union (EU) since the Commission is also a signatory) which collectively account for more than 90 per cent of world trade, Estonia is about to join, and thirty countries or independent customs territories are in the accession process, including Cambodia, China, the Russian Federation, Saudi Arabia, Chinese Taipei, Ukraine and Vietnam. The combined total of 165 is close to double the eighty-five contracting parties in the GATT in September 1986 when the Uruguay Round was launched. Clearly, the vast majority of countries now view membership in the WTO "club" as something very desirable—or at least, indispensable.

II CURRENT WTO COMMITMENTS

WTO commitments is a topic best discussed either very briefly or in considerable detail. For obvious reasons, the latter works best for this chapter. The official guide to current WTO commitments and procedures is the 558-page (in English) 1994 GATT publication, *The Results of the Uruguay Round of Multilateral Trade Negotiations*. However, this is an exceptionally "reader unfriendly" publication, partly because of the rhetoric, but mostly because of the organisation, and for most purposes a better reference is the WTO's 1999 publication, *Guide to the Uruguay Round Agreements*.

Along with the issue of countries' commitments under the WTO, the relationship or interaction between WTO commitments and those contained in the leading RIAs is also relevant. Because space limitations rule out any attempt to survey commitments under all the leading RIAs, the following discussion is limited to a brief consideration of the African FreeTrade Association (AFTA) and the Asia-Pacific Economic Co-operation (APEC).

Consider a hypothetical country which is a participant in the WTO, the AFTA and APEC.[11] The external policy commitments of these three agreements

---

[10] Language matters, especially in areas where sensitivities run high. For this reason, the term "global governance" is not a helpful way of describing this topic. Something along the lines of "the role of multilateral institutions in an integrated world" or "rules of the game in an integrated world" would be more likely to keep open the lines of communication and dialogue, rather than "global governance".

[11] Brunei, Tanzania, Indonesia, Malaysia, the Philippines, Singapore and Thailand fit this description.

are the "parameters" within which the country's trade policy makers must function if the country is to be in compliance with its international obligations. Generally speaking, the commitments (1) define what the policy makers can and cannot do in the area of trade-related policies, and (2) lay down certain required actions, such as those related to the transparency of national trade-related policies and procedures, and—in the case of the AFTA—the programme of required preferential tariff reductions.

WTO Commitments

A fundamental feature of the WTO is the "single undertaking" nature of the multilateral agreement. With certain very limited exceptions (primarily for the least developed countries), all members are subject to the same rules and disciplines. This is in sharp contrast to the situation in the GATT between 1979 and 1994, when participation in the so-called Tokyo Round codes—covering such areas as anti-dumping, subsidies and countervailing duties, customs valuation and technical barriers—was optional. If a country is a member of the WTO, then that country must abide by the WTO rules and regulations.

On a very general level, it is possible to divide WTO commitments into four categories:

(1) **Market access.** To achieve, and then not reduce, the levels of access to its market for goods and services specified in its two schedules of concessions, as agreed to in the Uruguay Round and in the subsequent agreements on basic telecoms, trade in information technology products (the ITA), and financial services.

(2) **Rules and procedures.** To observe the rules and disciplines governing trade-related policies (e.g. on the use of quantitative restrictions, subsidies, customs valuation, the protection of intellectual property, health and safety standards and many other policies—see below for details).

(3) **Transparency.** To fulfil the approximately 165 notification requirements agreed to in the Uruguay Round, along with obligations to publish regulations and to establish various enquiry points. The other principal transparency activity is the Trade Policy Review Mechanism (TPRM), designed "to contribute to improved adherence . . . to rules, disciplines and commitments . . . by achieving greater transparency in, and understanding of, the trade policies and practices of Members".

(4) **Dispute-settlement.** To follow, in disputes with other WTO members, the rules and procedures laid down in the "Understanding on Rules and Procedures Governing the Settlement of Disputes", and to abide by the decisions of panels and the Appellate Body.

More on rules and procedures

The rules and procedures in the second of the country's four categories of commitments cover four principal areas of economic activity: trade in goods, trade in services, the protection of intellectual property, and—to a lesser but not negligible extent—foreign direct investment.

Goods

The core principles of GATT 1947 have been carried over to GATT 1994. These are the MFN rule, the national treatment rule (once goods or services are inside the border, they is not to be discriminated against), and the prohibition—except in certain specified circumstances—of protective measures other than tariffs.[12]

Ten categories of policies are covered by WTO rules in the goods area:[13]

- anti-dumping;
- safeguards;
- customs valuation;
- rules of origin;
- technical barriers;
- subsidies and countervailing duties;
- trade-related investment measures;
- preshipment inspection;
- import licensing;
- sanitary and phytosanitary measures.[14]

The Uruguay Round agreements in the goods area also include separate rules in two important product areas—agriculture, and textiles and clothing. These evolved into special cases under the GATT 1947, and which are now (gradually) being reintegrated into the framework of GATT 1994.

Services

There are three main parts to the General Agreement on Trade in Services (GATS): a basic set of rules which closely follow the core principles found in the General Agreement on Trade and Tariffs (GATT), additional agreements which deal with specific sectoral and other issues (including air transport, financial services, telecommunications and maritime transport), and each member's national schedule of commitments on specific service activities.

---

[12] The major exception to the MFN rule continues to be the provision for preferential trading agreements (Art. XXIV).

[13] Government procurement is not on the list because the Agreement on Government Procurement is a *plurilateral* agreement (membership is optional).

[14] Technically, the SPS Agreement is part of the Agreement on Agriculture, but in effect it is a stand-alone agreement.

The core rules, which in principle are applicable to all services by all WTO members, regardless of whether they are in countries' schedules, include MFN (however, countries are allowed to establish exceptions), transparency requirements (publication of laws and regulations, establishment of enquiry points and so forth), regional trading agreements, state trading, restrictions for Balance of Payments (BOP) purposes, government purchases of services, and general and security exceptions. These and other rules follow more or less closely their goods-related counterparts in the GATT 1994. Negotiations on rules for two other categories of measures as they apply to services—safeguards and subsidies—were not completed by the end of the Uruguay Round and are continuing. As regards those service activities which a country has entered in its schedule of commitments on services, the most important rules cover market access (based on the four modes of supply) and national treatment.

Intellectual property

Nearly half of the TRIPS agreement is devoted to minimum substantive standards for the availability, scope and use of intellectual property rights, including the minimum protection which must be given by the national law of each WTO member to seven categories of rights:

- copyright and related rights;
- geographical indications;
- patents;
- undisclosed information (trade secrets);
- trademarks;
- industrial designs;
- integrated circuits.

Another one-quarter of the TRIPS agreement deals with the enforcement of intellectual property rights, specifying the procedures and remedies each WTO member must provide. Other rules specify MFN and national treatment.

Foreign direct investment (FOI)

The most significant FDI-related rules in the WTO are those related to the requirement in the GATS, that countries grant the right of establishment to foreign firms in those service activities which are included in their services schedule. Another example is the provisions of the TRIPS agreement, which help define the legal environment affecting FDI. A common denominator of the GATS and the TRIPS is that both put important obligations on governments with respect to the treatment of foreign nationals and companies operating within their territories—in other words, obligations with respect to the central issue of FDI policies.

While the provisions of the Agreement on Trade-Related Investment Measures (TRIM) apply equally to domestic and foreign-owned firms—and thus are not, strictly speaking, FDI-related provisions—the measures they cover often arise in connection with FDI. Such measures include, in particular, local content and trade-balancing requirements. Finally, the Agreement on Subsidies and Countervailing Measures (ASCM) prohibits:

> "investment incentives meeting the definition of a subsidy, and granted contingent upon exportation of goods produced (or to be produced) by an investor, or contingent upon use of domestic over imported goods. . . Even if not prohibited, incentives that cause 'adverse effects' as defined by the ASCM are potentially subject to compensatory action, either multilaterally or under WTO Members' national legislation".[15]

Interpretation and enforcement of commitments

In many instances it is a fairly straightforward matter to decide whether a particular policy or behaviour is or is not in conformity with the country's WTO obligations. But there are also many instances in which the issue of the conformity of a particular policy with the rules is not at all clear. In any case, the member countries have made it clear that the only source of definitive interpretations of WTO rules is that of the Dispute-Settlement Panel and Appellate Body reports.

External enforcement of legally binding commitments is carried out through peer pressure from WTO partners and—where that does not work, through the WTO dispute-settlement procedures. As long as trading partners are willing to ignore non-compliance with WTO commitments, a country can—if it wants—get away with non-compliance. This might happen occasionally with developing countries which are very small traders, but it is unlikely that trading partners would ignore, for any length of time, important examples of non-compliance on the part of non-marginal traders.

AFTA Commitments

It is not easy for someone approaching the AFTA for the first time to determine exactly what activities take place (exclusively or partially) under it—as distinct from the Association of South-East Asian Nations (ASEAN)—nor to determine which AFTA commitments are legally binding and which are simply "best endeavours". As far as I can judge, the only legally binding commitments are those in the Common Effective Preferential Tariff (CETP) scheme, which involve reductions in intra-regional tariffs and the elimination of non-tariff

---

[15] For a more detailed discussion of this point, see WTO *Annual Report 1996* (WTO, 1996), 69–73 (English version). As this report notes, the Agreement on Government Procurement 1979—now, under the WTO, the Plurilateral Agreement on Government Procurement—was the first important GATT/WTO move into the area of the treatment of foreign companies by host countries.

barriers. If this is correct, all other commitments under the AFTA/ASEAN are "soft" commitments whose impact on future policies is very difficult to predict.

APEC Commitments

APEC has identified a number of goals in the trade policy area, most notably free trade by 2010 for developed APEC countries and by 2020 for developing countries. It has also initiated a large number of co-operation projects. But, as far as I could determine, there are as yet no legally binding commitments, at least not in the trade policy area. However, that could change in the not-too-distant future. When APEC leaders met in Vancouver in November 1997, they gave the "green light" to plans for "early voluntary liberalisation" in fifteen sectors, with nine targeted for negotiations in 1998 and implementation in 1999. The nine sectors are environmental goods and services, fish and fish products, forest products, medical equipment and instruments, energy, toys, chemicals, gems and jewellery, and telecommunications (a mutual recognition arrangement). This process was again endorsed by trade ministers at the June 1998 meeting in Kuching.

Under APEC's principle of voluntarism, countries are free to decide which sectoral initiatives to participate in, as well as the implementation period. A key question is whether, once a country has "voluntarily" agreed on a set of commitments, those commitments become binding.

Interactions between commitments under the different Agreements

From a purely legal standpoint, there is not much to say on this topic because the ASEAN group and the APEC group have each repeatedly stressed the importance of making their actions within the WTO compatible. The possible exception to this generalisation concerns their compatibility with Article XXIV of GATT. Here it is helpful to keep in mind that a regional agreement cannot be in conflict with WTO commitments, and thus there is no need to bring Article XXIV into the picture if it is limited to (1) liberalising actions done on an MFN basis, or (2) actions in an area not covered by WTO commitments.

A great deal has been written in recent years about the broader issue of the "political" or "policy" interaction between the WTO and RIAs. Are they complementary or competing approaches to further trade liberalisation? In chapter IV of its 1995 study on multilateralism and regionalism,[16] the WTO addressed this question in considerable detail, concluding:

". . . to a much greater extent than is often acknowledged, regional and multilateral integration initiatives are complements rather than alternatives in the pursuit of more liberal and open trade. [Existing] Regional integration agreements contain both higher and lower levels of obligation than the WTO. In the latter case, the WTO complements [extends] the liberalization achieved at the regional level, while the converse is true in the former case".

[16] WTO, *Regionalism and the World Trading System* (WTO, 1995), 56.

III OPTIONS FOR THE NEXT DECADE

Two principal developments explain the previously mentioned expansion of the GATT/WTO agenda inside the border. One is the GATT's success in reducing the level of restrictions imposed at the border. Tariffs in the industrial countries have come down from more than 40 per cent in the late 1940s to under 5 per cent (tariff peaks are still a problem for certain products, such as fish, textiles and clothing), and quantitative restrictions are now largely under control (keeping in mind the scheduled phase-out by 2005 of the bilateral Quantitative Restrictions (QR) imposed under the Multifiber Arrangement). This process has both "exposed" impediments to trade other than tariffs and quotas, and led governments to look for other policies to protect politically influential special interest groups from foreign competition.

The other development is the ongoing integration ("globalisation") of the world economy. Between 1950 and 1974, the world's trade-to-GDP ratio doubled from 7 per cent to 15 per cent. By the end of this decade it will be close to 25 per cent and there is no reason to believe that it will not continue to rise in the foreseeable future.[17] Flows of FDI, which increased very dramatically in the second half of the 1980s, were up more than 20 per cent in 1997, to $400 billion. Small and medium-size enterprises in a broad cross-section of countries are following the multinationals in sourcing, marketing and investing across national boundaries.

As countries' "economic lives" become more intertwined, it is inevitable that, increasingly, many ostensibly "domestic" policies will have real or perceived spillover effects on trading partners. And it is equally inevitable, as a result, that members of the WTO, an organisation whose primary mission is to provide rules and procedures that reduce the uncertainty associated with transactions across national frontiers, will find themselves debating the pros and cons of further moves "inside the border".

When the ministers met in Marrakesh to sign the Uruguay Round Agreement, they were aware that not only bringing traded services under multilateral rules, and bringing agriculture back into the heart of the GATT/WTO system, were truly major achievements, but also that the member countries had not gone very far down the liberalisation (market-opening) road in either area. Their response was to mandate that another round of multilateral negotiations in each area should begin by the year 2000. Those negotiations, presumably, will be launched late this year at the WTO Ministerial meeting in Seattle (30 November through 3 December). The debate that has been going on for some time is whether to respond to the requirement to launch formal negotiations in those two areas by launching a much more ambitious round of multilateral negotiations—a so-called "millennium round".

Two factors are driving the calls for an ambitious, big-agenda round. One is a very pragmatic concern of the EU, Japan, Korea and other countries which

---

[17] WTO, *International Trade 1995* (WTO, 1995), 15–23.

still maintain very high levels of protection for agriculture. They know thast they will come under enormous pressure to reduce agricultural trade barriers in the new round, and they believe that they need a range of "successes" in other areas to make the final package they take home for ratification politically acceptable to their electorates. The other factor is the previously mentioned point that a combination of the ongoing integration of the global economy (with everyone living closer together in an economic sense), and the WTO's mission to reduce the uncertainty surrounding cross-border transactions, is constantly pulling the WTO further inside the border.

The result is a number of suggestions, including both traditional and new topics, for converting a two-topic round into a "millennium round". Combining the two mandated topics and the candidates that have been put forward thus far yields the following list of possible agenda topics that will, if adopted (partially or entirely), shape trade relations for the coming decades:

- agriculture;
- services;
- industrial tariffs;
- government procurement;
- state trading;
- trade facilitation;
- investment rules;
- competition rules;
- Internet/electronic commerce;
- environment-related WTO rule changes;
- other rule changes (e.g. Article XXIV);
- labour standards.

This will be in addition to whatever improvements in rules and procedures might evolve from the Marrakesh-mandated reviews/appraisals of existing WTO provisions in three key areas: dispute-settlement rules and procedures (this year), the TRIPs Agreement and the TPRM (in 2000).

Two very different groups are opposing calls for the kind of ambitious agenda outlined above. One is composed of developing countries in the WTO which feel that such an agenda, going beyond the mandated areas of agriculture and services, is premature because the system is still "digesting" the ambitious Uruguay Round results. How much support there is for this view among the 100 or so developing countries in the WTO, and the extent to which it is simply a bargaining strategy, is not clear, but India is promoting it with support from, among others, Egypt, Indonesia, Malaysia and Pakistan.

The other "group" is a heterogeneous collection of trade unions and non-governmental organisations (NGOs), collectively referred to in today's terminology as members of "civil society", united by their deep suspicion and dislike of globalisation in general, and of multinational firms and the WTO in particular. For the most part, their concerns focus on what they believe are the negative effects of globalisation and trade liberalisation on the environment, development, employment and income distribution.

It is impossible at this point to predict the likely impact of these two groups on either the agenda-setting process in Seattle or the eventual outcome of the new round of negotiations.

IV POSTSCRIPT

A recent and important development is the proposal to establish "An Advisory Centre on WTO Law" in Geneva. From an institutional and budget standpoint, it will be completely separate from and independent of the WTO. The broad purpose is to provide participating developing countries with a range of WTO law-related services, including education, counselling and (for a fee that varies according to the country's per capita income), professional legal assistance in WTO dispute-settlement cases. The project is now fully developed, and the organisers hope that it can be launched by mid-1999. Further details are available from:

Mme Claudia Orozco
Permanent Mission of Colombia to the WTO
Tel: (41 22) 919 05 10
Fax: (41 22) 734 60 94
Email: claudia.orozco@ties.itu.int

9

Global and Regional Regulatory Changes of Foreign Direct Investment: Challenges and Opportunities for the ASEAN in the Wake of the Recent Turmoil

SUTHIPHAND CHIRATHIVAT

I INTRODUCTION

The Association of South-East Asian Nations (ASEAN) is a region which consists of a population of over 500 million with a combined gross domestic product of roughly US $550 billion. The grouping has today fulfilled the dream of having all ten South-East Asian nations united now that Cambodia has become the last country to be part of the ASEAN.[1] Although these countries are known to be at different stages of economic development, success has been achieved in keeping members focussed on opening their economies.

The Asian crisis, beginning in Thailand, soon extended throughout the region, weakening the overall economy of the region. Each has been seriously affected by a shrinking economy, a weakened currency and a reduced purchasing power. The event provides for crisis-hit countries to look at how their political and corporate culture impeded adjustments to changing competitive conditions. Several changes have to be made to prepare for policy adjustments. Otherwise, the region risks a repetition of the worst of the crisis. The question is how the ASEAN is to emerge as a stronger unit after the crisis.

The region had done well prior to the crisis in terms of liberalising trade and attracting foreign direct investment (FDI). The so-called trade-investment nexus in the ASEAN has been the direct implication of the formation of the ASEAN

---

[1] With Cambodia finally joining the Association on 30 April 1999, thirty-two years since the ASEAN was formed in 1967 by Indonesia, Malaysia, the Philippines, Singapore and Thailand amid concern that the war and the communist threat could spill into their territory.

Free Trade Area for FDI flows and trade patterns in the region.[2] A continued commitment to outward-oriented policies has been expressed through the leaders, vision of ASEAN 2020 and the latest effort to create an ASEAN Investment Area (AIA) which aims to further indicate open regionalism in the ASEAN.

Against these backdrops, the effects of the economic crisis should not destroy years of progress pointing to globalisation leading to open borders for flows of trade, investment, finance, ideas and cultural values. The crisis should not be seen as a threat to the national well-being of the region.[3] Certainly, the crisis has caused the ASEAN to ponder more realistically on the costs and benefits of being a part of globalisation. At the country level, some ASEAN governments, including Malaysia, the Philippines, Singapore and Thailand, have welcomed the opportunity for reform.

This chapter aims to look at the importance of FDI to the economy, especially production and trade in the regional context up to the present. The crisis that hit the region should not deter its commitment to a liberal trading and investment environment. It is then interesting to point out the changes of the global context of FDI and the progress made at regional and country level. There are certainly more benefits to reap and the region needs to work seriously towards achieving the results which they consider vital to them.

II BACKGROUND ON FDI IN THE ASEAN

Until the economic crisis, FDI in developing countries was concentrated in Asia. The region accounts for over half of the total FDI flows to developing countries between 1986–1997, reflecting the strength of the region in attracting FDI. Within the region, China and the ASEAN countries represent the main recipients. Evidently, China has quickly emerged as the largest FDI recipient in Asia and the second largest in the world after the United States. Since 1993, China's FDI inflows reached the level of around US $30 billion or over 30 per cent of all developing countries, making the country more important in terms of the size of FDI inflows compared to the ASEAN region.

As for the ASEAN's FDI inflows, this has continued to increase in its overall value to stand around US $26 billion or over 20 per cent or one-fifth of all developing countries. In terms of inward FDI stock, the ASEAN record is quite impressive as the region continues to enjoy the FDI inflows in commutative terms which increased ten times between 1980 and 1997. The inward FDI stock in the ASEAN represents a share of almost 22 per cent of all developing countries, which is still larger than China, standing at around 21 per cent (see Table 1). Singapore was the

---

[2] See P. Petri, "The Interdependence of Trade and Investment in the Pacific", in E.K.Y. Chen and P. Drysdale (eds), *Corporate Links and Foreign Direct Investment in Asia and the Pacific* (Harper International, Australia, 1995); and P.-C. Athukorala and J. Menon, "AFTA and the Investment-Trade Naxus in ASEAN" (1997) 20 *The World Economy* 159.

[3] D.C. Gladney and C.B. Johnstone, "Let's Take Asian Fear of Globalization Seriously", *International Herald Tribune*, 26 April 1999.

Table 1: Inward FDI Stock, 1980–1997

Unit: US dollars (millions)

	1980	1985	1990	1995	1996	1997
ASEAN 10:	24794	49876	92076	175903	203073	228604
Brunei	19	33	30	62	71	76
Cambodia	—	—	—	198	849	1049
Indonesia	10274	24971	38883	50603	56797	62147
Laos	2	2	14	213	373	463
Malaysia	6078	8510	14117	36778	41450	45203
Myanmar	5	5	173	937	1037	1117
Philippines	1225	1302	2098	7158	8678	9931
Singapore	6203	13016	28565	58622	68062	78062
Thailand	981	1999	7980	17236	19504	23104
Vietnam	7	38	216	4096	6252	7452
China	57	4305	18568	131241	172041	217341
Hong Kong, China	1729	3520	13413	21769	24269	26869
India	1177	1075	1667	5566	7948	11212
Korea, Republic of	1141	1806	5727	10478	12491	14832
Taiwan	2405	2930	9735	15736	17600	19848
S, E, S.E. Asia	32302	65247	144543	367523	445192	527602
Developing	108068	209856	357815	768364	896023	1043666
Developed	371917	546808	1377609	1929336	2122668	2349442
World	479985	756663	1736326	2732649	3065299	3455509

Unit: percentage

	1980	1985	1990	1995	1996	1997
ASEAN 10:	22.9	23.7	25.7	22.8	22.6	21.9
Brunei	0.0	0.0	0.0	0.0	0.0	0.0
Cambodia	—	—	—	0.0	0.0	0.1
Indonesia	9.5	11.8	10.8	6.5	6.3	5.9
Laos	0.0	0.0	0.0	0.0	0.0	0.0
Malaysia	5.6	4.0	3.9	4.7	4.6	4.3
Myanmar	0.0	0.0	0.0	0.1	0.1	0.1
Philippines	1.1	0.6	0.5	0.9	0.69	0.9
Singapore	5.7	6.2	7.9	7.6	7.5	7.4
Thailand	0.9	0.9	2.2	2.2	2.1	2.2
Vietnam	0.0	0.0	0.0	0.5	0.6	0.7
China	0.0	2.0	5.1	17.0	19.2	20.8
Hong Kong, China	1.5	1.6	3.7	2.8	2.7	2.5
India	1.0	0.5	0.4	0.7	0.8	1.0
Korea, Republic of	1.0	0.8	1.6	1.3	1.3	1.4
Taiwan	2.2	1.3	2.7	2.0	1.9	1.9
S, E, S.E. Asia	29.8	31.0	40.3	47.8	49.6	50.5
Developing	100.0	100.0	100.0	100.0	100.0	100.0

Source: UNCTAD, *World Investment Report 1998* (Geneva 1998), Annex Table B3.

largest recipient of inward FDI stock in 1997 representing 7.4 per cent, followed by Indonesia (5.9 per cent), Malaysia (4.3 per cent), Thailand (2.2 per cent), the Philippines (0.9 per cent) and Vietnam (0.7 per cent). With the exception of Brunei, the rest of the ASEAN consists of new members, which still need to pave the way for their domestic economy and policy to attract more FDI in the near future.

FDI in South-East Asia can be said to play a crucial role among those market-oriented economies and even for those emerging transitional economies.[4] It has a particular role in the development of infrastructure such as energy, industrial sectors linked to the growth of manufactured exports. Trade and FDI have re-inforced each other, making ASEAN fuel the economic expansion known as trade-investment nexus[5] which suggests a positive correlation between foreign investment inflows and trade. Although the FDI inflows have grown significantly, these remain limited to some forms of investment financing except for Singapore, Malaysia and, more recently, Vietnam. The inward and outward FDI stock as a percentage of GDP ratio (see Table 2) reached 72.4 per cent in Singapore in 1996, 48.6 per cent in Malaysia and 40.2 per cent in Vietnam. The large FDI role in Singapore seems to reflect its strategy for foreign firms to pro-vide technological, managerial, organisational and marketing capabilities.[6]

Table 2: Inward and Outward FDI Stock as a Percentage of GDP, 1980, 1985, 1990 and 1996

	1980	1985	1990	1996
ASEAN 10:				
Brunei				
Inward	0.4	0.9	0.8	1.8
Outward	—	—	—	—
Cambodia				
Inward	—	—	—	36.3
Outward	—	—	—	—
Indonesia				
Inward	14.2	28.6	36.6	25.0
Outward	—	0.1	—	0.8
Laos				
Inward	—	0.1	1.6	20.1
Outward	—	—	—	—
Malaysia				
Inward	24.8	27.2	33.0	48.6
Outward	1.7	2.4	5.3	14.8

[4] S.T. Chia and N. Pacini, *ASEAN in the New Asia* (Institute of South-East Asian Studies, Singapore, 1997), 42.

[5] Given relatively liberal trade regimes, East Asian investments have become increasingly pro-ductive, favouring investments in efficient export sectors rather than inefficient protected sectors: Petri, above at n. 2, 42.

[6] Chia and Pacini, above at n. 4, 44.

	1980	1985	1990	1996
Myanmar				
Inward	0.1	0.1	0.7	0.9
Outward	—	—	—	—
Philippines				
Inward	3.8	4.2	4.7	10.4
Outward	0.5	0.6	0.4	1.3
Singapore				
Inward	52.9	73.6	76.3	72.4
Outward	82.6	54.7	25.8	39.9
Thailand				
Inward	3.0	5.1	9.3	11.6
Outward	—	—	0.5	1.9
Vietnam				
Inward	—0.2	3.3	40.2	
Outward	—	—	—	—
China				
Inward	—	1.5	4.8	24.7
Outward	—	—	0.6	2.6
Hong Kong, China				
Inward	6.3	10.5	17.9	15.7
Outward	0.5	7.0	17.7	71.9
India				
Inward	0.7	0.5	0.5	2.6
Outward	—	—	—	—
Korea, Republic of				
Inward	1.8	1.9	2.3	2.6
Outward	0.2	0.6	0.9	2.8
Taiwan				
Inward	5.8	4.7	6.1	7.3
Outward	0.2	0.3	8.1	12.0
S, E, S.E. Asia				
Inward	3.8	6.6	8.8	15.8
Outward	1.3	1.4	2.7	8.1
Developing				
Inward	4.3	8.2	8.5	15.6
Outward	0.6	1.2	1.8	4.9
Developed				
Inward	3.8	4.9	6.6	7.6
Outward	5.2	5.9	7.8	10.1
Total				
Inward	4.6	6.5	8.0	10.6
Outward	5.0	5.9	7.8	10.8

Source: UNCTAD, *World Investment Report 1998* (Geneva, 1998), Annex Table B4.

Likewise, the inward and outward FDI flows as a percentage of gross domestic fixed capital formation also reflect the point that has been made above (see Table 3).

The recent features of investment in th ASEAN correspond to the rapidly growing intra-regional investments in East Asia since the mid-1980s. The major investment flows are from Japan and Asian newly industrialised economies (NIEs). These rapid flows have been in accordance with the surge in Japanese outward FDI and the emergence of Asian NIEs as major regional investors compared to FDI inflows from the United States and the European Union. These US and European investors, before the recent crisis, were preoccupied with the major changes back home. Meanwhile, the East Asian developing countries have tried to attract FDI such as ASEAN. Evidently, the geographical proximity has helped to facilitate intra-regional investments from which many ASEAN countries have been able to profit. Intra-regional investments have facilitated the industrial restructuring of the more advanced economies and created new industrial capability in the next tier of economies.

Regional production and business networks have evolved strongly in the region. Of particular significance are the Japanese and overseas Chinese networks. Japanese manufacturers treated the region, especially the ASEAN, as part of an integrated production system, relocating units of production to complete regional and global networks according to production and transaction costs, technology and market segmentation. Since the 1980s, Japan has been

Table 3: Inward and Outward FDI Flows as a Percentage of Gross Fixed Capital Formation, 1986–1996

Unit: percentage

	1986–1991 (Annual Average)	1992	1993	1994	1995	1996
ASEAN 10:						
Brunei						
Inward	—	—	—	—	—	—
Outward	—	—	—	—	—	—
Cambodia						
Inward	—	—	—	—	—	—
Outward	—	—	—	—	—	—
Indonesia						
Inward	2.3	3.9	4.3	3.8	6.7	8.5
Outward	—	0.1	0.8	1.1	0.9	0.7
Laos						
Inward	—	—	—	—	—	—
Outward	—	—	—	—	—	—
Malaysia						
Inward	14.7	26.0	20.3	14.9	11.0	11.1
Outward	2.9	2.6	5.4	6.2	6.9	8.8

	1986–1991 (Annual Average)	1992	1993	1994	1995	1996
Myanmar						
Inward	3.0	3.3	2.4	1.0	0.8	0.5
Outward	—	—	—	—	—	—
Philippines						
Inward	6.6	2.1	9.6	10.5	8.9	7.8
Outward	—	—	2.9	2.0	0.6	0.9
Singapore						
Inward	37.6	12.4	23.0	35.0	28.9	27.5
Outward	6.9	7.4	9.9	15.7	14.0	14.0
Thailand						
Inward	5.5	4.8	3.6	2.3	2.9	3.0
Outward	0.4	0.3	0.5	1.3	1.3	1.2
Vietnam						
Inward	—	—	—	—	—	—
Outward	—	—	—	—	—	—
China						
Inward	2.9	7.4	12.2	17.3	15.0	17.0
Outward	0.7	2.7	2.0	1.0	0.8	0.9
Hong Kong, China						
Inward	10.7	7.4	5.3	5.1	4.9	5.2
Outward	14.9	29.9	55.9	55.0	58.6	54.6
India						
Inward	0.3	0.4	1.0	1.4	2.4	2.9
Outward	—	—	—	0.1	0.1	0.3
Korea, Republic of						
Inward	1.3	0.6	0.5	0.6	1.1	1.3
Outward	1.4	1.1	1.1	1.8	2.1	2.6
Taiwan						
Inward	3.6	1.8	1.8	2.5	2.7	3.2
Outward	11.1	4.0	5.0	4.7	5.2	6.6
S, E, S.E. Asia						
Inward	3.6	4.5	6.5	7.9	7.5	8.3
Outward	2.0	2.9	4.2	4.8	4.7	5.0
Developing						
Inward	3.4	4.2	6.1	7.6	7.4	8.7
Outward	1.3	1.7	3.0	3.4	3.2	3.3
Developed						
Inward	3.5	2.6	3.0	2.8	3.9	3.6
Outward	4.5	3.8	4.5	4.9	5.6	5.2
Total						
Inward	3.6	3.3	4.4	4.5	5.6	5.6
Outward	4.1	3.7	4.9	5.3	5.9	5.5

Source: UNCTAD, *World Investment Report 1998* (Geneva, 1998), Annex Table B5.

Table 4: FDI Outward Flow from South, East and South-East Asia, 1994–1997

	1994	1995	1996	1997	Percentage change 1996–1997
Billions of dollars and percentage					
Five most affected economies:					
Indonesia	0.6	0.6	0.5	2.4	369
Korea, Republic of	2.5	3.5	4.7	4.3	−9
Malaysia	1.8	2.6	3.7	3.1	−16
Philippines	0.3	0.4	0.2	0.1	−50
Thailand	0.5	0.9	0.9	0.5	−46
Total	5.7	8.0	10.0	10.4	4
China	2.0	2.0	2.1	2.5	18
Hong Kong, China	21.4	25.0	26.4	26.0	—
India	0.1	0.1	0.2	0.1	−50
Singapore	3.7	4.0	4.8	5.9	23
Taiwan	2.6	3.0	3.8	5.2	35
Total for S, E, SE Asia	35.6	41.8	47.4	50.2	6
Share of the five most affected countries in total for S, E, S.E. Asia	16.1	18.4	21.1	20.7	−2

Source: UNCTAD, *World Investment Report 1998* (Geneva, 1998), Annex Table A.VII9.

particularly successful in shifting its production in the East Asian region. Overseas affiliates are linked with parent companies through firm control and sourcing of capital goods, parts and components.

On the other hand, there is also a rising trend for Chinese firms in Hong Kong, Singapore and Taiwan, which are linking up with the local ethnic Chinese minorities in South-East Asia, to form various kinds of business ventures ranging from trading services to the production of set-up linkages between them. Tables 4 and 5 show FDI outward flows and stocks from the East Asian region. Hong Kong and Singapore have also played a crucial part for FDI outward flows and stocks especially since the beginning of the 1990s. Taiwan, Korea and, more recently, Malaysia and China have also seen a rise in outward FDI stocks and flows, which suggests a trend related to intra-regional investments, obviously related to the Chinese business and production network which is taking place.

Finally, benefits of FDI in the ASEAN should not be overstated without a careful analysis of such a trend. It is true that a large amount of FDI inflows creates opportunities for local businesses through joint ventures and backward and forward linkages for the manufacturing sector. However, the financial and technological ownership advantages of foreign affiliates could put domestic firms into doubt as competition could become more severe, both in the product and factor markets. In many ASEAN countries, the host governments have offered excessive investment incentives for foreign affiliates which could surpass those offered to the local firms. There is evidently a need to reflect how far these incentive structures have to be rationalised in order to ensure that they are not giving too much away. There are also reflections with regard to the macroeconomic impact such as its linkages to growth and development and income distribution. The rapid path to growth and development in the ASEAN and its linkage to FDI are still far from a foregone conclusion.

Table 5: FDI outward Stock, 1980, 1985, 1990, 1995, 1996 and 1997

Unit: US dollars (millions)

	1980	1985	1990	1995	1996	1997
ASEAN 10:						
Brunei	—	—	—	—	—	—
Cambodia	—	—	—	—	—	—
Indonesia[a]	—	49	25	1295[b]	1807[c]	4207[c]
Laos	—	—	—	—	—	—
Malaysia	414	749	2283[d]	8903[d]	12603[d]	15703[d]
Myanmar	—	—	—	—	—	—
Philippines	171	171	155[d]	909[d]	1091[d]	1227[d]
Singapore	9675[e]	9675[e]	9675	32695	37500[f]	43400[f]
Thailand	13	16	398[g]	2324[g]	3255[g]	3755[g]
Vietnam	—	—	—	—	—	—
China	—	131	2489[g]	15802[g]	17916[g]	20416[g]
India[a]	4	19	30	282[b]	521[b]	621[b]
Taiwan	97	204	12894[d]	25113[d]	28956[d]	34178[d]
Korea, Republic of	—	—	—	—	—	—
Hong Kong, China[c]	148	2345	13242	85156	111512	137152
S, E, S.E. Asia	10704	14013	43745	183013	229238	279395
Developing	15397	29516	74428	233914	281612	342202
Developed	509235	659367	1629834	2557415	2830918	3192496

Source: UNCTAD, *World Investment Report 1998* (Geneva, 1998), Annex Table B4.
a: estimated by using the inward stock of the United States as a proxy
b: estimated by adding flows to the stock of 1993
c: estimated by using the inward stock of the United States and China as a proxy and accumulating flows since 1994
d: estimated by adding flows to the stock of 1988
e: stock data prior to 1998 are estimated by subtracting flows
f: estimated by adding flows to the stock of 1988
g: estimated by adding flows to the stock of 1989

III FINANCIAL CRISIS AND TRENDS IN FDI

To some extent, investment diversion from the original ASEAN member countries towards China and Vietnam was a sign of the impending crisis in ASEAN. These countries, primarily relying on labour-intensive export promotion, had seen the erosion of their exports and the rapid shifts in locational attractiveness, which meant the structural adjustment was not rapid enough in the face of rising labour costs or currency appreciation in one country after another.[7] To varying degrees, those same countries have achieved this transition, but not always smoothly. Failure to do so has led to greater competition for the most footloose projects with countries such as China and Vietnam.

The impact of the financial crisis has clearly decelerated growth, with Thailand being among the first hit in 1997. Naturally a sharp decrease in private external capital inflows followed the turmoil which erupted in the financial markets of some countries in East and South-East Asia. On the other hand, outflows of private capital were on a sharp rise. In fact, FDI inflows in 1997 to the five most affected countries, namely Indonesia, South Korea, Malaysia, the Philippines and Thailand, taken together, remained at a level similar to that of 1996.[8] However, these capital inflows slowed considerably during the first quarter of 1998 when compared to the first quarter of 1997. Several countries found themselves in simultaneous crisis and the contagious effects were quite strong at that time. Strong exchange rates depreciation contributed greatly to such a sharp decline in private capital inflows.

A small increase in net private capital flows in the region in 1999 is expected compared with 1998, but these will still be below the level of the early 1990s. However, the most important type of inflow that is doing well during the crisis is FDI. FDI fell only slightly in 1998.[9] Indonesia was the hardest hit, while South Korea and Thailand survived relatively well. Large exchange rate depreciation had caused a potential fall in the wage share, hence reducing production costs for foreign companies. The collapse in asset prices offered some good bargains for buyers. In the manufacturing and service sector, there was also an increase in cases of mergers and acquisitions.[10] Japanese companies tried hard to save their affiliates by injecting more liquidity and technical assistance. European and US firms sought to make interesting deals in many types of projects. Thus, even if FDI or other measures of investments decreased greatly, production by those foreign affiliates was likely to decline far less, at least in the short term.

---

[7] These same countries were not seeking enough new, more capital-intensive projects, thus ensuring that existing investors remained by upgrading their production towards greater physical or human capital intensity or technological sophistication, embodying higher local added value.

[8] UNCTAD, *World Investment Report* (Geneva, 1998), 208.

[9] Both from the World Bank and IMF estimates: *The Economist*, 24 April 1999, 22.

[10] It is estimated that Indonesia, Malaysia, the Philippines and Thailand sold assets of US $11 billion to foreigners in 1997.

However, if the crisis and declines in FDI persist, then production can also be expected to fall over the medium term.[11]

The falling GDP growth rate and an unclear macroeconomic situation may cause the reduction of FDI in certain sectors,[12] especially for those who supply goods and services to the local and regional market. This is clear for investments in the automotive sector where purchases are usually made locally. Recession implies a cutback in production units, redundancies lower retained earnings, especially for affiliates established in the markets. On the other hand, firms with more outward-oriented production such as electrical and electronic products or even textile and garments, are more resilient, as their production is less affected and they are able to gain reasonable support from abroad.[13] While they will have little advantages over each other because all currencies have depreciated, these advantages could be offset to some extent by the high import content as many of the major exports in the ASEAN, such as electronics, have an import content which represents on average more than half of the export value.[14]

Finally, domestic-related companies in need of capital are more likely to sell shares, and sometimes a controlling interest, to foreigners. In addition, each government of the crisis-hit economies is under greater pressure to liberalise its inward investment regime. Several companies in these ASEAN countries are debt-ridden and need to recapitalise. This is obvious in the financial sector where a number of local banks and finance companies need to restore confidence and to recapitalise with greater foreign participation. Thus, the crisis seems to have influenced indirectly the schedule of commitments in the Financial Services Agreement by the ASEAN. Also, most ASEAN countries have liberalised their investment regimes to varying degrees as a result of the crisis. Greater privatisation is expected to lead to greater FDI flowing into the region, as has happened in other parts of the world. These countries have also discussed ways to attract more trade and investment through the possibility of accelerating regional integration.

IV INVESTMENT REGIMES IN THE ASEAN COUNTRIES

As in most countries, investment regimes are an important component of economic policy and strategy within the ASEAN region. Investment policy in the

---

[11] Certainly, there remains a lot of reflection and work to be done in order to predict how the recent crisis will affect FDI in the ASEAN.

[12] It is possible that rapid growth of TNC investment stocks in recent years may have created some excess capacity, and may further contribute to a decline of TNC investments in coming years: E.D. Ramsletter, "Turmoil in Asset Markets and the Prospects for Foreign Transnational Corporations in Southeast Asia" (1998) 10(3) *Chulalongkorn Journal of Economics*, 285.

[13] UNCTAD, above at n. 8, 216–21.

[14] Even for domestic producers, some are still dependent on foreign partners for imported parts and components. The automotive industry, in the ASEAN, imports engines and other technological parts and components from its Japanese counterparts.

ASEAN today gears toward more liberalisation as an easy way to promote growth and enhance domestic capital and technology. With the recent crisis, many members of the grouping seem to be even more obliged to adapt major changes in investment measures to attract more FDI in such turbulent times. The present reality of investment regimes is much different than before the mid-1980s, when ASEAN countries still showed wide differences in policies and attitudes towards FDI, which reflected more or less different historical experiences and priorities.[15]

In fact, investment policy liberaliation in the ASEAN came to be better known after the mid-1980s, when several countries were confronted with problems and made efforts to attract FDI as a way to move their economies ahead. As a result, governments embarked on unilateral liberalisation, deregulation and privatisation, resulting in more open trade and investment FDI which promotes manufacturing for export. In fact, Singapore has always maintained the most open economy with free capital flows. This has now spread to the ASEAN-Four economies, namely Indonesia, Malaysia, the Philippines and Thailand, where the governments pursue a more active policy with the use of investment incentives and investment promotion efforts to attract foreign investors for the use of national resources, land and labour and upgrading production and technology as a production base. Except for the Philippines, where political uncertainties disrupted some investors, the rest of the ASEAN-Four economies had changed fairly restrictive FDI policies.

At some point, there has been a convergence of FDI policies with regard to both the level and range of investment incentives offered and the relaxation of performance requirements and other restrictive regulations. The convergence of FDI policies has meant that the host countries have paid greater attention to other factors to maintain or secure a competitive edge. But it also raises questions with regard to the extent that ASEAN governments compete for investment among members. Obviously, incentives could become redundant as investors might have invested under less favourable conditions. But, overall, a remarkable level of regional convergence of investment rules and incentives has emerged in the ASEAN region from largely unilateral reforms:[16]

- full repatriation of profits is allowed for most investments in almost all ASEAN countries;
- fiscal investment incentives are broadly similar within the region;
- administration of FDI has been streamlined towards more efficient investment approval procedures and a greater transparency and consistency in applying investment incentives and performance requirements;

---

[15] S.Y. Chia, "Foreign and Intra-regional Direct Investments in ASEAN and Emerging ASEAN Multinationals", in Fukasaku, Kuchiro, Fukunari Kimara and Shijiro Urata (eds), *Asia and Europe: Beyond Competing Regionalism* (Sussex Academic Press, 1998), 63.

[16] Chia and Pacini, above at n. 4, 1997–8; D.E. Konan, "The Need for Common Investment Measures within ASEAN" (1996) 12(3) *ASEAN Economic Bulletin* 339.

- positive incentives have been implemented and there has been a move away from restrictions and performance requirements;
- liberalisation trend is towards a clear national treatment in policy formulation for both foreign and domestic investors;
- a favourable investment environment has been created for both local and foreign investors, such as the establishment of industrial estates and export processing zones and the provision of easier access to land and infrastructural facilities and services.

Although these similar investment rules and incentives occurred across the region, the history and motivations for liberalisation differ among ASEAN members. Some important distinctions in national policies remain.[17]

Most ASEAN countries provide investment incentives to attract and control FDI.[18] These incentives are often offered in conjunction with performance requirements to offset the benefits given to firms. Competition for FDI, however, has resulted in similar attraction for investment from abroad and an erosion of regional welfare. In some cases, benefits are being shifted from local firms to multinational corporations (MNC).

On the other hand, most countries also restrict a foreign equity participation and some other limitations to investors, such as sectors or industries which are not permitted foreign participation. Performance requirements could be observed in the ASEAN[19] which restrict employment of foreign personnel at managerial and technical levels.

For these reasons, many countries in the region have entered into bilateral investment agreements with a growing number of FDI home countries. Such agreements usually have the scope for: right of establishment and national treatment; right to repatriate capital and income without restriction; assurance that expropriation of foreign-owned assets is allowable under well-defined conditions and with fair and prompt compensation and avoidance of double taxation.

From these perspectives, unilateral investment liberalisation in the ASEAN has made much progress up to the present time. Together with numerous bilateral treaties signed with several major countries, the region is generally improving the scope for FDI from abroad. At the individual country level, Singapore is ranked as one of the most attractive investment locations in the world and has served as an example for other countries in the region. Malaysia, Indonesia, the Philippines and Thailand have significantly liberalised their investment policies. The recent crisis allows these countries to fine tune different investment regulations. Indonesia was the most affected by the crisis, followed by Thailand. Malaysia and the Philippines are also struggling with these difficulties. Even the

---

[17] Konan, ibid., 342.

[18] This includes tax holidays, accelerated depreciation and investment allowances, export incentives, preferential loans and subsidies.

[19] These limitations on foreign human capital are said to be having some significant impact on FDI in the ASEAN.

transitional economies like Vietnam, Myanmar and Laos need to adjust their policies in the present circumstances.

In general, the former restrictions on foreign equity participation are now much more relaxed in many sectors, including services such as banking and finance, energy, telecommunications and transport. Land ownership and entry and employment of foreign nationals have also been more relaxed than previously. It seems that the recent turmoil has strongly pushed many countries to open sectors formerly prohibited to foreign investment (see Table 6 at end of chapter).

V   GLOBAL CONTEXT AND REGIONAL RESPONSES FOR FDI

Investment policies within the ASEAN have developed independently with the conduct of a unilateral liberalisation and a number of bilateral investment treatments. It is only recently that the region has had to look more at regional and multilateral agreements. Investment issues have become part of the World trade Organisation (WTO) since the conclusion of the Uruguay Round in 1994, and the new round has planned to add investment issues in its discussion. The Asia-Pacific Economic Cooperation (APEC) has decided, since the Bogor Leaders' Meeting, to liberalise trade and investment by 2020 in the Asia-Pacific region. As a result, it has concluded with an APEC non-binding investment principle. The Asia-Europe Investment Promotion Action Plan, agreed at the First Asia-Europe Meeting in Bangkok, aims at generating greater two-way trade and investment flows between Asia and Europe. The ASEAN is increasingly faced with these challenges in its investment policy formulation.

Investment issues as part of the WTO

Investment issues in the GATT conclusion of 1994 figure largely in three agreements: the Agreement on Trade-related Investment Measures (TRIMS), the General Agreement on Trade in Services (GATS) and the Agreement on Trade-Related Intellectual Property Rights (TRIPS). To the extent that liberalised market access is induced under the new trade regime in the different sectors, there would be new sectoral patterns of inducement for both domestic and foreign investment. There is still a need for detailed analysis of the liberalisation offers made by different countries which would provide insight into the nature of the new investment opportunities that the latest GATT round would induce at the national and global level. For the ASEAN as a region, many elements that have entered the TRIMS, GATS and TRIPS have far-reaching implications for the investment regime and related policies in the future.

The TRIMS agreement has been enacted since July 1995 and restricts the use of local content requirements, trade balancing requirements, and foreign exchange balancing agreements. Developed countries were provided with a two-year grace period before measures agreed to be covered would come into full effect. Developing countries like the ASEAN were provided with a five-year grace period, and a seven-year period was permitted for the least developed countries. The ASEAN is particularly concerned with the prohibition of incentives related to export performance and local content requirements, as they will have to maintain transparency in regard to all these measures and they will have to conform to the dispute-settlement mechanism of the GATT 1994 in all matters relating to the TRIMS.[20] With regard to the dispute-settlement mechanism, there is discussion over the possibilities of cross-retaliation between the TRIMS, on the one hand, and other goods and services, on the other, which could further reduce the freedom of policy choices dealing with FDI activities open to the developing countries.[21]

As for the GATS, the agreement has covered international investment issues in a more comprehensive manner than the TRIMS. It has already provided for a liberal market access and a fair national treatment to foreign suppliers of services for which country commitments are undertaken. The ASEAN, as developing countries, need to gain experience as to how this new regime of service liberalisation will serve their national interests. As for the induction of a separate agreement on the TRIPS, the process of technology transfer has been, in a way, separated from the framework of capital movements, in the sense that technology transfer would be governed by a different set of disciplines than those applicable to the capital flows across countries. The TRIPS considers intellectual property as private property so needs to protect the rights of the owners. The obligations of the host governments are described in terms of protecting rights through appropriate legislative and institutional mechanisms. The agreement does not recognise the rights of the host governments to protect their national interests for promoting indigenous technological development.

Wider regional investment environment related to the ASEAN

At the regional level, the mix of investment issues is broader than that found at the country or bilateral level. Concepts and practical approaches to deal with them are less uniform, reflecting, among other things, differences in interests, needs, levels of development and perspectives on future development. There are now two major regional efforts to which the ASEAN is subject: the APEC Non-Binding Investment Principles and the Asia-Europe Investment Promotion Action Plan. These arrangements are generally aimed at the liberalisation of restrictions to entry and establishment of FDI, followed by the elimination of discriminatory operational conditions.

---

[20] V.R. Panchamukhi, "Multilateral Agreement on Investment (MAI)—What Should be the Response of the Developing Countries" (1996) 13 *RIS Digest* 42.

[21] There are many critical issues to be noted. It is for the ASEAN to ensure that positive flows of FDI outweighed the negative effects in the medium and long-term.

The APEC guidelines on foreign investment are a set of non-binding guidelines for the treatment of foreign investment as discussed at the Bogor APEC Leaders' Meeting in 1994. The report argued for a region-wide investment code which would stem the inconsistencies of bilateral investment treaties across the region. This includes, among others, liberalisation of investment and capital movements. Increases in such flows will contribute to economic progress in the Asia–Pacific region, and the programme recognises the central role played by the private sector in the regional integration process. The APEC Non-Binding Investment Principles adopted in 1994 apply to the entire APEC liberalisation and facilitation process to achieve the long-term goal of free and open trade and investment no later than 2010 in the case of industrialised economies, and 2020 in the case of developing economies.[22]

The ASEM Investment Promotion Action Plan (IPAP) was first called for in the inaugural Asia–Europe Meeting in Bangkok. The basic terms of reference of the IPAP are derived from the Chairman's Statement of the first ASEM. The draft document was reviewed and finalised at the second meeting of the ASEM Government and Private Sector Working Group in Luxembourg in July 1997. Its primary objective is to generate greater two-way investment flows between Asia and Europe through enhancing the investment climate between and within Asia and Europe. To attain this main objective, the IPAP has set several subsidiary objectives through the strengthening of business/government co-ordination and co-operation, with person-to-person contacts, linkages between the business sectors in each region, enhancing the information network, improving frameworks of investment policies and regulations, building and creating synergy among existing programmes designed to promote Asia–Europe investment activities, and taking a more proactive role in cross-flows of investment. The IPAP will focus on a number of activities under two broad pillars: investment promotion and investment policies and regulations, both of which involve a strong emphasis on government/business sector co-operation and co-ordination.[23]

Features of the ASEAN Investment Area

Until the recent crisis and the formation of the ASEAN Investment Area (AIA), regional co-operation to promote investment flows and industrial development had not produced impressive results. Industrial schemes introduced since the late 1970s and early 1980s, such as the ASEAN Industrial Projects (AIP), the ASEAN Industrial Complementation (AIC) and the ASEAN Industrial Joint Venture (AIJV) schemes, had not gone so smoothly and had mostly failed.

---

[22] One could try to assess these principles on different topics such as transparency non-discrimination, expropriation, settlement of investment disputes, tax measures, transfer of funds, capital movements, national treatment, performance requirements, investment incentives, etc. See the Asia–Europe Investment Promotion Action Plan (IPAP), 29 July 1997, 52–4 (mimeograph).

[23] Ibid., 8–10.

ASEAN governments dictated too strongly and designed these programs without really touching the difficulties behind these ideas.

As for the latest scheme, known as the ASEAN Industrial Co-operation (AICO), these efforts, launched in April 1996, aim not only to attract more investment to the ASEAN region, but also to increase intra-ASEAN investment by providing an institutional framework for private sector collaboration. It remains to be seen how the AICO could enhance production networking and regional specialisation to realise the benefits of clustering and economies of scale in order to enhance ASEAN international competitiveness.[24] By April 1999, only twenty-six projects had been approved by the ASEAN Secretariat with a certificate of eligibility, especially for the joint product of indigenous ASEAN car producers.[25] Hopefully, AICO will overcome the problems faced by earlier industrial co-operation schemes.

Because of the results produced and the experiences gained in this area, together with a rapidly changing investment environment, the fifth ASEAN Summit, held in December 1995, agreed to establish a regional investment arrangement to enhance the attractiveness and competitiveness of the region for direct investment flows. A Framework Agreement on establishing the AIA was signed in October 1998 by the ASEAN Economic Ministers. The implementation of the Framework Agreement was assigned to the AIA Council. The AIA now becomes the operative framework which was once part of the ASEAN vision 2020 which was announced by the Heads of Government at the Second ASEAN Informal Summit in Kuala Lumpur in December 1997.

Therefore the AIA Council has been changed in order to prepare for the implementation of the programmes and work plans to realise the AIA by 2010. The Council requested the Coordinating Committee on Investment (CCI) to begin work on the AIA, especially on the submission of the Temporary Exclusion List (TEL) and the Sensitive List (SL) for the opening-up of sectors for investment and the granting of national treatment. The Council also requested the CCI to table the specific schedules, programs and action plans to execute the three programs of the AIA, namely co-operation and facilitation, promotion and awareness, and liberalisation.

The primary objective of the AIA is substantially to increase the flow of direct investment from ASEAN and non-ASEAN sources by making the region a competitive, open and liberal investment area. This will entail, among other things, a number of activities such as:[26]

- the immediate opening of most industries, with some exceptions as specified in the TEL and the SL, for ASEAN investors by 2010 and for all investors by 2020;

---

[24] AICO products enjoy 0–5% tariffs immediately in the ASEAN upon approval. To qualify for AICO, a project has to involve at least two ASEAN countries and at least one company from each; the company must be incorporated in an ASEAN country with at least 30% national equity.

[25] Chia, above at n. 15, 66.

[26] From the Joint Press Release Inaugural Meeting of the AIA Council, 8 October 1998, Manila, the Philippines.

- granting immediately national treatment, with some exceptions as specified in the TEL and the SL, to ASEAN investors by 2010 and to all investors by 2020;
- implementing co-ordinated ASEAN investment co-operation and facilitation programs;
- implementing co-ordinated promotion programs and investment awareness activities;
- involving the private sector actively in the AIA development process;
- promoting freer flow of capital, skilled labour, professionals and technology among ASEAN members;
- providing transparency of investment policies, rules, procedures and administrative processes;
- providing a more streamlined and simplified investment process

This Framework Agreement on AIA, together with the 1987 ASEAN Agreement for the promotion and protection of investments and the 1996 Protocol, covers direct investment flows into and within the region. ASEAN members, once committed to the AIA, must gradually eliminate investment barriers, liberalise investment rules and policies, grant national treatment and open up industries initially in the manufacturing sector and, later, in other sectors.

The initial package of the TEL and SL for the opening-up of industries and granting of national treatment will be submitted to the AIA Council within six months after the signing of the Agreement. The implementation of the Framework Agreement is subject to review every two years. New members are accorded flexibility in the implementation time-frame.[27]

There are certainly benefits to be gained from AIA investors through the AIA arrangement and it will encourage, among other things:

- greater investment access to industries and economic sectors;
- national treatment;
- greater information and awareness of the investment climate as well as investment opportunities in the region;
- a more liberal and competitive investment regime.

VI PROSPECTS FOR AN INVESTMENT REGULATORY FRAMEWORK

FDI is an important component of the ASEAN policy framework. Until recently, the region was able to attract a large amount of foreign investors. The crisis has dashed the hope of many countries for strong growth, at least in the short-term. Hence, the key to recovery is to regain investor confidence in the region. The region needs to adapt consistent, transparent and practical

---

[27] Vietnam will phase out the TEL by 2013; Loa PDR and Myanmar will phase out the TEL by 2015.

measures related to investment and to persuade different countries to be involved in the recovery process.

The idea is for the ASEAN as a whole to adapt and adjust its own investment regulatory framework to better suit the changes in the global and regional context. This is to make sure that the region continues to send the right signal to investors, namely that all ASEAN member countries remain committed to economic liberalisation and welcome foreign capital. The ASEAN Free Trade Area (AFTA), which would be substantially in place by the turn of the century, aims at creating an increasingly barrier-free market place of 500 million people with which to attract investors. The Agreement Framework of the AIA aims to free investment among ASEAN investors by 2010 and for non-ASEAN investors by 2020. The ASEAN needs to show its openness to attract the synergy of trade and investment, thus making the ASEAN attractive as a free and open trading and investment area.

Recent regulatory changes in the ASEAN suggest that there is an even more flexible attitude toward FDI in the region.[28] Examining FDI determinants in the region, it is clear that regulatory frameworks have become open and hospitable to FDI. Business facilitation has been strengthened and promotional efforts have been accelerated. As for the economic determinants of investment, the crisis has allowed these countries to create opportunities for FDI, especially for efficiency-seeking and asset-seeking FDI in the form of currency-driven cost advantages and cheaper and more easily available assets. The combination of these factors should allow for cautious optimism for FDI flows in the ASEAN region. The variations may still exist depending on the adjustment to recovery and attractiveness for investment.

To characterise the ASEAN regulatory framework on investment, one can see that:

- Investment incentives have always been the major policy component in the past. Almost each member country has assigned the responsibility to some kind of national agency responsible for investment matters. Due to changes within the global and regional context, especially the WTO, the region has to work towards an adjustment to new rules and regulations governing at the multilateral level.
- Restrictions and investment protection have become important areas where the ASEAN needs to work more at the country level. There already exist a number of bilateral agreements taking care of these issues. In general, reducing restrictions have been considerably improved in the ASEAN where investment protection has covered well in the region.
- Liberalisation of FDI frameworks has become the dominant type of FDI policy change in the world and has also encouraged the ASEAN to adjust. AIA, which now operates under the Framework Agreement signed in October

---

[28] UNCTAD, above at n. 8, 237.

1998, is a good example of how the ASEAN has tried to improve the FDI policy framework.

Overall, great advancement has been achieved through unilateral reforms since the mid-1980s. At the same time, bilateral treaties on investment have been well respected in most ASEAN countries. Recent attempts to co-operative efforts of FDI at the regional level through AIA have emerged with substantial investment liberalising benefits. Co-operation on investment regulatory framework is likely to be beneficial to the region by promoting greater efficiency in the inducement and distribution of resource endowment through FDI, which would finally improve investment rules, and regulations and policy at the national level. The ASEAN's crisis is bad news for the ASEAN economies and investment, in general, in the region. The pace of the ASEAN's economic recovery will determine future economic confidence as the ground work related to investment framework might have begun to show some results.

Table 6: Changes in the Regulatory Framework Regarding FDI in some Major ASEAN Countries Affected by the Crisis, June 1997–June 1998

Indonesia:
—Eliminated the 49% limit on foreign share holdings in firms other than financial firms in September 1997.
—Allowed 100% foreign ownership of non-bank financial firms, including insurance companies.
—Guaranteed existing foreign ownership in financial institutions.
—Under the new "reformation policy on investment" announced by the Office of the Ministry of Investment/Investment Coordinating Branch on 29 May 1998, opened retail and wholesale trading and palm oil sectors to foreign investment. (Import-export trading had been opened earlier for foreign investment.) For the time being, foreign investment in retail and wholesale trading should be in the form of joint ventures with Indonesian nationals/companies.
—Under the above-mentioned "reformation policy" package, various simplified procedures apply to foreign investors.
—Presidential Decree Number 96/1998 revised the list of industries and activities fully or partially closed to foreign investment. The new list is valid for three years but subject to annual review, if necessary. All other industries and activities are open to FDI.

Malaysia:
—Relaxed the limits on foreign equity holdings. The limit now is 30% foreign equity, except for export-oriented industries, high-technology industries and multimedia companies with Multimedia Super Corridor (MSC) status. Foreign equity holding in the local licences basic telecommunications companies has been raised from a previous maximum of 30% to a new maximum of 49%. Malaysia is prepared to consider applications to raise the foreign equity holdings up to a maximum of 61%, provided the companies concerned reduce their foreign equity holdings to a maximum of 49% within five years.

—Guaranteed up to 51% foreign equity participation in existing insurance companies by current holders. Malaysia's revised offers following the WTO negotiation concluded in December 1997 in respect of foreign equity participation in the insurance sector are as follows:

* New foreign entrants into the local insurance industry will be restricted to an equity stake of 30%. However, foreigners with an existing presence in the local industry will be allowed a maximum of 51% foreign equity participation in the following circumstances:

    —a foreign direct insurer operating in Malaysia as a branch, and which locally incorporates its operation in compliance with the Insurance Act 1996, can retain up to 51% of the equity of the locally incorporated entity;
    —an existing foreign owner of a locally incorporated insurer which has yet to restructure can retain up to 51% of the equity of the restructured company, provided aggregate foreign shareholding does not exceed 51%;
    —the present foreign shareholders which were the original owners of locally incorporated insurance companies that have restructured in line with requirements under the National Development Policy, can increase their shareholdings to 51% provided aggregate foreign shareholdings do not exceed 51%.

* These restrictions do not apply to foreign professional reinsurers which are allowed to operate as branches in Malaysia, or in the case of locally incorporated joint venture reinsurance companies, the foreign partner may retain up to an aggregate of 49% of the equity in the joint venture company.

—Fully/majority foreign-owned fund-management companies will be allowed.
—Relaxed bumiputera policy. Relaxation of regulations on the release of a 30% share of listed firms owned by bumiputera to non-bumiputera. Approval on a case-by-case basis of acquisitions of bumiputera firms by non-bumiputera.
—The Minister of International Trade and Industry relaxed the country's equity policy for the manufacturing sector as follows (from 31 July 1998):

* With the exception of activities in a specific exclusion list,* all new projects in manufacturing, including those of expansion and diversification, will be exempted from both equity and export conditions. This means that project owners can hold 100% equity and will not need to meet any export requirements.
* This policy will apply to all applications received from 31 July 1998 to 31 December 2000, as well as applications already received, but for which decisions are pending.
* All projects approved under the new policy will not be required to restructure their equity after the period.
* The Government will review this policy after 31 December 2000.

Philippines:

Amendments were made to the Investment House Act (October 1997) and the Financing Company Act (February 1998). Key changes which affect foreign investment are:

—Allowable foreign equity participation has been increased to 60% for both investment houses and finance and leasing companies, subject to reciprocity rights.
—Paid-up capital for investment houses is now 300 million pesos.
—Paid up capital for finance and leasing companies is now:

Table 6: *cont.*

- at least 10 million pesos for those located in Metro Manila and other first class cities;
- 5 million pesos for those situated in other classes of cities;
- 2.5 million pesos in municipalities.

Thailand:

—Foreign equity holdings were limited to no more than 49% except for export-oriented projects with at least 80% export share located in Zone 3, where 100% foreign ownership was allowed. The Board of Investment relaxed this regulation in 1997 for companies with financial difficulties so that they could have foreign ownership of more than 51%, on condition that Thai shareholders of that company agree and confirm their acceptance in writing of the change in ownership to the Board of Investment.

—The Minister of Finance, upon the recommendation of the Bank of Thailand, may release the 25% limit for foreign interests in locally incorporated banks and finance and credit companies for ten years. The absolute amount of foreign equity holdings up to 100% will be protected if acquired during this period. Existing shareholding structures of foreign bank branches are guaranteed.

—Announced that majority foreign ownership of existing promoted firms in certain industrial zones would be permitted if agreed by existing Thai shareholders.

—The 30% export requirement for exemption of import duties used in the manufactures of exports has been eliminated.

---

* Paper packaging; plastic packaging (bottles, films, sheets and bags); plastic injection moulding components; metal stamping, metal fabrication and electroplating; wire harness; printing, and steel service centre.
Source: UNCTAD, based on information from national sources.

10

The Compatibility of the Chinese Anti-Dumping Regulations with the WTO Anti-Dumping Agreement

ZENG LINGLIANG AND HAN ZHEN

I INTRODUCTION

Background of the Regulations

The Regulations on Anti-Dumping and Countervailing Duties of the People's Republic of China (the Chinese Anti-Dumping Regulations) came into force on 25 March 1997. They evolved as a result of the increasingly urgent need for such regulations during the gradual opening of the Chinese domestic market to the outside world since 1978.

During the past twenty years, hundreds of anti-dumping cases have been filed against Chinese enterprises and companies. According to statistics, there have been more than 280 such cases amounting to the value of US $50 billion, from 1979–1997.[1] Within the single year 1997 there were on average three cases against Chinese exports per month.[2] The applicants of those cases came from more than thirty countries in five continents. Thousands of products had high anti-dumping duties imposed upon them, among which were not only raw material products, electrical apparatus, but also Chinese traditional export products like cotton cloth, clothes, shoes, etc. With the consequent contraction of the export markets, many Chinese exporters and producers concerned were badly injured. Some of them even went bankrupt in a short period of time. Hundreds of thousands of workers lost their jobs.[3]

While some Chinese industries were facing a serious export situation, there had been an increasing number of Chinese enterprises losing their domestic

---

[1] *People's Daily* (overseas edition), 13 May 1997.
[2] Wang Chuanli, "Chinese Anti-dumping legislation and Practice", in *Research on Issues of International Law*, (Chinese University of Politics and Law Press, 1999), 34.
[3] Chuanli, ibid.

markets. With the deepening transformation of the whole economic system in China, the foreign trade system changed. Exporters and importers, domestic and foreign, both enjoyed much more freedom than before. With better access to the Chinese domestic market and without the appropriate anti-dumping and countervailing measures, foreign products flooded into China at very low prices and soon received a high market share. The impact was depressing to Chinese national industries, some of them collapsing in the competition while others were struggling to survive and seriously threatened by foreign dumping, causing injuries.[4] They did not know how to protect themselves, and, more seriously, they had no idea what rights they had. The Government also had a hard time because what it was facing was completely new. The problem of foreign dumping into China remained untouched until 1994.

After a decade of preparations, on 4 July 1994 the Foreign Trade Act of the People's Republic of China (Chinese FTC) came into effect, with Articles 30–32 dealing generally with anti-dumping issues, which resemble Article VI of the GATT 1994. Article 30 provides that the Government may take necessary measures to abate and eliminate the injury or the threat of injury to relevant domestic industries caused by importing products at prices lower than normal values. Article 32 further stipulates that relative administrations of the State Council shall make investigations in such issues and settle the disputes therein.

Nearly three years later, the State Council issued the Chinese Anti-Dumping Regulations in accordance with the provisions of the Chinese FTC. For the first time in this country there emerged a systematic implementing act regulating anti-dumping (also countervailing) actions.

Significance of the Regulations

The importance of the Regulations cannot be overestimated, because they have filled a big vacuum in the Chinese foreign trade law system. As the first special anti-dumping and countervailing law in Chinese history, there is no doubt that it is a far-reaching, positive influence on the development of the Chinese economy.

First of all, it provides substantive rules to be followed by both government and domestic industries. Specific departments of government are respectively authorised to decide to initiate an anti-dumping investigation, to conduct the investigation, to make preliminary or final determinations, and to levy and collect provisional or final anti-dumping duties. All their actions must be taken under the Regulations.

As for domestic industries, they now have their own legal weapon to defend themselves against foreign dumping. They have begun to realise their legal rights and they learn problem-solving remedies in case these rights are violated

---

[4] Yang Wenhui and Gao Feng, "Chinese Anti-dumping Reality and Existing Problems" (1998) 5 *Chinese Economic Issues* 32.

or threatened. For instance, just six months after the entry into force of the Chinese Anti-Dumping Regulations, nine Chinese companies and factories filed an anti-dumping case on US, South Korean and Canadian newsprint with the Ministry of Foreign Trade and Economic Cooperation of the Peoples Republic of China (MFTEC). After the preliminary affirmative determination, provisional measures were taken on the export product in question.[5] It is reputed to be " a significant and remarkable case" in Chinese anti-dumping practice and that "there has never been another legislation strumming the heart of domestic industries as the Anti-Dumping Regulations do".[6] A year after that first case, Wuhan Iron and Steel Corporation filed another case against Russian steel products. The MFTEC decided to initiate an investigation on 12 March 1999. This second anti-dumping case is still under investigation.[7]

Secondly, the law contributes to the perfection of China's domestic market economy. Since 1978, China has undergone a persisting transformation of its economic system. With the inception of competition mechanism and an increasing number of laws passed to stipulate competitive actions of domestic competitors, the domestic economy has become more and more market-oriented. But it cannot be a real, mature market unless it integrates itself into the international market and can solve the problems brought about in the process of such integration. The Regulations badly need to preserve a fair competitive environment for domestic and foreign competitors and to keep the foreign trade order by fighting against foreign dumping actions.

Finally, the Regulations are highly consistent with the Agreement on Implementation of Article VI of the General Agreement on Tariffs and Trade 1994 (WTO Anti-Dumping Agreement) in terms of principles and main contents, which will be discussed in Part II below. Since China has been making great efforts to become a Member of the WTO, the promulgation of Chinese Anti-Dumping Regulations and their conformity with the WTO law has paved the way for its entrance to the WTO.

Purposes and main contents of this chapter

The following part of this chapter is designed to make some comparisons between the Chinese Anti-Dumping Regulations and the WTO Anti-Dumping Agreement in order to ascertain the consistency between them and also to clarify the defects of the Regulations. Implementation issues of the Regulation are also discussed. Next, the authors try to put forward some suggestions to perfect the Regulations and their implementation.

---

[5] *People's Daily*, 10 July 1998.
[6] Chuanli, above at n. 2, 28.
[7] *Wuhan Morning News*, 26 March 1999.

Legislative intention

It may be controversial to say that the Chinese Anti-Dumping Regulations were created with the same legislative intention as the WTO Anti-Dumping Agreement. National anti-dumping laws always represent intentions to protect domestic industries and to restrain foreign trade, while Article VI of the GATT 1947 was adopted to circumscribe national anti-dumping actions on which the WTO Anti-Dumping Agreement provides for more restrictive requirements.

Nowadays, almost every country is at the same time both an exporting country and an importing one. It can be well understood that each country has its own anti-dumping laws and different or sometimes completely contrary attitudes towards worldwide anti-dumping rules, since balancing various interests is no easy task for any government. There is a paradox between the rule that the development of national economy through optimal allocation of productive resources to a great extent lies in free trade, and the reality that the desires and interests of exporters, importers, producers and consumers cannot be ignored. The market order and stability of national economy are equally important. This paradox was usually dramatically demonstrated by those hard and time-consuming historical negotiations, especially of the Uruguay Round,[8] between nations concerned with anti-dumping issues and by the ambiguity in the final text of the WTO Anti-Dumping Agreement.

In the meantime, however, a certain balance was achieved. Compared with the 1979 Anti-Dumping Code, the WTO Anti-Dumping Agreement brought about numerous changes, which more strictly confine national anti-dumping actions. National anti-dumping laws are considered to be legitimate if consistent with the Agreement. It is not surprising that "the adopted changes cannot resolve the fundamental problems of an inflated dumping margin and the quasi presumption of injury" and that "anti-dumping measures remain as restrictions on trade and protection against foreign production".[9] But the Agreement tends to protect foreign trade against the abuse of powers of importing countries and forces them to improve transparency in their anti-dumping actions.

As far as Chinese Anti-Dumping Regulations are concerned, Article 1 says that the legislative intentions of the Regulations are to preserve foreign trade order and fair competition and to protect relevant domestic industries. The wording seems to show that its intentions are no exception to those of other national anti-dumping laws. But given their background, principles and contents, the legislative intentions of Chinese Anti-Dumping Regulations are still

---

[8] G.N. Horlick and E.C. Shea, The World Trade Organization Anti-Dumping Agreement" (1995) 29(1) *Journal of World Trade*.

[9] Gabrielle Marceau, *Anti-dumping and Anti-trust Issues in Free Trade Area* (Clarendon Press, 1994), xl.

rather distinctive to some extent. Unlike anti-dumping laws of WTO members, which were enacted a long time ago and had to be revised in accordance with the evolution of Article VI of the GATT 1947, the Chinese Anti-Dumping Regulations have been consistent with the newly implemented international anti-dumping rules from the very beginning. Anti-dumping measures will not be imposed upon foreign products until there is established existence of dumping injury and the causal relation between them. The regulations were not created to refuse foreign products and to protect domestic industries arbitrarily. They were intended to preserve a fair competitive environment. Its non-member status in the WTO does not prevent China from restraining its own actions in anti-dumping and other aspects. China carries out its "open-door" policy consistently and has established sound economic relations with the WTO members and other countries on the basis of reciprocity. The self-restrained anti-dumping legislation shows China's intention to co-operate with the WTO and its members and contribute to the improvement of world trade.

Principles

Principle of non-discrimination

The principle of non-discrimination is one of the fundamental principles of the WTO and applies to all fields regulated under the WTO laws, including the Anti-Dumping Agreement. For instance, the Agreement introduces "a fair comparison"[10] into the determination of dumping to eliminate the possibility of discriminating against foreign products by choosing inappropriate comparable prices and ignoring relevant factors having a bearing on price comparability. As to the imposition of anti-dumping measures, the Agreement provides that they shall be imposed "on a non-discriminatory basis on imports of such products from all sources found to be dumped and causing injury".[11] In a word, the spirit of the principle is embodied in the whole Agreement.

The Chinese Anti-Dumping Regulations do not explicitly and directly provide for the principle of non-discrimination, but imply it in relevant provisions. Article 6 of the Regulations provides that "the margin of dumping shall be determined on a fair and reasonable comparison between the export price of the imported product and its normal value". That is, a fair comparison is also required in Chinese anti-dumping law. Article 40 further stipulates that "the People's Republic of China may, in the light of real situations, take necessary measures against those countries or regions who impose discriminatory anti-dumping or countervailing measures on Chinese products".

It can be inferred that China will not practice its anti-dumping law in a discriminatory way, since it does not permit other countries to discriminate against Chinese products. In fact, this presumption has been proved in the first

[10] WTO Anti-Dumping Agreement, Art. 2.4.
[11] Ibid., Art. 9.2.

anti-dumping case in the country, in which the Chinese anti-dumping authorities determined, after the investigation, the dumping margins of products from Canada, South Korea and the United States respectively, and imposed appropriate provisional measures on them according to their different dumping margins.[12] The principle of reciprocity is indispensable, since China is still not a member of the WTO and cannot use the dispute-settlement mechanism of the WTO to settle disputes with other countries in respect to anti-dumping issues. If a country really discriminates against Chinese export products, under the principle of reciprocity, China can take countermeasures against those who discriminate against Chinese export products without violation of the principle of non-discrimination.

Principle of transparency

In the light of the intention of the WTO Anti-Dumping Agreement, it is very important that national anti-dumping measures be taken on a transparent basis. Each step of the measures will be made known in some way to interested parties, and also to the Committee on Anti-dumping Practices. Article 18(5) of the Agreement requires WTO members to notify their domestic laws and/or regulations relating to anti-dumping to the Committee, and members having no anti-dumping laws or regulations should notify that fact. Article 16.4 obligates members to submit a report of all anti-dumping measures they have taken, as well as lists of all anti-dumping measures in force, twice a year. It also requires, without delay, a report of all preliminary or final measures taken. In additon, Article 16.5 asks members to notify the Committee its authorities competent to initiate and conduct anti-dumping investigations. Furthermore, public notices of the initiation of an investigation, of any preliminary or final determination and of conclusion or suspension of an investigation are required to be given to interested parties.[13] Subject to the requirement to protect confidential information, evidence presented in writing by one interested party shall be made available promptly to other interested parties participating in the investigation.[14] The phrase "interested parties" is interpreted to include exporters, importers, producers, a trade or business association, the government of the exporting member, and the domestic producers or an association of them.[15]

As a non-member state of the WTO, China undoubtably need not notify the WTO of its anti-dumping laws. However, as soon as the Chinese Anti-Dumping Regulations were adopted, they was publicly issued both at home and abroad. Furthermore, if one looks into the provisions of the Regulations, it may easily be seen that they require almost the same provisions as the Agreement does in terms of the principle of transparency. The determinations of whether or not to

---

[12] See above at n. 5.
[13] WTO Anti-Dumping Agreement, Art. 12.
[14] Ibid., Art. 6.1.2.
[15] Ibid., Art. 6.11.

initiate an investigation, preliminary or final determinations, affirmative or negative, of the existence of dumping, injury and imposition of anti-dumping measures are all required to be notified.[16] The applicant and interested parties are permitted to see the materials concerned in a particular case when pursuant to the protection of confidentiality.[17]

Principles of material injury or threat of material injury and causal link

No anti-dumping measures shall be taken on foreign products unless material injury or the threat of such an injury is demonstrated to exist and the causal link between dumping and injury is satisfied. It is this principle that changed the direction of national anti-dumping laws, and made arbitrary anti-dumping actions only by the reason of price illegitimate. Therefore, Article 3(5) of the WTO Anti-Dumping Agreement expressly requires that "it must be demonstrated that the dumped imports are . . . causing injury within the meaning of this Agreement". The "injury" is interpreted to "mean material injury to a domestic industry, threat of material injury to a domestic industry or material retardation of the establishment of such an industry and shall be interpreted in accordance with the provisions of this Article".[18] There are special provisions which govern the determination of threat of material injury to a domestic industry.

The Anti-Dumping Regulations of China also introduce these principles in their provisions. For example, Article 2 of the Regulations provides that "anti-dumping or countervailing measures shall be taken under circumstances provided for in these Regulations that there is material injury or threat of material injury caused by an import product in the way of dumping or being subsidized". It can be inferred that no anti-dumping measures should be taken unless the requirements of material injury or threat of such an injury and the causal relationship between them have all been met with.

Structure and main contents

The Chinese Anti-Dumping Regulations resemble, to a great extent, the WTO Anti-Dumping Agreement in terms of logical structure. The Regulations consists of forty-two articles which are divided into six chapters, i.e., "General Principles" (Chapter 1), "Dumping and Injury" (Chapter 2), "Anti-Dumping Investigations" (Chapter 3), "Anti-Dumping Measures" (Chapter 4), "Special Stipulations on Countervailing" (Chapter 5) and "Supplementary Articles" (Chapter 6).

The main content of the Regulations, with the exception of Chapter 5 concerning countervailing measures, is generally the same as the Agreement.

---

[16] Chinese Anti-Dumping Regulations, Arts 17, 18, 19.
[17] Ibid., Art. 20.
[18] WTO Anti-Dumping Agreement, footnote 9.

Dumping and dumping margin

Articles 3 to 6 of the Regulations govern the determination of dumping.

According to Article 3, a product is to be considered as being dumped if its export price is lower than its normal value. Its normal value, as Article 4 says, can be :

(i)   the comparable price if the identical or the like product has a comparable price in the export country; or

(ii)   the comparable price when the product or the like product is exported to a third country; or

(iii) the price composed of the cost of production of the identical or the like product plus a reasonable amount for other costs and profits.

Article 5 provides for the determination of export price which shall be based on:

(i)   the export price that has been paid or is payable; or

(ii)   the price at which the imported product is first resold to an independent buyer; or

(iii) the price constructed on a reasonable basis by the MFTEC after its consultation with the General Administration of Customs (GAC).

The dumping margin is the difference between the export price of the import product and its normal value. Pursuant to Article 6, a comparison shall be made between the export price and the normal value of the import product on a fair and reasonable basis.

Injury

Articles 7–9 of the Regulations deal with the determination of injury.

Under Article 7, there are three kinds of injuries, i.e. the material injury to an established domestic industry, threat of material injury to an established domestic industry and material retardation to the establishment of a domestic industry.

According to Article 8, when ascertaining the injury caused by dumping, the authorities shall take the following factors into account:

(i)   the quantity of the dumped product, or the growth and the possibility of massive growth of the dumped product when compared with the domestic identical or like product;

(ii)   the price of the dumped product, i.e. the price cuts of the dumped product or the impact on the price of the domestic identical or the like product;

(iii) the impact of the dumped product on the domestic industry;

(iv)   the capacities of production, export and inventories of the product being dumped.

The Regulations provide for the same definition of domestic industry as the Agreement does. Article 10 of the Regulations defines domestic industry as referring to all the domestic producers of the identical or like product, or to those whose collective output of the product constitutes a major portion of the total domestic production of those products excluding the domestic producers who are related to the exporters or importers, or are themselves importers of the allegedly dumped product.

Initiation of investigation

Under the Regulations, before the initiation of investigation there shall be a written application filed by domestic producers or relevant organisations. Article 12 includes a list of required contents of the application and emphasises that necessary evidence shall be included in the application. A written application shall contain:

(i)   the names and the addresses of the applicant and the producers it represents;

(ii) the name and category of the imported product and its tariff number in the tariff schedule concerned, and the names and types of the domestic like product;

(iii) the quantity and price of the alleged dumped product and its impact on domestic industry;

(iv) the causal relationship between dumping and the injury;

(v)   other factors considered by the MFTEC.

The MFTEC shall examine the application and the evidence submitted by the applicant. After consultation with the State Economic and Trade Commission (SETC), the MFTEC shall make a decision on whether or not to initiate an investigation.[19] If, under special circumstances, the MFTEC has sufficient evidence that there is dumping, injury and a causal link between them, upon consultation with the SETC, it can automatically initiate an investigation.[20] This special provision for automatic investigation is equivalent to Article 5.6 of the WTO Anti-Dumping Agreement.

Conduct of investigation

After the initiation of an investigation, the MFTEC and the GAC will set out to find whether or not the alleged dumping exists, while the SETC tries to determine whether there is an injury. They are to make preliminary determinations separately according to their findings. If the preliminary determinations are affirmative, further investigations are justified.[21] If not, or if the applicant

---

[19] Chinese Anti-Dumping Regulations, Art. 13.
[20] Ibid., Art. 14.
[21] Ibid., Art. 17.

withdraws the application or the dumping margin or the volume of imports is negligible, the investigation shall be terminated.[22]

Article 15 of the Chinese Anti-Dumping Regulations provide the same duration as the WTO Anti-Dumping Agreement, in that the investigation shall be concluded within one year, except in some special circumstances, and in no case more than eighteen months after its initiation.

Article 6.8 and Annex II of the WTO Anti-Dumping Agreement provide for rules of best information available. Article 20 of the Chinese Anti-Dumping Regulations also provide that "a case in which an interested party refuses access to facts, or otherwise does not provide relevant information, or significantly impedes the investigation, the MFTEC and the SETC may make determinations on the basis of the facts available".

Anti-dumping measures

Provisional anti-dumping measures may be taken after the preliminary affirmative determination of the existence of dumping and injury. Provisional anti-dumping duties may be imposed on the product in question, or the exporters concerned may be asked to provide cash security or other forms of security.[23] The amount of the duties or the security shall not exceed the dumping margin and the duration of provisional measures shall not exceed four months, and in no case exceed nine months.[24]

The provisional anti-dumping duties may be retroactively imposed upon dumped products exported within ninety days before the notification of imposition of such duties, provided that:

(i)   the export product has a history of injuring domestic industry, or the importer of the product knows or should know the dumping facts and that the dumping will injure domestic industry; and

(ii)   the dumped product is exported in large quantities within a short period of time and has injured domestic industry.[25]

If the exporter in question or the exporting country promises to undertake effective measures to eliminate the injury to domestic industry, the investigation may be sustained.[26] But if the undertakings are not performed, the MFTEC may decide to resume the investigation.[27]

Final anti-dumping duties may be levied after the final affirmative determination. The collection of anti-dumping duties and the price undertakings shall be

---

[22] Chinese Anti-Dumping Regulations, Art. 18.
[23] Ibid., Art. 22.
[24] Ibid., Arts 22, 24.
[25] Ibid., Art. 32.
[26] Ibid., Art. 25.
[27] Ibid., Art. 26.

concluded in five years, during which the MFTEC may make a review automatically, or on request of interested parties.[28]

It is certain that the provisions of the Chinese Anti-Dumping Regulations illustrated above resemble the relevant provisions of the WTO Anti-Dumping Agreement.

III GAPS TO BE FILLED

Although the Chinese Anti-Dumping Regulations are on the whole consistent with the WTO Anti-Dumping Agreement, they still leave much to be desired. The wording of most of the provisions is too general to be operated. In spite of Article 41 providing that the MFTEC, the SETC and other relative departments of the State Council may make implementing ordinances pursuant to the Regulation, so far such implementing ordinances have not publicly appeared. Compared with the WTO Anti-Dumping Agreement, the Regulations need to fill gaps at least in the following aspects:

Further definition of "comparable price", "constructed price", "like products", "fair comparison" and other related concepts in determination of dumping

The Regulations require a fair comparison between the export price and the normal value of the allegedly dumped product, and the normal value is provided to be a comparable price in the export country or in the market of a third country. But there is neither definition of the "comparable price", nor provisions on how to choose a third country.

The Agreement, however, provides that a "comparable price" shall be the price for the like product when destined for consumption in the export country in the ordinary course of trade, or for the like product exported to an appropriate third country. The term "the ordinary course of trade" is defined in following articles and the price in the third country is required to be "representative".

The Agreement also provides that the fair comparison shall be made "at the same level of trade" and "in respect of sales made as nearly as possible at the same time". Due allowance shall be made in each case for differences which are demonstrated to affect price comparability.

As for the constructed price, the Regulations do not provide the exact meaning of the "reasonable costs", while the Agreement defines it in considerable detail.

In fact, no definition of the term "like product" can be found in the Regulations. In contrast, the Agreement interprets the "like product" to mean "a product which is identical, i.e. alike in all respects to the product under consideration, or in the absence of such a product, another product which, although

[28] Ibid., Art. 33.

not alike in all respects, has characteristics closely resembling those of the product under consideration".

Further standards and methodology for the determination of "threat of material injury" and "cumulative assessment of effects"

Article 8 of the Regulations makes a list of factors that shall be considered in the determination of injury. But the Regulations do not pay sufficient attention to the determination of a threat of material injury. According to the Agreement, the determination of a threat of material injury shall be "based on facts and not merely on allegation, conjecture or remote possibility".[29] The Agreement also requires an evaluation of all relevant economic factors and indices having a bearing on the state of injury.

Article 9 of the Regulations permits the authorities cumulatively to assess the effects of imports from more than one country when such imports are simultaneously subject to anti-dumping investigations. But the Regulations do not make further provisions on how cumulatively to assess such effects. In the light of the Agreement,[30] cumulative assessment can be made only if:

(i)   the dumping margin from each country is no less than 2 per cent of the export price;

(ii) the volume of imports from each country is not negligible, i.e. no less than 3 per cent of imports of the like product in the importing country or the imports from all the countries collectively account for 7 per cent of the like product in the importing country;

(iii) the cumulative assessment is appropriate in the light of conditions of competition between the imported products and the conditions of competition between the imported products and the like domestic product.

Standardisation and completion of investigation

Both the Chinese Anti-Dumping Regulations and the WTO Anti-Dumping Agreement stipulate that an investigation to determine the existence, degree and effect of any alleged dumping shall be initiated upon a written application by or on behalf of the domestic industry. However, the Agreement provides in detail when the application can be considered to have been made "by or on behalf of the domestic industry". No such provision is included in the Regulations.

As for evidence, Article 12 of the Regulations provides only that "necessary evidence" shall be attached to the application, while the Agreement requires "sufficient evidence" and uses a whole article stipulating issues of evidence. Such difference in wording seems to show that the WTO Anti-Dumping Agreement

---

[29] WTO Anti-Dumping Agreement, Art. 3.7.
[30] Ibid., Art. 3.3.

is stricter than the Chinese Anti-Dumping Regulations in terms of evidence requirements attached to an investigation application.

In cases where the number of exporters, producers, importers or types of products involved is so large as to make the determination of dumping and injury impracticable, the authorities may limit their examination by using samplings.[31] The Regulations do not stipulate it in sufficient detail as the relevant provisions of the Agreement do. The same sharp contrast can also be made in respect of on-the-spot investigation.

Article 18(4) of the Regulations provides that the investigation shall be terminated when the dumping margin or the volume of the dumped product is negligible. But the Regulations do not point out to what extent the dumping margin and the volume of the dumped product is *de minimis* and negligible.

Issues of anti-circumvention measures

Article 35 of the Regulations authorises the MOFTEC, the SETC and other related agencies under the State Council to apply appropriate anti-circumvention measures. Although the provision and practice of anti-circumvention measures have not been new in other countries, especially in the United States, their compatibility with the law of the WTO is by no means without doubt. Although in the Uruguay Round there had been draft provisions relating to anti-circumvention measures, the final Agreement did not include them because of disagreement among the negotiators. Even though there is a ministerial decision in the Final Act, recognising the issue of circumvention and referring the matter to the Committee on Anti-Dumping Practices for resolution, it does not expressly permit the WTO members to make anti-circumvention measures.

Necessity of provisions for judicial review

Article 13 of the WTO Anti-Dumping Agreement provides that each member shall maintain judicial, arbitral or administrative tribunals or procedures to review the administrative actions relating to anti-dumping determinations promptly. It further requires that such tribunals or procedures shall be independent of the authorities responsible for the administrative actions in question.

It is a pity that there is no provision concerning judicial review of the administrative actions relating to final anti-dumping determinations under the Chinese Anti-Dumping Regulations. However, there is an administrative review procedure in the Regulationss by the same administrative authorities which make the anti-dumping decisions in question, i.e. the MFTEC, the SETC and the TSC.[32] Nevertheless, interested parties may still doubt that these authorities can make impartial reviews of their own decisions.

---

[31] Chinese Anti-Dumping Regulations, Art. 19; WTO Anti-Dumping Agreement, Art. 6.10.
[32] Chinese Anti-Dumping Regulations, Art. 33.

However, an alternative legal remedy exists in this respect. In the light of Article 71 of the Administrative Proceedings Act of the PRC, foreign persons or entities may bring a lawsuit against administrative actions before the Courts of Justice in China. Article 11(1) of the same Act lists the administrative actions that can be used, and Article 11(2) states that the Courts of Justice shall hear other cases against actionable administrative measures set forth by other Chinese acts or regulations. But this should not be the excuse for the absent provisions concerning judicial review procedures in the Chinese Anti-dumping Regulations when China becomes a member of the WTO.

IV CONCLUSION

As mentioned at the beginning of this chapter, the adoption and coming into force of the Chinese Anti-Dumping Regulations are of far-reaching significance both internally and externally. The Regulations are a wonderful example of the Chinese legislature more and more obviously paying attention to the compatibility of its legislation with international law such as the law of the WTO in this case, although in reality there may still exist certain gaps between the former and the latter. And this consistency is particularly imperative to China in its striving for strengthening the market-oriented economic reform, and speeding up and completing its WTO entrance negotiations with trading powers.

However, legislation is one thing and its implementation another. More than two years have passed since the enactment of the Chinese Anti-Dumping Regulations, but so far there have been only two anti-dumping cases filed by domestic industries. This is partly because domestic industries have little knowledge of, and experience in, anti-dumping procedures, and partly because they still do not understand very well that they have to unite as one against foreign dumping in order to protect themselves. Some of the domestic factories or companies did not co-operate very well with others and the authorities during the course of anti-dumping investigation, while wanting to share the final victories.

It seems to these authors that it will take some time for China to perfect its anti-dumping legislation, to bring it into full play in economic and trade relations and to make it completely consistent with Article VI of the GATT and the WTO Anti-Dumping Agreement. At the moment, and in the near future, the related governmental authorities should speed up the formation and publicising of some implementary rules and methodologies of the present Regulations, such as a detailed schedule of investigation procedures, a standard form of questionnaire, rules of using sampling investigation, rules of hearing, rules of confidentiality, provisions of judicial review, etc.

On the other hand, it is highly recommended that the central government should set up a fixed group of officials and experts with sufficient knowledge and experience, especially responsible for anti-dumping issues, who come from the above competent authorities and legal and economic circles.

The last, but not least, suggestion is that both central and local governments, chambers of commerce, universities, institutes and associations should organise periodical personnel training programmes or workshops on anti-dumping issues, both for domestic industries and the authorities concerned, so as to raise their proficiency in dealing with anti-dumping matters. As the largest developing market-oriented country in the world, it is desirable and possible for China to get humane, financial, technical and facility assistance for such meaningful programmes from developed countries, the WTO and other international organisations.

11

China's Trade Policy and its Implications

HUANG WEIPING

I INTRODUCTION

Now ranking in the top 10, China is one of the major players in global trade. In 1998, the total trade of China with the rest of the world was more than US $ 320 billion, increasing by only 0.5 per cent on its worth in 1997. With the exchange rate unchanged for the whole year after that, the beginning of the East Asian Financial Crisis and the pressure from neighbouring countries' depreciation of currencies on China's exports, domestic economic development is becoming increasingly serious.

In the past 20 years, since China implemented policies of reform and openness to the outside world, China totally reformed its trade policies with the shift of the economic system from a planned economy into a market driven economy. The change in the trade policies and deregulation could be summarised as follows:[1]

1979–1987— breaking the monopoly of the state over the foreign trade of China, China established different kinds of trade companies up to 2020. The foreign funded companies, such as joint ventures, could do limited foreign trade business. The central government of China let the provincial level do some limited foreign trade business; combined the trade companies with the industrial enterprises; established the branches of trade companies in other countries; reformed the planning, accounting system of trade and introduced some responsibility system into the trade business;

1988–1990— broadly introduced the responsibility system into foreign trade business; introduced the foreign exchange retain and profit retain system into some trade companies such as light industry, garments and so on; reformed the trade business institutions such as license, quota; reformed the trade management system;

---

[1] See Wang Shaoxi, Wang Shouchun, *China's Foreign Trade* (Renmin University Press, 1995).

1991–1993—   abolished the fiscal subsidy to export; reformed the exchange retention system, leaving more to the trade companies;

1994–present—established the unified interbank market of foreign exchange; reduced the tariff; introduced and carried out the tax rebate for export; established the " Law of Foreign Trade"; abolished the planning system in trade business; established the quota bidding system; reorganised the state owned trade companies; unified the trade regulations and improved the trade transparency; allowed to established limited foreign funded trade companies;

China reduced the import duty several times during the 1990s. Today the weighted average import duty is 15 per cent. The non-tariff control over import has reduced seriously since reform in 1980s. Generally speaking, the rate of freedom of imports today in China is more than 90 per cent, the same as the level of freedom of Japan in the early 1980s.[2]

Although China carried out the free-trade driven policies, some disputes remain between China and its trade partners in the fields of import restriction tariff and non-tariff control; standards issues; government procurement; export subsidies; sanitary measures; transparency of trade policies; intellectual property protection; service barriers; banks and insurance industry services; telecommunication; information services and investment. China is considering and putting into practice measures to reduce these disputes.

By entry to the WTO, China will certainly follow the rules of the game in international trade with the basic benefits of the developing country guaranteed by its trade partners. With entry to the WTO, China will go further in the way of reform and become more open to the outside world, and will certainly make contribution to the world economy, and finally, will be one of the real members of the global village.

II THE REFORM OF TRADE POLICY

China has experienced rapid and market driven economic development for more than 20 years, and today is one of the major players in international trade ranking the tenth largest, while already deeply integrated into the present world economy. Most scholars both in China and world wide consider the reform of trade policies in China, which led the rapid development of imports and exports. Trade contribution to economic development during the 20 years is very great. Statistics show that net exports contributed to economic growth in 1990 (contribution rate was 37.53 per cent) and 1994 (contribution rate was 11 per cent) when China's economic circle was at the bottom of the development curve. On the other hand, the trade surplus gives China the foundation to sur-

---

[2] Song Ligang, Hwang Weiping, *Reform in China's Trade: Policies and Process* (Economic Science Press, 1997).

Table 1: Trade in China (1978–1998) US (billion dollars)

Year	Export	Growth Rate(%)		Import	Growth Rate(%)
1978	9.75	28.40	10.89	51.00	−1.14
1979	13.66	40.20	15.68	43.90	−2.02
1980	18.12	33.80	19.55	24.70	−1.43
1981	22.01	14.30	20.02	2.56	1.99
1982	22.32	1.36	22.02	10.01	0.30
1983	22.23	−0.43	19.29	−12.27	2.94
1984	26.14	17.61	27.41	28.14	−1.27
1985	27.35	4.63	42.25	54.15	−14.90
1986	30.94	13.14	42.90	1.54	−11.96
1987	39.44	27.45	43.22	1.01	−3.78
1988	47.52	20.49	55.27	27.89	−7.75
1989	52.54	10.57	59.14	7.01	−6.60
1990	62.09	18.18	53.35	−9.89	8.74
1991	71.91	15.81	63.79	19.58	8.12
1992	84.94	18.12	80.59	26.33	4.35
1993	91.76	8.03	103.95	28.99	−12.19
1994	121.04	31.90	115.69	11.30	5.35
1995	148.77	22.91	132.08	14.16	16.69
1996	151.07	1.54	138.84	5.10	12.23
1997	182.70	20.09	142.36	2.54	40.34
1998	183.76	0.50	140.17	−1.50	43.59

Source: Statistical Year Book, State Bureau of Statistics, 1990, 1995, 1999

vive its RMB currency exchange rate unchanged, which contributed to the stability of the monetary situation of the East Asian region as well as the recovery of the economy in the region. The development of and changes in China's external trade is shown in Table 1.

China's external trade ranked thirty-second in the world in 1978; eleventh in 1995; and tenth in 1998, which shows great progress since modernisation of economy. External trade also contributed greatly to the increase of the foreign exchange reserve, which was US $19.44 billion in 1992, US $51.62 billion in 1994, and reached US $144.9 billion in 1998. Meanwhile China's degree of dependence upon External Trade increased year by year, which showed that China is deeply involved or integrated into the world economy, and that the development of China is closely associated with the global economic changes. See Table 2.

Besides the progress of external trade, China introduced a large amount of foreign capital, especially foreign direct investment (FDI). FDI is working in different industries, such as light industry; telecommunications industry; other information technology related industry and finance industry, and today plays

Table 2: The Dependence of China's Economy upon External Trade

Year	GDP (RMB, Billion)	Export (USD, Billion)	Dependence on Export (%)	External Trade (USD, Billion)	Dependence on Trade (%)
1980	447.0	18.12	6.0	37.67	12.6
1985	856.2	27.35	9.5	69.60	24.1
1990	1768.6	62.09	17.0	115.43	31.6
1993	3417.2	91.76	16.8	195.65	35.8
1994	4379.9	121.04	23.8	236.73	46.6
1995	5768.3	148.77	21.6	280.85	40.7
1996	6380.0	151.07	19.6	289.91	37.8
1998	7955.2	183.76	19.2	323.93	33.8

Source: Statistic Year Book, 1990, 1995, 1999

a very important role in Chinese economic development. Foreign funded firms have made a great contribution to China's external trade. In 1998, foreign invested enterprises (FIEs) accounted for 48.68 per cent of China's total external trade, that figure was only 4.04 per cent in 1986. China has been the second largest FDI absorber in the world—just after the US—for 6 years. More than 400 of the 500 Giants in "Fortune" invested in China and have conducted business. On the other hand, the rapid growth of the FIEs' export left some issues to which China has had to pay attention.

One of the key incentives for introduction of foreign capital from the outside world by China is to encourage the development of trade. To this end, China allowed investment from some kinds of service companies whose business trade related to access the Chinese market, especially transportation, insurance, advertisement, law services, commodity retail and banking services. By the end of May 1999, there were 173 foreign funded banks doing business in China of which 24 were doing RMB business, and 14 foreign funded insurance companies in operation, either in property or life insurance. Besides that, there were 16 foreign funded companies in the shipment business, more than 300 foreign funded firms in advertising and about 280 foreign funded commissioning agent firms. There are still about 20 foreign invested commercial retail companies, 16 foreign funded commodity inspection firms and 92 law firm representative offices. All these foreign invested trade related service companies contributed considerably to China's rapid growth of external trade.[3] The general picture of the roles of the FDI in China can be found in Table 3.

The result of the external trade mentioned above is the real legacy of the reform of Chinese relations with the rest of the world. The reform of China's

[3] Kim Weixing, "Reform in Enterprise Offered Great Chances for Foreign Investment" *East Asia Economy and Trade News*, 14 June 1999.

Table 3: Roles of FDI in China (US dollars (billions) (%)

Year	Number of Projects	Contractual Value	Realised Value Export	% of China's Import	% of China's Trade	% of China's Assets	% of Fixed Output	% of* Industry Revenue	% of tax
1979–1982	920	4.96	1.77	—	—	—	—	—	—
1983	638	.92	0.92	—	—	—	—	—	—
1984	2,166	2.88	1.42	—	—	—	—	—	—
1985	3,073	6.33	1.96	—	—	—	—	—	—
1986	1,498	3.33	2.24	1.88	5.60	4.04	—	—	—
1987	2,233	3.71	2.31	3.07	7.81	5.55	—	—	—
1988	5,945	5.30	3.20	5.18	10.64	8.12	—	—	—
1989	5,779	5.60	3.40	9.35	14.87	12.28	—	—	—
1990	7,273	6.60	3.49	12.58	23.06	17.43	—	2.28	—
1991	12,978	11.98	4.37	16.75	26.51	21.34	4.15	5.29	—
1992	48,764	58.12	11.01	20.44	32.74	26.43	7.51	7.09	4.25
1993	83,437	111.44	27.52	27.51	40.24	34.27	12.13	9.15	5.71
1994	47,549	82.68	33.77	28.69	45.78	37.04	17.08	11.26	8.51
1995	37,011	91.28	37.52	31.51	47.66	39.10	15.65	14.31	10.96
1996	24,556	73.28	41.73	40.71	54.45	47.29	15.10	15.14	11.87
1997	21,001	51.00	45.26	41.00	54.59	46.95	14.79	18.57	13.16
1998	19,799	52.10	45.46	44.06	54.73	48.68	13.23	27.00	14.38
total	324,620	572.495	267.315	—	—	—	—	—	—

* Excluding tariff and land tax.
Source: Statistic on FDI in China, MOFTEC, 1999

external economic system has created a better climate for foreign investors, who have considered China as one of the best places to do business, especially during the period of East Asian Economic Crisis.

In December 1998, China's Enterprise Investigation System surveyed 4573 foreign investors of APEC member countries. The result suggested that most of the investors questioned considered China to be one of the most favorable places to invest in the Asia-Pacific Region. The stability of society and political situation, the good prospects for future macro-economic climate, the primary guarantee for the profitability of investment by the open policy all suggested that China has a large capacity for introducing FDI from all over the rest of the world. The survey showed that the foreign investors in China are quite satisfied with:

1. adequate labour resources with certain quality;
2. market capacity;
3. favourable policies and regulations for foreign investment;
4. stable legal system;
5. price stability of input and output.

Meanwhile, the foreign investors from APEC countries hope that China should make further efforts to improve:

1. the infrastructure of investment;
2. efficiency of the administrative management of different level of government;
3. legislative system;
4. the game rules for firm's activities in the market;
5. the social security system.

Foreign investors also held a positive attitude to the liberalisation of trade and investment in the APEC region and hoped China would get membership of WTO (World Trade Organisation) as soon as possible. 87 per cent of the APEC countries' investors in China considered that China is one of the most attractive countries for foreign investors in the region; 95.2 per cent of the investors had confidence to continue to invest in China; 73 per cent of the FIEs from APEC region had made a five year plan for business in China, and 70.5 per cent had a ten year plan. All the results of the survey suggested that China ranked as one of the top countries with the most favorable climate for investment.

As mentioned above, these important changes in China's external economic relations are a result of establishment of foreign trade law; law and regulation of foreign investment absorption; reform of foreign trade policies, regulation and other measures. The means of reform suggests that the liberalisation of trade is directed towards the game rules of the WTO and standardisation of the process of external trade by China's firms.

Before 1979, the external trade system in China was highly monopolised. Exports and imports were controlled by the Ministry of Foreign Trade and, under the unified instructive plan, unified management and all foreign trade was in the hands of the state owned trade companies classified by their business operation. For example, China National Cereals, Oil and Foodstuffs Import and Export Cooperation, was a state owned monopoly over imports and exports of grain, oil and foodstuffs. Even other state owned foreign trade companies could not deal with these kinds of business. By the end of 1978, there were about 130 state owned companies including the local branches of the provinces which monopolised foreign trade business. At that time, the financial arrangement for foreign trade was called unified control of foreign trade revenue and expenditure throughout China. The companies had to hand over all the foreign exchange income, including the profit, and applied to the central government for the import payment. In short, the system of the external trade during 1950s–1970s could be characterised as administrative control over the whole foreign trade.

Under the traditional external trade system before 1978, there was no relationship between the trade companies and the manufacturing firms. Manufacturing firms could not know that anything had changed in the world market and could not match the needs and opinions of the foreign consumers. Because of the direct control of trade by the administration, the state owned foreign trade companies had no right to organise the operation independently, and for the most part since the companies did not need to be responsible for the profit and loss of their external business, the companies had no interest and made no effort to improve their business operations. Compared with the "Four Tigers" rapid development of foreign trade, China had to improve and develop its trade system to make more of a contribution to economic development. The reform was necessary at that time because of pressures from outside and inside China.

1. China liberalises the external trade management system

China first broke down the highly centralised foreign trade management system. In 1979, Central Government of China offered to the local authorities of Fujian and Guangdong the power to do foreign trade business. Foreign funded manufacturing enterprises were allowed to bring exports and imports in their own scope of operation. Then the key state owned manufacturing enterprises were able to try their own external trade business, and even some large non-state owned enterprises, such as large private ones (a total of five today) were offered the right to conduct imports and exports as part of their own manufacturing operation. For some time, the companies affiliated to Army and Police could conduct foreign trade (now stopped). By the end of 1997, China established an experiment by which some of the foreign trade companies which reached the standards set by the trade regulations could do some certain external business in China, such as the Mitsubishi and other foreign trade companies (a total of six foreign companies) in Pudong region, Shanghai city. With these reforms, China has broken down the state monopoly system of external trade, and today in China there are more than 25,000 external trade companies doing business.

2. Reduction of the tariff and non-tariff external trade restriction

During the period of reform that began in 1978, the tariff in China reduced dramatically. The tariff income had accounted for a large percentage of the fiscal income of the central government: in 1985 the ratio was 29.4 per cent; in 1994 it was still 11.4 per cent[4] and the call for protection of the infant industries led to slow improvement of tariff reform. In 1991 China reduced the import tariff for 40 goods; the next year, for 225 commodities; by the end of 1992, for 3371 commodities, and in 1993 for another 2898. In 1996 China lowered the average import tariff from 42.1 per cent to 23 per cent, on 1 October 1997 it further lowered the average import tariff to 17 per cent, by the end of 1999, the average import tariff will lower to 15 per cent, and by the year of 2020, China will be a real free trade country. With the reduction of the import tariff, China also reduced its non-tariff trade restriction. Traditionally, China's non-tariff restrictions have included import and export licenses, import quotas, administrative control and other import restrictions. Since 1996 China has reduced the non-tariff control from 1,530 commodities to about 500; the level open in this field is about the same in Japan in early 1980's. For some quotas and licenses, China has carried out a bidding system instead of administrative allocation since the mid 1990s. The percentage of bidding is just 25 per cent, but it has shown the direction of reform in allocation of the quotas.

3. Let firms be responsible for their own operation, profit and loss

In the 1980s to 1990s, China reformed the management system of external trade. The first stage was to establish the responsibility system in trade: the firms were responsible for their own business and the state owned companies also for the profit to the Government. The State administration then reduced and finally abolished all the fiscal subsidies to exports and imports in the early 1990s. All trade companies had to be responsible for their own operation: the State would not subsidise the loss any more and companies could retain some part of the profit as their own financial resources. The firms could then establish stable relationships with the manufacturing enterprises, and even invest or create new enterprises. With the deepening of the reform, China introduced the shareholder system into foreign trade firms, and pushed the firms in the direction of establishing modern enterprises. The trade companies organised the business chamber and associations to serve their businesses by offering information and assistance. In short, the trade companies in China today are independent to make decisions and do business, and are not offered any financial support from the government.

---

[4] Song Ligang and Hwang Weiping, *Reform in China's Trade: Policies and Process* (Economic Science Press, 1997).

4. Reform in macro-level management in external trade

With the micro-level reform in trade, China also reformed several aspects of the macro-level trade management. First came reform in the foreign exchange business. In the traditional system, trade companies could sell their foreign exchange income to the Bank of China at the official rate. With reform, the retention system which allowed companies to keep part of the foreign exchange income (50 per cent in Special Economic Zones, 25 per cent in other regions) was established, and then in 1984 the wrap market was established, which meant that companies could buy and sell foreign exchange in the market (at that time there were two rates, official and wrap market, in China). In 1994, the interbank foreign exchange market was established and the rate of RMB to other currencies was set by the forces of supply and demand in that market. The rate of RMB to US $ in 1994 was RMB 8.70 = $1 and was RMB 8.29 = $1 in 1998 in the interbank market it appreciated slightly.

China has been increasing the transparency of the trade regime related law and regulation. Today, the publication of central and provincial level reports, laws, regulations, and other official trade related texts can be found easily in China. This has contributed significantly toward transparency. Moreover, the Chinese Government has established several web sites, accessible either in Chinese or English, carrying government news and the text of newly published laws and regulations (the most influential ones are, www.cei.gov.cn; www. moftec.com.cn).

The trade companies, even the state-owned, have been doing business independently. The Ministry of Foreign Trade and Cooperation and its provincial level agencies, has administrative responsibilities but never intervened in the business of companies. Only very few commodities (such as military goods) are under government control (for example, through plans and direct control). Most goods can be dealt with by the different firms in China without "instructive planning". In China, the commission agency system in external trade is very common. Small businesses without expertise in foreign trade business can ask trade companies to be commission agents, and commission is set by the market.

With the reform in foreign trade system of the last 20 years, though many issues remain to be addressed and there is still a long way for the Chinese to go further in reform, one can see that great progress has been made by China, and the direction of the reform in China's external trade suggested is very clear—toward the basic requirements of the World Trade Organisation (WTO), and in the way of the trade liberalisation.

III AREAS OF CONFLICT

Although great improvements have been made in the structure and operation of China's external trade system, disputes with trade partners have remained, and some conflicts remain serious in certain aspects of China's trade relations with other economies in the world. The core issues are about how far and how rapidly China should go in the way of trade liberalisation, and how it can learn from the shocks to Chinese economic development such as that of the financial crisis during 1997–1998. China's future trade development will present some difficulties, such as the instability in world price for particular products (with the given size and structure of China's trade). The WTO rules for developing countries are inadequate and the best solution for China is to commit to developed country rules in all areas, or at least to reach developed country rules within a finite period.[5] Frankly speaking, the disputes between China and its trade partners have to some extent, halted China's entry to the WTO and also hurt wider trade development in China as well as in the world. The areas of dispute, mostly raised by China's trading partners, are analysed below.[6]

Import Policy

Although in 1996 China lowered its average import tariff from 42.1 per cent to 23 per cent, and on 1 October 1997 further lowered the average import tariff to 17 per cent, on 6 January 1999, the Minister of Finance announced that there would be further import tariff cuts for the 1014 products in the textile and toy sectors. By the end of 1999, the average tariff rate will be 15 per cent, which will be the same as that in most of the developing countries.

China's trade partners complain that China restricts imports by a variety of means, including prohibitively high tariffs and domestic tax on imported products; non-tariff measures; limitations on which businesses can import and other trade barriers. For some motor vehicles the tariff reached 100 per cent. Besides the high tariff, the trade partners complain that unpredictable application of that rate created the import and export difficulties. The tariff might vary for the same product depending on the places of entry, the local tariff added, or some exemption measures applicable. In addition to tariffs, imports may also be subject to value-added and other taxes. The trade partners have complained about the current value-added taxing system (VAT). China's VAT is usually 13 per cent or 17 per cent. Thus, a product subject to a 17 per cent import tariff, 17 per cent VAT and consumption tax would be taxed at a rate in excess of 34 per cent.

Non-tariff barriers to trade are administered at national and provincial levels by the State Economic and Trade Commission (SETC), the State Planning Commission (SPC) and MOFTEC. Although on 1 January 1999, China Customs announced that the number of products requiring export licenses had been cut from 707 to 395, a 44 per cent reduction, trade partners complain that many products are subject both to quota and also to import licensing requirements. For these products, after permission has been granted by other administrations for importation, MOFTEC must decide whether to issue a license.

[5] Editor, *China and East Asia Trade Policy* (Australia and Japan Research Center, 1995).
[6] See USTR, "Foreign Trade Barriers in China", 2 June 1998.

Transparency

Although in recent years China's trade system has become significantly more transparent, trade partners suggest that they will sometimes meet difficulties in learning which regulations or rules apply to their operations in China.

Trading rights

Today, with 25,000 companies involved in external trade, China still restricts the type and number of entities within the country which have the legal right to engage in that trade. China's trade partners suggested that in the context of its WTO accession negotiations, China should pledge to liberalise the availability of trading rights, such as the rights to import and export, and access to China's distribution system. At the end of the transition period, all foreign and domestic businesses will have trading rights, avoiding having to go through intermediary firms who had the right to import goods into China.

Standards

China has retained the statutory inspection requirement on about 780 imported goods and several hundred exported products. China's trade partners complain of problems with the standards system in China, including the lack of transparency; difficulty in determining the appropriate standards; use of different standards on imports from different countries and different standards from domestic goods. For example, the US traders often argue that they encounter difficulty in learning which Chinese standards apply to their goods. Sometimes a particular good from the US may need to meet a different standard at the Chinese point of entry than does the same good coming from the EU. Another matter of complaint is that China's phytosanitary and veterinary import quarantine standards are overly strict, unevenly applied, and not backed up by modern laboratory techniques.

Government procurement

China's trade partners complain that government purchasing actions and decisions are subject to its law and regulations. Although China used to be committed to publishing all trade related laws and regulations, it has not published any laws on government procurement practices, and competitive procedure is not allowed in most public procurement in China. In that case it is argued that government procurement practices are unclear and that there is a lack of transparency.

Export subsidy

China's trade counterparts complain about export subsidies, although the Chinese government claims that direct financial subsidies on all exports including agricultural goods ended on 1 January 1991. Chinese exporters can benefit from loan policies (to get non-commercial terms loan), export tax rebate (to rebate the value-added tax), preferential tax policies (to get reduced income taxes), and preferential energy and raw material supply policies. The trade partners take these preferences as discrimination in trade.

Lack of intellectual property protection

China's trade partners complain that end user piracy of business software is widespread. One can easily find unauthorized copies of pirated software or audio and video products anywhere in China. For example, the US industry estimates of IP losses in China due to piracy, and so on have exceeded US $ 2 billion. Although Chinese authorities have investigated the issue, it still remains a serious problem and they do not feel that action against unauthorized software, audio and video products is effective.

Services barriers

China's trade partners complain that in most sectors, foreign service providers are only allowed to operate under selective "experimental" licenses. In their minds the Chinese market for services remains very closed. Restrictive operation and investment law and lack of transparency in administrative procedure limit the foreign companies service exports to China and investment in the country. It is of particular concern that service trade opportunities, particularly in financial, telecommunications, audiovisual, distribution, professional legal and accounting services and travel and tourism sectors, have been affected by a variety of limitations on foreign participation throughout the Chinese economy. Other obstacles, such as labour employment, representative office establishment and joint-venture requirements, make it very difficult to access China's market even though the market is huge.

In service provision, it is argued that information services in China remain a difficult and sensitive area for foreign firms to access. Foreign investors cite the example that, in April 1996, the State Council of China announced plans to apply severely restrictive regulations governing the activities of foreign information providers. The distribution services sector is another difficult issue; foreign companies are again restricted in the scope of their activities. Business licenses often do not allow firms to provide the full range of services, including marketing, after-sales services and customer support. Foreign firms do not have access to transportation services on a reasonable and non-discriminatory basis and are required to use state-owned companies to distribute their goods.

Anti-competitive practices

Anti-competitive practices in China come in the form of industrial conglomerates, created to improve the profitability of State Owned Enterprises (SEOs) and to keep unemployment low. Some are even authorised to fix prices and allocate contacts.

Electronic commerce

In fact, at present sales and contracts executed through electronic commerce are not regulated under Chinese law. As Chinese officials become aware of the potential of e-commerce to promote exports and increase the international competitiveness of Chinese firms, China will increase its regulation. All foreign investors are aware of the lack of an effective legal framework and this poses a challenge to development of e-commerce business in China.

Investment barriers

Although China's official policy is to welcome foreign investment, foreign investors believe that the Chinese government has established investment barriers, and control on foreign investment by channelling them to the areas that support China's economic development policies. China encourages foreign investment in priority infrastructure sectors such as energy production, communications, and transportation and restricts or even prohibits it in sectors where China has a specific need or where it wants to protect the local industry. In addition, China bans investment in certain industries in the name of "national security interest", and forces foreign firms into joint venture arrangements, insisting on foreign companies technology transfer.

Other criticisms

China's trade partners complain that smuggling in certain areas of China is very serious, and severely affects their business deals and investment. This is despite Chinas investigation and consequent establishment and use of the special Police Force to eliminate smuggling. Efficiency of administration is not satisfied, and this issue will not be easily solved for it is really an "old" problem in China.

All these criticisms indicate the views of China's trade partners: China should be required to liberalise trade and open its market further to the rest or the world; China should reduce the domestic economic and non-economic distortion in trade dramatically, and finally, it has to accept the costs of adjustment drawn from trade liberalisation in order to achieve the economic and non-economic gains which liberalisation will bring to China.

IV MOVES TOWARDS AN AGREEMENT

To answer the criticisms from its trade partners, foreign perspectives on the efforts that China should make are found in one important document from the United States Trade Representative (USTR) for China's entry to the WTO.

On 30 September 1997 the USTR submitted its Strategic Plan for FY1997–FY2002 to Congress.

> "China: WTO conclude a commercially meaningful WTO accession package with China that provides both effective market accesses for U.S. goods and service and conformity to international trade norms. Key factors include market access in sectors where the U.S. is competitive, such as agriculture, electronics, medical devices, pharmaceuticals, and services (including distribution, telecommunications and insurance)".[7]

On March 1997, in the *Draft Protocol on China WTO Accession*, the US offered the conditions for China's entry to the WTO. Amongst them are:

1. Uniform administration—including laws, regulations, rules, directives, policies and measures. All the above mentioned will affect trade in goods, services, trade-related aspects of intellectual property rights or the control of foreign exchange.
2. Transparency—All the laws, regulations, rules and policies of China's trade should be published and readily available to other WTO members. China should offer the trade related data and information to WTO members.
3. Non-discrimination—Foreign individuals, enterprises and foreign funded enterprises shall be no less favoured than other individuals and enterprises in respect of goods, services and other trade business either in nationwide or subnational level.
4. Right to Trade—All enterprises, including foreign funded ones, should have the right to trade in all goods throughout the customs territory of China, except for some very special goods which will be permitted by the GATT/WTO.
5. State Trading—China should ensure import and export procedures of state trading enterprises are fully transparent, and should provide full information on the pricing mechanisms and distribution of import licenses, ensuring that quotas are on an equal footing.
6. Foreign Exchange Control—China should accept Article VIII of the IMF's Article of Agreement, which means the free foreign exchange in the current account of the Balance of Payments.
7. Subsidy—China should stop all export and import subsidy to goods, services and other trade.
8. Taxes and Charges Levied on Import and Export—China should ensure that customs fees or charges applied or administered by national and sub-

---

[7] See p. 32 <<http://www.ansi.org/testsite/grace/public/news/natl.html>>.

national authorities should be in conformity with the GATT 1994, and foreign funded enterprises should be on a fully equal footing.

In addition to the conditions mentioned above, China should be following the regulations set by GATT for the agriculture and standards. On April 9, 1999, information from *Inside US Trade* indicated that the agreement reached was as follows:

China would lower its tariff for agriculture to an average level ranging from 14.5–17 per cent, and on industrial goods to an average tariff between 7.1–9.44 per cent. Two thirds of these cuts would be implemented by 2003 and others in 2005. China agreed to sign the Information Technology Agreement with most tariff elimination phased out by 2003 and others by 2005. It agreed that it would allow the retail distribution of cars in its market—auto imports would be covered by a quota worth US $ 6 billion that will grow by 15 per cent annually until 2005, when it would be phased out. China also agreed that by 2005, it would reduce tariffs on built-up vehicles to 25 per cent and tariffs on auto parts to 10 per cent. Other agreements were reached in the finance, value-added information and investment industries the direction of the all goods and services agreements is towards free trade.

The requirements of the foreign trade partners of China for trade liberalisation in China are concentrated in accession to China's market in goods, services, and other products, tariff and non-tariff reduction, State trading, financial and other services, transparency of the trade laws and regulations. Actually, trade liberalisation is consistent with China's policy of reform and opening up to the rest of the world, which is obviously in China's interest. On the other hand, China's trade liberalisation is also in the interest of the rest of the world, especially WTO members. As the tenth largest trade country in the world, China should contribute to the development of the world economy, such as the non-depreciation of RMB during the East Asian financial crisis, which would be benefit to both China and its trade partners. China's leaders suggested that in 2020, China would be a trade liberalised country, although there is still some way to go to meet that goal. China also fully realises the rights and obligations with trade partners would be balanced, in which case China should be prepared to practice the obligations of trade liberalisation as well as enjoy the due rights.

Every country in the world when opening up its market to the outside should only take a step-by step approach. China should not be exception to this. It will open its market in line with the current level of economic development. I consider that excessive demands or hasty actions in this regard would not only harm China's economic development but also endanger or harm the interests of China's trade partners. Recently China has gone further in the way of trade liberalisation (or as has been commented, in the way of WTO accession). It has reached agreement on agriculture with the US for the reduction of import tariffs, increase in the quotas of grain imports, and the elimination of export subsidies. China has also allowed foreign investors to establish the entities to do the value-added telecommunication business, first in Pudong Shanghai, and then in other places: for financial services, it further expanded the open area, and also the ratio of investment, then the RMB business will be opened to the foreign funded financial institutions. China has made commitments to reduce industrial tariffs and non-tariff import controls and to eliminate the export subsidy. In short, China is liberalising trade.

Economically, trade liberalisation in China has its benefits but also the negative effects on economic development. Some issues would become more serious with further free trade, such as unemployment and destruction of infant industries. Some analysis of these issues should be made before the open policy is pushed forward.

Lowering the import tariff would harm the domestic industries

This is a very common view when talking about trade liberalisation. There is a dilemma in China—the nominal tariff was high enough but the real tariff was as low as in the developed economies. Statistics show that in 1994 only 15.8 per cent of total import was levied and the rest were free of duty. During 1991–1995 the real import tariffs were only 5.6 per cent, 4.9 per cent, 4.3 per cent, 2.9 per cent and 2.7 per cent; tariff rebate was so common in China. Since that time Chinese industries have not been harmed by the rapid growth. In 2000, after more than 20 years of development of the Chinese economy, and the growth of the capacity of competition in China's industries, I believe there would be no serious negative effects of further opening to the outside world. During the reform China's productivity has shown rapid improvement, the current economic situation has shifted from "shortage" into a structural "surplus", the effective supply is greater than effective demand. With one third of the world capacity of TV, washing machine and refrigerator production today in China's market, the imported durable applicants would not find it easy to defeat domestic ones, even when the former is in a foreign brand. China has gradually taken the products made by foreign funded enterprises within the territory as Chinese made goods, a positive signal to the further opening to the outside world.

Economic structural transition creates difficulties in further market market liberalisation[8]

Some people believed that China's further opening to the rest of the world, especially in its entry to the WTO, would create more difficulties to the supply over demand in production and would increase unemployment. By studying the history of reform and open policy since 1978, one could find that China should be further opening to the rest of the world and joining the WTO during an

---

[8] Huang Weiping, "WTO Accession at Economic Difficult Time and Development in the Competition" *Trade Information & World Machine Electronic*, July 1999.

economically difficult time, because supply is greater than demand. When China's economy is in the situation of demand soaring high or inflation, any kind of goods and services could be sold in the market. Opening to the outside world means that foreign enterprises could cut profits easily by entering China. But during the difficult time of oversupplied production, foreign enterprises would have the same problems as Chinese enterprises, the same economic over-production, so they could not sell their output easily. Investment from other economies would help China rise from the bottom of the economic curve.

Lack of demand for domestic production is the key issue for China's economic development, but it could not be taken as the result of opening to the outside world or of trade liberalisation. It is really the result of the lowering willingness of people to consume. The evidence of the low willingness to consume in China could always be found in the growth of bank savings. Facing the uncertainty of the future life with the further reform in housing, medical care, education for children, retirement all of which used to be paid for predominantly by the government, people have to save extra money today to pay for the items mentioned above. The possibility of unemployment encouraged saving. People cut down today's consumption to ensure their future life. Only young people in their twenties and thirties are willing to consume with a loan—to make today's dream come true with tomorrow's income.

As for unemployment, this is really not caused by open policy but due to the transition of the economic structure. Statistics suggested that since the 20 year open policy has been carried out, foreign funded enterprises have absorbed 180 million people directly as workers and staff in China, and created another 7 million jobs indirectly, releasing the pressure of unemployment. Open policy has contributed to job creation. In fact the unemployment today in China is the result of transition of structure which every economy must deal with, the reduced production of "sunset" industries. Most of employees laid off at the age of forty to sixty, could not cope with the shift of structure. Only social security system could help them, for they learned only a very little during the 1970s great cultural revolution.

Benefits and losses from China's WTO accession and trade liberalisation

As mentioned above, I believed that trade liberalisation and WTO accession is consistent with the policy of China's reform and opening up, therefore it is in China's interest. The benefit of WTO entry and trade liberalisation could be classified in the short and long term as a fundamental one.

In the short term, the benefit drawn by China from WTO entry and trade liberalisation would be the great push for the reform in state owned enterprises. The large number of the state owned enterprises in China are in a period of transition, but the traditional management system halted their development in reform. The trade liberalisation and WTO accession will give them a push to hasten the pace in the way of transition. And in the short term trade liberalisation would also put more pressure on unemployment. The rather tough market for their products—this is the cost of transition.

In long run, the benefit drawn by China from trade liberalisation and WTO entry would be very great. With trade liberalisation, China would hasten to establish a perfect market driven economy with a matching economic system. This is the final target of the reform. In long run China will be a real part of the world economy, contributing with the other members to the global village. A fundamental benefit of China's trade liberalisation and WTO entry would be Chinese participation in the negotiation of world trade rules. Only with the entry to the WTO could China be deeply involved in the negotiation process. Today China still remains outside the international trade institutions. Bilateral negotiation and the exercise of power are the only measures for China to establish its trade relations with its counterparts, a negative influence both on the development of China's trade and on the world trade system.

It has been argued in some literature that with trade liberalisation and WTO accession, China would emerge in the APEC area, which would lead to severe competition in the market, first for labour-intensive goods and then for the standardised capital intensive market. Actually I believe this is not true: China's development would not limit the development opportunity of other developing economies, especially in neighbouring countries, as China's economic structure ranges widely, and is regionally diverse in endowed resources and traditional economic structure. Co-operation is good in the APEC region, but competition is better, for it will encourage development in both competitors. In the future the external economic relations between China and its counterparts will certainly be co-operation in the framework of competition, while competition is in the framework of co-operation, which will be of benefit to both.

12

Regionalism, Open Regionalism and Article XXIV GATT: Conflicts and Harmony

SUNG-HOON PARK

I INTRODUCTION

Over the last fifteen years or so regionalism has become increasingly prevailing in the world economy. After the first wave of regionalist tendency during the 1960s, the number of regional integration agreements (RIAs) has again surged especially since the 1980s. The WTO recently reported that of totally 184 RIAs notified to the General Agreement on Tariffs and Trade (GATT)/World Trade Organisation (WTO) so far, 109 agreements are still in force.[1] As the increasing regionalism in the world economy implies potential threat to the multilateral trading system governed by the WTO, the WTO established the Committee on Regional Trading Arrangements (CRTA), which should examine the existing and new RIAs for their conformity with the WTO rules. Article XXIV of the GATT provides rules and conditions under which the RIAs can be allowed under the multilateral trading system. In concrete, Article XXIV of the GATT stipulates several conditions for free trade agreements (FTAs) and customs unions to be treated as allowed exceptions to the most favored nations (MFN) treatment stipulated in Article I of the GATT/WTO Agreement as the most important principle of the multilateral trading system.

One of the consequences of the increasing regionalism in the world economy is that multilateralism and regionalism have been co-existing for a couple of decade, and are expected to do so for a while in the future, as well. In the light of the global economic governance for the new millenium, the question arises as to whether this phenomenon can continue to exist for a long time, and whether new attempts have to be started to contain regionalism and promote multilateralism.

---

[1] Of these 109 RIAs, eighty-four are notified under GATT, Art. XXIV, fourteen are notified under the Enabling Clause, and the remaining eleven are notified under GATS, Art. V. See WTO, "Regional Trade Agreements Notified to the GATT/WTO and in force in February 1999", available at http://www.wto.org/wto/develop/webrtas.htm.

The results of studies conducted independently by the WTO[2] and the OECD[3] contain some clues for this question. On the relationship between regionalism and multilateralism, both of the institutions conclude that regionalism so far has not been detrimental to the multilateral trading system, but was complementary to it. Does this mean that regionalism is always good for the world economy? The answer is, certainly "not". This leads us to another very important question: How can regionalism be overcome in such a way that multilateral trading system can be strengthened?

Discussions on this topic are concentrated on the following two central questions. First, will the rules stipulated in the Article XXIV of the GATT and the "Understanding on the Interpretation of Article XXIV of the GATT 1994" (the Understanding) be sufficient to reduce regionalism and strengthen multilateralism, or do they need to be revised? This question has already been addressed by several scholars, including, *inter alia*, McMillan[4] and Frankel and Wei.[5] Secondly, are there any new mechanisms that can lead regionalism to become conform to the multilateral trading system? What is the role of open regionalism in this regard? Several articles, including Bergsten,[6] Garnaut[7] and Park[8] have also attempted to answer this question.

This chapter mainly addresses the above-raised two questions rather in an integrated manner, considering the fact that so far they were dealt with more or less independently. The chaper is organised as follows. Part II sketches, in a brief manner, recent trends of regionalism, and discusses background and motivations of such regionalist tendency. In Part III, the main characteristics of the concept of open regionalism are discussed, and its merits and shortcomings in relation to GATT rules are identified. Part IV is devoted to the discussion of the main contents of Article XXIV GATT and the Understanding attached hereto, and presents a series of recommendations raised for their revision. Part V draws some important conclusions from the discussion.

---

[2] WTO, *Regionalism and the World Trading System* (Geneva, 1995).

[3] OECD, *Regional Integration and the Multilateral Trading System. Synergy and Divergence* (Paris, 1995).

[4] J. McMillan, "Does Regional Integration Foster Open Trade? Economic Theory and GATT's Article XXIV", in K. Andeson and R. Blackhurst (eds), *Regional Integration and the Global Trading System* (New York, 1993).

[5] J. Frankel and S.-J. Wei, "Open regionalism in a World of Continental Trading Blocs" (IMF Working Paper 98-10, 1998).

[6] Bergsten, "Open Regionalism" (IIE Working Paper 97-03, 1997).

[7] R. Garnaut, *Open Regionalism: An Asia Pacific contribution to the world trading system?* (Institute of South-East Asian Studies, Singapore, 1996).

[8] S.-H. Park, "Liberalizing the World Trade Through Open Regionalism: Options for APEC in the 21st Century", paper presented at the APEC Study Center Consortium Meeting/Conference, Malaysian ASC, 11–13 August 1998.

II THE CO-EXISTENCE OF REGIONALISM AND MULTILATERALISM

Regionalism in the post-war era

Table 1 shows the general trends of the number of regional integration agreements notified to the GATT/WTO.

Table 1: Number of RIAs notified to the GATT/WTO (1948–1999)

Period	1948–1959	1960–1969	1970–1979	1980–1989	1990–1994	1995–1999*	Total
Number	5	21	40	11	33	74	184

* This number was projected by the author using the two sources listed below.

Source: WTO, *Regionalism and the World Trading System* (Geneva, 1995); WTO, "Regional Trade Agreements Notified to the GATT/WTO and in Force in February 1999", available at http://www.wto.org/wto/develop/webrtras.htm.

We can identify several characteristics of regionalism during the post-war era. First, the number of notified RIAs has on average increased, reflecting the fact that despite the successive strengthening of multilateral trading system under the GATT and the WTO, countries resorted increasingly to regional economic integration. Secondly, the post-war world economy has witnessed an up-and-down of regionalism over the last fifty years. In terms of the number of RIAs notified to the GATT/WTO, the 1970s and then the 1990s can be regarded as the periods with the highest frequency of such notification. In contrast, during the 1960s and 1980s, the number of notified RIAs remained at very low level.

The figures in Table 1, however, does not reflect the "real" strength of regionalist tendency of each period, because they have largely been distorted by one unique event which was followed by many related bilateral agreements, which were then eventually notified to the GATT/WTO. This event was European integration. Therefore, the figures tend to overstate the strength of regionalism for each period. During the 1970s, it was the formation within Europe of Customs Union (CU) in 1968, which led, in 1970s, to many related bilateral agreements. During the period since mid-1980s, it was the EC's announcement to launch Single European Market by 1993 and the increasing outreach of European countries in the form of FTAs and CUs, that contributed to a surge in the number of RIAs. On average, however, it appears that regionalism has emerged as an additional force to multilateralism in the world economy, and the two have become eqully important.

The increase in inter-regional and inter-continental regionalism

Another important phenomenon related to regionalism is the fact that recently many inter-regional and inter-continental regionalism have been formed, or are under discussion and/or negotiation. The first such significant inter-regional regionalism was Asia–Pacific Economic Cooperation (APEC),[9] which has been officially launched in the Asia–Pacific in 1989. In the Americas, the heads of the states agreed upon establishing the Free Trade Area of Americas (FTAA) by 2005, which is now under serious negotiation, involving thirty-four countries in North and South America. The European Union (EU) and the United States, as well, reached an agreement to negotiate on a free trade agreement which is called Transatlantic Free Trade Area (TAFTA).

Such inter-continental regionalism has been pursued for different purposes. For instance, the formation of APEC, in which the United States has played a leading role, was motivated mainly by the intensification of European integration in the mid-1980s. The United States wanted to use APEC as a leverage in negotiations with the EU on further liberalisation of world trade during the Uruguay Round. The discussion on the establishment of the TAFTA was started after the EU–US Summit Meeting in Madrid in December 1995, and through the TAFTA the two parties would like to strengthen the already strong trade and investment ties between them through an approach called "deeper integration".[10] The formation of the FTAA can be regarded as an extension of North American Free Trade Agreement (NAFTA) towards countries belonging to Central and South America, and here again, the United States has been playing a crucial role. In fact, the change in policy directions in the United States around the mid 1980s—from one-sided multilateralism towards two-track approach regarding multilateralism and regionalism as equivalent policy alternatives—seems to have generated increasing cases of such inter-continental regionalism.[11]

[9] The terminology "regionalism" in the context of international law and economics is used usually for cases in which countries form free trade area and/or customs union, as specified in Art. XXIV of the GATT. APEC's approach differs slightly from these notions, because it envisages to achieve "free trade in the region" by 2010 for developed member economies, and 2020 for developing member economies. However, its basic idea is similar to FTAs, so that it could be regarded as quasi-regionalism. See APEC Secretariat, "Implementing the APEC Visioin", Third Report of the Eminent Persons Group (1995).

[10] Deeper integration differs from shallow integration in that the latter is concentrated on reducing tariff and non-tariff barriers, while the former focuses more on harmonising domestic rules and procedures. The Mutual Recognition Agreements (MRAs) and intensified business-to-business relations are major instrument used in the TAFTA approach. For the basic idea of deeper integration see, *inter alia*, P. Robson, *The Economics of International Integration* (London, 3rd ed. 1993); and OECD, *Regionalism and Its Place in Multilateral Trading System* (OECD, 1996).

[11] The Asia–Europe Meeting (ASEM), which was launched as a bilateral co-operation channel among twenty-five countries located in Asia and Europe, can be regarded as a response by the EU on such US approach, even though it is not expected to be developed into an FTA in the near future. For economic background and implication of the ASEM for the multilateral trading system, see Park "The Emergence of ASEM and Its Consistency in the WTO", paper presented at the Second International Conference of the European Union Studies Association of Korea (EUSA-Korea), in collaboration with the EC Delegation to Korea, 14–15 November 1997.

The co-existence of multilateralism and regionalism: background and relationship

Especially since the mid-1980s the increasing tendency towards regionalism coincides with the strengthening of multilateral trading system, which reached its apex in 1995 when the WTO was launched as a result of successfully completed Uruguay Round negotiations. This seemingly contradictory development implies that countries were, on the one hand, making efforts to strengthen multilateralism under the auspices of the GATT. On the other hand, they were at the same time resorting increasingly to regional economic integration.[12] As a consequence, the co-existence of multilateralism and regionalism has become one of the main characteristics of the recent world economy. Even though such situation is expected to sustain for a while, a fundamental question arises as to whether or not regionalism has been and will be detrimental to the multilateral integration process of world economy.

Two conflicting views exist for the relationship between regionalism and multilateralism. One is the view that regionalism has been (and will continue to be) a stumbling block to multilateralism. The other contends that regionalism has been (and will continue to be) a building block to multilateralism. The first view is well summarised by Bhagwati[13] and Bhagwati and Panagariya.[14] They argue that regionalism is detrimental to the multilateral world trading order, and is thus an obstacle to the integration of the world economy, mainly for the following reasons. First, regionalism by itself implies preferential trading arrangements that basically discriminate between members and non-members, not only in enforcing tariff barriers but also by erecting non-tariff barriers, such as rules of origin, regional content requirements, etc. As such, regionalism results in trade diversion. Even though they also expect some trade creation effects as well, the authors argue that trade diversion effect exceeds trade creation effect in almost all cases, and thus results in inefficient allocation of production factors in the world economy. Secondly, if regional integration is at work, then countries will focus more on regional integration efforts and less on the multilateral trading order which is more desirable.[15] Thirdly, scholars who prefer multilateralism refer to historical experiences that the proliferation and strengthening of regionalism, in many cases, have resulted in a serious political

---

[12] This seemingly contradictory posture can be explained by the following two reasons. First, European countries started to establish the Single European Market in the mid-1980s, which motivated countries in other regions to form their own regionalism. Secondly, as Uruguay Round negotiations at that time were not progressing very well, some countries wanted to reap the benefits of liberalisation earlier at regional level. See OECD, above at n. 3.

[13] J. Bhagwati, "Preferential Trade Agreements: The Wrong Road" (1996) 27(4) *Law and Policy in International Business* 865.

[14] J. Bhagwati and A. Panagariya, "Preferential Trading Areas and Multilateralism—Strangers, Friends, or Foe", in J. Bhagwati and A. Panagariya (eds), *The Economics of Preferential Trade Agreements* (AEI Press, Washington, 1996).

[15] This is usually called "interest diversion".

or military conflict between regions or countries. Thus, they are concerned about an excessive proliferation or strengthening of regionalism potentially having negative geopolitical impact in the longer term.

It is interesting to note, however, that many scholars are of an opposing view, arguing that regionalism has had positive effects towards multilateralism.[16] First, they regard regionalism as a building bloc to multilateralism, because they believe regionalism will expand horizons of "freer trade" and thus will inevitably lead to strengthening multilateralism. In other words, in contrast to the former view, the scholars argue that there will be more trade creation than trade diversion. Secondly, these scholars point out that regionalism contributes to the economic development of under-developed economies, in that they are able to gain access to external control mechanisms to continue their domestic reforms, which is necessary for the development process. Thirdly, they point to many cases in which liberalisation measures adopted in regional economic blocs have been successfully transmitted to the multilateral trade negotiations.[17] Fourthly, liberalisation initiatives on the regional level may have a demonstration effect to economic agents of a nation, such as bureaucrats, government, consumers and entrepreneurs, etc., so that an environment facilitating liberalisation is easily created. Finally, as can be conferred from regional integration arrangements such as the EC (Germany versus France), MERCOSUR (Argentina versus Brazil) and APEC (Japan versus China and East Asia), many regional integration arrangements have been created to ease political or military tensions or have effectively generated such results. Thus, the scholars counterargue against the concern that regionalism will increase geopolitical tensions.

It is too early to make a definite decision in favour of one argument against the other. However, almost all scholars and policy makers are of the same position that multilateralism is more beneficial to the world economy than regionalism which divides trade systems according to regions. Also, it is generally recognised that even those who argue for the positive effect of regionalism do have in mind the ultimate contribution of regionalism to the strengthening of multilateralism.[18]

---

[16] For example S. Young, "Globalism and Regionalism: Complements or Competitors?" (Korea Development Institute, Policy Monograph 93-02, Seoul, 1993); F.C. Bergsten, "Competitive Liberalization and Global Free Trade: A Vision for the Early 21st Century" (IIE Working Paper 96-15, 1996).

[17] See also WTO (1995).

[18] Studies conducted independently by the WTO, above at n. 2, and the OECD, above at n. 3, on the relationship between regionalism and multilateralism conclude that regionalism has so far been complementary to multilateralism.

III OPEN REGIONALISM: BACKGROUND, BASIC CONCEPTS AND PRACTICAL
INTERPRETATION

Background of open regionalism

Open regionalism is a concept that has been raised and discussed actively in the context of economic co-operation in the Asia–Pacific region.[19] It can be understood as a concept that was born in a world economic environment where opposing systems of multilateralism and regionalism co-exist. As noted above the world economy experienced two waves of regionalism since World War II, first in the 1970s and then in the 1990s. In both cases, regional integration arrangements in which European countries are members accounted for a major part.[20]

In the context of relationship between regionalism and multilateralism, RIAs which emerged after mid 1980s deserve more attention. During the first stage of Uruguay Round negotiations in the late 1980s,[21] European Community has started its initiative to create the Single European Market by early 1993, leading to deepening and widening of European integration. This has prompted other regions and countries to adopt strategic counter-measures and create regional economic blocs of their own.

Another very important stimulus for the emergence of this new regionalism was provided by the change in the policy direction of the United States around the mid-1980s. In fact, the United States was traditionally regarded as a guardian of multilateralism, playing leadership role in the liberalisation of world trade and global integration of world economy ever since the creation of the GATT. However, the United States showed increasing interest in regionalism since the beginning of 1980s when Europe gained more economic "clout" in the world through its ambitious economic integration programmes. For example, since the mid-1980s the United States has intensified its effort to participate in regional integration arrangements, including the FTAs with Israel and Canada, which came into effect in 1985 and 1989, respectively. Also, APEC, which can be considered as a quasi-regionalism initiative, was created in 1989, in which the United States exercised a strong influence. The NAFTA, which inaugurated in 1994, has now become the first pillar of US regionalism policy.

Parallel to a strong move towards regionalism, the United States has also been looking for ways to overcome the proliferation of regionalism. In this respect, United States has been striking a certain degree of balance between multilateralism and regionalism in its external policy, and has adopted this approach

[19] According to Garnaut, above at n. 7, the concept was first articulated by the Pacific Economic Cooperation Conference (PECC) in 1980, and then continuously adopted by APEC as an ideal for the future development of economic co-operation within Asia–Pacific region.
[20] See WTO, above at n. 2, Appendix Table 1.
[21] The Uruguay Round had originally targeted 1989 to conclude the negotiations, but it this was extended to 1993.

because it had to establish a mechanism to counter deepening and widening of European integration.[22] Also, from a political and politico-economic point of view, the United States was not ready to be criticised as discarding multilateralism for national interest. These conflicting interests have led the United States to adopt a two-track strategy. As the result, United States has strengthened its participation in FTA agreements, on the one hand, and has adopted a strategy to use APEC as a tool to overcome regionalism, on the other.[23] Under these circumstances, the Eminent Person's Group (EPG) within APEC, which was formed by the initiative of the United States, proposed to adopt open regionalism as the basic concept of APEC.

As can be deduced from the objective of balancing multilateralism and regionalism, the basic spirit of open regionalism in APEC needs to be understood from a different perspective than the concept of regionalism that is stipulated in Article XXIV of the GATT. The objective of open regionalism in APEC is to contribute to world trade liberalisation by extending the benefits of trade liberalization measures implemented within the area of APEC to non-members. However, such unilateral liberalisation cannot be successfully exercised by APEC so far, because APEC member countries have yet to reach an agreement on the modality of implementing open regionalism. If it fails to do so, APEC's open regionalism runs the risk of becoming an "oxymoron", which embodies two seemingly contradictory concepts of openness and regionalism.

Basic concepts of open regionalism

Basic operational concepts of open regionalism in the context of APEC have been defined first by APEC's EPG in its second report,[24] and by Bergsten.[25] Garnaut[26] and Park[27] also elaborated basic concepts of open regionalism and its (potential) contribution to multilateral trading system. For the purpose of discussion in this chapter, three alternative definitions of open regionalism are presented and discussed below.

---

[22] As soon as the EC announced that it will create a common market in Europe by 1993 with the adoption of the Single European Act in the early 1980s, the United States and Japan expressed concern about "Fortress Europe".

[23] A similar analysis can be found in Garnaut, above at n. 7.

[24] The EPG interprets open regionalism as achieved if at least one of the following four conditions are fulfilled: (1) the maximum possible extent of unilateral liberalisation; (2) a commitment to continue reducing its barriers ro non-member countries; (3) a willingness to extend its regional liberalisation to non-members on a mutually reciprocal basis; (4) voluntary unilateral liberalisation and unconditional MFN. See APEC Secretariat, "Achieving the APEC Visioin" (Second Report of the Eminent Persons Group, 1994). For a more detailed discussion of these four criteria, see S.-H. Park, "Making APEC's Open Regionalism Consistent with the WTO" (Korea Institute for International Economic Policy, Survey Report 98-06, APEC Study Series 7, 1998) (in Korean).

[25] Bergsten, above at n. 6. Bergsten presented five operational definitions of open regionalism as follows: (1) open membership; (2) unconditional MFN; (3) conditional MFN; (4) global liberalisation; (5) trade facilitation. For a more detailed discussion of these definitions see Park, above at n. 24.

[26] Garnaut, above at n. 7.

[27] Park, above at n. 8.

1. *Unconditional MFN and unilateral liberalisation*

The interpretation of open regionalism as an instrument to adopt unconditional MFN principle implies that APEC's liberalisation will be implemented without introducing any new exclusive benefits for members and any new discrimination against non-members. As mentioned above, at the time of formulation of the concept of open regionalism, the foremost concern was that it should be in line with provisions of Article XXIV of the GATT. In other words, the significance of this interpretation lies in the fact that it could ease the concern of outsiders that APEC may become closed in nature by too much emphasis on internal economic integration than on multilateral negotiations on liberalisation.

However, this interpretation has faced both internal and external problems in implementation. Internally, there is still a gap between the interests of the group of developing member economies and developed member economies. Therefore, it is not clear whether all APEC members will be willing to agree on unilateral liberalisation measures, without securing reciprocal liberalisation by major trading partners, such as the EU. Externally, if this definition were adopted officially, APEC does not possess any effective mechanism to control free-riding countries that want to enjoy the benefits of APEC's liberalisation measures without any reciprocal commitment to liberalisation.

2. *Conditional MFN and reciprocal liberalisation*

The purpose of this interpretation is to provide an answer to the moral hazard issue that accompanies free riding. If APEC adopts this definition, APEC will apply measures to liberalise internal trade flows on a reciprocal basis to countries (regions) that have committed similar liberalisation levels or conditions. Bergsten estimated that many trading partners would be willing to accept this concept, which will lead a very positive relationship between regionalism, open regionalism and multilateralism. He predicted global liberalisation led by the WTO to be eventually realised through the application of conditional MFN treatment.

However, the concept of conditional MFN will be faced with obstacles, if such major trading countries as the EU refuse to accept reciprocal liberalisation. The fundamental limitation of this interpretation is whether APEC develops into a regional integration agreement, such as an FTA and a CU, because GATT allows only these two RIAs to be exceptions to MFN treatment. Therefore, APEC in the current status does not possess any legal instrument that can effectively confine the benefits of liberalisation among APEC member countries. Thus, if APEC, which did not reach the status of an FTA or a CU, tries to achieve liberalisation within APEC and does not extend the internal liberalisation to non-member countries, it will violate provisions of Article I of the GATT.

Therefore, in order to be able to adopt conditional MFN as an operational definition of open regionalism, APEC does have only two options. First, APEC should eventually be developed into an FTA or a CU as defined in Article XXIV of the GATT, and then adopt one of the two strategies: first, APEC should concentrate on internal liberalisation without expecting reciprocal liberalisation by other trading partners; secondly, APEC should reach out to major trading partners and negotiate agreements to establish FTAs and/or CUs. Among the two, the second strategy could be offered as a way effectively to realise an open regionalism concept.

The second option for APEC to adopt before reaching the status of an FTA or a CU is to begin its effort to revise the provisions of Article XXIV of the GATT. Especially in the context of open regionalism, the priority of APEC's efforts could be placed on the issue of allowing liberalisation based on reciprocity. If this is possible without concluding FTA or CU agreements, then it could contribute potentially to multilateral integration of world trade by widening the horizons of freer trade and overlapping regions in which trade flows are liberalised.

3. Global liberalisation

Where the liberalisation timetable of APEC is implemented in line with that of the WTO, the concept of open regionalism is implemented in the form of "global liberalisation". Bergsten[28] suggested that if open regionalism is interpreted in this way, the emergence of any new discrimination factors by way of APEC may be controlled. So far, this interpretation has been adopted by APEC in two liberalisation schemes, leading to different results: It has proved successful in the case of the Information Technology Agreement (ITA), which was first negotiated within APEC and brought to the WTO for multilateral negotiation , and then officially launched in February 1997 within the WTO. It proved a failure in the case of early voluntary sectoral liberalisation (EVSL) approach, which was a major item of APEC agenda in 1998, due mainly to differing interests of member countries in the speed and scope of liberalisation in nine selected industries.

Even though this operational definition of open regionalism possesses the potential to play a crucial role in facilitating global trade liberalisation in the future, its successful implementation depends on several factors. First, an agreement among APEC member countries on the speed and coverage of liberalisation should be secured. Secondly, after reaching internal agreements, APEC should make efforts to convince as many trading partners as possible to secure the so-called "critical mass" ready to participate in liberalisation deals. In this context, global liberalisation through open regionalism will be possible only in specific sectors.

---

[28] Bergsten, above at n. 16.

Attempts to implement open regionalism within APEC

Even though almost ten years have passed since APEC was created, it seems that APEC failed so far to find an appropriate operational definition of open regionalism or agree on a detailed modality to implement open regionalism in its external relationships. Instead, APEC appears to have experimented with diverse concepts of implementing open regionalism in its short history as follows.

First attempt: unconditional MFN

At the initial stage of APEC's substantial progress in official economic co-operation, which was around the time of its first Summit Meeting held in Seattle in 1993, APEC pursued open regionalism based on the principle of unconditional MFN as proposed by the EPG in its second report. However, this initiative failed to gain momentum because of the rising concern about free riding by non-member countries. The developing member countries of APEC were also not ready to accept an extensive liberalisation package, even within APEC, and were therefore unwilling to adopt unilateral liberalisation which could be extended unconditionally to non-members of APEC.

Second attempt: conditional MFN

A second attempt by APEC to implement open regionalism was based on the principle of conditional MFN, which accommodated the opposing position of some member countries. However, APEC met with another obstacle in this attempt, because a step was needed before the implementation was made possible under the provisions of Article XXIV of the GATT. In other words, under the condition that APEC did not develop itself into an FTA or a CU, it was not at all possible for APEC practically to apply conditional MFN treatment to non-members. The declaration adopted in Bogor Summit Meeting in 1994 (Bogor Declaration) did not suffice to provide APEC with the legal status of FTA or CU. If APEC had adopted a clear vision of developing such a RIA, its attempt to implement open regionalism in the form of conditional MFN would have been possible, especially through conclusion of agreements to establish an FTA or a CU with non-members.

Third attempt: concerted unilateral liberalisation

A third attempt by APEC to exercise open regionalism was the so-called "concerted unilateral liberalisation" approach. Instead of pursuing agreed liberalisation, APEC opted to pursue liberalisation in a "concerted" way in a move to address concerns about free riding and to be in line with the WTO rules. The concrete steps taken by the member countries were to prepare individual action plans (IAPs) and to agree on collective action plans (CAPs) to liberalise trade and investment at individual level and collectively, as agreed upon in the Osaka Summit Meeting in 1995. In other words, at this stage APEC pursued voluntary and non-binding liberalisation, and wanted to extend such initiatives to non-members, with the hope that both problems of free riding and "unconformity with the WTO rules" will be solved at the same time.

Even though APEC member countries welcomed this method, it also met with many limitations, mainly due to the inherent ambiguity of such non-binding procedures and the inability to reach an agreement on the basic issue of the degree of "concertation". In reality, some member countries' IAPs only contained liberalisation steps which they committed in the framework of the WTO, with the hope of enjoying the free-rider status by taking advantage of the ambiguous situation, leading to a failure of this liberalisation programme.

Fourth attempt: early voluntary sectoral liberalisation

The APEC member countries have come to realise that they need to be more specific on the degree of bindingness in order to address the problem of ambiguity. Thus, in 1988 APEC adopted early voluntary sectoral liberalisation (EVSL)[29] which is an advanced form of concerted liberalisation with detailed procedures of liberalisation specified and a degree of binding elements. Fifteen (nine for 1998 and six for 1999) sectors were selected as candidate sectors for which liberalisation of trade within APEC should first be proceeded. If APEC members had agreed upon the coverage and speed of liberalisation in these selected sectors, this then would have been transferred to the multilateral negotiation channels, such as the WTO, for negotiations to achieve global liberalisation using the APEC's liberalisation package as a leverage.

However, in the process of selecting the sectors for early liberalisation, sharp disagreements among member countries have been observed. In addition, even after the agreement was reached on the sectors to be liberalised, disagreement among member countries on the coverage and extent of liberalisation was prevalent. Due to these difficulties and the reluctance, especially of Japan, to accept liberalisation in fisheries and forestry, the EVSL package could not be adopted officially in the Kuala Lumpur Summit Meeting of APEC in 1998. Had the EVSL package brought about success in liberalising the selected fifteen sectors, it would have been the second success of such attempt, the first being the Information Technology Agreement (ITA) of 1997. In fact, ITA was only possible because there had already been an agreement, albeit unofficial, among the member countries of the Quad (the US, Canada, Japan and the EU), before it

---

[29] As was the case with the ITA in the WTO, the procedure of this interpretation is to initiate global liberalisation by reaching an agreement at a certain level within APEC or creating a critical mass through APEC, first, and then negotiating with non-APEC members through the WTO prior to implementing the liberalisation measures. See C.-S. Kim, "Early Voluntary Sectoral Liberalization: Current Status and Korea's Response", paper presented at the policy seminar, Korea Institute for International Economic Policy, April 1998 (in Korean).

was negotiated within APEC. In the case of EVSL package, such pre-agreement among the major trading countries was practically non-existing, and some member countries feared about free-rider problems, in case EVSL failed to bring about global liberalisation in these selected sectors.

IV PROVISIONS OF THE GATT/WTO ON RIAs: WHETHER AND WHAT TO CHANGE

In line with the emergence of the concept of open regionalism, regionalism-related GATT provisions including Article XXIV are subject to controversy about whether and how to reform. A reason for this controversy is that the procedural specifications in these provisions work only to the extent that the drafters of the GATT intended.[30] Considering the potential contribution of open regionalism to bringing about multilateral integration of world trade, this section investigates whether the GATT provisions on RIAs should be reformed to accommodate such new developments in the world economy.

GATT/WTO provisions on RIAs

GATT, Article XXIV

Article XXIV of the GATT constitutes a central article of the multilateral trading system on RIAs. It contains several specifications on the conditions of RIAs to be allowed as exceptions to the MFN principle. These specifications mainly aim at minimising the negative effects of RIAs on the member countries of the GATT/WTO. The main provisions stipulated in Article XXIV are:

1. The establishment of a free trade area is acceptable under the GATT so long as its purpose is *to facilitate trade within the region* and not to raise barriers to trade with outside economies (Article XXIV:4).
2. Duties and other restrictive regulations of commerce *shall not be on the whole higher or more restrictive* than the corresponding duties and other regulations of commerce existing in the same constituent territories prior to the formation of the free trade area (Article XXIV: 5b).[31]
3. Duties and other restrictive regulations of commerce shall be *eliminated on substantially all trade* between the constituent territories in respect of products originating in such territories (Article XXIV: 8b).
4. Entry into an FTA shall be *promptly notified to* the GATT/WTO (Article XXIV: 7a).

---

[30] Until 1994, over sixty nine previous working parties on individual CUs or FTAs had been unable to reach unanimous conclusions as to the GATT's consistency of those agreements. On the other hand, no such agreements have been explicitly disapproved.

[31] With respect to CUs, they shall not, on the whole, higher or more restrictive than the general incidence of duties and regulations before the CU was formed (Art. XXIV:5a).

5. Any interim agreement shall include a plan and schedule for the formation of FTA or CU *within a reasonable length of time* (Article XXIV: 5c).[32]
6. If any country imposes higher tariffs on non-members than before the forming of CU, it should *compensate* for them (Article XXIV: 6).

The basic idea behind provisions in Article XXIV is that the GATT will, in principle, permit discrimination but only in return for full fledged liberalisation among the members of an FTA or a CU. A violation of the principle of MFN treatment can, therefore, only be accepted if the countries involved in any RIAs are willing to liberalise "substantially all trade" within the RIAs. Furthermore, external tariffs should not be raised by countries concluding FTAs, and in the case of CUs the common external tariffs of the group toward third countries should not "on the whole" be more restrictive than the "general incidence of" duties and regulations before the CU was formed. The rules also allow these conditions to be met gradually. They particularly allow for "an interim agreement"—, i.e. one that leads to a CU or an FTA "within a reasonable time"—to depart from these provisions. Finally, the GATT requires countries to notify all such final and interim agreements for examination by a working party to ensure their conformity with GATT rules. It is not necessary for agreements to be explicitly approved—they may be implemented unless the working party formally objects.

Enabling Clause

Regional agreements among less-developed economies are accorded special treatment, through the so-called Enabling Clause agreed upon in the Tokyo Round in 1979. The purpose of the Enabling Clause is to enable developing economies to overcome their underdevelopment and carry out their duties as GATT members after achieving their economic development.

1. A mutual reduction or elimination of tariffs and non-tariff measures may be permitted notwithstanding the provision of the GATT, Article I (paragraph 2).
2. Members shall not raise barriers to, or create undue difficulties for, the trade of any other contracting parties (paragraph 3).
3. The arrangement shall not constitute an impediment to the reduction or elimination of tariff and non-tariff barriers on an MFN basis.
4. Members shall notify the arrangement to the WTO (paragraph 4).
5. The contracting parties shall afford adequate opportunity for prompt consultation.

The Enabling Clause does not direct any specific forms of RIAs, such as FTAs or CUs, so arguably any form of RIAs might be permitted under this Clause.

---

[32] During the Uruguay Round, the "Understanding on the Interpretation of Article XXIV of GATT 1994" was adopted, which states that "a reasonable length of time should exceed ten years only in exception cases".

The provision by developed countries of the Generalised System of Preferences (GSP) to underdeveloped nations has been possible based on this Clause. It appears that the provisions in the Enabling Clause contain more ambiguous and loose rules than the Article XXIV.

Article V of the GATS

The General Agreement on Trade in Services (GATS) was a product of Uruguay Round negotiations, and specifies the articles on multilateral rules on trade in services. As the Article I of the GATT, the Article II of the GATS provides for the principle of non-discrimination. However, Article V of the GATS specifies conditions of exceptions to the MFN principle, as Article XXIV of the GATT does so to the unconditional MFN principle.

Under Article V of the GATS, RIAs are allowed, provided such agreements:

1. have substantial sectoral coverage (Article V:1.a); and
2. provide for the absence or elimination of substantially all discrimination between or among the parties, in the sectors covered under (1), or prohibition of new or more discriminatory measures (Article V:1.b).

In addition, Article V confers flexibility on the developing countries as follows:

1. Where developing countries are parties to an agreement of the above type, flexibility shall be provided for in accordance with the level of development of the parties concerned, both overall and in individual sectors and sub-sectors (Article V:3).
2. An agreement shall not, in respect of any member outside the agreement, raise the overall level of barriers to trade in services within the respective sectors compared to the level applicable prior to such an agreement (Article V: 4).

As mentioned above, what Article V of the GATS regulates is generally similar to its GATT counterpart in Article XXIV. However, there are two important differences between the two. First, provisions in Article V of the GATS apply to individual sectors and sub-sectors, whereas provisions in Article XXIV of the GATT explicitly require newly introduced tariffs and non-tariff barriers be "not on the whole higher or more restrictive". Secondly, the rules for RIAs to be found in Article V of the GATS seem, as a whole, to be weaker than those in the GATT, considering the fact that, in the GATS, no liberalisation in services is explicitly required for an agreement to be acceptable. Rather, a simple standstill on existing measures is sufficient according to Article 1:b of the GATS.

Proposals to reform GATT/WTO provisions

In the context of increasing regionalism in world economy, especially since the beginning of 1990s, and of increasing complexity in the institutional relationship between regionalism and multilateralism, many proposals have been put forward to reform the GATT/WTO provisions concerning regionalism. These proposals stem from the observation that the existing rules are not the first-best ones, or are not sufficient in restricting the prevalence of regionalism. The major line of criticism is focused on the following five aspects.

(1) Requirement to liberalise "substantially all trade"

The requirement to liberalise "substantially all trade" within an RIA has been criticised by several analysts. For Bhagwati[33] this notion needs clarification because it is not clearly defined how much "all" is "substantially" all. This ambiguity is likely to lead to loopholes, thereby contributing to exclusion in related agreements of sensitive sectors such as agriculture and steel. To avoid this kind of loopholes, it is suggested that the notion be changed into a phrase that requires liberalisation of "all the trade". Setting a certain percentage, for instance 80 per cent or 90 per cent, of liberalisation across all sectors can also be considered as an alternative to the "all the trade" requirement suggested by Bhagwati.

Although there is a need to clarify "substantially all trade" requirement, and the two suggestions of reform discussed above will contribute to successfully mitigating regionalist tendency of the current world economy, they also entail shortcomings. Bhagwati's suggestion, for instance, seems to be too ambitious and idealistic, and it is also uncertain whether a total elimination of trade restrictions will increase overall welfare.[34] If adopted by the WTO, Bhagwati's suggestion is also expected to give rise to unfair treatment between the existing and new regionalism. Moreover, it considers only the liberalisation aspect of RIAs, thus leading to insufficient consideration of deep integration, which is also one of the main effects of regional economic integration.

The suggestion to liberalise 80 per cent or 90 per cent of total trade among member countries of an RIA may be in line with the welfare argument raised by Frankel,[35] which established an econometric model generating more favourable welfare effects through partial liberalisation rather than through a total liberalisation. However, it also entails problems. Trade volume in one sector is not the result of one single factor—"trade impediments"—but of many factors influenc-

---

[33] J. Bhagwati, "Regionalism and multilateralism: an overview", in J. de Melo and A. Panagariya (eds), *New Dimension in Regional Integration* (Cambridge University Press, 1993).

[34] The analysis by J. Frankel, *Regional Trading Blocs* (Institute of International Economics, 1997) is illustrative in this respect. His econometric model generates a more favourable welfare effects in case of partial liberalisation than in case of total liberalisation. Based on this result, he argues that a removal of 100 % intra-bloc trade barriers may not need strict enforcement, although he recognises the danger of accepting partial liberalisation as a rule.

[35] Frankel, ibid.

ing trade relations. Consequently, it will not be easy to identify the product lines, for which tariffs should be eliminated, to come to the specified percentage. Also, shifts in demand and supply may affect the trade flows differently, which will also make it quite impossible to reach the exact value of 80 per cent or 90 per cent of all trade.

Considering the merits and shortcomings of these reform suggestions, the "substantially all trade" requirement might be interpreted as incorporating "constructive ambiguity", which effectively prevents countries from applying selective and/or sectoral liberalisation in just a few areas. This effect is expected also to strengthen if the international organisation, which possesses the power of ruling and enforcement, has enough authority to judgment on it. Therefore, it seems that the problem we have currently is not the ambiguity incorporated in the "substantially all trade" requirement, but that we have not yet found an appropriate governance system for regionalism to prevent the misuse of the existing rules.[36]

(2) Requirement for new trade restrictions to be "not on the whole higher"

The requirement to be "not on the whole higher or more restrictive" concerns, in principle, the trade diversion effects to non-members of an RIA, and has been a more controversial issue. Preferential treatment provided to a partner country of an RIA leads to a reduction of demand for products from non-member countries even though external tariffs are not raised. Besides the compensation in case of raising external tariff rates, the GATT fails to address such trade diversion and ignores the impacts such arrangements might have on outsiders even when they do not raise external tariffs.

One way to effectively avoid trade diversion was proposed by McMillan,[37] who suggested that any RIAs have to design external barriers, so that trade volume with outsiders remains at least at the old level. With agreements leading to FTAs or CUs which inherently contain preferential market access provisions to member countries, this would be possible by a corresponding reduction of external barriers. Along the same line with this proposal is the one raised by Bhagwati,[38] suggesting that the lowest pre-union tariff be adopted as a common external tariff.[39] By eliminating the effects of trade diversion, this proposal would confine the effects of preferential agreements to trade creation, leading to improvement of welfare for the countries involved. Another merit of this proposal is that it will provide the members of RIAs with an incentive to continue expanding membership of the agreement until all the important trading partners

---

[36] Whether the Committee on Regional Trading Arrangement (CRTA), which is established within the WTO, can take up this task, needs still to be proved.

[37] McMillan, above at n. 4.

[38] Bhagwati, above at n. 33.

[39] Adopting this rule would make countries with low tariffs less attractive partners for a CU, and would thus lead to a reduction in the number of RIAs. However, high-tariff countries will also be inclined to form CU, strengthening the trade diversion effect.

are included. If adopted by the WTO as a governing principle of regionalism, and the effect mentioned above comes to be realised, then this proposal has the potential to become an important instrument to widen the possibility for regionalism to become open regionalism, which leads eventually to the strengthening of multilateralism.

However, this prescription also confronts with both conceptual and practical problems. In reality, in order to implement McMillan's suggestion, countries should know, prior to the agreement, what kind of compensation they would have to pay. But, beforehand, there will inevitably be greater uncertainty about the extent of trade diversion likely to occur. Moreover, after the agreement comes into effect, separating the effects occurring because of the trade-diverting aspects of the agreement from other economic changes will be difficult, because a reduction in imports from the rest of the world may be influenced by other factors as well. Also, RIAs could have dynamic effects that lead to increased intra-RIA investment flows and to accelerated economic growth. In the long run, therefore, outsiders could gain from increased imports induced by higher income generated by these dynamic effects even though in the short term they may lose as a result of trade diversion.

Considering the merits and shortcomings of suggested reform proposals, one cannot easily make a final decision about whether the provisions should really be reformed. If the GATT rule is maintained, it should be regarded as a minimum restriction on new RIAs. A reduction of external tariffs is desirable in global liberalisation, but in the current setting that is what the RIAs by themselves have to decide, either in a voluntary manner or influenced by pressure from trading partners. Here, the potential of open regionalism to contribute to the strengthening of multilateralism can be identified: if there is a sufficient number   of countries willing to exchange liberalisation, members of an RIA may be peer-pressured to do the same, thus leading regionalism open to outsiders.[40]

(3) Distinction between CUs and FTAs

Article XXIV of the GATT allows for both FTAs and CUs. Krueger[41] has proposed that only customs unions be allowed, "because rules of origin . . . extend the protection accorded by each country to producers in other FTA member countries . . . they can constitute a source of bias toward economic inefficiency in FTAs in a way they cannot do with customs unions".

Members of FTAs differ in their external tariffs. They are normally confronted with the problem that, without rules of origin, imports from outside the

---

[40] This will be possible if the WTO allows reciprocal liberalisation as one of governing principles of regionalism, as discussed in Part III above.

[41] A.O. Krueger, "Free Trade Agreements versus Customs Unions" (National Bureau of Economic Research Working Paper 5084, Cambridge, 1995).

free trade area could be brought into the low-tariff countries and then shipped duty free to members with higher tariffs.[42] Rules of origin that define eligibility for duty-free access for members of an FTA provide an opportunity for raising barriers against outsiders while leaving tariff levels unchanged.[43] Krueger also argues that the existence of rules of origin in which insiders are protected is likely to give firms a vested interest in maintaining protectionism and thus reduce the willingness of an FTA to engage in external liberalisation. This would suggest that only CUs should be permitted by the GATT rules for preferential arrangements.

Adopting this suggestion would lead many countries potentially willing to join an FTA to discard the idea, because they do not want to give up independent trade policies, which will in turn contribute to reducing the regionalist tendency. Therefore, it is not hard to conjecture that had such a rule been in effect, NAFTA would never have been concluded. It would surely be preferable to constrain FTAs in their ability to use these rules to meet the protectionist demands of certain industries.

However, the proposal ignores an important advantage of FTAs, namely that members can mitigate the harmful effects of trade diversion by lowering their barriers toward the outside world. Indeed, since trade diversion is harmful not only to outsiders but also to members of an FTA, countries have an incentive to do precisely that, under the condition that they find partners willing to exchange this liberalisation. A tentative conclusion concerning rules of origin is that even though the problem of rules of origin is an important one, dealing with it through banning FTAs is too extreme a solution. One approach that would allow FTAs to remain in conformity with the spirit of the GATT would be to permit only a single definition of rules of origin applicable for all products.[44]

(4) Enabling Clause and Article V of the GATS

The provision in the 1979 Enabling Clause, which exempts integration agreements among developing countries from the requirements laid down in Article XXIV of the GATT, is another source of concern related to WTO's rules on RIAs, leading to potential conflicts between the two provisions. For example, a heated debate was observed between Argentina, Brazil and Uruguay, on the one hand, and many developed countries, on the other, as to whether MERCOSUR

---

[42] That is called "trade deflection" or "circumvention".

[43] Over the years, different ways of defining origin have been used. The OECD, above at n. 10, identifies three such procedures: change of tariff heading, requirement of specific processes to be completed, and value-added. Customs authorities have generally opted for combinations of the different approaches in order to balance the objectives of predictability and flexibility against the minimum costs in implementing the rules.

[44] The EPG of APEC has proposed a series of characteristics of rules of origin for APEC, which can be benchmarked by any other RIAs. According to the EPG, rules of origin supporting free trade should be simple, transparent and applicable across-the-board, as well as contain substantial transformation rule.

agreements should be notified to the GATT under Article XXIV or under the Enabling Clause.[45] Recently, however, as developing countries increasingly adopt outward-looking development strategy, they regard the provisions of Article XXIV of the GATT as an instrument to lock in recent policy reforms. This has led to a reduction of tensions between developing and developed members of the WTO.

It was noteworthy that, despite the increasing number of RIAs at the time when the Uruguay Round was concluded, the rules for regional integration laid out in the GATS were considerably weaker than those to be found in the GATT. They only have provision on "substantial sectoral coverage", and this appears to be far more lenient than the requirement to liberalise "substantially all trade" for goods. Furthermore, in the GATS no liberalisation in services is required for an agreement to be acceptable. Instead, a simple standstill on existing measures is regarded as sufficient, because the GATS provision stipulates that participating countries should ensure elimination of existing discriminatory measures *or* prohibition of new or more discriminatory provisions. One explanation for this loose condition in the GATS is that the GATS had been worded with a view to ensuring that all existing RIAs be consistent with it.[46] However, this approach does not justify the substantial imbalance between conditions for the goods sector and those for the services sector.

(5) Enforcement and surveillance

A fundamental problem attached to many proposals raised is that they do not take into account the fact that in practice the GATT has not been effective in enforcing the strict rules contained in Article XXIV. Indeed, although many FTAs have excluded agriculture and numerous other sectors, they have not been rejected by the GATT. The GATT has also not been strict enough in enforcing the rules relating to transition periods. Some agreements have such long periods for implementation that they can justify discriminatory treatment without full internal liberalisation for extensive periods. In addition, many agreements between developing countries have not come closer to meeting the GATT rules at all.[47] This is unfortunate because failure to meet these rules can lead to agreements that are potentially attractive but which increase trade diversion. In this respect, it is to be welcomed that the "Understanding" has addressed this issue by specifying that the "within a reasonable length of time" is to mean, in principle, within ten years.

---

[45] See WTO, above at n. 2.

[46] See R. Lawrence, *Regionalism, Multilateralism and Deeper Integration* (Brooking Institution, 1996).

[47] See J.M. Finger, "GATT's influence on Regional Arrangements", in J. de Melo and A. Panagariya (eds), *New Dimension in Regional Integration* (Cambridge University Press, 1993).

V   CONCLUSION

This chapter investigated the increasing tendency towards regionalism, the emergence of open regionalism as a concept to overcome regionalist tendency, and discussed major contents and problems of the GATT/WTO provisions relating to regionalism. It identified open regionalism as a potential way of over-coming regionalism and promoting multilateral trading system. However, it was also pointed out that the current practices of APEC in implementing open regionalism are faced with two imminent problems, the free-rider problem, on the one hand, and violation of MFN principles, on the other.

The chapter has drawn the following conclusions from the discussion so far. First, major problems facing the GATT in relation with regionalism seem not to be found in the specific paragraphs of GATT, Article XXIV, but in other WTO rules, such as the GATS and Enabling Clause. They should be revised so as to ensure transparency and balance between goods and services sectors, as well as between the interests of developing countries and developed countries.

Secondly, another source of concern was identified in the insufficiently specified mechanism of enforcement of provisions relating to regionalism.[48] The newly established CRTA is a welcomed decision, but it needs to be provided with stronger hands to monitor, investigate and under certain circumstances, prevent the operation of RIAs.

Thirdly, considering the potential contribution of the concept of open region-alism to expanding the horizons of liberalised trade within the multilateral trad-ing system, this chapter cautiously proposed reciprocal liberalisation, among RIAs or involving RIAs on the one side, to be established as one of governing rules of Article XXIV of the GATT. However, a strong condition has to be attached to this provision, such that it should lead to RIAs being opened to non-members, which will contribute to the expanding and overlapping of horizons of freer trade within the multilateral trading system. This is expected to strengthen multilateralism, rather than regionalism in the world economy.

---

[48] The WTO Secretariat, above at n. 2, suggested three measures to be established to reinforce the transparency and surveillance of Art. XXIV: (1) establishment of a common forum, within which individual agreements can be examined; (2) revival of biennial reporting of the developments of RIAs and preparation of standard format of reports; and (3) establishment of a periodic moni-toring exercise covering all regional agreements.

13

*Economic Law Reform Dealing With the Asian Financial Turmoil**

ZHANG YUEJIAO

The crisis that struck Thailand, Indonesia, South Korea and much of Southern Asia in the second half of 1997 had adverse economic, financial and social impacts on these affected countries and regions of the world. Meanwhile, it has produced much literature, explanation and scholarly debate. From different angles, academics and practitioners have written analytical papers on how the "Asian miracle" suddenly became a financial crisis. As a result, they have drawn lessons for recovery and future improvement in order to ensure sustainable development in Asia. Most of these papers focused on economic and financial aspects and institutional structural reforms of Asian Financial Turmoil.

This chapter focuses on the legal aspects of the Asian financial crisis and attempts to draw some lessons learned on legal reforms in Asia and in other regions of the world. The chapter is divided into three parts: Part I is a briefing on the evolution of the Asian financial turmoil and analysis of its causes; Part II focuses on law reforms relating to company law, insolvency law and banking reform and regulations; Part III presents the Asian Development Bank's efforts in assisting its developing member countries (DMCs) to deal with financial and bank restructuring and law reforms in order to help crisis-affected economies recover from the Asian financial crisis as quickly as possible.

I ASIAN FINANCIAL TURMOIL

Evolution of the Asian financial turmoil

The Asian financial crisis began on 2 July 1997 when the Thai baht was floated. It depreciated by 15 per cent in the first week alone. The crisis spread quickly to

* The following observations of Zhang Yuejiao reflect her personal views and do not represent an official position of the Asian Development Bank or any of its officers. Based on a number of articles published in the Annual Reports of the Asian Development Bank, articles and speeches at the High Level Regional Workshop on the Asian Financial Crisis in March 1999, and informal consultation on the Asian Financial Crisis held at the Bank in October 1998.

the Philippines and Indonesia and, by mid-October, it moved north-east to the Republic of Korea. The Korean currency had depreciated up to 70 per cent compared to the US dollar. In mid-November the crisis moved back to South-East Asia to Indonesia, and then to Russia and to some Latin-American countries, affecting one-fifth of the world's GDP. It is estimated that the downward revision translates into an output loss of $600–800 billion, most of it attributable to the Asian financial turmoil.

Since much of the Asian success story depended on export-led growth, it is understandable that any slow-down in international trade would affect these economies more than other economies. Due to the sudden reduction of foreign exchange reserves, huge debt burdens of companies and the larger-than-estimated number of countries affected, imports of the affected economies have been reduced tremendously. The initial years of trade surplus and high export growth had motivated many of these economies to invest heavily in real estate steel industries, and semi-conductors. Consequently, excess capacity of these exporting countries and slackening of world demand had an adverse effect on the exports of these countries. The terms of trade became worse and exports further slowed down.

In addition, the social impact of the Asian financial crisis is significant. In the very short period between 1997–1998, the official unemployment rate rose from 6.7 per cent to 15 per cent in Indonesia, from 1 per cent to 9 per cent in Thailand, and in South Korea to 7.6 per cent. Poverty has increased accordingly.

Causes of the Asian financial turmoil

The Asian financial turmoil has revived the long-standing debate on two competing views of currency crisis: one view regards crises as emanating from macroeconomic fundamentals, while the other view blames self-fulfilling prophecies and financial panics. A preliminary consensus has now emerged on the crisis of the confidence-cum-structural weakness view. First, it was a crisis of confidence—a capital account crisis, not the traditional type of current account crisis. Secondly, its root causes were structural, namely premature financial liberalisation (liberalisation of financial markets prior to the institution of adequate supervision and regulation), capitalism and policy mistakes in managing private capital inflows—and not macroeconomic fundamentals. The crisis involves private-to-private capital flows, not fiscal profligacy, monetary expansion or sovereign debt. Thirdly, it was a liquidity crisis.[1]

The Asian Development Bank study shows that many Asian economies had records of rapid economic growth in combination with relative openness of the economy that attracted significant capital inflows, which fueled further growth.

---

[1] "The East Asian Financial Crisis-Issues in designing and sequencing macroeconomic policies— A Regional Macroeconomic Policy Paper based on RETA 5770", study of financial markets in selected member countries for a high-level regional workshop on the Asian Financial Crisis, 25–26 March 1999.

These economies also had access to a large pool of domestic resources supported by savings rates in the range of 35–40 per cent of gross domestic product (GDP). However, there were a number of financial sector weaknesses such as underdeveloped bond markets, poor corporate governance, lack of regulation and supervision of financial sectors. The crisis has demonstrated that these capital flows were not managed properly in the affected economies.[2]

Inefficient banking sectors

In many affected Asian countries, big banks are state-owned and large state-owned banks become structurally disadvantaged for a number of reasons, for example: badly performing portfolios resulting from directed lending to state-owned enterprises with heavy debts; policy motivated lending and social lending requirements; large numbers of redundant employees; strong union influence; and large inefficient branch networks.

Underdeveloped bond markets

Compared to the equity markets, the region's bond markets are underdeveloped. When its long-term bond market remains underdeveloped, any economy pays a high price in the form of foregone benefits. Most lending to the private sector in the region has continued to take the form of short-term bank credit (bank loans took 79 per cent of their combined GDP, while capital market borrowing using long-term corporate bonds amounted to a mere 9.82 per cent).

Poor corporate governance practices

Poor corporate governance is singled out as one of the most critical underlying causes of the difficulties faced by the banking and corporate sectors in the crisis-affected economies.

Most Asian corporations involve extensive state-ownership and control over business and financial assets. Korea has close involvement with the government through the *Chaebols* (most have a debt-to-equity ratio exceeding 500 per cent and an estimated 20 per cent of *Chaebol* debt will need to be written off.) Indonesian direct government ownership of banking insurance amount to roughly 50 per cent and government direct credit in state banks and private banks are about 20 per cent. The negative factors of Asian corporations controlled by government or family or big conglomerates are: exclusion of outsiders, reducing competitive pressure and allowing incumbents to become lazy; sub-optimising capital allocation; tendency toward large concentrations and concentrated cross-holding within a very few companies; sustaining weak companies at the expense

---

[2] Some scholars argued that international financial speculators took advantage of developing member countries' (DMCs) tremendous need of capital.

of strong companies; encouragement of excessive collusion (sometimes tacit); and cover-up of problems, thus defeating transparency.

Corporate governance issues cover the following angles: (i) the lack of competitive capital markets; (ii) inadequate legal protection for investors, both shareholders and creditors; (iii) ill-defined and marginal role of outside shareholders; (iv) inadequate information disclosure; and (v) lack of cross-checking and supervision.

Inefficient regulatory structure and coverage of securities markets

According to the International Organisations of Securities Commissions (IOSCO), three major objectives of securities market regulations are (i) protection of investors; (ii) maintenance of fair, efficient and transparent markets; and (iii) reduction of systemic risk. As the regulatory frameworks in the region are beset by enforcement problems and rising monitoring costs, three key weaknesses are identified: (i) fragmented regulatory structure and coverage; (ii) overemphasis on the merit-based regulations; and (iii) under-utilisation of securities regulatory authorities (SROs). The principal responsibility of SROs is to ensure that there is an efficient and sound licensing system for investment firms and security houses with sufficient capital to cover their risks. It is essential to ensure that the regulatory policy framework protects the investors' rights and their securities and resources from unfair practices. Any overt or covert actions by securities companies or shareholders should be closely monitored to avoid any insider trading.

Weak prudential regulation and supervision

There was no prudential system and sufficient disclosure requirements. Therefore, there are heavy bad debts, weak capital, mergers hampering banking systems, management changes and even bankruptcy.

In addition, there was overemphasis on merit-based regulations instead of disclosure-based regulations. In many financial-crisis-affected economies, there were no independent and qualified accountants, lawyers or evaluators to supervise the necessary procedures.

Outdated and inefficient legal framework

From the above-mentioned causes, a lesson which can be drawn is that many financial-crisis-affected economies lacked legal and regulatory systems and institutions. Either their legal framework was outdated without adequate laws to follow or there was poor implementation and enforcement of law. For example, there was no adequate company law, insolvency law, securities law, banking law or capital market regulations in many affected countries. There is an urgent need to pass new laws or amend existing laws to address problems adversely affecting governance practices, such as: (i) highly concentrated ownership which allows majority shareholders to make decisions without taking into account the interests of minority shareholders; (ii) ineffective company boards and directors that fail to exercise proper oversight functions; (iii) violation of legal, financial and other regulations including related party transactions: (iv) passivity among both minority shareholders and institutional investors; (v) underdeveloped equity markets having a limited role which could be played by institutional and other investors in strengthening governance; (vi) primacy of debt financing and weak banking systems; and (vii) nexus between conglomerates.

Another problem is that of weak enforcement of law. Delivery of justice is difficult in some countries. Court congestion constitutes an obstacle for settlement of debt-related disputes and recovery of bad debts. An inadequate legal framework makes it difficult and time-consuming for banks to seize or transfer collateral behind delinquent loans. There are no adequate secured transaction registration and enforcement systems. Many banks lend money relying on personal relations without seeking collateral, mortgages or other forms of guarantees for repayment of debts. Asia needs good bankruptcy laws to close down badly performing enterprises under financial crisis. Even though some laws and regulations did exist, they are no longer suitable to meet the current situation. For example, Indonesia Bankruptcy Ordinance 1904 is based on the Dutch Bankruptcy Act of 1896.

There are essentially three ways of dealing with insolvency: liquidation, rescue and informal workout.[3] Many countries do not have adequate insolvency laws or rescue arrangements. Some countries have insolvency laws, but procedure and time consumption is so lengthy that creditors cannot adequately solve problems. Many countries still do not have informal workout experience.

Furthermore, many judges and governmental officers have inadequate knowledge of financial markets and the banking industry. This makes it even more difficult to settle financial problems and to set up modern banking and capital markets. Above all, endemic corruption, corrosive of the institutional structure, together with weak enforcement, make the legal framework dead and the banking system a disaster.

II LEGAL REFORM UNDER THE ASIAN FINANCIAL TURMOIL

We can all draw lessons from the Asian financial crisis in terms of poor governance, banking supervision, capital market regulatory framework, corporate

---

[3] Insolvency procedure covers liquidation (formal court-administrated sales of most or all of the assets, usually in piecemeal fashion. At the end of the process, third parties become owners of the assets. Rescue is formal court administered rehabilitation, reorganisation or restructuring in an attempt to preserve the concern as an ongoing income producing entity. The end result is that one or more creditors become in some way owners of the enterprise through debt or equity swaps). Informal workout is an informal process that does not involve court proceedings. The debtors remain in possession of the assets. Creditors accept either reduction or rescheduling of debts.

restructure, integrity, transparency and accountability. In one word, good governance is the main requirement to end the Asian financial crisis and to einsure sustainable economic development. The Asian Development Bank (the Bank) was the first multilateral development institution formally to adopt a governance policy in 1995, which was a key step in helping to transform the Bank into a broad-based development institution. The Bank has made considerable progress in implementation of governance policies: strong policies on anti-corruption, law and development; intensive "awareness-raising" and technical dissemination activities; greater consideration of governance in projects, and a number of governance-focused programs in Thailand and Indonesia.[4] How is good governance to be ensured? It should be governed by law but not governed by man. Therefore, in my view, "the rule of law" is the core of good governance.

The "rule of law" has been understood by some to indicate generally that decisions should be made by the application of known principles or laws without the intervention of discretion in the application. (See *Black's Law Dictionary* (6th ed. 1990). The "rule of law" in terms of constitutional law was invoked by English writers as early as the twelfth and thirteenth centuries to restrain the powers of monarchs, and was articulated in the Massachusetts Constitution of 1780, which spelled out the principle of separation of powers to the end that the government may be a government of laws, and not a government of men. In modern constitutional law, the "rule of law" translates into principles of law-abiding governmental power, independent courts, transparency of legislation, and judicial review of the constitutionality of laws and other norms of lower order.[5]

Recognising that the importance of law to economic development has been more assumed than studied, the Bank in 1996 commissioned a comparative study on "The Role of Law and Legal Institutions in Asian Economic Development, 1960–1995" in six Asian economies. The evolution of legal systems in Asia during this thirty-five-year period offers important insights into the causal relationship between legal and economic development. The study suggests that the strongest causal links range from changes in economic policy both to economic development and to the legal system, which then further affects economic development. The relationship is multi-causal. Thus, for rule-based law to play an effective role in economic development, economic policies must be in a position that reduces direct state management of economic activities. This is a critical conclusion.

The Asian financial crisis further indicates the need for a sound legal framework. A sound legal framework should, I believe, cover: (a) a comprehensive set of binding laws and regulations both predictable and enforceable; (b) an easy

---

[4] The Bank approved a $1.5 billion financial sector governance loan in Indonesia in 1999.

[5] See "Good Governance and the Role of Law in Economic Development", by Ibrahim F.I. Shihata, Senior Vice-President and formal General Counsel of the World Bank; Secretary-General, International Center for Settlement of Investment Disputes.

procedure to implement and enforce laws and regulations so that if there is a default or violation of law, the injured party can solve the problem through judicial courts or arbitration or other informal ways; and (c) a well-functioning public institution with competent and trained staff to implement the laws and regulations and a clean and efficient judiciary to enforce laws and regulations.

The current legal reforms under the Asian financial turmoil are pursuing the above three areas by means of: publication of new laws or amendment of existing laws; and training of implementing officers, judges and professionals, and judiciary reform. This chapter will introduce the current law reform activities relating to corporate governance, insolvency law and banking reforms in three affected countries: Korea, Thailand and Indonesia.

Making new laws and amending existing laws and regulations

Currently, many Asian economies are preparing new laws and amended some existing laws and regulations in order to facilitate financial crisis recovery and long-term sustainable development, mainly covering the following laws and regulations: amendment or preparation of company law; insolvency law; cross-Border insolvency; social security law; banking supervision regulations; capital market regulatory regimes; securities law; secured transactions; registration of land titles; accountancy law; mutual funds; regulations on management of non-financial institutions; foreign direct investment; regulation on merger and acquisition; and regulations on assets management.

Company law

Company Law is a basic law to regulate the organisation a structure of a company and function of an entity in the market. One of the main causes of the Asian financial turmoil is poor corporate governance. The corporate governance of Asian economies has generally been associated with a high concentration of ownership and control by a few families, low level of property right protection and weak enforcement, high leverage of corporations, loose monitoring and screening by lending institutions, and ineffective banking regulations. Governmental intervention into companies' day-to-day management including decisions of borrowing and investment is lacking. Consequently, many bad loans and dead projects have been produced. Lack of transparency and independent supervision provides loopholes for directors or managers to abuse their power and to transfer a company's money to their own pockets. Disclosure of bad loans and serious financial problems is very inadequate and very often delayed, or disclosed by some creditors only when it has become very serious.

In order to recover from the Asian financial crisis, the Korean legislative body passed new regulations aimed to improve corporate governance by the following:

- minority shareholders with more than 0.01 per cent ownership are allowed to file suits;
- minority shareholders are entitled to propose items on the agenda at the general shareholders' meetings;
- beginning in 1999, public companies are required to fill at least one-quarter of the board of directors with outside directors;
- public companies with assets of 100 billion won or more are required to appoint at least one full-time statutory auditor;
- Korea's financial accounting standards have been amended to be substantially consistent with international accounting standards, effective from 1 January 1999;
- thirty of the largest business groups are to file the combined audited financial statements from the fiscal year ending 31 December 1999;
- financial accounting standards for the financial service industry have been fully upgraded to be consistent with international the best practices, effective from 1 January 1999;
- poor performance of auditing is to be subject to increased reviews and heavier sanctions;
- fiduciary duty of managers to the Board of Directors has been introduced.

Korea passed reform bills through the National Assembly in February 1998, including many incentives to promote corporate restructuring, for example:

- the Tax Exemption and Reduction Control Act, which provides a tax break for company restructuring, including exemption of Small and Medium-sized Enterprises (SMEs) from capital gains on the sale of real estate used to repay debts to financial institutions and for real estate transfers through Mergers and Acquisitions transactions;
- the Bank Act, thus increasing the limit on bank ownership of a corporation's equity from 10 per cent–15 per cent, or higher with the Financial Supervisory Commissions (FSC) approval;
- a Corporate Tax Act, which advances non- deductibility of interest on "excessive" debts from 2002 to 2000;
- the Foreign Direct Investment and Foreign Capital Inducement Act, which permits takeovers of non-strategic companies by foreign investors without government approval and raises from 10 per cent–33 per cent the shares which a foreign investor can acquire without board approval;
- the Antitrust and Fair Trade Act, prohibiting any new cross-guarantees and eliminating existing cross-guarantees by March 2000.

Despite the above-mentioned law reform measures, some scholars and practitioners criticise these Korean reforms since the International Monetary Fund (IMF) and World Bank have not made progress. Also it does not settle internal problems of corporate governance, but focuses only on external problems of *Chaelbols*. There is monopolisation of 40 per cent of the stock exchange market by five major *Chaelbols*. The government-promoted corporate restructuring fails to embrace employees' participation in the ownership and management as an integral part. Workers are excluded from the decision-making process of corporate restructuring.[6]

Thailand passed the Public Company Act in 1993. The law offers the protection of basic shareholders, but some requirements reduce small shareholders' rights. For example, the right to call an emergency shareholders' meeting requires 20 per cent of total eligible votes, where, in most other countries, only 10 per cent is necessary. Small shareholders are minimally involved in corporate decision-making and receive little information regarding corporate decisions. Now under financial crisis, small shareholders are demanding accountability on the part of management and directors for corporate failure, and access to accurate and timely corporate information. With regard to the implementation of the fiduciary duty of the board, the Thai police filed a charge against twelve directors and executives of two defunct companies. These cases will set a precedence with respect to the legal interpretation of a board's accountability to the shareholders.

Indonesia adopted the Limited Liability Company Law in 1995. Public and state companies are regulated by a government regulation of 1998 regarding limited liability companies. Indonesia's company law has a minimum authorised capital requirement ($100,000 for a public company). Indonesian company law has requirements on disclosure, accounting standards liability of the Board of Directors and fiduciary duty of managers. However, implementation and supervision is poor. Judiciary enforcement is slow and inadequate.

Insolvency law

The Asian financial crisis demonstrated that the lack of a legal framework for systematic restructuring of debt or the efficient liquidation of businesses incapable of being restructured poses an impediment to economic recovery. All Asian financially affected economies have a bankruptcy law but with deficiencies or which is outdated. One of the legal reforms in Asia is to modernise the bankruptcy law. They have taken measures to amend the existing bankruptcy law including speeding-up liquidation procedures, establishing special bankruptcy courts, training judges and liquidators; improve rescue procedures and create informal workout through negotiation between debtors and creditors, similar to the informal workout in the United States and England.[7]

In February 1998, the Korean National Assembly passed three measures to reform Korea's insolvency regime:

---

[6] See "Intervention" by Yoon Youngmo, International Secretary, Korean Confederation of Trade Unions, 3–5 March 1999.

[7] The concept of informal workout emerged more than ten years ago in some countries, notably the United States and England, as an alternative to the application of formal insolvency law processes. This informal workout between banks and debtors has become known as the "London approach" and "pre-package" Chapter 11 of the US Bankruptcy law.

- first, the Bankruptcy Act, which concentrates authority over insolvency cases in district courts;
- secondly, the Composition Act, which introduces an administrator for asset preservation, requires debtors to report on implementation, and requires creditors to evaluate debtor implementation;
- thirdly, the Reorganisation Act, which establishes expedited dealings, promotes specialisation within the courts, and strengthens creditors by reorganising creditors' committees.

Corporate restructuring

In July 1998 210 financial institutions entered into a Corporate Restructuring Agreement (CRA).

The requirements for corporate restructuring include the conclusion of voluntary workout agreements within three to six months after an initial standstill; selection of a seven-person Corporate Restructuring Coordination Committee (CRCC) to arbitrate inter-creditor disagreements; submission of proposed workouts that lack 75 per cent approval to the CRCC for arbitration, and significant penalties for violation of the CRA, including failure to honor CRCC arbitration decisions.

Thailand has amended its Bankruptcy Act passed in 1940, which had provided only for court-supervised liquidation into a provision of an option for court-supervised reorganisation in 1998.

The adoption of Bangkok rules for voluntary corporate restructuring encourages Thailand to adopt informal workout for the settling of debt disputes due to their cultural and historical background. Thais are characteristically non-confrontational and conflict-averse in their approach to business. Negotiation and compromise are the normal practice. Litigation is reverted to relatively infrequently. Thais are always reluctant for the bank or other creditors to sue their borrowers for non-payment in the courts, as opposed to looking for informal workout.

Indonesia adopted its bankruptcy law in August 1998. This law covers formal liquidation procedure and two kinds of "rescue" processes. The debtor filing a petition for bankruptcy starts the procedure. A stay or suspension of all actions takes ninety days. If, within that time, the debtor coporation presents a plan of composition approved by creditors, the plan takes effect. The second process starts by a coporation filing a request for suspension of payment of debts. There follows forty-five days for temporary suspension and a negotiation between the debtor and the creditors. The affairs of the debtor corporation are jointly managed by court-appointed administrators and by the debtor. The creditors vote on the proposal. In the case of the failure of the two rescue procedures, the court may proceed with the liquidation of the debtor corporation. Indonesia has taken an informal workout initiative called the "Jakarta Initiatives Task Force", appointed by the President. Its principal functions are to facilitate negotiations, refer cases of public interests to the courts under bankruptcy law and to provide a central reference point for obtaining necessary government and other approvals to implement plans of restructure.

Banking and financial reform

The Government of Korea has issuance of about 20 trillion won by the Korean Asset Management Cooperation in bonds for the purchase of 44 trillion won in face value of non-performing loans. Banks have restructured their balance sheets and assumed lending. They have strengthened insolvency laws and prudential norms, consolidating the supervisory function.

The Government of Indonesia has established specialised agencies for bank restructuring (IBRA) and external debt restructuring (NDRA), and taken a medium-term approach to institutional capacity-building and loan recovery. The Government has announced the closure of thirty-eight banks. Other measures include the tightening of the prudential framework, and development of a deposit insurance scheme.

The Government of Thailand has provided about 300 billion baht in capital incentives for banks to strengthen their capital positions and balance sheets as a supplement to the roughly 1.1 trillion baht supplied in liquidated support. Thailand's bank-led approach to restructuring, combined with a strengthening of the legal framework and incentive structure, including amendment of bankruptcy law and tightened prudential regulation, have improved bank management and corporate governance.

Improved judicial system to strengthen law enforcement

Most affected Asian economies are taking measures to strengthen their judicial systems to reduce court congestion. Korea has established a special bankruptcy court. Thailand has established a judicial reform committee aimed at improving court efficiency.

Since the above-mentioned law reform measures have been recently introduced, it is still too early to make a thorough assessment of the law reforms. But experience shows that any of company law or insolvency law cannot adequately function without a sound legal institution framework with competent law officers, judges, lawyers, a well-equipped information system of laws and court cases, and an efficient and just court system to enforce the law. Many DMCs are undertaking law and judiciary reforms.

III ASIAN DEVELOPMENT BANK AND DEVELOPMENT ACTIVITIES

As the Charter of the Asian Development Bank indicates that "the purpose of the Bank shall be to foster economic growth and co-operation in the region of

Asia and the Far East" and "to contribute to the acceleration of the process of economic development of the developing member countries in the region", facing unprecedented Asian financial turmoil and request of DMCs the Bank has taken important measures to assist financial-crisis-affected DMCs in providing emergency loans and technical assistance in its banking reform to reduce bad debts.[8] Meanwhile, the Bank has provided technical assistance on law and development activities to assist its DMCs' law and judicial reform, strengthening good governance to recover from the Asian financial crisis in particular.

In recent years, the Bank's operations have focused on social and economic structures as a complement to the Bank's traditional focus on physical infrastructure projects. With the adoption of the Board Paper on Governance, Sound Development Management in 1995,[9] the Bank has identified law and development assistance and legal framework for private sector development as areas for bank operations to encourage greater predictability, transparency, accountability and participation in development management in the Bank's DMCs. A principal instrument for law and development programming has been technical assistance (TA), under which consulting services are provided for training and institutional development.

Recognising the importance of the "rule of Law" in the economic development process, the Bank has worked closely with its DMCs in response to the Asian financial crisis, complementing the Bank's ongoing law and development assistance in twenty-three DMCs in support of the Bank's five strategic objectives of promoting economic growth, reducing poverty, supporting human development, improving the status of women, and protecting the environment. The Bank has completed one 101 law and development-related projects for DMCs. The Bank has undertaken 250 law-related technical assistance projects. The Bank's law and development activities mainly cover assistance in the preparation of economic laws, strengthening judiciary enforcement capacity and training of public legal officers.

How do we define "law and development"? Some international scholars define "law and development" as "law and social change".[10] The Bank's law and development assistance has focused on economic law-related activities, avoiding activities of a political nature, which are prohibited under the Charter.[11]

---

[8] The Bank has taken many initiatives in supporting recovery of Asian financial-crisis-affected economies, such as: the Asian Currency Crisis Support Facility (ACCSF), as part of the Bank's Japan Special Fund to help crisis-affected member countries, and amounting to 367.5 billion Japanese yuan; the Asian Growth and Recover Initiative (AGRI). It aims at resource mobilisation ($5 billion for Bank and corporate restructuring) for the crisis-affected Asian economies through a multilateral framework comprising Japan, the United States, the World Bank and the Bank.

[9] See the Asian Development Bank Board Paper R151–95.

[10] See J.H. Merryman, "Comparative Law and Social Change: On the origins, style, decline and revival of the Law and Development Movement" (1977) 25 *American Journal of Comparative Law* 457.

[11] See "A Strategic Review of the Law and Development Activities of the Asian Development Bank", 28 April 1997 (GC97BM463).

One feature of the Bank's law and development projects is demand-driven. In the last two years, since many DMCs of the Bank have been affected by the Asian financial turmoil, they have needed to amend existing laws or prepare new laws to deal with financial crises, strengthen good governance and improve the judiciary system and the retraining of public servants. The Bank has provided TA to Indonesia, Thailand the and People's Republic of China for the preparation of securities law, and the amendment of insolvency law, accountancy law and capital market supervision regulations. The Bank provided the first loan to Pakistan in supporting its Legal and Judiciary Reform Project to the amount of US $80 million. The Bank has provided regional technical assistance projects on a grant basis to Mongolia, Vietnam, India, the People' Republic of China, the Pacific region, the Maldives and other DMCs, for the retraining of governmental legal officers and judges.

In 1998, in response to the need for legal reform under the Asian financial crisis, the Bank processed a regional technical assistance project on insolvency reform, covering eleven Asian economies, including Japan, Korea, Thailand, Singapore, Malaysia, Indonesia, the Philippines, Pakistan, India, Hong Kong, China and Taipei. This project covers an individual economy's report on insolvency law reform, and a comparative report on Asian practices of insolvency procedures, including liquidation, rescues and informal workout, and recommendations. The comparative study report and discussions indicate that further efforts should be focused on: insolvency case statistics and insolvency law implementation information-gathering; training of judges, liquidation administrators, governmental officers and leading banks on insolvency matters; co-operation of research work on cross-border insolvency; protection of secured creditors; effective reorganisation of debtor corporation; informal workout; and good corporate governance and sanctions. Under this RETA, a Symposium on Insolvency Reforms was held at the Bank in January 1999, and was well received by legislatures, governmental officers, scholars and practitioners on insolvency issues. A new round table seminar on insolvency and secured transaction will be held at the Bank later this year.

The Bank's assistance to DMCs affected by the crisis in its earliest days focused on reforms of their legal and policy frameworks for regulation of financial institutions, and of their financial and capital markets.

The Financial Markets Reform for Thailand deals with problems arising from non-performing loans to finance companies and rehabilitation of unliquidated finance companies by improving the legal framework for debt recovery. The programme required action an amended bankruptcy law, ensuring autonomy of the Securities and Exchange Commission, increasing accountability of the Stock Exchange of Thailand, preparing a corporitisation law, allowing conversion of existing state-owned enterprises to privatised companies, and enacting amendments to the alien business law to permit participation of foreign and majority foreign-owned domestic securities companies in securities brokerage and dealer businesses.

The Financial Sector Program for the Republic of Korea involved the reform of significant financial sector laws and regulatory policies. The Program involved amendments to the Bank of Korea Act to guarantee the operational independence and autonomy of the Bank of Korea, the passing of an act for the establishment of the financial supervisory institutions to consolidate supervision of all commercial and specialised banks, and issuance of guidelines reforming the insurance industry. In August 1998, the Republic of Korea's Bank Supervisory Authority, after reviewing prudential standards in accordance with the requirements of the Program, announced revised core principles relating to the treatment of financial assets and the revision of loan classification criteria. The Korean National Assembly enacted, at the end of 1998, the Mortgage-Backed Securitisation Companies Act.

The Bank's 1998 Financial Governance Reforms-Sector Development Program in Indonesia addressed bankruptcy law reforms and secured transaction law reform and reform to Indonesia's anti-corruption legislation and regulations. Pursuant to this Program, Indonesia enacted the 1998 Banking Law and approved regulations providing a framework for Bank mergers and acquisitions, as well as for the liquidation of commercial banks and approved new loan-loss regulations. A 1998 Presidential Decree established the State Ministry for the Empowerment of State Enterprises, which will commence performance audits and recommend measures to improve accountability and transparency. Under a parallel technical assistance loan, the Bank is making available financing to the Government for training of bankruptcy personnel and for the development of a secured transaction registration system.

The Bank has provided a small-scale technical assistance grant to the People's Republic of China (PRC) in supporting the drafting of the Securities Law. The Securities Law was approved on 29 December 1998. It strengthens the legal framework for the PRC securities market, increases transparency and accountability of the China Securities Regulatory Commission (CSRC), facilitates disclosure-based initial public offerings, and prohibits such practices as insider trading and brokerage firms mixing their own and clients' money to trade shares. Another TA for supporting the regulatory framework of the CSRC offered by the Bank is under being prepared.

Assistance of judiciary reform

Enforcement of law is a critical pillar of the "rule of law". From the lessons learned from Asian financial crisis, we can see court congestion, low efficiency of judges, poor facilities of courts, and long procedures of case-handling and corruption as obstacles to the enforcement of laws.

Many countries are undertaking judicial reform and combating corruption. The Bank is processing a regional technical assistance program to support a survey and in depth study on court congestion in five DMCs in order to make recommendations on further judiciary reform in the region.

Implementation of the law requires sound governmental legal services. The Bank is processing a regional technical assistance program aimed to improve organisation and management of governmental legal services in DMCs.

Human resources is the fundamental issue for the implementation of the "rule of law" and economic development. Continuing legal education and the ongoing training of public sector lawyers and judges constitute primary forces of the Bank law and development programs. The Bank has provided regional technical assistance programmes on retraining of trainers, judges and governmental officers in Vietnam, Mongolia, Nepal, India, Pakistan, the PRC, the Maldives, Thailand and the Pacific region.

In order to enhance legal knowledge and awareness in DMCs, the Bank, together with the Dutch Government, are processing a regional technical assistance programme on legal literacy for governance.

Many DMCs need information and cross-border experience in pursuance of their law and judiciary reforms as well as to meet the needs of training their personnel. The Bank has provided a regional technical assistance program on Development of the Internet for Asian Law (DIAL). Project DIAL provides policy makers, law reform personnel, and interested members of the public free access from 40,000 legislative precedents from more than forty countries worldwide. In addition to the texts of legislative materials, Project DIAL gives selected "authorised users" e-mail access to panels of international experts who can provide preliminary guidance for their research with such materials.

The Bank has also provided technical assistance projects to the PRC and Tajikistan to support the collection and translation of their laws and regulations, in order to make the legal system transparent and facilitate dissemination of laws and regulations.

As most DMCs need information of the laws and regulations of other countries to share their experience, the Bank, in 1996, launched LAW-DEV on the Internet to provide a forum for the worldwide exchange of information on current law and development activities, research, teaching and publications. Similarly, a prototype Internet resource for legal research (Project DIAL) has been created to make available the full texts of legislation and regulations and related law reform reports to legislative draftsmen and law practitioners in the Bank's DMCs.

IV CONCLUSION

Legal reform includes law reform and judiciary reform. There are three kinds of law reform: tinkering, which accepts the existing system and seeks to keep it operating and improve efficiency; following, which adjusts the legal system to social change; and leading, which uses the law to implement changes. Law reform, as refereed to in this chapter, is a mixture of all three kinds law reform. Reform is progress in order to achieve a better society. Therefore, all economies need law reforms. Along with rapid economic development, every economy's law is under a constant process of evolution.

Law is a binding custom or practice of a community, a rule of conduct or action prescribed or formally recognised as binding, or enforced by a controlling authority. The law reflects each economy's culture, history, policies and stage of economic development. Occasionally we may focus too strongly on "international best practice" and "foreign experts", and, in relative terms, give too little attention to the contributions of local consultants and to the breadth of the effective deliberative process among affected stakeholders. It reminds us that the best laws are those which can specifically suit an economy.

Legal systems and social science are the common heritage of mankind. Every economy should share other legal systems and law-drafting skills to use for the development of their own legal regime building.

There are many common features in economic laws. Harmonisation of international commercial law is a world trend, such as the International Sales of Goods Convention, and the Recognition and Enforcement of Foreign Arbitrage Awards Convention. UNCTRAL (United Nations Commission on International Trade Law) arbitration rules become many economies' internal rules. Therefore, during the process of law reform, economies need to take into consideration international conventions and practices, in order to reduce conflicts between international law and domestic law.

The passage of a law is easy, but most important is the implementation and fair enforcement of law. In the process of law reform, capacity-building is crucial. The legal and judicial functions in most DMCs are seriously under-resourced, with low budgets and a lack of capable and well-trained legal officers and judges. Strengthening capacity-building and training of governmental officers and judges will ensure implementation and enforcement of law.

Law and economic development are interrelated and linked. The current Asian financial crisis once again confirms the linkage and mutual effects between law and development. The Asian financial crisis has disclosed the deficiencies of legal systems of affected economies and resulted in many law reforms to address those shortcomings. Finally, the improved legal framework will assist the recovery from financial crisis and prevent eventual new crisis in these areas. Naturally, problems will be occur in other fields and new laws will be introduced accordingly. By doing so, society is making progress, and the sustainable economic development objectives can be achieved.

Index